Doolittle's
Tokyo Raiders

Doolittle's Tokyo Raiders

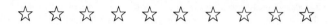

by CARROLL V. GLINES

VNR VAN NOSTRAND REINHOLD COMPANY
NEW YORK CINCINNATI TORONTO LONDON MELBOURNE

First published in paperback in 1981
Copyright © 1964, 1981 by Carroll V. Glines
Library of Congress Catalog Card Number 64-3287
ISBN 0-442-21925-3

Van Nostrand Reinhold Company
A division of Litton Educational Publishing, Inc.
135 West 50th Street, New York, NY 10020

Van Nostrand Reinhold Ltd.
1410 Birchmount Road, Scarborough, Ontario M1P 2E7

Van Nostrand Reinhold Australia Pty. Ltd.
17 Queen Street, Mitcham, Victoria 3132

Van Nostrand Reinhold Company Ltd.
Molly Millars Lane, Wokingham, Berkshire, England RG11 2PY

Cloth edition published 1964 by Van Nostrand Reinhold Company

Eight cloth impressions

16 15 14 13 12 11 10 9 8 7 6 5 4 3 2 1

Excerpts in this book are reproduced by special permission as follows: *Global
Mission,* by Henry H. Arnold, Harper & Row Publishers, Inc., copyright,
1949, by H. H. Arnold; *Way of a Fighter: The Memoirs of Claire Lee Chennault,*
Robert Hotz, ed., G. P. Putnam's Sons, copyright, 1949, by Claire Lee Chen-
nault; *The Amazing Story of Corporal Jacob DeShazer,* by C. Hoyt Watson, Seattle
Pacific College; *Ten Years in Japan,* by Joseph C. Grew, Simon & Schuster,
Inc., copyright, 1944, by Joseph C. Grew; *Admiral Halsey's Story,* by William F.
Halsey and J. Bryan III, McGraw-Hill Book Company, copyright, 1947, by
William F. Halsey, copyright, 1947, by The Curtis Publishing Company; *Fleet
Admiral King, A Naval Record,* by Ernest J. King, Fleet Admiral, USN, and
Walter Muir Whitehill, Commander, USNR, W. W. Norton & Co., Inc., copy-
right, 1952, by Ernest J. King; *Thirty Seconds Over Tokyo,* by Captain Ted Law-
son, edited by Robert Considine, copyright, 1943, by Random House, Inc.;
The Amazing Mr. Doolittle, by Quentin Reynolds, Appleton-Century, copy-
right, 1953, by Quentin Reynolds; *The Public Papers and Addresses of Franklin
D. Roosevelt,* 1942 Volume, by Samuel I. Rosenman, Harper & Row Publishers, Inc., copyright, 1950, by Samuel I. Rosenman; *Midway, The Battle That
Doomed Japan,* by Mitsuo Fuchida and Masatake Okumiya, copyright, 1955,
by U.S. Naval Institute, Annapolis, Maryland.

Dedicated to

EIGHTY BRAVE MEN

FOREWORD

THE B-25 RAID ON JAPAN has gone down in the annals of World War II as a classic example of the courage and ingenuity of American airmen in combat. Led by the incomparable Jimmy Doolittle, the raid came at a time when the Japanese were advancing steadily across the Pacific. Guam, Wake, Hong Kong, and Singapore had fallen. In the Philippines, General Wainwright and the remnants of his force were making a brave but hopeless last stand on Corregidor.

The appearance of 16 B-25s over Japan on April 18, 1942, lifted the gloom that had descended upon America and her Pacific allies. The bomb damage that resulted was not great, compared with that inflicted later in the war, but the raid had some far-reaching effects. The Japanese were forced to retain fighter units for the defense of the home islands which had been intended for the Solomons, and they felt compelled to expand their Pacific perimeter beyond the area where it could be defended adequately. The full impact of the raid on the minds of the Japanese military leaders and its consequent influence on the course of the war in the Pacific were not realized until long after that conflict.

For America and her allies the raid was a badly needed morale booster. Besides being the first offensive air action undertaken against the Japanese home islands, the Tokyo raid accomplished some other "firsts" that augured well for the future. It was the first war action in which the United States Army Air Forces and the United States Navy teamed up in a full-scale operation against the enemy. The Doolittle raiders were the first (and last) to fly land-based bombers from a carrier deck on a combat mission and first to use new cruise control techniques in attacking a distant target. The incendiary bombs they carried were the fore-runner of those used later in the war. The special camera recording apparatus developed at Colonel Doolittle's request was adopted by the AAF and the crew recommendations concerning armament, tactics and equipment were used as the basis for later improvements.

It was twenty-six months before American bombers went back to Japan. During those months of bitter fighting America was slowly building her land, sea and air forces and with them driving the enemy, island by island, back across the Pacific. In 1944 and 1945 mighty fleets of B-29s penetrated the skies over Japan and finished the job begun by Jimmy Doolittle and his raiders in 1942.

January, 1964   GENERAL CURTIS E. LEMAY
Chief of Staff
United States Air Force

PREFACE

Each year on April 18, about half a hundred men gather for a three-day reunion at a hotel in a large city somewhere in the continental United States. While most of the program for the three days is light-hearted, part of one day is set aside for a business meeting and luncheon. The good-natured kidding is dropped. Guests are ushered from the room. The men sit down to serious discussion of group affairs.

Following the meeting the group is served a luncheon. Before each man is set a silver goblet with his name engraved on its side. Waiters pour wine for each man and then they, too, are asked to leave.

The chairman for the group that year rises and the group follows his cue. He lifts his goblet high and says, "Gentlemen, I propose a toast to those who gave their all in the success of our mission in 1942 and to those who have since joined them—our fondest memories, sincere appreciation and gratitude. May they rest in peace."

The solemn men facing the chairman lift their goblets and answer, "To those who have gone." They drink to conclude the toast, each man knowing that before another reunion is held, he may be included among "those who have since joined them."

The men who pay this annual tribute to their departed comrades are members of an exclusive military fraternity that no one else can join. Of the original eighty members only a few more than fifty are still alive. Some day, like the Civil War veterans of yesteryear, they too will hold their last reunion and the group will be no more.

While the men may slowly fade away, the deed that brings them together each year will remain forever etched on the pages of American military air history. They performed a military miracle by bombing an enemy capital at a time when the nation's morale had reached the lowest ebb ever recorded. They began the reverse of the tide of Japanese conquest and brought the first good news for America and her Allies in the beginning months of the most devastating war in all history.

The full story of the Tokyo Raid could not be told without the wholehearted cooperation of the surviving Raiders and the Army, Navy, and Air Force archivists who guard the official records. The records, classified until now, revealed a major portion of the story. However, there was some missing data which could only be supplied by the principals themselves. Therefore, the information contained in the following pages is based on both official records and the recollections of those who took part in this historic mission. All dialogues have been reconstructed from the best available evidence. When persons are quoted without reference to the source of information, it is to be understood that this information was obtained from interviews or correspondence with the persons concerned. Most of the survivors were interviewed in person by the author; others patiently provided details by mail. Many elusive details concerning the preparatory phase were not found in the records and were known to only one man—the leader of the Tokyo Raiders, Lieutenant General James H. "Jimmy" Doolittle. Without his personal assistance, interest, and encouragement, many of the valuable human interest items would not have come to light.

This story of the Tokyo Raid is divided into three parts. The first part concerns the birth of the idea of a carrier-borne raid of land-based bombers and the planning, preparation, training and launching of the operation. It also contains never-before-released information concerning the Task Force that brought the B-25's to the launching point.

Part II contains narratives by one member of each of the sixteen planes on the raid. Part III explains the aftermath and the effects of the raid on the Chinese who befriended the American airmen, the Japanese who were humiliated by it and the American people who were proud that there were men who had the courage to fly it. Most important, it tells of the significance of the mission and its effect on the outcome of the war in the Pacific.

This is the true, complete story of eighty brave men. It has never been told in its entirety before.

McLean, Virginia   CARROLL V. GLINES
                                                          Colonel USAF (Ret.)

ACKNOWLEDGMENTS

This book could not be written without help. Besides the principals involved who willingly granted interviews or provided information when requested, the author is grateful for the assistance provided by the following: Brigadier General S. L. A. Marshall, USA (Ret), former Chief Army Historian; Captain F. Kent Loomis, USN (Ret), Assistant Director of Naval History; Lieutenant Commander David M. Cooney, USN, Head, Magazine and Book Branch, Office of Navy Information; Mr. Dean C. Allard, Head, Classified Operational Archives, Navy Department; Mrs. Mildred D. Mayeux, Archives Assistant, Classified Operational Archives, Navy Department; Mrs. Alice Martin, Information Specialist, Magazine and Book Branch, Office of the Secretary of the Air Force; Lieutenant Colonel Gene Guerny, Deputy Chief, Magazine and Book Branch, Office of the Secretary of the Air Force; Miss Minerva A. Snoddy, Chief, Reference Section, Administration Services Division, Headquarters, U. S. Air Force; Miss Marguerite K. Kennedy, Chief, Archives Branch, USAF Historical Division, Aerospace Research Institute; Mrs. Virginia G. Fincik, Mrs. Stella K. Turner, Mrs. Bernice L. Weis, and Mrs. Frances M. Lewis, Research Specialists, Aeronautical Charting and Information Center, Alexandria, Virginia; Mr. Wilbur J. Nigh, Chief, Reference Branch, National Archives and Records Service, World War II Records Division, General Services Administration, Alexandria, Virginia; Mr. Edwin Alan Thompson, Research Specialist, Manuscript Division, Library of Congress; Mr. Charles J. Graham, North American Aviation, Inc.; and Mr. Richard M. Bueschel, Japanese Air Historian.

All photographs, unless otherwise indicated, are official U. S. Air Force photographs.

TABLE OF CONTENTS

PART I

PLANNING AND PREPARATION

PART II

THE MISSION

PART III
AFTERMATH

APPENDICES

Part I

PLANNING AND PREPARATION

The planning and preparation for a military air operation often require hundreds of man-hours. The objective of the operation is first determined and an assessment of the available resources is made to ascertain what it will take to achieve the objective. Operations specialists go over every aspect of the tasks assigned and prepare detailed plans outlining exactly what is needed in the way of manpower, planes, materiel and facilities. The air units are specified and missions are then "laid on."

Although born in the haste of war, the historic air action described in this documentary required the same painstaking planning and preparation; however, the need for absolute secrecy precluded most of the written formalities required in "normal" war planning. The following pages contain an account of the planning and preparation for one of the most daring and imaginative air raids in history. The result of that single raid was to change the course of war and signal the beginning of the end of Japanese militarist tyranny.

Chapter 1

"IT HAS NEVER BEEN DONE BEFORE . . ."

The large clock on the wall behind Speaker of the House Sam Rayburn showed 12:28 P.M. The joint emergency session of the Congress he was about to open was to be the most significant in his 55 years of Government service. Before him, the House chamber was jammed with not only the nation's legislators but the Justices of the Supreme Court, Cabinet members and top military leaders.

In the packed gallery above and behind the Speaker were accredited members of the Capitol Hill press corps. In the front row of the visitor's gallery was Mrs. Eleanor Roosevelt, the wife of the President. Near her, by special invitation, sat the widow of President Wilson. The conversations that filled the air were clipped and terse.

On the House floor, there was a sudden stir of excitement. Rayburn rapped his gavel for silence. The Doorkeeper of the House arrived at the center aisle and announced, "Mr. Speaker, the President of the United States!"

From a side door President Roosevelt slowly entered the packed chamber leaning heavily on the arm of his son, James, who was dressed in the dark green of a Marine captain. There was a hush and then a roar of applause as the entire assemblage rose simultaneously and watched the President make his way slowly to the dais just below Rayburn.

The genial Rayburn allowed the applause to continue briefly, then held up his hands for quiet. A chaplain gave a brief prayer and then Rayburn motioned for the audience to be seated.

The President spread open a black loose-leaf notebook, grasped both sides of the lectern firmly and paused to look at his audience. Then, in those measured resonant tones that the whole world had come to know, he began to speak:

"Yesterday, December 7, 1941—a date which will live in infamy—the United States of America was suddenly and deliberately attacked by naval and air forces of the Empire of Japan."

Describing the events of the previous 24 hours, the President recited the list of Japanese conquests and announced, "As Commander-in-Chief of the Army and Navy, I have directed that all measures be taken for our defense. But always will our whole nation remember the character of the onslaught against us. No matter how long it may take us to overcome this premeditated invasion, the American people in their righteous might will win through to absolute victory."

Cheers, whistles and applause interrupted the President at this point. He looked up at the audience, smiled and raised his hand in acknowledgment. Continuing, the President put into words what the whole nation and the non-Axis world hoped he would. He had given the promise of revenge and hope for victory that everyone needed. He concluded by saying, "I ask that the Congress declare that since the unprovoked and dastardly attack by Japan on Sunday, December 7, 1941, a state of war has existed between the United States and the Japanese Empire."

In the few minutes that the President had spoken, a national resolve was formed. Millions of Americans began the slow recovery from the state of shock which had gripped them during the previous 24 hours when the ugly news from the Pacific first poured in. If the Japanese had calculated that the American people would be cowed into submission by the disaster in the Pacific, they had not studied American history. The same nation that had coined such phrases as "United We Stand—Divided We Fall" and "Remember the Maine," proclaimed a new one: "Remember Pearl Harbor!"

The policeman at the White House gate stepped out of his guard house as the Army staff car approached. He held up his hand to the driver indicating he wanted to check the occupants in the rear seat. The officer peered inside and instantly recognized the stony, unsmiling face of General George C. Marshall, Army Chief of Staff. Seated on Marshall's left with the ever-present grin that had earned him the nickname of "Hap," sat General Henry H. Arnold, Chief of the Army Air Forces. The guard smiled back at Arnold and waved the car inside the White House grounds.

It had been exactly two weeks almost to the hour that the first news of the Pearl Harbor attack had reached the White House. Upon Marshall and Arnold had fallen the unprecedented burden of planning and directing the mobilization of the most powerful Army and Air Force the world had ever known. Daily since that infamous Pearl Harbor Sunday, Marshall had reported Army problems and plans to the President, along with his Navy counterpart, Admiral Ernest J. King. Today, Arnold had been invited and the group assembling outside the President's study included Harry Hopkins, Roosevelt's special advisor, Admiral Harold R. Stark, Secretary of War Henry Stimson, Secretary of the Navy Frank Knox, and Admiral King.

They were shown into the study and the President greeted his visitors cordially one by one. Although the weight of responsibility on him was greater than on any president in history, he did not show it. When the visitors had taken their seats, Roosevelt announced that Sir Winston Churchill and his top military leaders would arrive the next day and asked that the group be ready to discuss the strategic problems confronting the two countries at subsequent meetings.

General Marshall gave the President his estimate of the entire global war situation, after which the President discussed the war situation in Africa and England and then turned his attention to the Far East. He was interested in striking back at Japan at the earliest possible moment and asked everyone present to consider ways and means to attack Japan as soon as possible. He then asked what had been done so far.

Marshall briefed the President on plans to "militarize" the ex-Army and Navy officers who were flying for Colonel Claire L. Chennault with the American Volunteer Group in China. Roosevelt emphasized that he wanted a bombing raid on Japan proper as soon as humanly possible to bolster the morale of America and her Allies. This emphatic request, which was repeated over and over again, made a profound impression on everyone present. The President's sense of urgency was immediately transferred by Marshall, Arnold, and King to their respective staffs when they returned to their offices.

Arnold was greatly encouraged by this meeting. He had been apprehensive about the President's understanding of airpower's potential but Roosevelt's grasp of the total war situation was impressive and Arnold's fears were now gone. "From that time forward," he later wrote, "there was no doubt about the Commanding General of the Army Air Forces being a member of the President's staff." [1]

When Arnold returned to his office from this White House meeting, he immediately dictated his notes to a secretary. The resulting memorandum, passed from Arnold to the War Plans Division of the Air Staff, became a directive to begin planning for retaliatory air strikes against Japan.

At 10:30 A.M. on the day before Christmas, Arnold met with the British Army, Navy, and Air Force leaders who had come with Churchill. Air Chief Marshal Sir Charles Portal, Arnold's British counterpart, had some very definite ideas about what the American military forces should do to stem the spread of the Axis cancer. He was particularly firm in his advice about the Japanese.

Portal told Arnold that an attack on Japan was a Navy task, because carriers could sneak up on Japan and make the same kind of attack that the Japanese had made on Pearl Harbor. The risk would be no different than that taken by British carriers at Taranto or by the Japanese carriers near Hawaii. This kind of strategy, he reasoned, would cause the Japanese fleet to return to its home islands and allow the Allies to strengthen themselves in the Pacific.

Arnold was not impressed with Portal's logic. "I always thought that Portal mixed wishful thinking in with his reasoning concerning the Pacific air strategy," Arnold said later. "I thought he was afraid if our Air Force planned to use heavy bombers against Japan it would cut down the number he would receive." [2] In addition, Arnold felt it would be suicide for the Navy to bring their carriers within range of Japanese land-based aviation. The situation was not the same as Portal had intimated. At that moment, the only way to attack Japan seemed to be to operate heavy bombers from East Chinese bases as the President obviously wanted.

The conferences with the British (to be known as the Arcadia Conferences) lasted through January 14, 1942. During the time the British war leaders were in the States, meetings were held

almost daily with the President, the Prime Minister and the
Combined Chiefs of Staff in attendance.[3] These were always
formal gatherings and were usually followed by meetings of
"working committees" made up of representatives from each
country's Army, Navy, and Air Force. The subjects discussed and
strategy agreed upon covered every phase of the war against the
Axis powers.

At 5:30 P.M. on January 4, the Combined Chiefs met with
Roosevelt and Churchill in the White House. One of the principal subjects on the agenda was the unsettled French situation
in North Africa. Admiral King voiced his opinion about the
U.S. Navy's part in the intended landing operations saying that
three carriers should be sent to the area. He thought that one
carrier should have about 75 or 80 Navy fighters aboard and
another should carry about 80 or 100 Army fighters. The third
should be used to transport Army bombers and carry gas, bombs,
and ammunition.

Arnold did not take issue with King's suggestion but he knew
there would be some problems to solve. That night, back in his
office in the Munitions Building, Arnold transcribed his notes
and wrote, "By transporting these Army bombers on a carrier,
it will be necessary for us to take off from the carrier, which
brings up the question of what kind of plane—B-18 bomber
and DC-3 for cargo?

"We will have to try bomber take-offs from carriers. It has never
been done before but we must try out and check on how long it
takes."[4]

The War Plans Division of the Army Air Forces staff studied
this unusual memo from Arnold and began the necessary checking of technical data to work his idea into the North African

invasion plan. Army fighters could probably be launched either from the deck of a carrier or by catapult. But a loaded B-18 bomber or a DC-3 cargo plane? It would take some experimentation to find out.

The fact that "it has never been done before" did not bother the flyers assigned to planning tasks. The Army Air Forces owed its very existence to the fact that it had done things that had no precedent, that it dared to proceed unhampered by tradition. "Hap" Arnold had said that it must be tried out and that is what would be done. Therefore, the requirement to consider the feasibility of launching land-based heavy planes from carriers was turned over to the Air Staff officers assigned to plan for the invasion of North Africa. Simultaneously, other flying officers were writing and rewriting plans to bomb Japan from China. They were also to consider any other possibilities of conducting attacks against the Japanese homeland and forward those plans to Arnold for his consideration in line with the President's desires.

The seed of the idea of using a Navy carrier to transport Army planes to an area of operations had been planted by Admiral King but King did not envision medium bombers and large transports actually flying from a carrier's deck. This innovation was conceived in the brilliant mind of General Arnold on that bitter cold fourth day of January, 1942. However, Arnold did not realize just how good his idea was. Its value was not to be evident until three and a half months later. Different airplanes were to be launched from carriers against the enemy and it was against a different enemy in another theater of war.

NOTES TO CHAPTER 1

1. Henry H. Arnold, *Global Mission* (New York: Harper & Brothers, 1949), p. 274.

2. *Ibid.*, pp. 276-277.

3. The title "Joint Chiefs of Staff" was adopted for the Americans and "Combined Chiefs of Staff" for the American and British Chiefs of Staff when they met together.

4. Memorandum of White House meeting, January 4, 1942, General Henry H. Arnold files, Library of Congress.

Chapter 2

A CONCEPT IS BORN

The first month of war found the defensive structure of the Allied nations crumbling along every front. In the Pacific, one Japanese victory followed another with alarming rapidity. United States forces in the Philippines had retreated into the Bataan Peninsula. The British Army, having surrendered the base at Penang, was retreating southward and the Japanese were able to continue their advance upon Singapore at almost a marching pace with only token resistance. In the Dutch East Indies, enemy forces had landed on Borneo, Timor, Celebes and New Guinea.

The rapid pace of Japanese successes was not offset by any showing of Allied power. The sinking of the British battleships *Prince of Wales* and *Repulse* in the Gulf of Siam on December 10, added to the gloom of the Allies. The fall of Wake Island on December 23, only confirmed the worst fears of the public that the U.S. Navy had been rendered impotent by the raid on Pearl Harbor. Wake Island was closer to Hawaii than Japan, which further proved Japanese boldness. The fact that the U.S. Navy could do nothing about it convinced the general public that the situation was desperate.

In the Philippines at the close of the year there was no doubt that organized resistance to the Japanese onslaught was practically at an end. On December 30, President Manuel Quezon and Vice President Sergio Osmeña had been sworn in for their second terms as guns roared in the distance. Quezon, confined to a wheel chair, had read a message to the small crowd assembled at the entrance to Malinta Tunnel. It was from President Roosevelt and was a sincere attempt to bolster the morale of the Filipinos and their gallant American defenders. The message read: "News of your gallant struggle against the Japanese aggressors has elicited the profound admiration of every American. . . . I give to the people of the Philippines my solemn pledge that their freedom will be redeemed and their independence established and protected. The entire resources in men and materials of the United States stand behind that pledge."

Roosevelt's message gave the fifteen thousand Americans and sixty-five thousand Filipinos who had escaped to Bataan renewed courage and hope. Behind the rugged terrain of Bataan they were supposed to hold out for six months if need be and await the coming of massive fleets of ships and planes from the States. These massive fleets did not exist but the men still alive on Bataan did not know it. They could only wait and fight and try to stay alive.

On December 18, Amon G. Carter, publisher of the Fort Worth *Star Telegram* and well-known aviation enthusiast, wrote to his old friend, Major General Edwin M. "Pa" Watson, military Secretary to the President. Carter, like hundreds of other well-meaning Americans, thought he had an original idea which would help win the war. He naively suggested that five hundred long-range bombers should bomb Tokyo using airline pilots, each plane carrying two to four thousand pounds of bombs.

Watson forwarded Carter's letter to General Arnold on December 30 for his comment. On January 7, knowing that his planners were considering all possible ways to bomb Japan, Arnold replied that, "the fundamental idea is sound but the problem of execution is something more than that expressed by Mr. Carter. However, we will have a solution in the near future which we hope will get the results desired." [1]

Admiral Ernest J. King, Chief of Naval Operations, was tired from the Arcadia Conference meetings he had been attending all day. He left his office in the Navy Building about eight in the evening and ordered his driver to take him to the Washington Navy Yard, where a former German yacht, the *Vixen,* was moored. The *Vixen* was serving as his flagship and second office where he could work undisturbed far into the night. Several key members of King's staff also lived and worked aboard with their chief. For them the war was an around-the-clock business, especially since the bad news of Japanese conquests had been coming in daily, apparently without an end in sight.

Earlier that day, Saturday, January 10, the President had reiterated his desire to strike Japan and asked King, Marshall, and Arnold to keep their respective staffs thinking of ways and means to carry the fight to the enemy and bolster public morale. So far none of them had yet come up with a definite plan.

After dinner, King retired to his cabin. Captain Francis S. Low, a submariner and operations officer on King's staff, waited a few minutes and then decided to speak to his superior alone. King was not an easy man to talk to and few outside the small circle of his staff felt comfortable in his presence. He had an aloof, serious demeanor, not unlike that of his Army counterpart, Marshall. Neither man smiled much; indeed in those days there wasn't much to smile about; the nation's fate in large measure rested in their hands.

Low knocked and King invited him inside. "Yes, Low, what's on your mind?"

Low got right to the point. "Sir, I've got an idea for bombing Japan I'd like to talk to you about."

King was immediately interested. Like Arnold, he had sent memos to his staff after every meeting with the President and Roosevelt's frequent mention of air raids against Japan had been transmitted to them.

Low continued, "I flew down to Norfolk today to check on the readiness of our new carrier, the *Hornet,* and saw something that started me thinking."

Low paused, then talked faster. "The enemy knows that the radius of action of carrier aircraft is limited to about 300 miles. Today, as we were taking off from Norfolk, I saw the outline of a carrier deck painted on the airfield which is used to give our pilots practice in taking off from a short distance . . ."

King was patient with Low, but so far Low hadn't told him anything new. "I don't understand what you're getting at, Low."

"Well, Sir, I saw some Army twin-engine planes making bombing passes at this simulated carrier deck at the same time. If the Army has some longer-range planes than our Navy fighters— maybe a medium bomber like the B-25 or B-26—and if they could take off in the length of a carrier deck, then it seems to me a few of them could be loaded on a carrier and used to bomb Japan. It would be a mighty big surprise to the Japanese and would certainly build up the morale of the American people."

King leaned back and said nothing for a minute. Low felt uneasy and expected a curt rebuff—it would not have been his first when he advanced a new idea to King.

"Low, you may have something there. Talk to Duncan about it in the morning."

"Yes, Sir," Low said pleased and turned to go. This back-handed favorable reaction of the Old Man was like getting a Commendation Medal.

"One thing, Low," King cautioned. "Don't tell anyone else about this."

Low immediately phoned Captain Donald B. "Wu" Duncan, at his Washington apartment. Duncan, a 1917 graduate of the Naval Academy, was King's air operations officer and was highly respected for his planning ability and knowledge of carrier aviation. "Wu, I've got something important I'd like to talk to you about," Low told him. "Can you meet me at the office tomorrow morning?"

"Sure," Duncan replied. Although King had promised that his overworked staff would have Sunday off, Duncan knew that Low, his senior and personal friend, wouldn't be calling without good reason. When they met next morning, Low explained his idea and how he had conceived it the day before ("fortuitous association" he later called it). "As I see it," Low told Duncan, "there are two big questions to be answered: first, can such a plane—a land-based twin-engine medium bomber—land aboard a carrier? And secondly, can such a plane, stripped down to its absolute essentials, and loaded with gasoline and bombs, take off from a carrier deck? If either one or both questions can be answered affirmatively, we may have a whole new concept of operation to go on."

"The answer to your first question is a definite negative," Duncan told him. "In the first place, a carrier deck is too short to land an Army medium bomber safely. Even if one could stop in time, there would be no place to stow it because it wouldn't fit on an elevator to be taken below and make way for the next plane. Both the B-25 and B-26 have tricycle landing gear. This design increases landing speeds and the tails are so high off the deck that there is no way to install a landing hook. Besides, if we could figure out a hook design, the tail structures are too weak to take the shock of hard sudden-stop landings."

"And my second question?"

"That will take some figuring. I'll get to work and let you know."

"All right," Low told him, "but the Admiral said to be sure that not another soul finds out what you're working on." Low recounted years later that "Duncan normally would have had available to him all sorts of talent to perform computations that had to be made in order to determine the feasibility of the study. Instead of that, Duncan had to lock himself up for a few days and do everything himself."

"Wu" Duncan found a vacant office and buried himself in the details of his study. He made discreet inquiries of the Army concerning the B-25 and B-26 aircraft asking for such information as landing speeds, dimensions, range, and load capabilities. He checked Navy files for the figures on deck space of the various carriers. Historical records were consulted to see what experience the Navy had had previously with taking off heavily loaded planes in short distances. Weather patterns were studied to determine the best time for raids against the islands of Japan. And most important, Duncan carefully checked distances to be flown against the capabilities of each airplane.

At the end of five days, Duncan came up with a 30-page analysis, handwritten since he had not wanted to entrust his study to a typist. He made only one copy and, so far as is known, it is the only complete document concerning the planning for the raid the Navy ever made. Its whereabouts today are unknown.

Duncan, a perfectionist and brilliant staff officer, who later rose to four-star admiral and Vice Chief of Naval Operations, had done a thorough job of thinking through the problems that would

have to be faced and solved. The one vital element in any plan
to strike Japan from carriers would be surprise. Surprise meant
absolute secrecy, for any Naval task force in the Pacific would
be a prime target and encourage the Japanese to attack with every
weapon at their command to finish the job on the U.S. fleet they
had started at Pearl Harbor. All operations therefore, should be
Top Secret and few, if any, records should be kept of arrangements. The lives of over ten thousand men would be at stake
if the plan leaked out.

For the planes, Duncan settled on the North American B-25
as the only plane that could possibly be used. Four-engine planes
were out of the question. The Martin B-26's required too much
take-off distance. The Douglas B-23 had too much wingspan to
get by the "island" on a carrier and its predecessor, the Douglas
B-18, didn't have the range nor could it carry a worthwhile
bombload if it were modified to carry extra gas. The B-25, properly modified, could carry two thousand pounds of bombs and
make a two thousand mile flight provided extra gas tanks were
installed. Normally, it would need at least twelve hundred feet
of runway with that kind of a load. If it were lightened, however,
it might be made to leap off in a little over a third of that distance,
especially with the aid of the forward speed of a carrier and a
wind of about 25 knots.

Duncan felt that the carrier *Hornet* would be the ideal vehicle
to transport and launch the B-25's. Commissioned in October,
1941, and completing her shakedown cruise at the time of his
report, she was due to sail from Norfolk in February for the
Pacific. Her decks would take 16 B-25's and she could steam
ahead at 25 knots or better. Using a screening force of one other
carrier, cruisers, destroyers and tankers, the *Hornet* could be
brought to within about five hundred miles of the Japanese coast
and the 25's launched. After bombing selected targets in Japan,

they could proceed to China and the task force could retreat to safer waters.

Army pilots, Duncan knew, were not trained to take off in extremely short distances. The pilots selected would have to practice on land with varying loads until they could all take off in the distance the length of a carrier's deck.

Modifications would have to be made to the B-25 to give it added gas capacity. Every extra mile that the B-25's could add to their range meant one less mile that the task force would have to risk inside the range of Japanese land-based aviation. But this meant added weight and weight meant either more take-off distance required or less of a bomb load. It would not make sense to have the planes so loaded with gas they could not carry enough bombs to do any damage. There would have to be a compromise and in Duncan's study these computations were fairly well worked out. However, to be perfectly sure, he knew an experimental run should be made; otherwise it meant risking the lives of many men.

At the end of the fifth day, Duncan told Low he thought he had the answers and suggested they both see Admiral King. Once inside King's office, Duncan briefed his superior on his conclusions.

King, unsmiling as usual, leafed through the handwritten sheets while his two subordinates stood by uneasily. When he had finished reading, King was thoughtful for a moment and then said, briskly, "Go see General Arnold about it and if he agrees with you, ask him to get in touch with me. But don't mention this to another soul!"

The two officers turned to leave and King called them back. "Duncan, if this plan gets the green light from Arnold, I want you to handle the Navy end of it," he said and then dismissed the pair with a wave of his hand.

Duncan nodded. He hadn't realized that he would have a part

in implementing the plan but he was delighted. He and Low immediately made an appointment to see General Arnold the next day, January 17.

NOTE TO CHAPTER 2

1. Memorandum to Major General Edwin M. Watson, January 7, 1942, General H. Arnold files, Library of Congress.

Chapter 3

A PLAN IS MADE

With each passing hour in the closing days of 1941, the news from the Pacific got worse. General Arnold pushed his staff day and night to plan the rapid expansion of the Army Air Forces to cope with the widening spread of enemy power. His greatest need, he soon found, was for strong, capable air leaders who could build the Air Force being formed on paper into lean, hard-fighting units capable of gaining back the initiative from the enemy. But good men with flying experience, leadership ability—and guts—were hard to find. "Our reservoir of skilled and experienced officers was so shallow," Arnold later wrote, "that every time we lost one he was almost irreplaceable." [1]

One of Arnold's "irreplaceable" air officers was Major James H. "Jimmy" Doolittle, master of the calculated risk, who had won nearly every aviation trophy there was and some of them twice. Racing and test pilot, aeronautical scientist, and holder of many aviation "firsts," Doolittle was a man whose fast-paced activities certainly belied his name. Not only was he the first man to fly across the United States in less than 24 hours, but also the first to do it in less than 12. He was the first to fly an outside loop and first to take off, fly a set course, and land without seeing the ground—thus pioneering the science of blind flying. He had won

the Schneider, Bendix, Thompson, Mackay, Harmon, Guggen-
heim, and Wright Brothers trophies besides a number of foreign
awards and had earned his doctoral degree in aeronautical engineering from Massachusetts Institute of Technology. He was, and
is, without a doubt, the most famous flyer in the world.

Doolittle had missed seeing service in World War I, and he
has never gotten over this oversight. He enlisted for flight training
in November, 1917 and became a flying instructor after graduation. In 1921, he participated in the Mitchell-directed battleship
bombings off the Virginia capes. Between then and the late 1930's,
his name became synonymous with dare-devil piloting. Contrary
to popular belief, Jimmy stayed in the Air Corps during his
record-shattering days until 1930 when he resigned his regular
commission as a First Lieutenant to go into commercial aviation.
He was given a reserve commission as a Major, however, and
maintained an active association with the struggling peacetime
Air Corps.

When war broke out in Europe in September, 1939, Doolittle
was sure that war was eventually coming to America. After a trip
to Europe where he saw the growing Luftwaffe firsthand, he got
in touch with "Hap" Arnold, his friend of many years, and asked
to be called back to active duty. On July 1, 1940, orders were
issued assigning him as a Major to Indianapolis, Indiana with
duty as Assistant District Supervisor of the Central Air Corps
Procurement District. Four months later Doolittle was transferred to Detroit. These two assignments were not an attempt to
shelve the world-famous flyer and keep him out of the cockpit.
President Roosevelt's plans to make America the "arsenal of
democracy" meant mass conversion of American industry from
peacetime goods to war materiel. Retooling and reorganizing was
a mammoth, almost impossible, task. Arnold knew that Doolittle
was one of the few men in the country who had not only the

necessary engineering background but the tact and finesse needed
to deal with industry as well.

In Detroit, Doolittle's ingenuity and talent for getting things
done paid off. The conversion of the auto industry to production
of airplane parts was one of the most difficult in American history.
By December 7, the entire automotive industry had agreed on
their "terminal quotas"—last private cars for the duration. Representing the Army Air Forces, Jimmy helped make the conversion
to war production as smooth as possible.

Throughout the time that Doolittle had been in Indianapolis
and Detroit, he had kept in close touch with Arnold. Although
not on Arnold's staff and far beneath him in the chain of command, no one ever tried to stop Doolittle from going "out of
channels" to contact Arnold directly when he had a problem.
He did not abuse the privilege which their friendship had given
him, however, and always used it in the best interests of getting
his assigned job done.

The day before Christmas, 1941, Arnold telephoned Doolittle
in Detroit.

"Jim," Arnold said, "I'd like to see you here in Washington.
How soon can you come?"

Doolittle, the man who can never stand still, gave the answer
Arnold expected. "I'll be there in about four hours."

When Doolittle strode briskly into Arnold's office in Washington, the conversation was brief. "I want you to move down here
and be on my staff," he told Jimmy. "I've got to be sure that we
get the equipment we really need in the months to come and that
the stuff coming off the production lines is operationally ready
when we get it. I'd like you to clean up your projects in Detroit
and move on down here as soon as possible."

Doolittle understood the problem perfectly. Between wars the Army's step-child air arm, because of budgetary limitations, had to be more interested in aircraft performance than in the purely military requirements in support of a doctrine for air warfare. The airplane was now going to war and it had to do other things besides fly high and fast. It had to be capable of carrying the fight to the enemy's homeland and destroying his war-making potential. Doolittle was to be Arnold's trouble-shooter and this role appealed to the indomitable airman who had an unmatched reputation of accomplishment. Doolittle's only concern, however, was that he might have to "fly a desk" for the duration. He had missed one war and he didn't want to miss another.

It was several days before Doolittle cleared up the loose ends in Detroit and moved to Washington. Official records show he was promoted to Lieutenant Colonel on January 2, 1942, and transferred to Headquarters, Army Air Forces on January 9. However, correspondence in official files proves that he was at his desk in Washington and working on vital problems concerning the B-26 *Marauder* at least a week previously. "It was an 'unforgiving' airplane," Doolittle recalled, "and it was killing pilots because it never gave them a chance to make mistakes. Hap Arnold wanted me to check into the airplane and recommend to him whether it should continue to be built or not. I checked it over, flew it and liked it. There wasn't anything about it that good piloting skill couldn't overcome. I recommended it continue to be built and it was."

General Arnold confirmed this in his memoirs:

"Our new pilots were afraid of the B-26," he wrote, "and we had one accident after another. Seemingly, all that was necessary was for one engine to go sour on a B-26 while in flight, and it would crash.

"At the time the B-26 trouble was at its height, I called Doolittle to my office, told him I would like to have him go out, take a B-26, fly it under any and all conditions, and then go down to the B-26 outfit, take command, and show those boys that flying this ship was no different from flying any other. Doolittle did this, and before he left the outfit he had the boys flying the B-26 on one engine, making landings and taking off with one engine, just as easily as they had formerly done with two." [2]

The B-26 problem was the first project Arnold had assigned him. Although he did not know it yet he was soon to be involved with another airplane and again to show that with the right equipment and the right training "impossible" things could be done.

When Captains Low and Duncan presented their idea to Hap Arnold on January 17, Arnold, as Low said later, "was most enthusiastic" about a carrier-based raid against Japan. He did not tell them that he had already asked his staff to check into the feasibility of just such a plan in connection with the forthcoming invasion of North Africa and that his staff was still pondering his memo of January 4. Staff members had not yet made their recommendations to him because of the work load imposed by the Arcadia Conference which was just ending. No one was really sure if a land-based bomber could actually take off from the rolling, pitching deck of a carrier. There would be only one way to find out.

Arnold liked the idea and immediately got in touch with King. After they had settled the fundamental division of responsibility between them, it was decided that Captain "Wu" Duncan would be the overall Navy coordinator to handle all Navy logistic planning for the operation. Whomever Arnold chose to handle the Army Air Forces side of the task would have the job of overseeing the modification of the planes and training the crews.

The man Arnold needed for this kind of mission had to be a man who was used to doing the impossible with an airplane. He had to be not only an experienced pilot but someone who could inspire others by example and who knew airplanes not only as a pilot knows them but as an aeronautical engineer. There was only one man in the whole Air Force who could meet those specifications. Arnold sent down the hall for Jimmy Doolittle.

"The selection of Doolittle to lead this nearly suicidal mission was a natural one," Arnold later explained. ". . . he was fearless, technically brilliant, a leader who not only could be counted upon to do a task himself if it were humanly possible, but could impart that spirit to others." [3]

Doolittle saluted and returned Arnold's ever-present smile as he entered his chief's office. After a little friendly chit-chat, Arnold was suddenly serious.

"Jim, what airplane have we got that will get off in five hundred feet with a two thousand pound bomb load and fly two thousand miles?"

Doolittle pondered a moment before answering. The Air Force had planes that could take off in five hundred feet but none that could do that and fly such a bomb load for such a distance. Still, if properly modified, maybe the B-18, B-23, or the B-25 could do it. The B-26 needed too much take-off distance and the heavy four-engined bombers could never be souped up to get off in that short a distance . . .

"General, I'll need a little time on that one. Give me a day or two and I'll have an answer for you."

"OK, Jim, but keep this under your hat and let me know as soon as you can."

Next day, Doolittle reported back to Arnold. "It narrows down to either the B-23 or the B-25, but either one will take some modifying."

"One more fact you should know that I didn't tell you is that the plane must take off from a narrow area not over 75 feet wide."

"Well, then the only answer is the B-25. It has a 67-foot wing span. The B-23 would never make it off safely. Now, what's behind all this?"

Arnold quickly passed on the basic idea to Doolittle who caught his boss's enthusiasm immediately. "Jim," he said, "I need someone to take this project over, get the planes modified and train the crews . . ."

"And I know where you can get that someone," Doolittle interjected.

Arnold grinned. He knew that was the way it would be. "OK, it's your baby. Let me know what you need and I'll see that you get it."

This was the kind of problem-solving Doolittle liked. Arnold then talked briefly with Admiral King. "We'll get your men within striking distance of Japan," King said, "then it's up to them. We'll shoot for a West Coast departure of about the first of April. If that's OK with you, I'll send Duncan to Pearl Harbor when the time is right and relay the plan to Admiral Nimitz. I'll let you know when we're ready for you. As I see it, the biggest problem will be security. The fewer who know what we're doing, the better."

Arnold agreed. Not only would the lives of hundreds of men in the naval task force depend on how well the secret was kept but the crews of the bombers, too. If the element of surprise were lost, the Japanese could have their numerically superior naval forces out waiting to catch what they missed at Pearl Harbor. Clouds of fighters would be ready to pounce on the Mitchells as they neared the home islands. No one had to remind Arnold of the consequences if word of the mission got out. The two veteran airmen—Duncan and Doolittle—had their orders and went their separate ways. Both knew by instinct and experience exactly what they had to do.

In spite of its informal beginnings, the plan for a carrier-based raid on Tokyo was not to be a hastily conceived devil-may-care operation. Some writers, not knowing the whole story, have described the raid as a desperate attempt to inflict indiscriminate damage on the enemy's stronghold and perhaps kill the Emperor himself. Such was not the case. The B-25 raid on Japan was only a piece of a master plan to build up American power in the Far East, assist China in driving the invaders out and carry the war to the Japanese homeland.

At the highest levels of the War Department, concepts of operations for the future conduct of the war in the Far East were not yet firm in the first week of January, 1942. General George C. Marshall, Chief of Staff of the Army, did not agree with Secretary of War Stimson's views on how the war was to be fought in the Orient. Stimson wanted a full-scale theater of operations established; Marshall and his planners, led by a staff officer named Dwight D. Eisenhower, seemed to favor a military mission with an emphasis on airpower. The idea was to lend American Army advisors to the Chinese to help them whip their almost limitless manpower resources into a powerful ground force. The paper prepared by Eisenhower's experts in the War Plans Division expressed the War Department's official view as:

1. To provide equipment to the Chinese Army to enable it to continue operations against the Japanese. This includes assistance in the maintenance of communications.

2. Instigating Generalissimo Chiang Kai Shek to intensify Chinese effort and to restore the waning spirit of the Chinese in carrying on the conflict.

3. To secure, maintain, and operate air bases for air operations
against the Japanese.

4. To organize various types of American units by enlistment
in the American Army to carry on guerrilla warfare.[4]

Proposals had already been made to Generalissimo Chiang
Kai Shek in Chungking asking him to accept the nomination as
Supreme Commander of an Allied China Theater. The Generalissimo accepted about January 5 and asked that Roosevelt
send a high-ranking American Army general to be chief of the
Allied staff. General Joseph W. "Vinegar Joe" Stilwell, blunt,
outspoken, indefatigable infantryman, was nominated, accepted,
and duly assigned. His job, as he saw it, was to "coordinate and
smooth out and run the (Burma) road, and get various factions
together and grab command." [5]

As the days passed relentlessly by and American policy in regard
to the China situation was being painfully formulated, the Japanese continued their daily advance south and westward. The
Burma Road, vital ground transportation link to China, had to
be kept open. It would take prodigious Allied effort—ground and
air—to stop the enemy's advance and keep the supply lines from
being shut off. At the end of January, T. V. Soong, Chinese
Ambassador to the United States, gloomily forecast the closing of
the Burma Road and asked for one hundred DC-3 transports to
fly war materiel over the "Hump" and keep China fighting. The
underrated Japanese forces had shattered all Allied estimates of
their ability to fight and did so with such bewildering speed that
war maps in Washington were continually out of date.

The importance of U.S. air aid to China grew as more and more
territory was lost to the enemy. By the beginning days of February, there was no doubt that Soong was right and that eventually
a major air effort would be needed which would have to be
predominantly American. If air transport routes were to be established, they would have to be well organized and coordinated and

they would have to be protected. Any offensive efforts by Allied ground armies could only be made under an umbrella of friendly air cover. The end of resistance in Burma was now definitely in sight. If the pressure were not relieved and more attention given to the ever-worsening situation in the Far East, it appeared there would be no end to Japanese aggression.

Even before the Chinese Ambassador's dire prediction, plans were well advanced by mid-January in the Air War Plans Division to establish a major fighting air command, the Tenth Air Force, in Burma. An advanced detachment, under the code name AQUILA, was organized to be the nucleus of the build-up of American air power in China. There were to be five separate but related projects in this initial build-up:

1. The flight of B-25's to be dispatched from a carrier, were to provide the first medium bombardment aircraft for use in China. Pilots and crews were to be absorbed into the Tenth Air Force after their mission.

2. Thirty-five DC-3 transports were to be provided to form the aerial lifeline of supply.

3. A group of 33 A-29 attack planes under the command of Colonel Leo H. Dawson, were to be ferried from the factory to the Chinese Air Force under the lend-lease agreement; the pilots were then to be assigned to the Tenth Air Force.

4. Twenty-three B-24 heavy bombers, under command of Colonel Harry A. Halvorsen, were to be the first long-range bombers assigned to the Tenth. It was this unit, known as the Halpro Group, that was to open up long-range strategic attacks on Japan from Chinese bases.

5. Fifty-one P-40E's were to be assembled at Takoradi, West Africa and ferried to China for the use of Chennault's AVG, whether or not it was absorbed into the American Air Forces.[6]

These five separate projects, once approved, were assigned to the various leaders chosen to carry them out. The last four projects, to be carried out independently of the others, were given Secret status. The first, now assigned to Lieutenant Colonel Jimmy Doolittle, was Top Secret because of the mission his planes were to perform en route from the carrier to the destination in China. In the beginning only five men, King, Arnold, Doolittle, Duncan, and Low, knew that this project had been approved. Records do not reveal but it is believed that Arnold let one other person in on the plan: President Roosevelt. However, there is some doubt that the President was told any details until later.[7]

At 2 P.M. on January 28, 1942, Arnold again met with the President, Secretary of War, Admiral King, General Marshall, and others in the White House. Discussions of strategy centered around the situation in the Pacific and the Far East. In his report of that meeting, Arnold noted that the President asked about the progress being made on plans for bombing Japan.

"At that time, the Doolittle Project was underway," Arnold recalled, "but all those present did not yet know about it and we didn't want it to be common knowledge so I steered clear of it and talked about bombing Japan from China and Russia." [8]

The official memorandum of that meeting reports:

> General Arnold stated that at present a man is working on this proposition of bombing from China or Russia; that it will take a few months to get the gasoline and fields available, after which bombing from China could start. Also that a route across the Aleutians is being developed for a way down the coast of Siberia.
>
> The President stated that, from a psychological standpoint, both of Japan and the United States, it was most important to bomb Japan as soon as possible; that he had been studying on a map the location of the latest Sino-Japanese lines, and in the northern part of China he was surprised to see that the line was considerably closer to Japan than he had previously thought.

General Arnold stated that plans for bombing from China contemplated that the bombers would fly to advanced bases in the evening, land, re-gas, fly over Japan, land at the advance bases, and then return to a base in the rear.

The President directed that the possibilities of establishing bases in Northern China be looked into. He also asked if there were any possibilities of bombing from the Aleutian Islands, but it was pointed out that the distances involved were too great.[9]

While Arnold thus concerned himself with broad air strategy on a global basis, the orders detailing those selected to carry out the thousands of tasks in support of that strategy began to flow out of Headquarters, Army Air Forces. Doolittle needed no orders. Sitting as he did at the elbow of Arnold, his position and his fame were all the authority he needed. "Special Aviation Project No. 1" was underway.

NOTES TO CHAPTER 3

1. Arnold, *Global Mission,* p. 259.
2. *Ibid.,* p. 299.
3. *Ibid.,* p. 299.
4. *Aide-Memoire,* Notes on China, prepared by Brigadier General Dwight D. Eisenhower for Lieutenant General Hugh A. Drum, January 2, 1942.
5. Stilwell diary.
6. Charles F. Rommis and Riley Sunderland, *U.S. Army in World War II: The China-Burma-India Theater* (Office of the Chief of Military History, U.S. Army), p. 79.
7. Admiral Ernest J. King in his book, *Fleet Admiral King: A Naval Record* (by Ernest J. King and Walter Muir Whitehill, New York: W. W. Norton & Company, Inc., 1952), p. 376, wrote that ". . . until twenty-four hours before the raid only seven people—King, Low, Duncan, Arnold, Doolittle, Nimitz and Halsey—knew of the *complete* plan. When *Hornet* was already in the western Pacific and fast approaching the point where the planes would be launched, King put on his cap and went to the White House to tell the President. That was the first detailed information that Mr. Roosevelt had of the raid on Tokyo."
8. Arnold, *op. cit.,* p. 289.
9. Memorandum of White House meeting, January 28, 1942, General Arnold files, Library of Congress.

Chapter 4

THE PREPARATION

In Washington, Captain Duncan had quickly set the wheels in motion for the Navy's part in the coming raid with his request that a submarine be dispatched to send back weather data. Lieutenant Commander William L. Anderson, skipper of the *U.S.S. Thresher,* was instructed to take his ship into Japanese waters via Midway Island, observe enemy shipping and attack targets of opportunity. In addition, he was to surface at regular intervals and make weather observations. Temperature, pressure, wind direction, wind speed, ceiling, and visibility were to be meticulously noted. Knowledge of the weather over and around the Japanese islands was important to such a mission and could easily mean the difference between its success or failure. Not only the aircraft but the entire task force used to get the planes to their launching points could be endangered by running into unexpected typhoons or severe storms.

The mission of the *Thresher* was only the first of the many arrangements Duncan had to make. A force of ships had to be planned to escort and protect the carrier carrying the Army B-25's. Destroyers, cruisers, oilers, submarines and at least one other carrier would be required. This meant obtaining provisions, fuel, ammunition, and manpower. Gathering such a force would put a severe strain on the Pacific Fleet—still trying to recover from

Pearl Harbor. The risk of loss to the Navy was great. There could be no slip-ups.

One vitally important question had to be answered before plans went too far. Both Duncan and Doolittle had carefully and independently calculated that it was mathematically possible for a combat-loaded B-25 to lift off a carrier deck. But could their figures be wrong? Could there be some mysterious aerodynamic reason that the as-yet-untried Mitchell bomber might not be able to get itself airborne in a deck length of a little over 450 feet? Duncan was determined to find out—personally.

The *U.S.S. Hornet,* the Navy's newest carrier, was due in Norfolk on January 31 to be readied for her first war mission. There would be no better chance, Duncan figured, to see how right—or wrong—he was. Besides, the *Hornet* might be the very carrier that would be used for the raid. He made arrangements with Arnold's office to have three B-25's waiting at the dockside when the *Hornet* arrived at the huge Hampton Roads installation. He then radioed Captain Marc A. Mitscher, skipper of the *Hornet,* that he would come aboard at Norfolk to discuss urgent business.

The Army Air Force crews selected for the experiment had been well trained for the mission. Lieutenant John E. Fitzgerald,[1] a 1940 graduate of Advanced Flying School, had about four hundred hours in the B-25 when war was declared. About the middle of January he received orders to proceed to Norfolk where he was put in charge of two other crews also assigned to the mission.

In Norfolk he flew about 30 test runs at one of the auxiliary fields, as did the pilots of the other two planes. One of the planes lost an engine and did not participate thereafter.

On the afternoon of February 1, Duncan, brisk and business-like, reported to Mitscher aboard the *Hornet* and discussed the experiment with him. Early the next day, Fitzgerald's two B-25's were towed to dockside. A huge loading derrick was attached to a specially constructed sling and the Mitchells were swung aboard the *Hornet* and lashed down.

On February 2, 1942, the *Hornet* was underway and about the middle of the afternoon the fliers were advised to man their planes.

Duncan and Mitscher stood together on the port side of the ship's bridge in their foul-weather gear and watched the preparations below them on the wind-swept deck. The first B-25 was maneuvered into position and the launching officer signaled to Fitzgerald to rev up his engines to the maximum. At the proper instant, the "go" signal was given. The Mitchell raced down the gently sloping deck and lifted easily into the air with space to spare.

From the pilot's point of view, the take-off was not without its moment of excitement. "When they spotted the planes for take-off," Fitzgerald said, "I was surprised to observe that we had been provided almost 500 feet of usable deck and that the plane's air-speed indicator showed about 45 miles per hour just sitting there. This meant we had to accelerate only about 23 miles per hour.

"When I got the "go" signal, I let the brakes off and was almost immediately airborne—well ahead of my estimate. One thing that worried me, though, was the projection of the 'island' out over the flight deck on which the skipper stood so he could have a clear view of the deck operations. The wing of my plane rose so rapidly that I thought we were going to strike this projection. I pushed the control column forward and the wing just barely passed underneath. I climbed and circled back to watch Lt. McCarthy take-off."

Lieutenant James F. McCarthy's plane was jockeyed into position and roared seaward. It, too, was airborne safely before reaching the end of the deck. The two Mitchells joined up and disappeared over the horizon; their crews were unaware of the significance of their experiment.

Duncan was now satisfied that his calculations were correct. The wind had been about 20 knots and the speed of the *Hornet* had been only 10 knots at the time of the second launch. At a top speed of 25 knots and an average wind, there was now absolutely no doubt that a combat-laden B-25 land bomber could make a carrier take-off.

While Duncan was busy working out the Navy's part in the coming operation, Doolittle continued necessary actions to co-ordinate the Air Force share. Modification of the planes had to be accomplished as soon as possible. New gas tanks had to be designed, drawings made, a contractor found, the planes scheduled into the modification center and tests made of the installations. All this had to be done before the crews were selected and trained. To make the April 1st deadline meant Doolittle would have to have top priority and carte blanche everywhere he went. As Arnold knew, it would take all the Doolittle energy, know-how, and personality to get the job done.

Taking first things first, Doolittle checked into the contractors best qualified to modify the B-25's. On January 22, he formally requested "that one B-25B airplane be made available to the Mid-Continent Airlines at Minneapolis, Minnesota on January 23, 1942, or at the earliest possible moment thereafter." He further asked "that 17 more B-25's be delivered to Mid-Continent Airlines for alteration as required." [3]

On January 23, Doolittle arrived at Wright Field to confer with Brigadier General George C. Kenney. He explained to Kenney what he needed in the way of assistance for "the B-25B Special Project" but he did not tell him why. Kenney called in his top civilian and military experts [4] and Doolittle laid out his requirements succinctly, again without mentioning the reasons. Not only were extra gas tanks to be installed and the associated plumbing designed but new bomb shackles and other special equipment would be needed. Several planes were to be equipped with small electrically-operated cameras which would take 60 pictures at half-second intervals, starting automatically when the first bomb dropped. The others were to carry 16mm cameras similarly mounted. Landing flares were to be relocated forward of the rear armored bulkhead to protect them better against enemy fire.

The toughest part of the job, Doolittle told them, would be the installation of the auxiliary gas tanks. A 265-gallon, leak-proof tank would have to fit into the bomb-bay, leaving room underneath for four 500-pound bombs. The second tank should be a collapsible rubber bag affair that could be put into the crawlway between the front and rear compartments.

In the week between his visits to Wright Field, Doolittle had set other wheels in motion. He asked General Arnold to have the Intelligence staff select the best targets in Japan for the mission.

On January 31, Brigadier General Carl Spaatz, Arnold's deputy for intelligence, replied with a list of industrial targets located in Tokyo, Kobe, Nagoya, Yokohama, and six other major cities. Iron, steel, magnesium, and aluminum industries were listed, along with aircraft plants, petroleum refineries, and naval objectives. Beside each target suggestion was the reason for its selection. From this basic list, Arnold directed that target folders be prepared without delay.

A few days after Doolittle had been tapped to plan for his mission, the other projects of which the carrier-based raid was only a part, also began to take shape. The Halpro Project of locating a heavy bombardment group in China was in the final planning stages and on January 26, the Air Staff was directed to activate the Headquarters and Headquarters Squadron. President Roosevelt, impatient for air action against the Japanese homeland, had inquired as to the feasibility of operating heavy bombers from Mongolia. Without specifically mentioning either the Halpro or Doolittle projects, Arnold replied to the President on January 28:

> In reply to your recent inquiry, please permit me to advise you that there is no present means of operating heavy bombardment aircraft from Outer Mongolia, viz., east of Urga, and between Urga and the Outer Mongolia-Manchukuo border without the definite cooperation of the Russian Government.
>
> The Chinese Government has had no effective control of Outer Mongolia for the past several years, and no control is attempted by the Chungking Government to any important extent beyond Lanchow in Kansu Province, the Gobi Desert north of Kansu forming a fairly effective natural barrier.
>
> For this reason I feel that the plan which is now in progress, for carrying out an attack upon the Japanese enemy's center of gravity, by making use of facilities for which the Chinese Government can guarantee us a reasonable degree of security on the Eastern Asiatic mainland, is the logical and most effective plan.[5]

When the energetic Doolittle was reasonably sure that he had gotten all the different phases of his project started, he returned to his office in Room 4414 of the Munitions Building. Closing the door, he sat down at his desk and began to ponder over what he had done in the previous month. Had he really tied up all the loose ends? The blueprints from Kenney's experts were completed and planes were being modified; crews were to be selected; armament was being prepared. What else needed to be done?

Reaching into his desk drawer, Doolittle withdrew a pad of lined tablet paper and began to write: [6]

Subject: B-25 Special Project
To: Commanding General, Army Air Forces
    The purpose of this special project is to bomb and fire the industrial center of Japan.

It is anticipated that this will not only cause confusion and impede production but will undoubtedly facilitate operation against Japan in other theaters due to their probable withdrawal of troops for the purpose of defending the home country.

An action of this kind is most desirable now due to the psychological effect on the American public, our allies and our enemies.

The method contemplated is to bring carrier-borne bombers to within 400 to 500 miles (all distances mentioned will be in statute miles) of the coast of Japan, preferably to the south south east. They will then take off from the carrier deck and proceed directly to selected objectives. These objectives will be military and industrial targets in the Tokyo-Yokohama, Nagoya and Osaka-Kobe areas.

Simultaneous bombings of these areas is contemplated with the bombers coming in up waterways from the southeast and, after dropping their bombs, returning in the same direction. After clearing the Japanese outside coastline a sufficient distance, a general westerly course will be set for one or more of the following airports in China: Chuchow, Chuchow (Lishui), Yushan and/or Chienou. Chuchow is about seventy miles inland and two hundred miles to the south southwest of Shanghai.

After refueling, the airplanes will proceed to the strong Chinese air base at Chungking, about 800 miles distant, and from there to such ultimate objective as may, at that time, be indicated.

The greatest non-stop distance that any airplane will have to fly is 2,000 miles.

Eighteen B-25B (North American Medium Bomber) airplanes will be employed in this raid. Each will carry about 1,100 gallons of gasoline which assures a range of 2,400 miles at 5,000 feet altitude in still air.

Each bomber will carry two 500 lb. demolition bombs and as near as possible to 1,000 lbs. of incendiaries. The demolition bombs will be dropped first and then the incendiaries.

The extra gasoline will be carried in a 275-gallon auxiliary leakproof tank in the top of the bomb bay and a 175-gallon flexible rubber tank in the passageway above the bomb bay. It is anticipated that the gasoline from this top tank will be used up and the tank flattened out or rolled up and removed prior to entering the combat zone. This assures that the airplane will be fully operational and minimizes the fire and explosion hazard characteristic of a near empty tank.

In all other respects the airplanes are conventional. The work of installing the required additional tankage is being done by Mid-Continent Airlines at Minneapolis. All production and installation work is progressing according to schedule and the 24 airplanes (6 spares) should be completely converted by March 15th.

Extensive range and performance tests will be conducted on #1 article while the others are being converted. A short period will be required to assemble and give special training to the crews. The training will include teamwork in bombing, gunnery, navigation, flying, short take-off and at least one carrier take off for each pilot.

If the crews are selected promptly from men familiar with their jobs and the B-25B airplane the complete unit should be ready for loading on the carrier by April 1st.

General operational instructions will be issued just before take-off from the carrier.

Due to the greater accuracy of daylight bombing a daylight raid is contemplated. The present concept of the project calls for a night takeoff from the carrier and arrival over objectives at dawn. Rapid refueling at the landing points will permit arrival at Chungking before dark.

A night raid will be made if, due to last minute information received from our intelligence section or other source, a day-light raid is definitely inadvisable. The night raid should be made on a clear night, moonlight if Japan is blacked out; moonless if it is not.

All available pertinent information regarding targets and defenses will be obtained from A-2, G-2 and other existent sources.

The Navy has already supervised takeoff tests made at Nor-folk, Va. using three B-25B bombers carrying loads of 23,000 lbs., and 26,000 lbs. and 29,000 lbs. These tests indicate that no difficulty need be anticipated in taking off from the carrier deck with a gross load of around 31,000 lbs.

The Navy will be charged with providing a carrier, (probably the *Hornet*), loading and storing the airplanes and with deliver-ing them to the takeoff position.

The Chemical Warfare Service is designing and preparing special incendiary bomb clusters in order to assure that the maximum amount that limited space permits, up to 1,000 lbs.

per airplane, may be carried. 48 of these clusters will be ready for shipment from Edgewood Arsenal by March 15th.

About 20,000 U. S. gallons of 100 octane aviation gasoline and 600 gallons of lubricating oil will be laid down at Chuchow and associated fields. All other supplies and necessary emergency repair equipment will be carried on the airplanes.

Ist Lt. Harry W. Howze, now with the Air Service Command and formerly with the Standard Oil Company of New Jersey, will be charged with making arrangements for the fuel caches in China. He will work through A-2 and A-4 and with Col. Claire Chennault, a former Air Corps officer and now aviation advisor to the Chinese government. Col. Chennault should assign a responsible American or a Chinese who speaks English to physically check and assure that the supplies are in place. This man should also be available to assist the crews in servicing the airplanes. That the supplies are in place can be indicated by suitable radio code signal. Work on placing supplies *must* start at once.

Shortly before the airplanes arrive the proper Chinese agencies should be advised that the airplanes are coming soon but the inference will be that they are flying up from the south in order to stage a raid on Japan from which they plan to return to the same base.

Radio signals from the bombing planes immediately they drop their bombs may be used to indicate arrival at gasing points some six or seven hours later.

Care must be exercised to see that the Chinese are advised just in time as any information given to the Chinese may be expected to fall into Japanese hands and a premature notification would be fatal to the project.

An initial study of meteorological conditions indicates that the sooner the raid is made the better will be the prevailing weather conditions. The weather will become increasingly unfavorable after the end of April. Weather was considered largely from the point of view of avoiding morning fog over Tokyo and other targets, low overcast over Chuchow and Chungking, icing and strong westerly winds.

If possible, daily weather predictions or anticipated weather conditions at Chungking and the coast should be sent, at a specified time, in suitable code, in order to assist the meteorologist on the carrier in analyzing his forecasts.

Lt. Col. J. H. Doolittle, Air Corps, will be in charge of the preparations for and will be in personal command of the project. Other flight personnel will, due to the considerable hazard incident to such a mission, be volunteers.

Each airplane will carry its normal complement of five crew members; pilot, co-pilot, bombardier-navigator, radio operator and gunner-mechanic.

One crew member will be a competent meteorologist and one an experienced navigator. All navigators will be trained in celestial navigation.

Two ground liaison officers will be assigned. One will remain on the mainland and the other on the carrier.

At least three crew members will speak Chinese—one in each of the target units.

Should the Russians be willing to accept delivery of 18 B-25B airplanes, on lease lend, at Vladivostok, our problem would be greatly simplified and conflict with the Halverson project avoided.

It had taken Doolittle about two hours to draft this memorandum. He knew now that there were still some things to be done. Each of the elements of the plan had to be followed up. There would probably be some compromises and changes but if any single one of the important details were overlooked or not completed on time, the success of the mission would be in doubt. Most worrisome of all was the installation of the extra gas tanks. The matter of gas tank capacity could mean the difference between landing in enemy or friendly territory—between death or survival. The only thing that would be more important to the crews than gasoline would be their defensive guns. Both gas and gun problems were almost to doom the entire mission.

On January 30, Colonel John Y. York of General Arnold's staff penned his signature on a "directive memorandum" to the Materiel Division requesting that the number of B-25B airplanes to be modified for the Doolittle project by Mid-Continent be increased from the original number of 18 to 24. Twenty-four bombers were needed to assure at least 15 for the mission and that number could be obtained most handily from the three squadrons of the Seventeenth Bombardment Group, located at Pendleton, Oregon, and its associated Eighty-Ninth Reconnaissance Squadron. The choice of the airplane for the operation had actually determined the choice of the units that would furnish the crews. It was easiest to draw all crews from the squadrons furnishing the planes rather than leave them without equipment.

On February 3, the group received orders to transfer without delay to the Columbia Army Air Base, Columbia, South Carolina. The new commanding officer of the Seventeenth, appointed just before the group left Pendleton, was Lieutenant Colonel William C. Mills. While his unit was getting ready to move its ground and air echelons, Mills was instructed to pass the word among his squadrons and the Eighty-Ninth, commanded by Major John A. Hilger, that volunteers were needed for an extremely hazardous mission which would require the highest degree of skill and would be of great value to the war effort. By the time the four squadrons reached Columbia, the response was overwhelming.

On Mills' recommendation Doolittle selected Hilger as his deputy and explained that he would be responsible for taking 24 qualified crews and such ground personnel he would need to Eglin Field, Florida, to get started on a training program. They would prepare themselves for a mission that would require a take-off from a carrier, bombing a target enroute and a landing in China, where the planes would probably be delivered to the Chinese Air Force. Doolittle would commute between Washington and Eglin and handle all the planning. Hilger would be in charge of the group at Eglin in Doolittle's absence.

Colonel Mills had delegated to his three squadron commanders —Captain Edward J. York, Captain Al Rutherford and Captain Karl Baumeister—the task of coming up with the names of the men they recommended for the mysterious mission. All three had volunteered but Mills could allow only York to go. Since practically every man in the three squadrons of the Seventeenth and the Eighty-Ninth had volunteered, the four squadron commanders concerned made up rosters of an approximately equal number of men to make up the 24 crews. Mechanics, armorers, radio men, and other ground support personnel were also designated and ordered to proceed to Eglin as fast as planes could be made available to transport them.

Hilger and the major part of the contingent arrived at the Florida base between February 27 and March 3. No one except Hilger yet knew anything about the project nor what was expected of them. Hilger had cautioned them all not to speak to anyone and to get their planes ready for combat training missions as soon as possible. The men's previous combat experience was limited to submarine patrol missions off the Oregon and Washington coast. Although one crew had sunk a Japanese submarine, most of these missions were uneventful, and the men had not yet flown over enemy territory against anti-aircraft fire.

At Eglin they were assigned barracks and an operations building on the flight line apart from other units on the base. The commanding officer of the base had been informed only that this detachment was to undergo "special training" and that he was to provide such facilities and supplies as they required. Before Doolittle had left Columbia for Washington, Hilger had suggested that it might be a good idea if a Navy flying instructor were assigned to the project for a short time to teach the pilots about carrier take-offs. Army Air Forces pilots were not trained in getting heavily-loaded bombers off in the distance of a carrier flight deck; Navy pilots were required to be proficient in carrier take-offs and landings before graduation from flying school.

Lieutenant Henry L. Miller, USN, flying instructor at Pensacola Naval Air Station, was ordered to Eglin to train the Army pilots in carrier take-off procedure. Years later he recalled his impressions:

I reported to the commanding officer of the field. It was from him that I learned that Lieutenant Colonel Jimmy Doolittle was the commanding officer of the B-25 detachment. I figured something big was cooking.

When I arrived at the B-25 headquarters, I met Captains "Ski" York, Davey Jones and Ross Greening. I told them why I was reporting aboard. They seemed surprised. I didn't know that the whole operation was still a mystery to them.

After we chatted a while they asked me if I had flown a B-25 before. I had to be honest. I had never even *seen* a B-25 yet. They took me outside and I got my first look. Man, how I wanted to get my hands on that airplane.

After taking a look at some of the performance data and pilot's handbooks, we all climbed into the plane on that Sunday afternoon, proceeded to an auxiliary field that had been set aside for the group and made two practice take-offs. I acted as co-pilot for Davey Jones and Ski York while Ross Greening observed. I gave them instructions and they followed me to the letter. On the first take-off, the indicated airspeed was 50 miles an hour. The three Army pilots were skeptical and would not believe that we could take that plane off with a gross weight of 27,000 pounds, at 50 miles an hour. They agreed that the airspeed indicator must be off.

On the second take-off, with Davey Jones at the controls, we got off at an indicated 60 miles an hour because Jones held it on the ground a bit longer than York had done. Even so, the three of them were convinced. They didn't know it then but before they were finished, they would be able to take off from 350 feet in a 40 knot wind with the plane loaded to 31,000 pounds— 2,000 pounds over its designed maximum load.

Pilots assigned to the "Special B-25 Project" monitored the short field take-off practice of their flying mates at Eglin. Shown here checking stop watch times are, left to right, Lts. Knobloch, McElroy, Joyce, and Farrow.

On March 3, Doolittle landed at Eglin and the entire group of about 140 men assembled to hear him. It was a typical Doolittle pitch—short and to-the-point:

"My name's Doolittle. I've been put in charge of the project that you men have volunteered for. It's a tough one and it will be the most dangerous thing any of you have ever been on. Any man can drop out and nothing will ever be said about it. The operation must be made up entirely of volunteers. If anyone wants to bow out, he can do so right now."

Doolittle stopped talking and the room was quiet. Several hands went up simultaneously and Doolittle nodded toward a young second lieutenant nearest him.

"Sir, can you give us any more information about the mission?" the lad asked.

"No, I'm sorry, I can't right now," Doolittle answered. "But I'm sure you will start getting some ideas about it when we get down to work. Now, that brings up the most important point I've got to make to you and you're going to hear this over and over again. This entire mission must be kept top secret. I not only don't want you to tell your wives or buddies about it, I don't even want you to discuss it among yourselves."

Doolittle paused again to let his words sink in and continued. "The lives of many men are going to depend on how well you keep this project to yourselves. Not only your lives but the lives of hundreds of others will be endangered because there are a lot of people working on this thing. Don't start any rumors and don't pass any along. If anybody outside the project gets nosy, get his name and give it to me. The F.B.I. will find out all about him.

"Our training here will stress teamwork. I want every man to do his assigned job. We've got a lot of work to do on those planes to get them in shape. There's a lot of training in store for navigators, bombardiers and engineer-gunners. For the pilots the main thing is to learn how to take the B-25 off in the shortest possible distance with heavy loads. We've got about three weeks—maybe less. Remember, if anyone wants to drop out, he can. No questions asked. That's all for now."

As the project commander, Doolittle set up his organization along standard squadron lines. Major Jack Hilger was appointed executive officer; Major Harvey Johnson, adjutant, Captain "Ski" York, operations officer; Captain David M. Jones, navigation and intelligence officer; Captain C. Ross Greening, gunnery and bombing officer; First Lieutenant Bill Bower, engineering officer; and First Lieutenant Travis Hoover, supply officer.

During the first few days at Eglin, Doolittle took these officers aside and told them the general nature of their mission without specifically telling them what the targets were to be. He told them they would learn their destination only when aboard the carrier and on their way. He brought them up to date on how and why certain decisions had been made, such as the selection of the B-25, the main objective of the raid and how the airplanes were to be carried within reach of the targets. This was done because Doolittle knew that these factors would affect the training program. Secrecy was again stressed. It seemed to be uppermost in his thoughts; he saw to it that it was in everyone else's as well.

From the first day of training, it was clearly understood that all 24 crews would take the training and go aboard the carrier even though only about 15 planes would be taken. This was done for two reasons: no word could leak out from disappointed crews if they were on the carrier and there would be plenty of extra crew members available to replace those who might become ill or decided to withdraw from the mission at the last minute.

The first part of the flying training program was quick take-off practice. For the Army pilots, unaccustomed to near-stall take-offs, this practice was a harrowing experience. Throughout their cadet training days they had been taught always to have plenty of airspeed before flying a plane off the ground. They were used to flying from five-thousand-foot runways. Yanking the B-25 off with the tail skid almost dragging the ground was a most unnatural attitude to them. But with Hank Miller's encouragement and criticism, they soon learned.

"All pilots," Miller recalled, "with the exception of a few con-servatives, caught on quickly. Doolittle, Gray and Jones were particularly outstanding. But it was found that constant practice had to be given because pilots were prone to switch back to the conventional take-off."

In addition to take-off practice at the Eglin auxiliary fields, other training missions were scheduled concurrently. Originally it was decided that each crew would receive 50 hours of flying time to be spent on day and night navigation, gunnery, bombing, and formation flying. However, maintenance problems and troubles with the gas tank installations and gun turrets cut this time down considerably. Consequently, most crews flew only about half the number of hours planned.

Before navigation flights could be made, Doolittle required all engine and flight instruments calibrated and fuel consumption checked. Since each plane was to fly not less than nineteen hundred miles on a little over eleven hundred gallons of gas, all engines had to operate at maximum efficiency. All during the practice and testing, the gas tank modifications were a constant source of trouble. The 265-gallon steel tanks leaked profusely and new 225-gallon self-sealing tanks were installed in their place. Still there were leaks in the connections and other mechanical problems. A third tank of 60-gallon capacity was later installed in the position from which the lower gun turret was removed. The filler neck of this tank was accessible to the rear gunner in flight. Ten 5-gallon cans of gasoline were to be carried in the rear compartment and poured into this tank as the gasoline level went down. The total gas capacity, theoretically, amounted to the following:

Main wing tanks	646	gallons
Bomb bay tanks	225	gallons
Crawlway tank	160	gallons
Rear turret tank	60	gallons
Ten 5-gallon cans	50	gallons
Total	1,141	gallons

This B-25 is an exact replica of the plane piloted by Lt. Col. Jimmy Doolittle on the Tokyo Raid. The plane has a wingspan of 67 feet, 7 inches, its length is 53 feet, 5¾ inches, height 16 feet, 4-3/16 inches, and weight when empty approximately 20,300 pounds.

De-icing boots were installed on the leading edges of the wings and tail surfaces and anti-icing equipment for the propellors. (At this point in the planning, it had not yet been decided whether East China or Vladivostok was to be the destination, and icing conditions did prevail along the northern route to Vladivostok.) Two landing flares were installed forward of the armored bulkhead behind each pilot. If they were needed, they would have to be thrown out of the rear hatch by the gunner.

Since the mission required absolute radio silence and weight was a problem, the 230-pound liaison radio set was to be removed from each plane. In order to prevent unintentional broadcasts by improper use of the interphone, the coils were also to be removed from the command transmitters and stowed elsewhere within each plane for use upon arrival at the destination.

While all of these modifications and installations were important, none of them was more important than the armament. Unless a bomber is properly equipped to defend itself, its chances of survival against a determined enemy are slim. The B-25B's of 1942 vintage were woefully deficient in their firepower. They were equipped with top and bottom turrets, neither of which was satisfactory. The tail was unprotected and the nose contained a single .30 caliber flexible machine gun that the bombardier had to move from one gun port to another.

Ross Greening, armament officer for the project, met and solved a host of problems at Eglin.[8] For example, with Doolittle's approval he instructed that two wooden .50 caliber dummy guns made out of broomsticks be stuck out of the extreme tip of the tail, to deceive enemy pilots attacking from the rear. They were painted black and were somewhat longer than the actual .50 caliber machine gun to make their presence more noticeable.

Then, since the lower gun turret functioned improperly, if at all, it was decided to remove it. Colonel Doolittle actually made this decision, remarking, "A man could learn to play the violin good enough for Carnegie Hall before he could learn to fire that thing."

Greening himself developed a simplified bombsight for the B-25's that he called the "Mark Twain."[9] He reported that "actual low altitude bombing tests carried out at 1,500 feet showed a greater degree of accuracy with this simplified sight than was obtained with the Norden by the same bombardiers. This not only permitted greater accuracy in bombing but obviated the possi-

Replica of the "Mark Twain" bomb sight used by all sixteen bombers on the Tokyo Raid. The sight was constructed in the Eglin Field shops to the specifications of Capt. Greening; materials cost only about 20 cents. (The sight shown here was reproduced by Lt. Col. Horace E. Crouch, USAF (Ret.) navigator on the crew of Lt. Joyce; it cost about 75 cents in 1963.) Knowing airspeed and altitude, the bombardier could compute the angle at which the sighting bar should be set. When the target passed the line of sight, bombs were released. For low altitude bombing this improvised sight was more accurate than the famous (and secret) Norden bomb sight. (Photo by Francis N. Satterlee)

bility of the highly classified Norden sight from falling into enemy hands." [10]

Most of the gunners who had volunteered for the project had never fired a .50 caliber gun nor operated a power turret before. Gunnery practice was so delayed because of the amount of work that had to be done on the turrets that the men had little chance to get the feel of their guns under flight conditions. Precious days were lost while armament personnel tried desperately to get the turrets in working order.

By the end of the training period, most of the gunners had ground-fired their guns on the range, had bore-sighted them and fired a few bursts in the air; however, not one of them had fired on a moving target. Looking back on his training at Eglin, one gunner reflected, "I guess I should have been concerned at the time but I don't remember being worried about anything in those days. Somehow, I knew that if the Boss thought things were O.K., then we'd come out of it all right."

The Boss, meanwhile, was busy deciding, among other things, what types of bombs should be used on the raid. He was aided in this by Colonel Max F. Schneider, an ordnance expert, and Chemical Warfare Service personnel at Edgewood Arsenal, Maryland.

While Doolittle and Captains Ross Greening and Ski York were busy with their respective responsibilities, other officers of the group were carrying out their assigned chores. Captain Davey Jones was responsible for obtaining maps, photographs, target charts, target folders, and weather records from the Intelligence Section in Washington. Lieutenant Trav Hoover worked around the clock checking supplies and obtaining spare parts and equipment. Lieutenant Bill Bower spent all of his waking hours on the flight line supervising the maintenance crews when not in the cockpit. Lieutenant Royden Stork, a professional photographer before entering the service, haunted the base photo lab to obtain film to document the training phase and for the cameras being installed in the planes.

Another volunteer who had duties to perform, in addition to his crew training, was Dr. (First Lieutenant) Thomas R. White, a physician attached to the Eighty-Ninth Reconnaissance Squadron as Aviation Medical Examiner. As soon as "Doc" White had heard of the call for volunteers for a special mission while enroute to Columbia, he wired Major Hilger, his squadron C.O., to "squeeze me in somewhere."

Hilger was delighted that the squadron doctor, a favorite among the pilots, wanted to go along. "But, you'll have to train as a crew member, Doc," he told him.

"That's the way I want it, Major," White answered. "I've always wanted to be a gunner." And that's what he was. In subsequent practice at Eglin with the enlisted gunners, he scored the second highest score with the twin .50's. But no one needed to tell Doc White what his additional job was to be. Between stints on the gunnery range, he checked the immunization records of all prospective crew members and immediately innoculated them all for pneumonia, typhus, tetanus, bubonic plague, yellow fever, and smallpox. "I got a lot of static from the fellows," White recalled, "because for some of them it meant as many as eleven shots over a three-week period."

One day during the second week at Eglin, Doolittle flew back to Washington to report to Arnold how things were going. When he had outlined his problems and told how he was solving them, he added, "General, it occurred to me that I'm the only guy on this whole project who knows more about it than anyone else. You asked me to get the planes modified and the crews trained and this is being done. They're the finest bunch of boys I've ever worked with. I'd like your permission to lead this mission myself."

Arnold stared at Doolittle a moment, his grin faded, then he said, "I'm sorry, Jimmy, I need you right here on my staff. I can't afford to let you fly every combat mission you might help to plan."

Today, Jimmy Doolittle recalls the whole incident with a chuckle. "I launched into my sales pitch," he recalls, "and finally Hap shrugged his shoulders and said, 'OK, Jimmy, it's all right with me provided it's all right with Miff Harmon.' When he said that, I quit talking and got out before he changed his mind."

"Miff Harmon—General Millard Harmon who was later killed in the war—was Hap's chief of staff and had his office right down the hall. I thought I smelled a rat so I ran down the corridor and burst into Miff's office. 'Miff,' I said, 'I've just been to see Hap and gave him my report on this project I've been working on. I told him I wanted to lead the mission and he said it was OK with him if it's OK with you.'

"Miff was caught flat-footed which is what I intended. 'Sure, Jimmy,' he answered, 'whatever is all right with Hap is all right with me. Go ahead.'

"I thanked him and just as I closed the office door, I heard Miff's intercom buzz. It was Hap and I heard Miff say plaintively, 'But, Hap, I just gave him my permission since he said it was OK with you.'

"I didn't wait to hear any more. I beat it back to Eglin and hoped Hap wouldn't later order me to stay home. He never did." [11]

On his return to Eglin, Doolittle went about his own personal training program in earnest. "Naturally, I wanted to fly the mission as first pilot," he said, "but I wanted to go only on the basis that I could do as well as or better than the other pilots who had already started in their training program. So I took Hank Miller's course and was graded along with the others. I made it, but if I hadn't I would have gone along as a co-pilot and let one of the younger, more proficient pilots sit in the left seat."

All the crews flew as teams, which was very important to Doolittle's way of thinking. He knew that if a group of five men fly together day after day and get to know each other's mannerisms and techniques, it is not long before that crew has high morale and is willing to tackle anything. So it was with these men and, if personality differences appeared or individual proficiency was lacking, adjustments were made.

For his crew, Doolittle chose Lieutenant Richard E. Cole as co-pilot; Lieutenant Henry A. Potter, navigator; Sergeant Fred A. Braemer as bombardier; and Sergeant Paul J. Leonard as engineer-gunner. The original pilot, Captain Vernon L. Stintzi, had become ill, and Doolittle flew with them.[12] He had never known any of them before but he liked the way they worked together. From his first flight with them, he was satisfied they knew their jobs.

Doolittle depended on his officers to ramrod the project at Eglin while he flew back and forth to Washington. He kept no records and did all of his arranging on a man-to-man basis without a single one of his contacts ever knowing what he was up to. By the middle of March, he knew time was getting short. The *Hornet* had passed through the Panama Canal and was en route to San Francisco by way of San Diego. Duncan had made all the necessary arrangements with Admiral Nimitz's headquarters in Honolulu and had passed the word to General Arnold that he would soon tell him when arrangements were complete.

Doolittle kept in personal touch with Arnold on each of his many trips to Washington. Whenever Doolittle had trouble persuading someone to provide equipment or services for the project, that someone got the word direct from Arnold's office shortly thereafter. The word was quickly passed around that whatever Doolittle asked for, Doolittle was to get—no questions asked. Slowly, but surely, the men and their equipment were nearing the day of departure for the West Coast.

At the end of the third week in March, "Wu" Duncan wired from Honolulu: TELL JIMMY TO GET ON HIS HORSE. Arnold picked up the phone and passed the same message to Doolittle at Eglin.

"Thanks, Hap. See you around," was all his friend said. That simple message was launching eighty brave men and ten thousand naval personnel into an adventure they would never forget.

NOTES TO CHAPTER 4

1. Fitzgerald is now a Colonel assigned to the Air Force Communications Service.
2. This is the first time that the names of these pilots have been revealed. Contrary to popular belief, neither General Doolittle, Captain Duncan, nor any of the Tokyo Raiders were the first to fly a B-25 from a carrier.
3. Memorandum for Chief of the Air Staff, Subject: B-25 Alterations, from Lieutenant Colonel J. H. Doolittle, January 22, 1942.
4. The military men were Colonel K. B. Wolfe, Colonel R. C. Harmon, Lieutenant Colonel F. R. Cook, Lieutenant Colonel E. M. Gavin, and Major J. H. Carter. The civilian experts were Otto Spevacek of the Service Engineering Division, Kenneth Traber, James C. Dugan, and D. D. Delameter, of the Aircraft Laboratory, and Henry G. Roganti, of the Photographic Laboratory.
5. Memorandum for the President, January 28, 1942.
6. This remarkable document is the only known record of the planning phases of the Tokyo Raid up to this point. Although undated, it was believed written during the first week of February, 1942, but it was never actually sent to General Arnold. When queried about this in 1962, Doolittle replied, "It is definitely in my handwriting but I do not recall preparing this letter. It may have been done at the request of General Arnold, or it is possible I may have jotted some of my ideas down in letter form to clarify my thinking in connection with the various phases of the project."
7. On February 17, a letter had been dispatched to Eglin directing that the base provide the necessary accommodations. The letter concluded by saying that "inasmuch as this is an extremely confidential project, it is directed that no information be permitted to get out regarding the arrival, departure or activities of these airplanes and crews."
8. Colonel Charles R. Greening, "The First Joint Action," prepared for the Armed Forces Staff College, Norfolk, Virginia, December 21, 1948.
9. This sight was manufactured in the Eglin Field shops at a cost of approximately 20 cents for materials.
10. Greening, *op. cit.*
11. General Doolittle told the author, "I'll have to admit that I really counted on leading the mission from the moment I first heard about it. My only problem was how to approach Hap so he would say 'Yes.'" Further proof of this is his plan reported earlier in this chapter.
12. Stintzi did, however, go along on the *Hornet* as a spare pilot.

Chapter 5

THE ADVENTURE BEGINS

In the weeks between the middle of January and the day Jimmy Doolittle got the signal to head west with his B-25's, the war news had gone from bad to worse to the blackest in the country's entire history. The situation in the Philippines was hopeless. Manila had been declared an open city on the day after Christmas. During the first week of January, American and Filipino troops fought delaying actions as they backed their way down the Bataan Peninsula. Lacking everything but courage, the heroic defenders were reduced to eating dogs, iguanas, monkeys, mules, and snakes to stay alive. On February 22, General Douglas MacArthur was ordered to leave Luzon and go to Australia to assume command of Allied forces when—and if—those forces were provided. He finally left on March 22 and upon arrival in Darwin announced: "The President of the United States ordered me to break through the Japanese lines and proceed from Corregidor to Australia for the purpose, as I understand it, of organizing the American offensive against Japan, a primary purpose of which is the relief of the Philippines. I came through and I shall return." [1]

While the battle's end was nearing in the Philippines, Hongkong and Singapore, the other centers of Allied power in the Far East, fell under the onslaught of Japanese air, ground, and

sea might. Next on the timetable was Burma and the teeming
city of Rangoon fell on March 7. Soon after the fall of Singapore,
Sumatra was smothered, Java was shut off from the West and
on March 9, the Netherlands East Indies surrendered with its
ninety-eight thousand troops.

With these successes behind them, the Japanese turned their
attention to the next strategy in their master plan: the subjuga-
tion of Australia. Port Darwin, the only major naval base in
Northern Australia was attacked by the Nipponese in February.
The next two months were spent cutting off the island continent
from the north by occupying New Britain, New Ireland, part of
New Guinea, the Admiralty Islands and the Gilberts. Within
less than four months of that infamous Sunday, the war strategists
in Tokyo had masterminded unbelievable conquests. A seemingly backward island nation had quickly expanded itself into a
gigantic empire and acquired control over three million square
miles of land rich in natural resources. The entire Pacific Ocean
west of a line drawn from Alaska to Hawaii to Australia was
dominated by Japanese military and naval forces.

The fall of the Philippines, Malaya, Burma, and the Dutch
East Indies had encouraged a push westward as well as southward. When the Andaman Islands in the Bay of Bengal fell,
there became a very real possibility that Japan would seek to link
arms with its Axis partner, Germany. If German forces were to
push eastward through the Middle East, a link-up was possible
in India. The combined forces would then consolidate their
gains and gradually undertake to conquer and subjugate the rest
of the eastern hemisphere. Their goal of world conquest would
then be half won.

On February 16, 1942, Brigadier General Martin F. Scanlon,
assistant chief of the Air Staff for Intelligence, wrote a memorandum to General Arnold citing the possibility of this pincer

movement on India. He predicted that "the two Axis powers will attempt a pincer operation on a world scale, with the employment of aircraft within present ranges of design, while forcing the United Nations on a continuous defensive over lines of supply and communications more tenuous and difficult than those of the Axis powers."

Scanlon concluded that "the only effective and immediate attempt to frustrate the aerial offensive of the Axis nations must be made at Japan's long line of communications." [2] He listed several ways in which his conclusion could be translated into military actions:

1. By the immediate restoration of General MacArthur's position as one capable of severely restraining the freedom of Japanese movements through the China Sea. This should be a major operation which then would assure adequate aerial reinforcement and sufficient increase in the supplies and surface combat forces to assure the success of our operations.
2. By the immediate dispatch into China of available heavy bombardment units; these to commence at once a series of raids upon Japanese communications in China and in the China Seas, and Japan itself.
3. By the seizure, upon diplomatic pretexts, of Russian bases such as Kamchatka for direct air assault upon the Japanese homeland.
4. In conjunction with the above, air raids from carriers against Japan.
5. By continuing pressure upon the Malay barrier from the continent of Australia with the use of long-range air bombardment of Japan's central position at Singapore, with diversions aimed at tactical surprise by carrier-based aircraft such as our naval forces recently achieved in the Marshall Islands.

Although General Scanlon was a highly trusted member of Hap Arnold's staff, he was not aware of Jimmy Doolittle's plans. He knew that his recommendations were sound but, being a

military realist, he thought that it would be many months before
they could be carried out.

It was early morning when Admiral William F. "Bull" Halsey's
Task Force Thirteen put to sea from Pearl Harbor. On board
his flagship, the *Enterprise,* Halsey squared his long-billed baseball cap and watched the destroyers *Balch* and *Maury* as they
zigzagged and screened ahead. The cruisers *Northampton* and
Salt Lake City plodded off to port and starboard. Task Force
Thirteen was headed for Wake Island.

On February 24, Task Force Thirteen was standing 75 miles
off Wake waiting to launch her planes. At 7:10 A.M., the cruisers,
closer in, opened up with their 8-inch guns. A dozen fires immediately erupted among the buildings on the tiny island. Then
the planes from the *Enterprise* roared in and raked the atoll with
bullets and bombs. Three flying boats were destroyed and one
small boat sunk. As a surprise, the raid was a success; from the
standpoint of damage done, the risk was hardly worth the effort.
Halsey decided to make a bolder raid. After zigzagging on erratic
courses for several days to throw off any possible pursuit, he set
course for Marcus Island, a tiny speck in the Pacific, less than a
thousand miles southeast of Tokyo. On March 4, while the moon
was full, 40 of Halsey's planes zoomed in on the few buildings
and airstrip and laced them with .50 calibers. The buildings and
a gasoline dump were left burning. No enemy planes were
sighted but anti-aircraft fire was heavy and one American scout
bomber was shot down.

These two raids were planned only as diversionary moves to
attempt to convince the Japanese they should pull their forces
up from the south and release the pressure on the Philippines.
The Japanese, however, were not to be deterred. It would take

more than hit-and-run raids on two mid-ocean atolls to slow down their steam-rollering toward Australia.

"Wu" Duncan was dead tired by the time he landed in Honolulu. He had flown from Washington to Hawaii for only one purpose and that was to inform the Commander-in-Chief, Pacific Fleet, of the plan to bomb Tokyo with Army bombers. He made his way directly to the office of Admiral Chester W. Nimitz. His orders gave no clue to his mission, merely stating that he was to be on temporary duty for a period in excess of 72 hours. Admiral King had informed Nimitz that Duncan was coming to see him and that the plan he was to discuss had his backing and support. Nimitz had no idea what it was but knew it had to be important to send an officer all the way to Hawaii to talk it over.

Nimitz was truly a man "of cheerful yesterdays and confident tomorrows" as his Academy class yearbook had noted. The calmest of men, he was a genius for making prompt, right decisions and had a tremendous capacity for work. He created an atmosphere of quiet efficiency wherever he was and had immediately restored confidence to the defeated Pacific Fleet upon his assignment after the Pearl Harbor debacle.

Duncan's plan was to his liking. It would be just the job for Bill Halsey, now waiting for his next orders. Nimitz called in Halsey to meet Duncan and tell him the plan. Halsey recalled their meeting later: [3]

> ... Miles Browning and I were called to CINCPAC'S headquarters for a conference with Rear Admiral Donald B. Duncan, from CINCUS. (Ernie King, not liking the implication of "CINCUS," may have changed his title to "COMINCH" by then; I'm not sure.) 'Wu' Duncan told us that something big was in the air,

something top secret; Lt. Col. James H. Doolittle, with Navy cooperation, had trained sixteen Army crews to take B-25's off a carrier's deck, and the Navy had promised to launch them for Tokyo. They might not inflict much damage, Wu said, but they would certainly give Hirohito plenty to think about.

Chester Nimitz asked me, "Do you believe it would work, Bill?"

I said, "They'll need a lot of luck."

"Are you willing to take them out there?"

"Yes, I am."

"Good!" he said. "It's all yours!"

I suggested that the operation would run more smoothly if Miles and I could discuss it man-to-man with Doolittle, whom I had never met. Chester agreed and gave us orders to proceed to San Francisco.

Duncan stayed in Hawaii long enough to make sure that Halsey and the CINCPAC planning staff had all the facts they needed. He then wired Washington the message to have Doolittle proceed to the West Coast.

Duncan left Pearl Harbor for San Diego to meet Mitscher who had just come through the Panama Canal in the *Hornet*. This was Mitscher's first knowledge of the forthcoming mission and he was delighted that he was to have a part in it. It was not until then that he realized why Duncan had come aboard in Norfolk the previous month and had him launch the two B-25's.

Fron San Diego, Duncan went to San Francisco to await the arrival of Doolittle from Eglin and Halsey from Hawaii.

When the crews had all reported to the flying line at Eglin in the morning of March 23, Doolittle gave them a short talk.

"Today's the day we move out," he told them. "Those who are going know who you are. Those not going with us will clean things up here and report back to Columbia. Remember what I've told you time and time again. Don't tell *anyone* what we were doing down here. Even if you think you've guessed what our mission is, just keep in mind that they are your buddies who are going and their lives depend on you not breathing a word of this to another soul." He dismissed all but the crews of the 22 planes chosen for the trip (two planes had been damaged during the training at Eglin). These men were then told to fly their planes to McClellan Field, near Sacramento, California.

Doolittle arrived at McClellan on March 26 and met with the Commanding Officer of the Sacramento Air Depot, Colonel John M. Clark, and his top engineering personnel to discuss the inspection job on the B-25's. He insisted that nothing be tampered with or removed—the airplanes were simply to be inspected. He explained that a number of installations would be made, among them new propellers, the 60-gallon rubber gas tanks in the rear compartments where the lower turrets had been removed, new covers for the leak proof bomb-bay tanks (the original covers had been made too small, causing wrinkles and, consequently, leaks), hydraulic valves for the gun turrets, back-type parachutes to replace the seat-type, and other important details. The liaison radio was to be removed, and new glass navigational windows were to replace the present plexiglass ones. Doolittle was informed that not all of this material had been received at the depot as yet.

Doolittle did his best to instill a sense of urgency in the civilian maintenance men at the depot but he did not have much luck. As one of Doolittle's pilots said later, "There's always someone who doesn't get the word." The sense of urgency had not filtered down with the instructions. The civilian maintenance crews went ahead in a leisurely way checking the planes and equipment. Doolittle advised his crews to stay with their planes and watch the work being done. They were to report anything they did not like to him or Ski York. It was not long before the complaints started. Ted Lawson described his experience in his book *Thirty Seconds Over Tokyo*: [4]

> . . . I had to stand by and watch one of the mechanics rev my engines so fast that the new blades picked up dirt which pock-marked their tips. I caught another one trying to sandpaper the imperfections away and yelled at him until he got some oil and rubbed it on the places which he had sandpapered. I knew that salt air would make those prop tips pulpy when they had been scraped.
>
> The way they revved our motors made us wince. All of us were so afraid that they'd hurt the ships, the way they were handling them, yet we couldn't tell them why we wanted them to be so careful. I guess we must have acted like the biggest bunch of sore-heads those mechanics ever saw, but we kept beefing until Doolittle got on the long-distance phone, called Washington and had the work done the way we wanted it done.

Doolittle had indeed called Washington. He refused to speak to anyone except Hap Arnold.

"Things are going too slowly out here," he told his chief. "I'd appreciate it if you would light a fire under somebody. They're treating this whole project as 'routine' and that won't get the job done in time."

Arnold reacted immediately. What had been treated as a routine inspection of combat-bound airplanes suddenly became the most important project on the base and the men and machines of the B-25B Project became a focal point of interest. These *were* strange aircraft when one thought about it. Broomsticks instead of guns in the tails. No liaison radios. Shiny new propellers which were promptly painted as soon as they were installed. A strange looking gimmick in place of the bomb sight. Rubber gas tanks and no lower gun turrets. And the crews seemed like an odd bunch, too. If they were asked what it was all about, their answer was, inevitably, "mind your own business!" A clannish group, they avoided the regular personnel on the base and, without regard for rank, stuck together off duty as well as on.

Jack Hilger, Ski York, Ross Greening and the other pilots practically lived on the McClellan flying line fretting about the condition of their planes during the week after their arrival. None of them was satisfied with the speed or the quality of the work being done. The grumbling of the crews reached Doolittle and he conveyed the complaints to the civilian supervisors. Improvement was still not forthcoming.

The series of annoyances reached a climax one afternoon when Doolittle was talking with Jack Hilger and several other pilots in McClellan base operations. Outside, a civilian mechanic was attempting to start one of the B-25's. An engine churned briefly then backfired violently. Doolittle stopped talking, saw black smoke pouring out of the recalcitrant engine and literally exploded out of the building on a dead run. As he ran he shouted at the man to shut down the engine but was rewarded only by more backfiring. Doolittle ripped open the forward hatch, leaped up into the cockpit and almost yanked the man from the pilot's seat.

The reason Doolittle was angry was obvious to his pilots. The carburetors on all the planes had been carefully bench-checked at Eglin and were in perfect condition. They were so finely tuned that the engines had to be started with a precise procedure. Careless starting which would cause backfiring could throw them out of adjustment and increase fuel consumption dangerously. Doolittle knew better than anyone else that lives would depend on the most efficient engine operation possible.

When Doolittle calmed down, the mechanic explained that he was merely running the engines up as he was required to do after the carburetors had been adjusted.

"What? Do you mean that somebody fooled around with these carburetors without my OK?"

"All I know is that they were checked, found way out of adjustment and fixed up," was the reply.

To Doolittle, this remark was the last straw. He ordered his men to check over everything being done to their planes and let him know what was wrong. He conveyed their collective complaints to the engineering officer and the base commander. In addition, he again called General Arnold and told him what had happened. Arnold called the Air Service Command at Wright Field and demanded a report.

Colonel Clark's teletyped reply, received the day after the B-25's had left McClellan, defended the depot men and pointed out that frequently pilots tended to worry too much about the condition of their airplanes as their departure date for overseas approached. Clark admitted, however, that the depot was having a hard time finding and keeping experienced personnel.

During their stay at McClellan, Doolittle and Hilger had roomed together in the bachelor officers' quarters. On the morning of March 30, Doolittle mentioned that he had to go into San Francisco to meet his wife, Jo, who was coming in from Los Angeles where she had been visiting her ill father. What Hilger did not know was that, coincidentally, Doolittle had received a message from Washington saying that he was to meet Admiral Halsey that night in a downtown restaurant.

That evening, over dinner in an out-of-the-way dining room, Halsey, Captain Miles Browning, his chief of staff, Duncan and Doolittle discussed details of the forthcoming raid candidly. The *Hornet,* in company with the cruisers *Nashville* and *Vincennes,* the oiler *Cimarron* and the destroyers *Gwin, Meredith, Monssen* and *Grayson* of Destroyer Division Twenty-two, were to be designated as Task Group 16.2 and leave San Francisco on April 2 with Captain Marc Mitscher as Task Force Commander. Halsey on the carrier *Enterprise,* would leave Hawaii on April 7, accompanied by the cruisers *Northampton* and *Salt Lake City,* the oiler *Sabine* and Destroyer Division Six consisting of the *Balch, Benham, Ellet* and *Fanning.* This group of ships would be Task Group 16.1.

Rendezvous of these two forces, to be known as Task Force Sixteen after they merged, was to take place on Sunday, April 12th at Latitude 38°00′ North—Longitude 180°00′. This combined armada would steam westward and refuel from the *Cimarron* and *Sabine* eight hundred miles off the coast of Japan. The oilers would then detach themselves and the rest of the force would dash toward the enemy homeland for the launch.

Halsey later reported that ". . . our talk boiled down to this: we would carry Jimmy within 400 miles of Tokyo, if we could sneak in that close; but if we were discovered sooner, we would have to launch him anyway, provided he was in reach of either Tokyo or Midway.

"That suited Jimmy. We shook hands and I wished him luck. The next time I saw him he was Lieutenant General Doolittle, wearing the Medal of Honor." [5]

What Halsey did not mention but what Doolittle fully appreciated when he left that meeting was that the Navy was taking a magnificent risk in the operation. If any word leaked out to the Japanese the U.S. Navy could suffer a loss almost as great as at Pearl Harbor. Sixteen surface ships, the largest American naval force that could be mustered in the Pacific, would be heading westward together. They would be ideal targets for a small, marauding Japanese submarine force. Coupled with Japanese land-based aviation attacks, the Halsey force could be intercepted many miles before the planned launching point. If a heavy enemy task force were alerted and given the mission to sail eastward to engage Task Force Sixteen, it could mean the end of American naval strength in the Pacific.

Doolittle also knew what would happen if Halsey's ships were attacked and they were not within reach of Japan with his B-25's. The Mitchells would be summarily kicked over the side so the *Hornet's* planes could be brought up on deck and launched to protect the fleet. All he could hope was that his continual pleas for secrecy had prevented any information about the raid from getting to the enemy.

After he left Halsey, Doolittle telephoned Jack Hilger at McClellan. Double-talking in such a way that Hilger would be the only man in the world who could understand if the conversation were being overheard, he told him to spread the word that the B-25's were to be loaded aboard the *Hornet* the next day.

That night, Hilger put out the order to his pilots to round up their crews and report to the flight line at daybreak. All crews were to check their planes over carefully and fly them to nearby Alameda Naval Air Station. "This is it," he told them. "When we get over there we'll want to know if there is anything wrong with your ships. Give them a good test flight and put at least an hour's time on them."

Giving the order to his crews did not mean that he was not going to have trouble getting his planes out of the hands of the McClellan maintenance crews. Since all the work had not been completed, regulations would not allow the planes to be released to their crews. But Hilger had his orders and after heated arguments with base engineering personnel finally got his planes on their way one by one.

Doolittle arrived and made out his flight plan for the short hop to Alameda. He was handed a report form to fill out which asked for his opinion of the work performed on the planes while at that station. He took one look at it and wrote diagonally across the form a single word "LOUSY!"

The base operations officer looked startled when he saw the remark. "Just a minute, Colonel. You will have to give me a detailed report. This simply will not do!"

"I haven't got time," Doolittle snorted as he turned and headed for his B-25.

"I won't sign your clearance then, Colonel," the young officer called after the disappearing Doolittle. He stared in disbelief as the man climbed into his airplane, started the engines and took off.

The infuriated operations officer turned to Jack Hilger and shouted, "Who does that guy think he is? I can tell you he's heading for a lot of trouble!"

Hilger had watched the whole incident with a smile on his face. "He sure is," he drawled. "He sure is!"

As the planes landed at Alameda, Doolittle and Ski York were on hand to greet each pilot. "Anything wrong with your ship?" they asked. If the pilot admitted some engine or other plane malfunction, he was directed to a near-by hangar instead of the wharf. When 16 planes had been parked at the wharf, Doolittle told York, "these planes will go. If you have any last-minute malfunctions, substitute one of the other planes. Tell all the crews to get aboard the *Hornet* whether or not their plane is on the dock." Those who had to leave their B-25's at the hangar were the crews who would not fly the mission—unless somebody dropped out.

Navy handlers swarmed over the B-25's as soon as their crews shut down the engines. Gas was drained out of the tanks. A Navy "donkey" hooked a tow bar to the nose gear of each plane and towed it down to the pier. The crews walked solemnly behind their respective planes and watched silently as the huge dockside crane reached down and picked them up as if they weighed only a few pounds. Once their planes were aboard, the crews filed up the gangplank of the *Hornet* where Hank Miller waited for them on deck.[6]

"I was proud of those fellows that day," Miller recalled. "As each man came aboard, he saluted the National Ensign and then the Officer of the Deck and said, 'Sergeant or Lieutenant or Captain so-and-so reporting aboard for duty, Sir.' They were a smart-looking outfit and I was mighty proud of the way they responded to my teaching. They looked smarter in all respects than the Navy personnel that were going to and fro."

The crew of the *Hornet* was mystified by the requirement to hoist the B-25's aboard, but went about their tasks as if they handled Air Force bombers on their decks everyday. The night before, Miller had gone aboard the *Hornet* to make final arrangements for hoisting the planes. "Of course," he recalled, "I met many officers whom I had known before and all of them were obsessed with curiosity as to where they were going. Everyone tried to find out from me, but I kept mum. Several officers who knew that I was from Alaska speculated that the mission would be somewhere around the Aleutian Islands. They were completely in the dark until the announcement was made later."

On one of the flights Doolittle made to Washington before leaving Eglin, he talked at length with Hap Arnold about arrangements to receive his planes in China. It had been decided a month before that secrecy could not be maintained in dealing with Chiang Kai Shek's staff. On February 9, Brigadier General John Magruder had sent a wire to General Marshall concerning conferences with the Chinese and noted:

". . . Despite my request for confidential treatment of matter, at height of interview an unexpectedly drawn curtain disclosed four servants absorbing the facts. This is characteristic and indicates futility of efforts to maintain secrecy regarding any military matters." [7]

Marshall immediately sent a memo to Arnold saying, "with relation to the highly Confidential project you and King have on, please read Magruder's telegram of yesterday regarding lack of secrecy in all discussions at Chungking." [8]

With this information, Arnold decided not to tell anyone in Chungking about the Doolittle mission although General Joseph E. "Vinegar Joe" Stilwell had been told the bare essentials of the project before he left the States in February to take over the China, Burma, India Command. The need for preparation of five airfields to receive the "First Special Aviation Project" was discussed but Stilwell was not told from where the planes were to come. No word was forthcoming from Stilwell's headquarters concerning airfield preparation after his arrival. On March 16, Arnold requested information on the progress of airports and bomb and gas supplies at the agreed-upon airports in Eastern China. Two days later Arnold sent Stilwell another urgent message:

REFERENCE SPECIAL AIR PROJECT DISCUSSED WITH YOU BEFORE DEPARTURE, TIME FOR SPOTTING GAS AT AGREED POINTS GETTING SHORT.

Four days later Stilwell wired Arnold that the Standard Oil Co. of Calcutta had five hundred gallons of grade-120 oil in five-gallon tins and thirty thousand gallons of 100-octane gasoline. He wanted to know why it was needed and requested authority to move it to China.

Stilwell's lack of appreciation for the growing urgency expressed by Arnold's wires was understandable. He was not an airman and did not sympathize with the problems of flyers. Because of the extreme need for secrecy to protect Halsey's task force as well as Doolittle's crews, the communications between Washington and Chungking were limited to the essentials of advising both Stilwell and the Generalissimo what needed to be done, without informing them of the details or the strategic purpose of the project. Still it was necessary to have Chiang's approval of the undertaking before the bombers could land in China. The Generalissimo did not want the B-25's to land there after bombing Tokyo because he feared a violent Japanese reaction. His wishes were, in effect, overruled.[9]

By March 25th, Arnold was getting more concerned that arrangements were not shaping up in China. He sent a message to Stilwell specifying the amounts of high-octane gasoline and aviation oil that would be needed, the airports in China where they were to be located, and the arrangements to be made at the airports for landing the B-25's.

On the 29th, Stilwell radioed Arnold that he recommended the use of Chinese gasoline instead of attempting to fly in American gasoline from India "due to lack of communications, time shortage and impossibility of secrecy." He advised Arnold that Kweilin and Chuchow were the only fields safe for heavy bomber operations according to the Chinese. Chiang Kai Shek had disapproved the use of Yushan, Kian or Lishui by heavy bombers unless an inspection was made by an American officer.[10]

As soon as Stilwell's message was received in Washington, Arnold dictated a memo for Admiral King and asked that he forward the information on to Doolittle. Arnold mentioned the quantities of gasoline and oil available at the five Chinese fields and added that "these figures were furnished on personal directive of Generalissimo by Chief, Chinese Air Force and are believed reliable." [11]

Arnold then dictated a message to Stilwell:

SPECIAL PROJECT WILL ARRIVE DESTINATION ON APRIL TWENTIETH. SHOULD A CHANGE IN ARRIVAL DATE ARISE AN ATTEMPT WILL BE MADE TO NOTIFY YOU. YOU MUST HOWEVER BE PREPARED FOR VARIATION WITHOUT NOTICE.

After his conference with Halsey, Doolittle boarded the *Hornet* and conferred with Mitscher. Fifteen B-25's had been hoisted aboard and tied down.[12] "I think she'll take one more," Doolittle told the little skipper with the leathery face and bright blue eyes. "Since none of the lads have actually made a carrier take-off, it would give them a lot of confidence to see a B-25 take off. About one hundred miles out we could send that sixteenth plane back. We could take Hank Miller along and let him co-pilot."

Mitscher rubbed his jaw thoughtfully a moment and then answered, "OK, Jimmy, it's your show." He ordered the sixteenth B-25 hoisted aboard and told Miller to find himself a bunk.

At 3 P.M. on April 1, the *Hornet* unmoored, moved to Berth #9 in the middle of San Francisco Bay at dusk, and anchored. The crews of the B-25's had been assigned quarters throughout the ship and had settled down as best they could. Much to their surprise, Doolittle called them together and after a brief lecture about secrecy let them go ashore for the evening.

The sudden freedom gave the crews a last chance for a fling in San Francisco and most of them took advantage of it. Several of the pilots made their way to the "Top of the Mark" Hopkins Hotel to view the sights. Lieutenant Dick Knobloch, co-pilot on the crew of Lieutenant Edgar E. McElroy, began to wonder. There below them in plain sight of whoever cared to look was the *Hornet* with their planes lashed criss-cross on her deck. He nudged Ross Greening and whispered, "I hope they rounded up all the Japanese spies. If they didn't I hope they think those things are just being transported to Hawaii."

Greening nodded and grinned. "What's the matter, Knobby, don't you know that you can't take a B-25 off a carrier?" he asked mockingly. Knobloch grinned in reply. He hoped Greening was only kidding.

NOTES TO CHAPTER 5

1. Statement issued to the press at Alice Springs, Australia, March 17, 1942.

2. Memorandum for Chief of the Army Air Forces, Subject: Possibility of Joint Air Attack by Germany and Japan, from Brigadier General Martin F. Scanlon, Assistant Chief of the Air Staff, A-2, February 16, 1942.

3. William F. Halsey and J. Bryan III, *Admiral Halsey's Story* (New York: McGraw-Hill Book Company, Inc., 1947), pp. 101-105.

4. Ted W. Lawson, *Thirty Seconds Over Tokyo* (New York: Random House, Inc., 1943), p. 32.

5. Halsey and Bryan, *op. cit.,* p. 101.

6. A total of 70 officers and 64 enlisted Air Force personnel boarded the *Hornet*.

7. Telegram from General Magruder to General Marshall, February 9, 1942. Magruder was head of the lend-lease mission to China.

8. Inter-office memo, Marshall to Arnold, February 11, 1942.

9. Marshall later apologized to the Generalissimo for failing to consult him.

10. Stilwell still did not know of the exact nature of the project and probably assumed that Arnold was referring to the Halpro Project which was to ferry B-24's via the Atlantic, North Africa, and India.

11. Memorandum for Admiral King from General Arnold, Subject: Operations in China (Special Project), March 31, 1942.

12. It had been decided previously that the *Hornet's* deck could not safely accommodate the 18 planes originally planned. The Navy had recommended only 15 planes be brought aboard.

Chapter 6

LAUNCH PLANES!

After giving his men their last night on the town, Jimmy Doolittle went to the hotel where his wife, Jo, was staying while in San Francisco for a few days. On the morning of April 2, he packed his B-4 aviator's bag, kissed her tenderly and said, casually, "I'll be seeing you. I may be out of the country for a little while. Call you when I get back."

Jo Doolittle, after many years of hellos and goodbyes, had grown used to it—almost. Jimmy always used the same casualness with her and she never knew until after the fact that he had risked his neck in some way and had set a new record, won a race or achieved another aviation "first." This time, as all other times before and since, she held back the questions and began a wait that was to last almost two months.

Returning to the *Hornet,* Doolittle went to Mitscher's cabin. The two discussed the departure plans and agreed that all hands should be told their destination after the force was a day out of port. At that time the sixteenth plane would be sent back to the mainland. As they concluded their conversation there was a knock on the door. It was the intelligence officer with messages from Washington. It was then that Doolittle learned that the arrangements for gas, oil, and airport marking he had requested in China were being made. Along with this message, relayed from Stilwell, were two other messages, both dated March 31, 1942:

MAY GOOD LUCK AND SUCCESS BE WITH YOU AND
EACH MEMBER OF YOUR COMMAND ON THE MISSION
YOU ARE ABOUT TO UNDERTAKE.

ARNOLD

AS YOU EMBARK ON YOUR EXPEDITION PLEASE GIVE
EACH MEMBER OF YOUR COMMAND MY DEEP APPRE-
CIATION OF THEIR SERVICES AND COMPLETE CONFI-
DENCE IN THEIR ABILITY AND COURAGE UNDER
YOUR LEADERSHIP TO STRIKE A MIGHTY BLOW.
YOU WILL BE CONSTANTLY IN MY MIND AND MAY
THE GOOD LORD WATCH OVER YOU.

MARSHALL

There was also a personal message to Mitscher from Admiral
King. It read: "I hope—and expect—that the first war operation
of the *Hornet* will be a success. I am confident that it will be
insofar as her officers and crew—under your able leadership—can
make it so. Good luck and good hunting."

The log of the *Hornet* for Thursday, April 2, 1942, records the
following:

> . . . 0430 Commenced fueling from oil barge. 0600 Lighted fires
> under #2 boiler. O710 Completed taking oil from barge. Received
> 153,329.4 gallons of oil. 0750 U. S. S. NASHVILLE underway.
> 0800 Lighted fires under boilers Nos. 8 and 9. 0810 Cut No. 9
> boiler in on main steam line. GWIN and GRAYSON under-
> way . . . 0900 MONSSON underway. 0915 MEREDITH under-
> way. 0940 NASHVILLE underway . . . 1010 DesDiv 22 standing
> out. 1018 Underway from San Francisco, California on various
> courses at various speeds while standing out of harbor. Captain at
> the conn, navigator on the bridge. 1020 VINCENNES underway.
> 1030 NASHVILLE, VINCENNES and CIMARRON fell in
> astern in column . . .

What the log does not record is that the San Francisco harbor
was basking in bright sunlight although visibility was poor. To

men like Hilger, York, Greening and others, it seemed like sheer madness to be sailing on their mission in broad daylight. As they passed under the Golden Gate and Oakland Bridges they could see the hundreds of automobiles crossing overhead. Thousands of people were watching them go with their B-25's lashed firmly on the *Hornet's* decks.

The Navy has never explained why such a risk was taken. However, the crews on these ships were not all old hands. Captain Frederick L. Riefkohl, skipper of the *Vincennes,* commented in an interview that "I was rather skeptical about our crew at the time, as many of my old-time men who had been on her almost a year had left and we sailed from there with a crew that was practically 50 percent recruits." It is perhaps for this reason that it was decided not to attempt a night departure.

While his men worried about their chances of survival, their leader had a different kind of worry. Ever since he had wangled permission from Arnold to lead the mission, he was afraid that he would be pulled off at the last moment. Just before the *Hornet* started down the channel, he was ordered ashore in the captain's gig to answer an urgent telephone call from Washington. Doolittle recalled:

"I thought it was going to be Hap Arnold telling me I couldn't go. My heart sank because I wanted to go on that mission more than anything since I had planned it and worked on it from the beginning. When I got ashore, it turned out that it was General Marshall calling. I might have tried to argue with Hap but not General Marshall. Now I *knew* that the jig was up.

" 'Doolittle?' Marshall said. 'Yes, General,' I answered. 'I just called to wish you the best of luck,' he said. 'Our thoughts and our prayers will be with you. Good-bye, good luck and come home safely.' All I could think of to say was, 'Thank you, Sir, thank you.' I went back to the *Hornet* feeling much better."

At 11:48, the *Hornet* and her protectors passed Channel Buoy No. 1 "abeam to starboard (and) entered swept channel." Captain Mitscher was relieved by the Officer of the Deck and the crew settled down into their practiced routine. Mitscher's orders were to take a meandering, circuitous route to the point of rendezvous with Halsey's force on the 12th.

Unknown to anyone on the *Hornet,* Halsey was having a little difficulty getting back to Hawaii. "Miles and I had expected to be back in Pearl on the second," he wrote later, "in ample time to polish our plans for the mission, but stray westerly winds grounded all westbound planes. We telephoned the air operations officer at Alameda and Pan American every day, and every day we were given the same report. On the fifth, we had to notify the *Hornet* to postpone our rendezvous for twenty-four hours. On the sixth, already sore and sour, I added a touch of flu to my other worries and took to my bed, loaded with dynamite pills. Naturally, this was the afteroon that the winds died and our flight was scheduled. When I boarded the plane, I was so full of pills that I rattled, but I slept until a nosebleed woke me as we lost altitude for our landing, and I stepped off at Honolulu with the flu licked." [1]

At dusk on April 2, the first of many *Hornet* battle drills was called. All Navy personnel raced to battle stations. The B-25 crews rushed to their planes and simulated getting them airborne. The gunners on each crew practiced unlimbering their turret guns. From that time on, every morning at dawn and every evening at dusk, Mitscher ordered all personnel to battle stations. If an emergency arose, the B-25 crews would know the most expeditious method of getting to their planes and either flying them off or pushing them over the side.

Just before noon the next day, Hank Miller was on the flight deck talking to Lieutenant Dick Joyce. According to the plan, the two of them were to take the 16th plane back to the mainland that afternoon. While they were chatting, Jimmy Doolittle approached.

"Talk to you a minute, Hank?" he asked.

"Yes, Sir," Miller answered.

The two walked over to Joyce's plane. Doolittle looked quizzically down the deck toward the bow a moment, then climbed up into the cockpit and settled into the pilot's seat. Miller followed and dropped into the co-pilot's seat.

"That distance looks mighty short to me, Hank," Doolittle said, motioning toward the gently plunging bow.

"You know, Colonel Doolittle," Miller answered confidently, "this is a breeze. You see that tool kit that is away up the deck there—that is where I used to take off in fighters."

Doolittle was quiet a moment, then smiled at Miller and said, "Hank, what do they call 'baloney' in the Navy?"

The two pilots, both with a healthy respect for the other, chatted briefly and then parted. Doolittle made his way to the bridge. Miller went below to the pilot's wardroom for lunch. Just as Miller was finishing dessert, the ship's loudspeaker blared: "Lieutenant Miller, report to the Captain on the bridge."

When Miller got to the bridge Doolittle was just leaving. Obviously Doolittle and Mitscher had been talking about his flight. When Doolittle was gone, Mitscher asked him how he felt about making the take-off. "We probably can't give you 40 knots of wind over the deck today, Miller. Still want to try it?"

Miller assured him that he did. "We won't need 40 knots, Captain, because we'll have 460 feet to take off. We can make it easily with what you can crank up in the *Hornet*, Sir."

Mitscher looked at Miller thoughtfully a moment and then asked, "Do you have any of your clothes aboard?"

"Yes, Sir. I brought my clothes aboard because we are going to deliver this plane back to Columbia, South Carolina. Why do you ask, Sir?"

"Well, if there is no strain in getting off, we'll take that extra plane."

Miller was surprised. "Well, that's fine, Sir. But would you drop me off at the next mail buoy, please? I've been traveling half way around the world on the strength of a phone call. When I get back to Pensacola, I'll probably be an ensign again."

Mitscher just grinned. If the B-25's got off successfully and the *Hornet* survived this dangerous intrusion into Japanese waters, he was sure the Navy would see to it that the career of one lieutenant, senior grade, would suffer no ill effects.[2]

A short time after Miller's discussion with Mitscher, a Navy blimp arrived over the *Hornet*. Two boxes containing the navigators' windows Doolittle had ordered were lowered to the flight deck. Air coverage was being provided by PBY patrol planes from the Western Sea Frontier. Below decks, the B-25 crews were settling themselves into their assigned quarters.

The relationship between the Air Force and Navy personnel was, as Ross Greening described, "slightly strained and defensive." Doolittle's men, remembering their leader's continual warnings about secrecy, refused to give any information to the curious Navy men. "There were no evidences of open dislikes," Greening reported, "only a defensive aloofness." He added that "it was only natural the Navy men would think the Army was overdoing its part and the Army was in no mood to jeopardize its security until it was completely safe for the Navy to know the nature of the mission."[3]

On the afternoon of April 2, Mitscher decided to tell Task Group 16.2 where they were going. He told his chief signal officer to notify the rest of the ships by semaphore that "this force is bound for Tokyo." On his own ship, the *Hornet,* he made the same announcement over the loudspeaker.

The reaction to Mitscher's words was immediate. "Cheers from

Shortly after leaving San Francisco, the *Hornet* was intercepted by a Navy blimp, the L-8, which dropped supplies for the B-25's on the deck.

every section of the ship greeted the announcement," he said, "and morale reached a new high, there to remain until after the attack was launched and the ship was well clear of combat areas." [4]

Now all rumors were dispelled. Doolittle had encouraged his men, if pressed, to further the idea that the B-25's were only being transported to Hawaii. No one on the West Coast knew of their take-off training at Eglin and anyone familiar with airplanes knew that combat-loaded medium land-based bombers could never lift themselves from a carrier deck. But it was official now that Jimmy Doolittle and his men were going to try.

The effect on the part of both Navy and Air Force men was immediate. "Relationships improved in a matter of seconds," Greening recalled, "and immediately all hands, Army Air Force and Navy, joined together to accomplish all that was necessary to satisfactorily complete the mission." [5]

The Air Force crews had already been told where they were going. Doolittle had called them together in the empty mess hall after breakfast that morning and said, "For the benefit of those of you who have not already been told or have been guessing, we are going to bomb Japan. Our targets will be in Tokyo, Yokohama, Nagoya, Osaka and Kobe. The Navy will get us in as close as possible and launch us off the deck. After hitting our targets we'll head for small fields in China, gas up, and then fly on to Chungking. Everything's set and you'll be getting all the dope you'll need during the days ahead."

Doolittle concluded this brief meeting by giving all of the crew members a chance to withdraw and be replaced by one of the spare crews. No one did.

The entire Air Force contingent aboard the *Hornet* was relieved to find out at last where their mission was taking them. The long period of enforced silence had inhibited the group so badly that many of them later admitted they could not really get serious about the mission until they knew where they were going. Now that they knew, the whole scheme suddenly fitted together like a jig-saw puzzle. The take-off practice, the over-water navigation flights, the concern about the carburetors, the new props, everything, now added up.

Instinctively, the thoughts of all the flyers went to the condition of their planes. Pilots, navigators, bombardiers, and gunners, almost as if by order, went to their respective crew positions in each plane. There now was a clear purpose to the whole affair and they were glad to be a part of it.

The greatest burden of concern fell on the pilots. All 16 of them, at one time or another, paced off the distance between the "island" and the bow of the ship. Singly and in pairs they would measure the distance, counting as they went and ending up with similar conclusions. That distance *was* mighty short and not a one of them had ever taken their 25's off in those few feet at Eglin. Doolittle had assured them it could be done but he had never done it. Miller had said it would be "no strain" but, again, he did not know from actual experience. Doolittle had been told that two B-25's had been launched from the *Hornet* earlier but he hadn't *seen* them do it. There was only one thing they could do: put their trust and faith in "the Boss." They knew he would piloting the first plane off and would have the shortest length of deck. If he could do it, so could they.

The next day after all hands knew where they were going and why, Doolittle introduced two Naval officers—Commander Apollo Soucek and Lieutenant Commander Stephen Jurika. Soucek was Air Officer for the *Hornet* and gave them instructions on carrier operations. Jurika was the *Hornet's* Intelligence Officer. As soon as he was introduced, it was obvious why he had the job.

"My connection with the Doolittle Raid actually began in Tokyo, in 1939," he recalled years later.[6] "I was assigned as

Assistant Naval Attache and Naval Attache for Air to the American Embassy in Tokyo. We did not have bombing maps of Japan and one of my principal tasks during the ensuing two years was to make these. I spent most of my time locating and pinpointing industries, industrial areas and all manner of bomb target information.

"One of my greatest sources of information at this time was the Soviet Naval Attache who had a wealth of information on Japanese industry. He used liberal quantities of vodka in an attempt to elicit information from me. But I was able to pour a great many of his drinks into his potted palms without his knowing it. He attempted to get information from me about our forces in the Far East but he was a great source of information on Japanese industry.

"Among other ways we had of obtaining information was sailing in the bay from Tokyo to Yokohama, journeying on American ships from Yokohama to Kobe, and photographing the ports and shipyards we passed enroute. At the end of my two-year tour, we had quite a dossier on Japanese industry."

In 1941, Jurika returned to the United States, served briefly in the Office of Naval Intelligence in Washington and was then assigned to the *Hornet*. He knew the target cities the B-25 crews were going to attack better than he knew his home town.[7]

Jurika spoke to the crews almost every day, telling them of the history of Japan, the customs and political ideologies. He discussed the strange (to the American way of thinking) psychological differences between the Occidental and the Oriental and the physiological differences between the Chinese and Japanese. Most important, however, he showed the crews the best route to enter Japan, pass over the industrial areas and depart, which would keep the planes away from the anti-aircraft batteries and yet give them good aiming points to hit their targets.

"During the briefings," Jurika said, "I covered the locations of the Japanese industries, anti-aircraft batteries and such wonderful aiming points as the Diet Building towers and the three radio towers near the Navy Ministry in downtown Tokyo. I showed them where the Imperial Palace was and how to avoid that. In general, I covered all the escape and evasion tactics which could be used to get in and out in one piece."

Jurika also recalled that many of Doolittle's men did not seem to pay much attention to his lectures. "I felt that most of the pilots, with the exception of Colonel Doolittle, were far more interested in getting their aircraft off the flight deck of the *Hornet* than they were in any possible troubles they might encounter over Japan. There were very few questions during these briefings."

Other lectures were arranged by Doolittle for the benefit of his crews. He asked Doc White of Lt. Don Smith's crew to give them talks on first aid. Doc cautioned them particularly to take immediate care of any scratch or cut. "As you know, they use 'night soil' for fertilizer in China," he told them. "Everything is tremendously infected with a very potent organism. The Chinese themselves are immune to it or else they die in infancy. The tiniest scratch will get a raging infection in it within a few hours. Whatever you do, take every nick and scratch seriously, as if your life depended on it because it will."

Commander Frank Akers, the *Hornet's* navigator, gave an air navigation refresher course to the B-25 pilots. He, too, was dismayed that his students did not seem to take the instructions seriously. "The pilots were a carefree, happy group and seemed little concerned as to the danger of the mission or what might happen to them if they were shot down over Japan," he said.

". . . a great many of them grew beards and our suggestions that this was giving the Japanese an additional torture device in case they wished to pluck them out had no effect." [8]

While the Navy personnel may have thought Doolittle's men were taking their forthcoming mission too lightheartedly, their self-imposed training program would not bear this out. The gunners were given practice sessions with their turret guns at kites let out behind the *Hornet*. When they weren't firing and cleaning their guns, they worried about the general condition of their planes. Since all gunners (with the exception of Dr. White) were airplane mechanics as well, they tinkered and fixed from morning to night, stopping only long enough to eat and sleep. Their "ground school" consisted of aircraft identification classes as well as the lectures by Dr. White.

It was Doolittle's practice to speak to his men as a group two or three times each day. After he had told them what their target cities were to be and Jurika had given them their first lecture on the geography of Japan, he allowed each pilot to choose the target city he wanted to bomb and the airfield in China where he wanted to land. Each of the 16 crews, after studying the selection had a brief discussion among themselves, finally agreed on their choices and target folders were then passed out.

"You are to bomb only military targets," Doolittle told them, "and I don't want any of you to get any ideas that you're going to bomb the Temple of Heaven—the Imperial Palace. And avoid hospitals, schools, and other non-military targets.

"Most planes will carry three 500-pound demolition bombs and one 500-pound incendiary. You will drop the demolitions in the shortest space of time, preferably in a straight line, where they will do the most damage. You will drop the incendiary cluster as near to the others as possible in an area that looks like it will burn. If you can start a couple of good fires in a Japanese city, their buildings are so inflammable they'll never put them out. Avoid all stone, concrete and steel targets because you can't do much damage to them."

One pilot, wondering if Doolittle wanted them to bomb Japanese civilian homes deliberately asked, "Colonel, should we save the incendiaries for the residential area?"

"Definitely not. You are to look for and aim at military targets only, such as war industries, shipbuilding facilities, power plants and the like."

Doolittle repeated his admonition many times not to bomb the Emperor's Palace. He reminded them that bombing industries was an act of strategic warfare but that bombing the Palace deliberately could be interpreted by friend and foe alike as an inhuman and barbaric act. "It isn't worth a plane factory, a shipyard, or an oil refinery, so leave it alone," he told them again and again.

While the Army Air Force crews sweated and fretted about their planes and their forthcoming mission, they were unaware of the events that were taking place in China. On the day the *Hornet* had finished loading and moved to its anchorage in the middle of San Francisco Bay, raids were begun by Japanese bombers and fighters on the Chinese fields the Doolittle flyers were to use. Fortunately, negligible damage was done but these forays presaged the movement of Japanese ground forces southeastward. It would probably not be long before the entire area surrounding the five fields would be lost.

In addition to the threat of losing the bases, difficulty was being experienced in providing radio homing beacons at the five fields. General Arnold wired Chungking on April 2, requesting that transmitter frequencies between 200 and 1600 kilocycles be made available for the First Special Aviation Project. However, no one in China yet knew the full reason for the requests which now had to be complied with before the night of April 19. On April 5, it was reported that with the exception of Yushan, the other four fields could provide adequate radio facilities for homing use. On

April 6, General Arnold ordered that the numbers "57" be used for identification.

On the surface it appeared that the details of the raid were all being taken care of. However, misunderstandings were developing between Chungking and Washington because of the necessity for secrecy. Generalissimo Chiang Kai Shek had reluctantly given his assent to the project on March 28 without knowing any of the details. He was apprehensive about the use of Chinese air bases after a raid on Japan because of the possibility of massive retaliation against his people by the Japanese.

The details of the project were also kept from Colonel Claire L. Chennault, Commander of the famous Flying Tigers who were flying for Chiang. Even though he was given a short briefing by Stilwell and Colonel Clayton Bissell, Stilwell's air officer, on March 29, he was not told when or from where the B-25's were to come. It was a precaution that, ironically, might have saved some of the planes because the East China Air Warning Net had been perfected by Chennault and was under his control. Unfortunately, Stilwell did not know just how good that net was nor the life-saving role Chennault's system could have played if only he had been informed.

Bissell made several attempts to carry out Arnold's orders regarding landing and refueling facilities. He commandeered an ancient C-39 cargo transport and sent it out to survey the fields in China. Records do not reveal exactly what happened to the C-39 or its pilot but the plane crashed and the mission was never completed. Ten days later, on April 12, Bissell tried again, this time sending two U.S. fliers in Chinese Curtiss Hawk fighter planes to avoid stimulating enemy interest. However, weather conditions were so poor that after a number of hazardous and unsuccessful attempts, they were forced to postpone the project. Both planes were wrecked in the process.

After the C-39 had failed in its mission, sometime between April 3 and 6, Generalissimo Chiang Kai Shek began to have severe misgivings about supporting the special project. On the 11th, he asked Colonel Bissell to inform Marshall that he wanted the project delayed until the end of May so that his ground forces could try to prevent Japanese occupation of the Chuchow area.

Marshall replied the next day that he was unable to recall the special project since it was so imminent. He further affirmed that the planes would pass into Stilwell's permanent control after one landing for fuel. On the 13th, Hap Arnold also wired Chungking saying that the "first project" could not be stopped because of its advanced stage. He added that "we are depending upon your assistance as regards flares for landing and guidance and supplies for refueling."

The Generalissimo was still not pacified and on the 14th, Bissell reiterated that "special project requiring only one landing the Generalissimo wishes delayed." [9] Bissell also noted that "details on mission cannot be given to Generalissimo since they are not known here."

Marshall immediately replied on the 15th and directed Stilwell to explain the timing and reasons for the first special mission to the Generalissimo. This message was followed up by Arnold on the 16th, in which it was again stated that "no changes in plans or additional discussion of information feasible re project at this late date." [10]

If Task Force Sixteen were carrying out its orders, Marshall knew that it was only a matter of hours before the B-25's would be winging their way to Japan. On the 18th, he sent a final message to Chungking directing that an "atmosphere of total mystery will surround special project. Stilwell to deny any connection with project, in re to public information. No publicity desired for project. Desire Generalissimo to observe same policy. Report any information on results of project immediately to War Department."

As soon as Halsey returned to Pearl Harbor from San Francisco, he conferred with Admiral Nimitz and the final details of the forthcoming mission were conveyed to the planning staff. On April 7, Nimitz approved Operation Plan No. 20-42 which stated "this force will conduct a bombing raid against the enemy objective specified in Annex 'C' which is being furnished Commander Task Force Sixteen only."

Besides the Task Force ships Halsey had arranged for, there were two more vessels which only Halsey knew about. Two submarines were to maintain patrol stations beginning on April 15 as follows:

> U.S.S. *Trout*—Area bounded by Latitudes 31°00' and 31°30'
> North and Longitudes 142°30' and 144°30' East.
> U.S.S. *Thresher*—Area bounded by Latitudes 34°30' and 34°50'
> North and Longitudes 142°30' and 144°30' East.

The missions of the *Trout* and *Thresher* were to report to Nimitz via Commander Submarines, Pacific Fleet, information of any enemy forces which might threaten Task Force Sixteen. Halsey had been told that any and all surface ships and submarines he would sight west of the rendezvous point could be presumed unfriendly. During the month of April, all U.S. subs proceeding to and from patrol stations would not be routed north of Latitude 0°30' North.

On April 8, Halsey, flying his flag from the carrier *Enterprise*, steamed out through the submarine nets at Pearl Harbor and headed northwest. The heavy cruisers *Northampton* and *Salt Lake City* plowed obediently alongside while the destroyers *Balch, Benham, Ellet* and *Fanning* fanned out in protecting positions.

The oiler *Sabine,* slowest ship in the force, set the pace and trailed behind the "Big E."

During the five days that the *Enterprise* and her protectors were steaming northwestward, Mitscher and his ships were having their troubles as they marked time to delay reaching the rendezvous point. The weather was foul with high winds, heavy seas, rain squalls and poor visibility. The high winds loosened the cables holding the B-25's on the *Hornet's* slippery deck and induced severe vibrations into their control surfaces. On the 9th, Mitscher signalled for the *Cimarron* to refuel the *Hornet* but the swells were so hazardous it was impossible. Two men were thrown overboard from the *Cimarron* and refueling operations were discontinued. It was not until the 12th, that the *Cimarron* could resume her task.

On the morning of April 13, the two task forces merged at the rendezvous point of 38°00′ North—180°00′. The 16 ships maneuvered to take up their cruising stations and when all were in position, Task Force Sixteen steamed due west at a speed of 16 knots.

As the days dragged on, the B-25's were being continually checked over by their crews. Various minor difficulties developed. Generator failures, spark plug changes, leaky gas tanks and hydraulic system troubles plagued the B-25's. The *Hornet* maintenance shops below decks were kept busy repairing and replacing parts brought to them by the B-25 flight engineers.

While the 16 ships had been plunging toward their rendezvous, the American garrison on Bataan was fighting its last. On April 9, Bataan was surrendered but General Jonathan Wainright and thirty-five thousand of his troops had escaped to Corregidor for a last ditch stand. The whole world knew then that the Americans were doomed. For all practical purposes, the fall of Bataan had ended formal resistance on Luzon. The next day, April 10, thousands of American and Filipino soldiers began a series of forced

This photo shows the aft section of the *Hornet's* deck several days before entering enemy waters. Other ships in the sixteen-ship task force can be seen flanking the *Hornet*.

marches which historians were to refer to ever after as the Bataan Death March. American history would never record a darker period.

The war news had been so consistently good for the Japanese by April that they had become complacent. Their defenses against ground invasion were inadequate. In fact, they never seriously considered there might be an invasion of Japan because it had become a national myth that the homeland was divinely protected. In 1281, Kublai Khan had organized a mighty Mongol armada to invade and conquer the Japanese islands. A great typhoon destroyed or dispersed the Mongol ships and from that time on, the Japanese credited the *Kamikaze*—the Divine Wind—with their salvation.

The Japanese military planners were more practical in their thinking about air defense however. At a meeting of military councillors on November 4, 1941, Premier Tojo made the following reply to a question asked by Admiral Hyakutake regarding their defenses against attack from the air:

"I do not think the enemy could raid Japan proper from the air immediately after the outbreak of hostilities. Some time would elapse before the enemy could attempt such raids. I believe that enemy air attacks against Japan proper in the early stages of the war, would be infrequent and would be carried out by carrier-based planes. If it should become possible for the enemy to raid Japan from bases in the Soviet Union we might face considerable danger, but I think that this is not likely in the early stages of the war." [12]

Tojo was correct in his estimate but he miscalculated one vital point: he was counting on American carrier-based planes with a range of only three hundred miles which would have to return to a carrier. Not a single Japanese intelligence officer would have ever believed that the B-25's lashed to the *Hornet's* flight deck could fly from that deck, much less carry a bomb load of any size and make a flight of two thousand miles or more.

While Japanese intelligence was weak in its estimates of American ingenuity, it was strong in its ability to intercept and deduce from radio messages what the American Navy was doing. At 6:30 A.M. on April 10, the Combined Fleet radio intelligence unit heard radio messages being flashed between the Halsey and Mitscher forces and Pearl Harbor. Their radio experts deduced that an American task force built around two or three carriers was located in the vicinity of latitude 28°00′ North, and longitude 164°00′ East.

One Japanese historian [13] described the reaction in the Combined Fleet headquarters when the intelligence report was delivered:

"Under mounting tension, the Combined Fleet made accurate calculations. If the enemy were to proceed westward, Toyko would be attacked from the air around the 14th, because even if the carriers came at full speed they would have to approach within three hundred miles of the home islands in order to fly the planes they carried. However, our surveillance net was 700 nautical miles off-shore and the enemy, in order to break through this net and penetrate 300 nautical miles inward, would require 15 or 16 hours, so it would be possible for us to attack the enemy at our leisure the day before he launched his planes."

American intelligence did not know of the line of Japanese picket ships forming the early warning surveillance net. In spite of the many forays by submarines into Japanese waters, the fact that a line of 100- to 300-ton fishing trawlers was being maintained on station had escaped their notice. Japanese radar had a very limited capability of detecting planes and the air raid warning system was, therefore, mainly dependent on visual observation on land by military and civilian observers. The Japanese Navy had added to this system by stationing about 50 of these radio-equipped patrol boats six hundred to seven hundred miles off shore.

The state of Japanese air defenses was also an unknown factor. The air defense of Japan was conceived as a joint effort of the Army and Navy, with the air arms of both services being most vitally concerned. Although an actual ground invasion of Japan was not seriously considered, it was recognized that small scale retaliatory air raids, launched for political or morale purposes, might well be an inevitable consequence of the outbreak of war. Emphasis was, therefore, laid on preparing an air defense system which would frustrate such raids and discourage their continuance.

Local defense of cities against sporadic or occasional air raids was to be accomplished by land-based fighters and anti-aircraft artillery. Army and Navy bombers would cooperate in striking at the source by attacking enemy carriers and in knocking out air bases which might be established in China. The Doolittle raiders, unknowingly, were sailing into the enemy homeland where the land-based air defense strength consisted of approximately three hundred 75mm anti-aircraft artillery pieces and about one hundred Type-97 (Nate) single-engine fighters. Compared with the Japanese forces in the overseas areas, the air defense units in the home islands were poorly equipped and trained. Nevertheless, if properly alerted and ready, this was still formidable opposition for 16 lightly armed medium bombers.

On the 10th, when the radio intelligence reports were received, Vice Admiral Matoi Ugaki, Chief of Staff of the Japanese Combined Fleet, immediately assessed the Naval air forces available to meet the American task force, estimated to arrive within flying distance on the 14th. The immediate naval strength consisted of the First Fleet in the Inland Sea and the Second Fleet which was heading home from the Indian Ocean and would not reach Japan until the 18th, too late to engage the Americans. However, the Twenty-sixth Air Flotilla with its 69 bombing and scouting planes could augment the home defenses.

Ugaki and Vice Admiral Seigo Yamagata, Commander of the Twenty-sixth Air Flotilla, agreed on the plan of attack. When the American carriers were within six hundred miles of land, the first bombers would be dispatched. If any carriers remained after this attack, a sustained torpedo attack would be made early the next morning. If successful, they estimated that American carrier strength in the Pacific would then be completely wiped out.

The intelligence staff was discouraged when no more radio messages were intercepted and the American carriers were not sighted on the 14th. Either their radio intelligence system was unreliable or the Americans had slipped away and headed off in another direction. However, until it was known where the Americans were, preparations against a raid would continue.

Halsey's Task Force Sixteen steamed westward uneventfully on its course from the 13th to the 17th.[14]

Except during very poor weather, planes from the *Enterprise* maintained continuous inner and intermediate air patrols during daylight hours when weather permitted. Search flights were made at dawn and dusk up to two hundred miles in an arc of 60° off each bow.

During the afternoon of the 15th, Halsey sent a message to the other ships:

INTENTION FUEL HEAVY SHIPS 1,000 MILES TO WEST-
WARD X THENCE CARRIERS AND CRUISERS TO POINT
500 MILES EAST OF TOKYO LAUNCH ARMY BOMBERS
ON HORNET FOR ATTACK X DDs AND TANKERS

REMAIN VICINITY FUELING POINT REJOIN ON RE-
TIREMENT X FURTHER OPERATIONS AS DEVELOP-
MENTS DICTATE.

Each passing hour was now more fraught with danger. The tenseness was evident everywhere. It could be felt in the ward-room, the crews' mess, on the bridge and in the engine room. How close to Japan could they go without being spotted? No one knew. To add to the uncertainty was an English-speaking radio news program originating in Tokyo: "Reuter's, British News Agency, has announced that three American bombers have dropped bombs on Tokyo. This is a most laughable story. They know it is abso-lutely impossible for enemy bombers to get within five hundred miles of Tokyo. Instead of worrying about such foolish things, the Japanese people are enjoying the fine spring sunshine and the fragrance of cherry blossoms."

The log of the *Enterprise* for April 16, shows the increasing tension as Task Force Sixteen plowed into enemy-dominated waters:

"0501—Launched first inner air patrol of 6 fighters, followed throughout the day by patrols of 5, 4 and 6 fighters each. No contacts. Launched first scouting flight of 13 scout bombers to search sector 204-324 to distance of 200 miles, followed in the afternoon by scouting flight of 8 torpedo planes to search sector 204-324 to distance of 150 miles. No contacts.

Activity increased the next day. At 5:37 A.M., the *Enterprise* launched 18 scout bombers for three-hour search missions. During the morning, the *Sabine* pumped aviation gasoline and fuel oil aboard the Big E and then, along with the *Cimarron,* topped off the cruisers and destroyers. At 2:45 P.M., the destroyer *Monssen* and both tankers left the formation to await the return of the larger ships after the B-25's were launched. A short time later the other destroyers were detached. The two carriers and four cruisers left now increased their speeds to 20 knots. Hardly had the destroyers and tankers receded from view when the wind picked up and increased to gale force.

Meanwhile, the B-25's had been spotted on the deck for take-off. The lead bomber, Doolittle's, had 467 feet of clear deck; the last one, Lieutenant Bill Farrow's, hung precariously out over the stern ramp of the carrier. Two white lines were painted on the deck—one for the left wheel and one for the nose wheel of the bombers. If the pilots kept their plane on these lines they could be assured of clearing the carrier's "island" with their right wings by about six feet.

The excitement aboard the *Hornet* increased when its refueling was completed and the Mitchells positioned. Up on the bridge of the *Hornet,* Mitscher and Doolittle huddled over a map table.

"Jimmy, we're in the enemy's back yard now," Mitscher said calmly. "Anything could happen from here on in. I think it's time for our little ceremony."

Doolittle agreed. He had not yet read the messages to the group that he had received from Marshall and Arnold and he wanted to do this. When the *Enterprise* had merged with the *Hornet's* force, mail had been exchanged and Mitscher had received some official correspondence from the Secretary of the Navy, Frank Knox. Enclosed were some medals which had been presented to H. Vormstein, John B. Laurey, and Daniel J. Quigley, ex-Navy enlisted men, to commemorate the visit of the U.S. Battle Fleet to Japan in 1908. Vormstein and Laurey, both working in the Brooklyn Navy Yard at the time, had asked in their letter of January 26, that Secretary Knox "attach it to a bomb and return it to Japan in that manner." Quigley, formerly of the U.S.S. *Kearsarge,* wrote from his home in McKees Rocks, Pennsylvania, on March 2:

"Following the lead of my former fleet mates in forwarding

thru you, Sir, their Jap commemoration medals via bomb to
Tokyo, I herewith enclose the one issued to me and trust that
it will eventually find its way back in company with a bomb that
will rock the throne of the "Son of Heaven" in the Kojimachi Ku
district of Tokyo."

Knox had forwarded the medals to Nimitz at Pearl Harbor,
asking that the request be complied with at the appropriate time.
"The appropriate time seems to have come sooner than they
realized," Mitscher said, grinning. "Let's get your boys together
and comply with these instructions from on high."

Over the loudspeaker came the announcement, "Army crews,
report to the flight deck!" When everyone had gathered around
a bomb that had been brought on deck, Mitscher made a
short speech about the medals and handed them to Doolittle. Lieutenant Steve Jurika, having heard about the ceremony, added the
medal he had received from the Japanese in 1940.[15]

The group posed for pictures and kidded each other good-
naturedly. Several of them wrote slogans on the bomb like "I
don't want to set the world on fire, just Tokyo" and "you'll get
a BANG out of this!" They knew the time for departure was
drawing nigh. Dog tags were checked and last innoculations made.
Already their survival equipment had been handed out and the
eighty men who were going on the raid had been loaded down
like over-eager Boy Scouts. Each crew member had been issued
a Navy gas mask, a .45 automatic, clips of ammunition, a hunting
knife, flashlight, emergency rations, first aid kit, canteen, compass
and life jacket. Besides their clothes, most had added an assort-
ment of extras to their B-4 bags such as cigarettes, candy bars and
extra razor blades. "Shorty" Manch, six-foot, six-inch co-pilot on
Bob Gray's crew, planned to take along his phonograph and
records. "Sally" Crouch, navigator on Dick Joyce's crew, ever
mindful of the lectures about the lack of cleanliness in the Orient,

jammed rolls of toilet paper into his bags. They were hoping for the best but being prepared for the worst, and their lightheartedness soon became forced as each man wondered about his personal chances for survival.

Mechanical difficulties had been cropping up on every plane almost hourly. On the 16th, Lieutenant Don Smith's right engine cracked its blower while he was running it up. Navy carpenters hurriedly rigged up a platform so an engine change crew could remove it. It was taken below decks to the machine shop, quickly repaired and replaced.

Gun turrets did not function correctly, hydraulic lines still leaked, spark plugs fouled and gas tanks dripped. The anxiety of the crews mounted as Doolittle went from plane to plane, questioned the crews, and inspected their planes from the nose wheel tires to the false broomstick guns in the rear. On the afternoon of the 17th, he called the crews together.

"The time's getting short now," he told them. "By now every single one of you knows exactly what to do if the alarm is sounded. We were originally supposed to take off on the 19th but it looks like it'll be tomorrow instead.[16] This will be your last briefing. Be ready to go at any time.

"We should have plenty of warning if we're intercepted. If all goes well, however, I'll take off so as to arrive over Tokyo at dusk. The rest of you will take off two or three hours later and can use my fires as a homing beacon."

Doolittle reiterated the plan in full and, for the last time, gave the men a chance to back out. Again, no one took him up on his offer. He then gave instructions about the 5-gallon gas cans which were to be stowed in the rear compartment. "Don't throw out the empty cans as you use them," he cautioned. "If you do, you'll leave a trail directly back toward the *Hornet*. When the cans are all empty, punch holes in them and throw them overboard all at the same time. Now, any questions?"

There was one question that had bothered many of the men but no one had yet brought it up. One of the pilots, however, decided that he wanted to know what the Boss's answer would be so he asked, "Colonel, what should we do if we lose an engine or something else goes wrong and we have to crash land in Japan?"

Doolittle's answer was quick. "Each pilot is in command of his own plane when we leave the carrier," he answered. "He alone is responsible for the decision he makes for his own plane and crew. Each man must eventually decide for himself what he will do when the chips are down. Personally, I know exactly what I'm going to do."

The wardroom fell silent. Doolittle didn't elaborate so one of the group asked, "Sir, what will you do?"

"I don't intend to be taken prisoner," the scrappy little man answered. "If my plane is crippled beyond any possibility of fighting or escape, I'm going to bail my crew out and then dive it, full throttle, into any target I can find where the crash will do the most damage. I'm 46 years old and have lived a full life. Most of you fellows are in your twenties and if I were you, I'm not sure I would make the same decision. In the final analysis, it's up to each pilot and, in turn, each man to decide what he will do." [17]

He then cautioned them to get rid of any and all identification, letters, orders and diaries that would link them with the *Hornet,* their unit in the States or their training.

The B-25 crews labored all day on the 17th preparing their planes for battle. Ammunition and bombs were loaded aboard. Last minute engine run-ups were made and crew survival equipment placed in each plane. Doc White had thoughtfully climbed on board the *Hornet* in San Francisco with 80 quarts of bourbon

—a quart for every man going on the raid. During the voyage, he exchanged it with the Navy medics for pints of medicinal rye. These would be easier to carry in the B-4 bags he reasoned and, if they had to bail out, could be stuffed into their flight jackets. He admonished the group again to take care of any cuts they might get. There was now an air of extreme urgency that was felt by all on the *Hornet*.

Earlier that day, Commander Apollo Soucek, the *Hornet*'s Air Officer had issued "Air Department Plan for Friday, 17 April 1942":

> The Big Bombers on the flight deck will be loaded with bombs during the day. The sequence of events in connection with loading and respotting will be as follows:
> (1) Complete fueling ships; tanker shoves off.
> (2) Push ♯02268 and ♯02267 clear of number 3 elevator.
> (3) Bring incendiary bombs to flight deck via number 3 elevator; commence loading on accessible airplanes.
> (b) Start bringing heavy bombs to flight decks via regular bomb elevators; commence loading on accessible airplanes.
> (5) When all incendiary bombs are on flight deck, secure number 3 elevator and pull ♯02267 and ♯02268 forward far enough for loading purposes.
> (6) One half hour before sunset, respot the deck for take-off.
> Note: All loading will be done under the direct supervision of Captain Greening, U.S.A.

By sunset, loading and positioning were complete. All planes had been fueled; only personal baggage had to be stored aboard. Twenty-four hours later, if all went well, the 16 bombers would be gone. As had been the practice during the voyage, poker games started below decks the instant work was done. The night of April 17 was no exception.

At midnight on the *Hornet,* Ensign Robert R. Boettcher had relieved Ensign J. A. Holmes on watch as Officer of the Deck. He noted in the ship's log that the *Hornet,* in company with Task Groups 16.2 and 16.5, was steaming darkened on a course of 267° at 20 knots. The ship's bell chimed off the half hours as the midnight-to-four shift went about its routine chores. Boettcher's task was to stay alert for signs of any enemy sea or air activity and keep the *Hornet* knifing ahead on course.

When the six bells signalling 3 A.M. were chimed, Boettcher stretched, yawned and asked for a cup of coffee. He had drained the last waning drops when a message was flashed from the *Enterprise* that knotted his stomach: "Two enemy surface craft reported." The Big E's radar had spotted two enemy ships off the port bow at a distance of twenty-one thousand yards. All watch hands stared into the inky blackness; two minutes later a light appeared on the horizon.

The *Enterprise*'s short range, high frequency radio crackled out a curt order for all ships to come right to a course of 350° to avoid detection. As the ships obeyed, general quarters was sounded and every man on the six ships fought his way to his assigned battle station. A half hour later, the enemy ships faded from the radar screen and the westerly course was resumed at 4:11 A.M. For the Task Force, the day had begun even though the "all clear" had been sounded at 3:41. The B-25 crews went back to their cabins to resume their interrupted sleep.

At 5:08 the dawn search flight and fighter patrol consisting of eight F4F Grumman fighters and three SBD Douglas scout bombers took to the air from the *Enterprise* to search to a distance of two hundred miles. Three more scout bombers were launched for a combat air patrol above the Task Force.

The weather, which had been moderately rough during the

night, was worsening. Low broken clouds hung over the area; frequent rain squalls swept over the ships and the sea began to bellow up in 30 foot crests. Gusty winds tore the tops off the waves and the spray blew across the decks of the ships, drenching the deck crews.

The three SBD pilots climbed to the bottom of the broken clouds in a "single plane relative search." At 5:58, Lieutenant O. B. Wiseman sighted a small patrol craft. He quickly reversed course for the *Enterprise*. Fixing his position as best he could on his small plotting board, he jotted down a message:

Enemy surface ship—latitude 36-04N, Long. 153-10E, bearing 276° true—42 miles. Believed seen by enemy.

Wiseman handed the message back to the gunner in the rear seat and made a throwing motion with his hand.

The gunner knew what to do. He reached in his pocket for a bean bag message container, stuffed the paper inside and peered over the side as Wiseman dived for the Big E's flight deck. Wiseman put flaps down to slow his plane and the gunner opened the canopy. When the SBD was directly overhead, the message plopped down on the deck and was scooped up on the run by a deckhand and delivered to Halsey on the bridge.

Halsey's reaction was immediate. He ordered all ships in the Task Force to swing left to a course of 220° to avoid detection. The question uppermost in everyone's mind was whether or not Wiseman had been seen. About an hour later, at 7:38, another enemy patrol vessel of about 150 tons was sighted from the *Hornet* only twenty thousand yards away. If the *Hornet* could see the small vessel, there was every reason to believe that the Task Force had been sighted and reported. It became a certainty when the *Hornet's* radio operator intercepted a Japanese message which had originated from somewhere close by.[18] Still further confirmation came at 7:45 when Ensign J. Q. Roberts sighted the enemy vessel only twelve thousand yards away.

The moment of decision had come. Halsey ordered the *Nashville* to sink the patrol boat. In the log of the *Enterprise* was noted the following:

By previous agreement with Lt. Col. Doolittle, flight commander of the 16 B-25 planes on the *Hornet,* the plan was to launch one plane from a position approximately 400 miles east of Inuboe Saki at a time to permit arrival over Tokyo at sunset. The other planes were to be launched at local sunset to permit a night attack on Tokyo. However, in case the presence of the force was de-

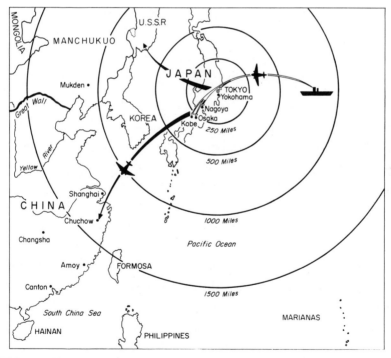

This map shows how the aircraft carrier *Hornet* carried the B-25's to within 600 miles of Japan. The planes, after bombing Tokyo, Yokohama, Nagoya, Osaka, and Kobe, as indicated by arrows, continued to the China mainland.

tected, it was understood the planes were to be launched immediately. If launched from 550 miles from Inuboe Saki, the arrival at arranged destination was remote possibility. If launched from a point in excess of 650 miles, it was calculated to be impossible to arrive at Yushan, the arranged destination. These factors were all considered and as our position was known to have been reported by the patrol vessel previously contacted, Adm. Halsey ordered the planes launched.

The message Halsey flashed to Mitscher on the *Hornet* was sent at 8:00 A.M.:

LAUNCH PLANES X TO COL. DOOLITTLE AND GAL-LANT COMMAND GOOD LUCK AND GOD BLESS YOU.

Doolittle, on the *Hornet*'s bridge when the message came, hurriedly shook hands with Mitscher and leaped down the ladder to his cabin, shouting to everybody he saw, "O.K. fellas, this is it! Let's go!" At the same time, the blood-chilling klaxon sounded and the announcement came over the loudspeaker: "Army pilots, man your planes!"

The B-25 crews had not been fully aware of the drama going on around them up to this point. Some had finished breakfast and were lounging in their cabins; others were shaving and preparing to eat; several were still asleep. A few had packed their B-4 bags but most were caught completely unawares when the call came.

Although their collective goal was the same, the 80 men all reacted differently. "Shorty" Manch had his own ideas about what to take. He grabbed his portable phonograph as well as two .45 caliber pistols and a carbine. He had his records in a cake tin but decided at the last minute to ask his buddy, Lieutenant Bob Clever, navigator on Ted Lawson's "Ruptured Duck," to put the precious platters under his seat. Clever reluctantly agreed.

Doc White hurriedly passed out the two pints of liquor to each man. Lieutenant Dick Knobloch ran from plane to plane handing up bags of sandwiches he had gotten from the galley.

Army and Navy men poured all over the *Hornet's* deck in seemingly wild confusion. Engine and turret covers were ripped off and stuffed up into the rear hatches. Ropes were unfastened and wheel chocks pulled away. A "donkey" pushed and pulled the 25's into position along the back end of the flight deck.

The *Hornet's* speed was increased and her bow plunged viciously into the towering waves. The deck seemed like a crazy seesaw that bit into the water each time the bow dipped.

Once each plane was in position, the job of loading could be completed. The gas tanks were all topped off. Navy crews rocked the bombers back and forth to break up any air bubbles in the tanks so they could pour in a few more quarts of precious gasoline. Sailors quickly filled the ten 5-gallon gas cans allotted each ship and passed them hand-to-hand up into the rear hatches.

The *Hornet's* control tower displayed a huge blackboard which noted the compass heading of the ship and the wind speed. As the crews jammed their personal belongings aboard, Hank Miller climbed up into the forward hatch of each plane, wished the crew good luck and said, sadly, "I sure wish I could go with you guys. I'll be holding up a blackboard to give you any last minute instructions. Give me a glance before you let your brakes off."

On signal, Doolittle in the lead plane started his engines and warmed them up. Near the bow on the left side, Lieutenant Edgar G. Osborne stood with a checkered flag in his hands. He began to swing the flag in a circle as a signal for Doolittle to ease the throttles forward. Osborne swung the flag in faster and faster circles and Doolittle pushed more and more power on. At the precise instant the deck was beginning its upward movement, chocks were pulled from under Doolittle's wheels and Osborne gave him the "go" signal. Doolittle released his brakes and the Mitchell inched forward.

Ted Lawson, waiting his turn in the "Ruptured Duck," described their leader's takeoff: [19]

> With full flaps, motors at full throttle and his left wing far out over the port side of the *Hornet,* Doolittle's plane waddled and then lunged slowly into the teeth of the gale that swept down the deck. His left wheel stuck on the white line as if it were a track. His right wing, which had barely cleared the wall of the island as he taxied and was guided up to the starting line, extended nearly to the edge of the starboard side.
>
> We watched him like hawks, wondering what the wind would do to him, and whether we could get off in that little run toward the bow. If he couldn't, we couldn't.
>
> Doolittle picked up more speed and held to his line, and, just as the *Hornet* lifted up on top of a wave and cut through it at full speed, Doolittle's plane took off. He had yards to spare. He hung his ship almost straight up on its props, until we could see the whole top of his B-25. Then he leveled off and I watched him come around in a tight circle and shoot low over our heads—straight down the line painted on the deck.[20]

The log of the *Hornet* for April 18 records that Colonel Doolittle was airborne at 8:20 A.M. ship time. Instead of following him three hours later, as originally planned, the second plane, piloted by Lieutenant Travis Hoover, had to take off just five minutes later.

"Hoover kept his nose in the up position too long," Lieutenant Hank Miller recalls, "and nearly stalled the plane. After the third plane took off, I put the words "STABILIZER IN NEUTRAL" on the blackboard. I'm pretty sure they saw and took my advice.

"Succeeding take-offs were all good except one—Ted Lawson's —because he either forgot his flaps or inadvertently put them back into the 'up' position instead of 'neutral.' But he got away with it.

The first B-25 to take off was flown by Lt. Col. Jimmy Doolittle. It is shown here just before its wheels left the deck. Observing the plane from his position on the "island" is Capt. Mitscher, skipper of the *Hornet*.

"The flaps on three other planes were up as they maneuvered into position, but the flight deck crew caught them before take-off. The only casualty to the planes themselves was a cracked nose glass on Lt. Don Smith's plane when it was rammed into the tail cone of the one ahead of it. There wasn't enough damage to worry about so he took off in order."

The last plane on the deck, piloted by Lieutenant Bill Farrow, seemed earmarked for disaster from the start. Since its tail was hanging out over the end of the deck, the loading of the plane's rear compartment could not be completed until the 15th plane, Smith's, had moved forward. Six deck handlers held down on the

The sixteenth B-25 on the crowded deck of the *Hornet* hung out over the fantail. The rear compartment could not be loaded until the airplane ahead was moved forward. A Navy plane handler, Robert Wall, lost an arm when he slipped on the wet deck and fell into the whirling propeller of this plane, piloted by Lt. Farrow, a few minutes before take-off.

nose wheel while Farrow taxied forward. Just as Smith revved up his engines, and the men moved away from Farrow's nose wheel, Seaman Robert W. Wall, one of the six, lost his footing. The sudden gust of air caused him to lose his balance and the combination of air blast and the slippery, pitching deck threw him into Farrow's idling left propeller. There was nothing Farrow could do. The prop chewed into Wall's left arm and threw him aside. His deck mates quickly rushed to him and carried him to sick bay where his arm was amputated a short time later.[21]

Farrow's plane was off at 9:20, exactly one hour after Doolittle's. Doolittle had 620 nautical miles to go to reach Inuboe Saki, the nearest point of land; Farrow's distance was calculated at an even 600 miles with the *Hornet's* position officially fixed at 35°55′N, 153°19′E.

While the Doolittle crews had been getting ready on the *Hornet,* the cruiser *Nashville* began pumping shells at the patrol vessel Ensign Roberts had sighted. Roberts made a glide bombing attack and dropped a 500-pounder but it missed. He strafed with a lone .50 caliber machine gun but could see no damage being done. Other planes joined the attack. The War Diary of the *Nashville* describes the action this way:

0748—Enemy ship bore 201°T at a range of 9,000 yds.
0752—Received order from Adm. Halsey to attack vessel and sink same.
0753—Opened fire with main battery firing salvo fire at range of 9,000 yds.
0754—Shifted to rapid fire.
0755—Checked fire. Target could not be seen.
0756—Resumed firing. Bombing planes made attack on enemy vessel. They returned the fire of the planes with machine guns and a light cannon.
0757—Enemy headed toward the *Nashville.*
0801—Bombing planes made another attack on enemy ship. This fire returned by the enemy.
0804—Opened fire. This fire was returned but enemy shells fell short.
0809—Bombing planes made another attack. Changed course to the left in order to close the enemy.
0814—Increased speed to 25 knots.

0819—Commenced firing salvo fire.
0821—Steadied a course 095T. Enemy vessel on fire.
0823—Enemy vessel sunk.
0827—Commenced maneuvering to pick up survivors. Attempts
       to rescue one man sighted proved unsuccessful.
0846—Went to 25 knots to rejoin mission.

The skipper of the *Nashville,* Captain S. S. Craven, added an additional note in the log to explain why it had taken so long to sink the small, apparently fragile vessel. He noted that "938 rounds of 6" ammunition were expended due to the difficulty of hitting the small target with the heavy swells that were running and the long range at which fire was opened. This range was used in order to silence the enemy's radio as soon as possible. The ship sunk was a Japanese patrol boat and was equipped with radio and anti-aircraft machine guns."

As soon as the 16th B-25 had left the deck, the entire task force reversed course to the east and proceeded at full speed in a maneuver the Navy calls simply "getting the hell out." The *Hornet,* now divested of its load of bombers, brought its own planes up on deck and assumed its aerial role of scouting in collaboration with the *Enterprise.* The fact that the enemy patrol vessel had gotten its message off before being sunk probably meant that every enemy plane and vessel within range of the American force would be searching for it. The assumption was well founded for aircraft were spotted on the radar screen of the retreating *Enterprise* but none came closer than 30 miles. The low clouds and poor visibility were proving to be allies.

At 11:30, Ensigns R. M. Elder, R. K. Campbell and J. C. Butler of Bomber Squadron Three were launched from the *Enterprise* on single-plane searches to the southwest. A few minutes later, Lieutenant R. W. Arndt led a three-plane flight off to attack enemy surface vessels reported 58 miles from the

This view showing the first B-25 taking off was made from the deck of the *Enterprise*. Waves broke over the deck as the bow dipped downward. The signal for take-off was given as the bow started its upward rise.

task force. Ensign Campbell was the first to make a contact. At 11:50 he sighted a 150-foot patrol boat painted dark gray with a tall radio antenna towering above its deck. Two dive bombing attacks were made but no hits were scored. Campbell pressed the attack firing both the .50 caliber and .30 caliber guns but only minor damage could be seen.

A few minutes after Campbell's attack, Lieutenant Arndt and his two wingmen attacked another vessel. Three 500-pound and five 100-pound bombs were dropped, again without success. As the War Diary of the squadron wryly noted, "there was no apparent damage from bombs except for one 100-lb. bomb near miss which evidently stopped the fire on one small caliber AA gun located aft. The enemy used radical maneuver and returned AA fire with what appeared to be a 1" gun."

Ensign Butler, searching another sector, sighted still a third patrol boat. It was about 125 feet long and was towing a smaller boat behind. He made three separate bomb runs, dropping one bomb each time. The two 100-pound bombs were duds but the 500-pound bomb landed close aboard on the port side causing fragmentary damage. After the bombing, Butler strafed both boats until his ammunition was gone. He thought he had sunk the smaller boat and damaged the larger one. After landing he reported that "own plane received three hits from enemy fire— not serious."

What Arndt and his squadron mates could not do, the *Nashville* did. As soon as the scout bombers retired, she opened fire on the bobbing patrol boat at forty-five hundred yards. Firing off and on for the next twenty minutes with her 5-inch and 6-inch guns as she closed the distance, she finally obtained results. Overwhelmed by the quantity of lead that filled the air, the Japanese ran up a white flag and the *Nashville* ceased firing. While the *Nashville* circled, the enemy boat slowly sank. Five survivors were spotted and quickly hauled aboard suffering from shock, immersion and fright. Only one, Seaman Second Class Nakamura Suekichi, was injured slightly with a bullet wound in his cheek.

There had been 11 men aboard the patrol boat, the *Nagato Maru*, according to Suekichi.[22] He reported in a letter to the author that ". . . the waves were high that day and I could not help worrying that our 70-ton *Nagato Maru* would capsize at any moment." He told Navy interrogators that he had spotted some planes while on watch and went below to rouse his skipper, Chief

Petty Officer Gisaku Maeda. The skipper assumed they were the usual morning patrol planes from Japan and stayed in his cabin. A short time later Suekichi tried again and said, "Sir, there are two of our beautiful carriers now dead ahead."

This time Maeda was wide awake. No Japanese carriers were supposed to be in his patrol area. He rushed on deck, studied them intently through his binoculars, and said sadly, "Indeed they are beautiful but they are not ours." He went below to his cabin, took a pistol from his sea bag, put it to his temple and pulled the trigger.

"At that time," Suekichi said, "we radioed the *Kiso*, the flagship of the Fifth Fleet, that the enemy had been sighted. When the American cruiser fired on us, I could actually see the approaching shells. The airborne attack by the enemy became more severe, but we really doubted whether they could hit us, so we pointed our small gun at the enemy. Looking back on our actions now, we acted foolishly. But, after all, we thought we were fighting for the great spirit of Nippon. Since we had communicated the discovery of enemy ships and planes, we were positive that no damage would occur in Japan."

While the *Nashville* was completing the action, the planes returned to the *Enterprise* to re-arm. One of them, piloted by Lieutenant L. A. Smith, however, could not make it. Without warning, the SBD's engine began to lose oil pressure and he had to ditch. His plane had been hit by the small caliber fire from the picket ship. He and his gunner, AMM2C H. H. Caruthers, were rescued shortly thereafter by the *Nashville*.

The excitement of the day was not yet over. A small enemy submarine was sighted and attacked before it hurriedly submerged undamaged. Other Japanese patrol vessels and freighters were sighted but not attacked. When the day's activities were studied by Halsey's staff, the number of enemy vessels found was surprising. Halsey reported that "in addition to the radar contact

with two craft made at 0310, actual contact showed one submarine, 14 PY's (patrol vessels) and 3 AK's (probably "mother
ships" for the patrols) concentrated in an area about 130 miles
by 180 miles. A similar concentration was reported by a submarine just returned from patrol in the East China Sea which
stated that 65 sampans had been sighted in an area just about
the same size as that mentioned above. These are indications of
the degree to which the Japanese are using these small craft for
patrols and screens around their vital areas." Halsey made no
mention of enemy land-based patrol planes which had also been
seen. If these planes had found the task force, there is no
doubt they would have attacked the carriers offensively, which
the patrol vessels could not.

The escaping task force steamed at full speed during the night
and at dawn the next day began its patrols again. No more enemy
ships were sighted but one scout bomber from the *Hornet*, over-
due from the morning patrol, ditched in the water out of gas
only seven miles from the *Enterprise*. The plane, piloted by
Lieutenant G. D. Randall with radioman T. A. Gallagher aboard,
sank in 30 seconds. Neither the plane nor the men were recovered.

It took Task Force Sixteen exactly one week to the hour after
launching the B-25's to reach Pearl Harbor. Before docking,
Halsey sent a "Well Done" to his skippers and termed the mission
a success. "The Japs chased us all the way home, of course,"
Halsey wrote later. "Whenever we tracked their search planes
with our radar, I was tempted to unleash our fighters, but I knew
it was more important not to reveal our position than to shoot
down a couple of scouts. They sent a task force after us; their
submarines tried to intercept us; and . . . even some of their
carriers joined the hunt; but with the help of foul weather and
a devious course, we eluded them . . ." [23]

The score for the Navy for this dangerous mission turned out
to be good. On the plus side of the ledger, the Army Air Forces

bombers had been launched without serious accident; three enemy patrol boats had been sunk and the entire task force had escaped without a scratch; five prisoners had been taken. When the *Thresher* and *Trout* returned to Pearl Harbor, their skippers reported exceptionally good hunting. The *Thresher* had sunk the *Sado Maru,* a 3,000-ton freighter right at the entrance to Yokohama Harbor. The *Trout* had damaged a 15,000-ton freighter, had beached or sunk in shallow water a tanker and freighter and had sunk a 7,000-ton freighter and a 1,000-ton patrol vessel. On the minus side, Halsey's force had lost three of its own planes and damaged three more in landing accidents. Two lives had been lost and one man was seriously injured.

Task Force Sixteen's work was done for the moment but Halsey made out his report and immediately prepared for his next combat mission. In reflecting on the results of the Doolittle raiders, he was moved to note that "in my opinion their flight was one of the most courageous deeds in military history."

The Japanese strategy of stationing a long line of picket ships six to seven hundred miles off the coast of the home islands was a natural one. Since their radar was primitive and the U.S. fleet was the only enemy force they had to fear, a line of expendable small fishing vessels was the logical way to gain early warning of any raiding force. The *No. 23 Nitto Maru* that had first sighted the Halsey force and sent the message and the other picket vessels were assigned to the Fifth Fleet under Vice Admiral Jushiro Hosogaya. The Twenty-sixth Air Flotilla, also under naval control, was led by Vice Admiral Seigo Yamagata. On April 1, the three squadrons of the 26th had been deployed to Kisarazu, Misawa and Minami Torishima for patrol duty. When the Continental Fleet radio intelligence unit discovered the American fleet carrying on lively "conversations" on the 10th, surveillance was increased. When the anticipated interception did not come on the 14th, vigilance was maintained nevertheless. However, since Halsey's task force maintained strict radio silence after the rendezvous, the report from the *No. 23 Nitto Maru* was the first real confirmation that the U.S. fleet was still definitely heading for Japan.

As soon as the *Nitto Maru*'s report was received a confirmation was requested but there was no answer. Vice Admiral Matoi Ugaki, commander-in-chief of the Combined Forces at Hashirajima, wrote in his diary that day that "we became tense over the report from *No. 23 Nitto Maru* and I immediately issued Order No. 3 against the American fleet."

The entire resources available to Ugaki were studied to see what strength could be brought to bear within 24 hours. Thirty-five land attack planes of the Twenty-first Air Flotilla, fresh from battle in the Philippines, had just arrived in Japan along with 63 carrier planes from the carrier *Kaga* which was berthed at Tateyama. All together, the Navy had massed 90 carrier fighters, 80 medium bombers, 36 carrier bombers and 2 flying boats to intercept the enemy force. At the same time, Vice Admiral Nobutake Kondo, commander of the Second Fleet, had returned victoriously from operations in the Indian Ocean with a large task force.

Upon receiving the order to intercept and engage the American fleet, Admiral Kondo left Yokosuka a few hours later with ten destroyers and the heavy cruisers *Aito, Takao, Maya, Nachi, Haguro,* and *Myoko.* The carrier group of the First Air Fleet, under Vice Admiral Tadakazu Nagumo, was also ordered to proceed at top speed to the estimated interception point. This task force, also returning from the Indian Ocean, was in the Bashi Channel south of Taiwan at the time and included the carriers *Akagi, Soryu, Hiryu, Suikaku,* and *Shokaku.*

The Eighth Submarine Fleet consisting of six vessels which

had departed from the Inland Sea on the 16th headed for the east coast of Australia, swung about. Three more submarines, under the command of Rear Admiral Shigeyoshi Miwa, of the Third Submarine Fleet, were cruising two hundred miles west of Halsey's task force. They, too, swung about and deployed for action. The entire Japanese fleet that could conceivably meet the enemy had almost instantly turned towards a single small area of the Pacific Ocean. If the American ships had continued westward to launch their carrier-based fighters three hundred miles out, only a miracle would have spared them. By the time the order had been dispatched and the various Japanese forces responded, Doolittle's 16 planes were already boring westward just above the wave tops.

By 9 o'clock, Hosogaya in Fifth Fleet Headquarters still had received no confirmation of the *Nitto Maru*'s report and could not verify his suspicions with the other picket boats. He expected the worst and warned the units under his command, "The enemy is definitely close by." Forty-five minutes later one of the patrol planes that had left Kisarazu at 6:30 on its regular morning run reported that it had met a two-engine land plane flying in the opposite direction at a point six hundred miles out to sea. This report was not believed because it was known that the American fleet did not have any twin-engined planes on its carriers.

As far as can be determined, the first person to sense something unusual from the fragmentary information available was Vice Admiral Yamagata at Kisarazu. At 10:30, the morning patrol plane should have reached a point 650 nautical miles at sea but no position report was forthcoming. When no report was received by 11:30, Yamagata dispatched three "second stage" patrol bombers as a spearhead to a point five hundred nautical miles out. Fifteen minutes later he ordered 24 fighters and 25 torpedo-carrying attack planes into the air.

While the weather over the Japanese islands was clear, the

frontal weather which Halsey's task force had been caught in, lay between the American ships and the Japanese air units. Visibility was reduced to three miles or less. Frustrated, the Japanese planes gave up one by one and started back at noon time. At that moment, Jimmy Doolittle was approaching Boso Peninsula. The planes behind him were spread out in trail in an arc about 50 miles wide because of high and changing winds, compasses that had been thrown off by the more than two weeks on the *Hornet* and the inability of navigators to take celestial sights of the sun due to the overcast. Although the Japanese were ready for something, they knew not what. Doolittle and his gallant avengers were about to achieve the surprise they had planned.

On the morning of April 18, a curious set of circumstances was developing in the city of Tokyo which was to influence the success of the oncoming American raiders as much as any other factor. From the time of the Pearl Harbor attack, Japanese domestic propaganda had assured the people that an air attack by the enemy on their cities was impossible, thus encouraging an optimism which tended to nullify their attempts at air raid precautions. Tokyo itself possessed a fairly efficient civil defense organization which was the model for the rest of Japan and had been set up several years before the outbreak of war. Each block had an air raid warden and air raid drills had become frequent enough to be accepted as routine, causing little disruption to the city's normal functions.

Tokyo papers announced on April 16, that there would be an air raid drill on Saturday the 18th. This information was conveyed to the restricted residents of the American and British Embassies on the night of the 17th by the city police. The drill began shortly after 9 o'clock on the morning of the 18th, just as the last of the B-25's were leaving the *Hornet*. The drill was a simulation of the "first alarm" under which the air raid wardens were notified but no sirens were sounded and the mass of the population did not seek shelter. However, the Tokyo fire fighting brigades demonstrated with their equipment in the streets and the air raid wardens stood by at their posts. At the British Embassy two fire-fighting units turned out briefly, and at the American Embassy certain of the designated personnel took the perfunctory steps required by the civil defense regulations. By 9:30, however, the Japanese air raid wardens at the British Embassy had returned to their normal household duties and by 11:00, the warden assigned to the American Embassy was teeing off at the local golf course.

Throughout the morning air activity over Tokyo increased but these were Army planes practicing for ceremonies and demonstrations for the Emperor's birthday and the dedication of the Yasukuni Shrine for the Japanese war dead on the 25th. During the period of the first alarm some Japanese Type 97 (Nate) fighters engaged in mock dog fights over the city; along the Tokyo waterfront barrage ballons were raised and lowered for practice. Curiously, while the Navy seemed fully aware of a threat developing, its concern had not been transmitted to the Army or Civil Defense organizations. Before noon, however, the Army Commander of the Tokyo area ordered three air defense fighters into the air and others to stand by on runway alert.[24]

By noon, Tokyo time, practice air raid defense activities were drawing to a close. The balloons at the mouth of the Tanagawa River were down, and only three air defense fighters under radio control were in the air although there were other planes flying in the area. A few fire-fighting teams were still in the streets. The American and British nationals in their respective embassies, although restricted, were allowed to make trips to take care of emergency needs. One American had been given permission to visit his physician and at 12:15 was taking a streetcar to make his appointment. The rest of his colleagues were just sitting down to their noon meal.

The traffic on the streets of Tokyo reached its usual high volume by noon. It was Saturday and hundreds were on their way to baseball games, flower festivals and other carefree activities. For those who had to work that afternoon in the war industries, it was time for the mid-day rest period. The weather was perfect with warming temperatures and gentle breezes. The weekend was full of beauty and promise. In a few moments, as Lieutenant Colonel Jimmy Doolittle crossed the coast 80 miles north of Tokyo and turned left, it was to be the day that Japan would forever mark as the beginning of the end of their dreams of global conquest. At exactly 12:30, Tokyo time, Doolittle's bombardier, Staff Sergeant Fred A. Braemer, pushed a toggle switch on his control panel marked "Bomb doors—open."

NOTES TO CHAPTER 6

1. Halsey and Bryan, *Admiral Halsey's Story,* p. 101.
2. At this writing Miller wears the two stars of a Rear Admiral. However, because the Navy's role in the Tokyo Raid was to remain secret for a year, his superiors at Pensacola had no idea what he had done to assure the success of the Doolittle mission. For his part in training the pilots he was awarded the Army Commendation Ribbon, one of the few Naval officers to receive this award.
3. Greening, "The First Joint Action," p. 21.
4. Marc A. Mitscher, Commanding Officer's Report of Action, to the Commander in Chief, U. S. Pacific Fleet, April 28, 1942.
5. Greening, *op. cit.,* p. 21.
6. From interviews conducted by the CBS Television Network for "The Doolittle Raid," produced by the Public Affairs Department of CBS News.
7. Before the war was over, Jurika learned that his mother had been executed by the Japanese in the Philippines on August 30, 1944. When the Japanese learned it was his intelligence, collected between 1939 and 1941, that provided the target information for the Doolittle raid, he was placed high on their list of war criminals. Jurika is now a Captain.
8. Letter to Captain C. E. Wakeman from Rear Admiral Frank Akers, November 14, 1955.
9. Message No. 519 from AMMISCA, Chungking to AGWAR, April 14, 1942.

10. Message No. 479, Marshall to AMMISCA, Chungking, April 15, 1942.
11. Message No. 501, Marshall to AMMISCA, Chungking, April 18, 1942.
12. Headquarters, USAFFE, and Eighth Army, "Homeland Air Defense Operations Record," Japanese Monograph No. 157.
13. An anonymous military analyst writing for the *Yomiuri Shimbun* newspaper on March 25, 1950, p. 2.
14. At midnight on April 13, Halsey ordered the time aboard the *Hornet* changed to Zone Minus Twelve and advanced one day, skipping Tuesday, April 14.
15. These medals were attached to a bomb loaded into the "Ruptured Duck," piloted by Lieutenant Ted Lawson.
16. A fact the Navy has never explained. Doolittle, however, was not worried about this early arrival at the launch point. He figured that the news of the bombing over Tokyo Radio and the approach of 16 bombers to the Chinese mainland would alert those preparing to receive them at the five Chinese fields. Since strict radio silence was maintained, he had no way of knowing of the difficulties at the Chinese fields and could not tell Chungking that his planes would arrive a whole day early. However, he did arrange with Halsey to have a coded message sent to Chungking via Pearl Harbor and Washington when his plane took off. This message was never sent.
17. Based on report of Colonel Merian C. Cooper to Commanding General, American Army Forces in China, Burma, and India, Subject: The Doolittle Raid on Japan, June 22, 1942.
18. The Japanese ship sighted was the *No. 23 Nitto Maru*. The message sent to Tokyo said: "Three enemy aircraft carriers sighted at our position 650 nautical miles east of Inubo Saki at 0630." (Tokyo time)
19. Lawson, *Thirty Seconds Over Tokyo*, pp. 55-56.
20. The take-off had been easy for Doolittle—so easy that he later wrote in his official report, "night take-off would have been possible and practicable." Asked later how he felt when he started to roll down the deck, he replied, characteristically, with one word: "Confident."
21. A collection of $3,000 was taken up for Seaman Wall by his shipmates. He was retired in November, 1942 and now lives in the state of Washington.
22. The names of the six crewmen lost were the captain, Maeda, and Seamen Saito, Ozawa, Naganuma, Suzuki, and Oki. Besides Suekichi, the survivors were Hiraga Yoshio, engine officer; Onuma Ken'ichi, steering officer; and deckhands Norio Ito, and Saguro Horie. When the five arrived at Pearl Harbor, they were interrogated by Naval Intelligence and then interned for the duration in POW camps in New Mexico, Wisconsin, and California. Suekichi is now employed as a day laborer in apple orchards in Iwate, Japan.
23. Halsey and Bryan, *op. cit.*, p. 105.
24. On April 17, the Japanese Navy had warned the Army's General Defense Command of the approach of a U. S. Fleet. Since the Army believed American carriers were only capable of launching short-range planes, they agreed with the Navy's estimate that the enemy would have to approach to a point about three hundred miles off shore. Basing time schedules on these conclusions, it was estimated that the attack would come in the early morning hours of the 19th. With so much naval air and sea strength amassed, the Army did not seriously believe an attack was possible.

Part II

THE MISSION

No group of airmen ever undertook a more dangerous combat mission with less chance of survival. Their valor has become a legend. In the following pages, one member of each crew tells what happened that fateful day from his viewpoint, some for the first time. These narratives have either come from their own combat reports or have been prepared especially for this book.

No doubt some of their crewmates will disagree with their recollections. This is understandable when it is realized that almost a quarter of a century has elapsed since their day of glory. Memories are admittedly dimmer, not only because of the passage of time, but because the lives of these men have been as full of excitement, travel, and adventure since then as those of any group of military men in history. Their own rugged individualism also contributes to any differences that may be noted, for they represent this keenly American trait to the ultimate degree.

Here then, are sixteen stories told by sixteen survivors of the sixteen planes that participated in the first air strike of World War II against the Japanese homeland.

Chapter 7

A PERSONAL REPORT

BY

JAMES H. DOOLITTLE

Took off at 8:20 A.M. ship time. Take-off was easy. Night take-off would have been possible and practicable.

Circled carrier to get exact heading and check compass. Wind was from around 300°.

About a half hour after take-off, was joined by A/C 40-2292, Lt. Hoover, pilot, the second plane to take off. About an hour out passed a Japanese camouflaged naval surface vessel of about 6,000 tons. Took it to be a light cruiser. About two hours out passed a multi-motored land plane headed directly for our flotilla and flying at about 3,000 ft.—2 miles away. Passed and endeavored to avoid various civil and naval craft until landfall was made north of Inubo Shuma.

Was somewhat north of desired course but decided to take advantage of error and approach from a northerly direction, thus avoiding anticipated strong opposition to the west. Many flying fields and the air full of planes north of Tokyo. Mostly small biplanes apparently primary or basic trainers.

Encountered nine fighters in three flights of three. This was

Crew No. 1 (Plane 40-2344): left to right, Lt. Henry A. Potter (Navigator);
Lt. Col. James H. Doolittle (Pilot); S/Sgt. Fred A. Braemer (Bombardier);
Lt. Richard E. Cole (Co-Pilot); S/Sgt. Paul J. Leonard (Engineer-Gunner).

about ten miles north of the outskirts of Tokyo proper. All this
time had been flying as low as the terrain would permit. Continued low flying due south over the outskirts of and toward the
east center of Tokyo.

Pulled up to 1,200 ft., changed course to the southwest and incendiary-bombed highly inflammable section. Dropped first bomb at 1:30 (ship time).[1]

Anti-aircraft very active but only one near hit. Lowered away to housetops and slid over western outskirts into low haze and smoke. Turned south and out to sea. Fewer airports on west side but many army posts. Passed over small aircraft factory with a dozen or more newly completed planes on the line. No bombs left. Decided not to machine gun for reasons of personal security. Had seen five barrage balloons over east central Tokyo and what appeared to be more in the distance.

Passed on out to sea flying low. Was soon joined by Hoover who followed us to the Chinese coast. Navigator plotted perfect course to pass north of Yaki Shima. Saw three large naval vessels just before passing west end of Japan. One was flatter than the others and may have been a converted carrier. Passed innumerable fishing and small patrol boats.

Made landfall somewhat north of course on China coast. Tried to reach Chuchow on 4495 (kilocycles) but could not raise.

It had been clear over Tokyo but became overcast before reaching Yaki Shima. Ceiling lowered on coast until low islands and hills were in it at about 600'. Just getting dark and couldn't live under overcast so pulled up to 6,000' and then 8,000' in it. On instruments from then on though occasionally saw dim lights on ground through almost solid overcast. These lights seemed more often on our right and pulled us still farther off course.

Directed rear gunner to go aft and secure films from camera. (Unfortunately, they were jerked out of his shirt front where he had put them when his chute opened.)

Decided to abandon ship. Sgt. Braemer, Lt. Potter, Sgt. Leonard and Lt. Cole jumped in order. Left ship on A.F.C.E. (automatic pilot), shut off both gas cocks and I left. Should have put flaps down. This would have slowed down landing speed, reduced impact and shortened glide.

Left airplane about 9:30 P.M. (ship time) after 13 hours in the air. Still had enough gas left for half hour flight but right front tank was showing empty. Had transferred once as right engine used more fuel. Had covered about 2,250 miles, mostly at low speed, cruising but about an hour at moderate high speed which more than doubled the consumption for this time.

All hands collected and ship located by late afternoon of 19th. Requested General Ho Yang Ling, Director of the Branch Government of Western Chekiang Province to have a lookout kept along the seacoast from Hang Chow Bay to Wen Chow Bay and also have all sampans and junks along the coast keep a lookout for planes that went down at sea, or just reached shore.

Early morning of 20th, four planes and crews, in addition to ours, had been located and I wired General Arnold, through the Embassy at Chungking: TOKYO SUCCESSFULLY BOMBED. DUE BAD WEATHER ON CHINA COAST BELIEVE ALL AIRPLANES WRECKED. FIVE CREWS FOUND SAFE IN CHINA SO FAR. Wired again on the 27th giving more details.

Discussed possibility of purchasing three prisoners on the seacoast from Puppet Government and endeavoring to take out the three in the lake area by force. Believe this desire was made clear to General Ku Cho-tung (who spoke little English) and know it was made clear to English-speaking members of his staff. This was at Shangjao. They agreed to try to purchase of three but recommended against force due to large Japanese concentration.

Bad luck:

(1) Early take-off due to naval contact with surface and air craft.

(2) Clear over Tokyo.

(3) Foul over China.

Good luck:

(1) A 25 mph tail wind over most of the last 1,200 miles.

Take-off should have been made three hours before daylight, but we didn't know how easy it would be and the Navy didn't want to light up. Dawn take-off, closer in, would have been better as things turned out. However, due to the bad weather it is questionable if even daylight landing could have been made at Chuchow without radio aid.

Still feel that original plan of having one plane take off three hours before dusk and others just at dusk was best all-around plan for average conditions.

Author's Note: The above terse summary of Jimmy Doolittle's first combat mission did not express the true feelings of a man who had been a fighter all his life. His first thoughts when he hit the ground were of his own crew and the other 75 men he thought were also down somewhere in the vast expanse of China. He had landed in a rice paddy with knees bent to favor his once-broken ankles and immediately fell into a sitting position up to his neck in the "night soil" fertilizer. Soaking wet and thoroughly cold, he scrambled out and began to look for some signs of habitation. Quentin Reynolds, in his book *The Amazing Mr. Doolittle,* explained what happened next: [2]

"He saw lights in what appeared to be a small farmhouse only a hundred yards away. He unharnessed his 'chute, dropped it and plodded through the mud of the field to the front door of the house. He banged on it and cried out the Chinese phrase all of the pilots and crewmen had learned, "Lushu hoo megwa fugi." (I am an American.) There was an immediate reaction to the phrase, but not the one he had anticipated. He heard a bolt rammed into place on the other side of the door, and at the same time the lights went out. Nothing he could do would arouse the people behind that door.

"Giving up the farmhouse as a bad job, he wandered on. He found a narrow road, followed it half a mile and then came across a very large box placed on two sawhorses. If he could get inside that box he would at least be protected from the chill wind. The box was merely covered with planks. He removed them, climbed up on one of the sawhorses, and then hopped down into the box. He found he had company—a very old Chinese gentleman whose hands were folded peacefully on his chest. The Chinese gentleman, however, wasn't asleep; he was dead, and Doolittle assumed, quite correctly, that he had stumbled into the local morgue. Doolittle had no prejudice against spending the night with a dead Chinese, but the box, made out of thin strips of wood, wasn't strong enough to keep out the rising wind. So Doolittle left the dead Chinese and continued up the road.

"He stumbled into an old water mill. The rain had increased now, and the ramshackle mill looked like a real haven. It was relatively dry inside. But he found that the bitter cold kept him from sleeping. He went through a series of bending exercises trying to generate some warmth in his chilled body. He didn't sleep at all that night.

"The morning was overcast, but the rain had stopped. He continued down the road and finally met an old Chinese farmer who looked at him curiously. The farmer spoke no English, nor did he respond to the 'I am an American' phrase, but Doolittle took out a pad and drew a picture of a locomotive on it. When he added a question mark, the farmer smiled and nodded. Evidently there was a railroad somewhere near. The farmer beckoned him to follow. He led him about a mile up the road, not to a railroad but to what was obviously a local Chinese military headquarters. A major who was in charge looked very suspiciously at Doolittle, and held his hand out for Doolittle's .45-caliber gun which he had spotted in its holster. Doolittle shook his head. He found that the major understood English fairly well. He explained that he was an American who had parachuted out of an American plane during the night. He also said that he was an ally of the Chinese army and therefore he would keep his gun.

"There was an uncomfortable silence for a moment while the major and three of his men, cradling tommy guns in their arms, looked at the mud-spattered American. The major hesitated a moment, and Doolittle felt he was on the point of giving an order to have him shot immediately.

" 'I'll lead you to where my parachute is,' he said, and the major nodded.

"Doolittle led them back along the narrow road, past the mill, the morgue, and then he located the farmhouse which had received him so inhospitably the previous night. He found the rice paddy and led them to the exact spot where he had landed. But the parachute he had left there had disappeared.

"The three soldiers were muttering to each other, and the major's eyes showed nothing but disbelief. Doolittle decided that the people in the farmhouse at least would remember the shouting and would remember his banging on the door. He asked the major to check with them. They walked to the farmhouse. The farmer, his wife and two children looked completely blank when the major interrogated them in rapid Chinese.

" 'They say they heard no noise during the night.' He turned to Doolittle. 'They say they heard no plane during the night. They say they saw no parachute. They say you are lying.'

"Doolittle was now beginning to sweat. He protested vigorously to the major that he was in fact an American officer, that he had bombed Tokyo, and that four members of his crew had bailed out with him. Nothing he said could remove the hard suspicion from the major's eyes. But then two of the soldiers who had gone into the farmhouse reappeared with broad smiles on their faces and the parachute in their arms. Obviously the farmer had thought that the parachute could be converted into something useful. The sight of the parachute completely dissipated the officer's suspicions. He shook hands with Doolittle and immediately ordered his men to get him something to eat. He ordered another to return to headquarters and send out searching parties for Doolittle's crew."

Later that day, Dick Cole, Hank Potter, Fred Braemer and Paul Leonard were located and they had had a similar experience. In his official report, Leonard told how he had spent the night wrapped in his parachute and then walked about six miles the next morning trying to find the other crew members. When he couldn't locate anyone, he decided to return to his starting point.

"Returning to where I landed," Leonard said, "I encountered four men armed with rifles. One motioned to me to raise my hands while the other three proceeded to cock their rifles. One took aim. At the same moment, I pulled my .45. The one who was aiming fired so I fired twice. They ran so I turned and climbed to mountain top where I could see men gathering around the foot of the hill. All of them had rifles. I hid myself as well as possible and they left. I then figured out a course to travel at night.

"After about an hour and a half, I saw a crowd of people returning back down the valley. In front I could see Lt. Potter and Sergeant Braemer. I reloaded my clip because I figured they were captured. I started yelling and ran down the mountain but found they were in good friendly company."

But Potter and Braemer had not been in "good friendly company" when they landed. As soon as they were discovered by a band of guerrillas, they were immediately robbed, tied up and marched off. Fortunately, they came across an English-speaking Chinese boy who led the guerrillas and their captives to his house and spread the word. Soon the guerrilla chieftain arrived and their belongings were restored. They had set off searching for Leonard when he found them.

Doolittle felt a little better when his crewmen came in but there were still seventy-five more men to be accounted for. Next day, he made his way back to the scene of the crashed B-25 with Paul Leonard. Potter, who had sprained an ankle in the jump, Cole, and Braemer decided not to go. When the two men arrived at the site, Doolittle's morale reached the lowest point in his entire career. The once-beautiful B-25 was spread all over two acres of a mountain top.

The two men picked through the wreckage and Doolittle found his Army blouse. However, it was oil-soaked and someone had removed all the brass buttons. That didn't help his morale either. He sat down dejectedly on the airplane with his head in his hands. He described his feelings to the author:

"As I sat there I was very, very depressed. Paul Leonard took my picture and then, seeing how badly I felt tried to cheer me up. He said, 'What do you think will happen when you go home, Colonel?'

"I answered, 'Well, I guess they'll send me to Leavenworth.'

"Paul smiled and said, 'No, sir. I'll tell you what will happen. They're going to make you a general.'

"I smiled weakly and he tried again. 'And they're going to give you the Congressional Medal of Honor,' he said.

"I smiled again and he made his final effort. 'Colonel,' he said, 'I know they're going to give you another airplane and when they do, I'd like to be your crew chief.'

"It was then that tears came to my eyes, and I told him that if I ever had another airplane and he wanted to be my crew chief, he surely could."

To Doolittle, or any pilot, the request Leonard made was the highest possible compliment. Doolittle, as always, kept his promise and Leonard became his crew chief on a B-26 in North Africa a few months later. The following February, the two of them landed at a forward Allied airdrome, near Youks-les-Bains, Algeria, when it was attacked by German bombers. Doolittle had taken a jeep to a nearby

Lt. Col. Jimmy Doolittle was convinced that his first combat mission was a failure. Several days after his bail-out, he made his way back to the wreckage of his plane to see what could be salvaged. Completely dejected, he sits beside a wing section of the plane. This photo was taken by his engineer-gunner, Sgt. Leonard.

fighter strip leaving Leonard to work on the plane when an air raid alarm sounded. As the German bombers came in low, Leonard manned his plane's top turret guns until the batteries ran down and the turret wouldn't work. He then made a run for an old bomb crater fifty yards away. In one of those soul-tearing freaks of war, a bomb hit the crater just as he reached it and exploded right in his face. In a fraction of a second, the life of the man who had dedicated himself to serving as "the Boss's" crew chief was snuffed out. To Doolittle it was the greatest personal tragedy of the war.

In the meantime, the other two of Leonard's predictions had come true. As soon as Doolittle had reached Chungking, he was notified of his promotion to Brigadier General on April 26, skipping the rank of Colonel.[3]

Instead of letting him wait until all of his crews were rounded up, Doolittle was ordered back to the United States and left China on May 5th. Traveling via Cairo, Khartoum, Accra, and Natal, he reached Washington about May 15th. Generals Marshall and Arnold, in the interest of secrecy to protect the raiders who had not yet been located, told Doolittle to remain in hiding for several days in his apartment at 25th and Q Streets in downtown Washington. He was not to even let his wife know that he was back in the country. Doolittle did as he was told and used the time to prepare his report and write letters to relatives of his men. Then, at noon on May 19th, Arnold called him on the phone and said, mysteriously, "I'll pick you up in about an hour in a staff car."

When the car arrived, not only Arnold but Marshall was also in the rear seat. Doolittle saluted respectfully. Arnold smiled and said: "Come on, hop in, Jimmy. We haven't got much time."

There was something suspicious in the air as the car sped downtown and no one spoke. When he could stand it no longer, Doolittle asked his superiors where they were going. Arnold only grinned and Marshall gave him a cold stare. "Well," Doolittle ventured, "I think there's something going on that I don't know about. I'm not a very smart fellow and if it involves me I think somebody had better tell me so they won't be embarrassed."

Hap Arnold could not contain his secret any longer and announced, "Jimmy, we're on our way to the White House. The President is going to give you the Medal of Honor."

No one could have been more surprised than Doolittle. He said, frankly, "That's ridiculous, Sir. I don't think I've earned the Big

Medal. I think it was wrong when they gave it to "Slim" Lindbergh for crossing the Atlantic and I think it's wrong to give it to me now!"

Arnold was taken aback and, as Doolittle described later, "got mad as hell at me." But a grateful people and their President were to have their way. When the three officers arrived at the White House, they were shown into an anteroom outside the President's office. While they waited, a side door opened and in stepped a surprised Jo Doolittle, who had been flown all the way from Los Angeles "looking like a carpet bagger because I didn't have a chance to change clothes or even go to the ladies' room." She had absolutely no idea why she had also been mysteriously whisked to the White House after landing at National Airport.

The famous flyer and his wife were completely dumbfounded. As they embraced briefly, Hap Arnold chuckled happily in the background. A few moments later the four people were shown into President Roosevelt's office, where Jimmy was decorated with the highest award this nation can bestow. To this day, however, Doolittle does not believe he should have been awarded the Medal of Honor. "I'll spend the rest of my life trying to earn it," he says. No one agrees that he has to.

As soon as the news was released that the famous Jimmy Doolittle had led the raid, he was deluged with congratulatory letters and telegrams. School children, veterans organizations, unions, and industrial firms sent money and war bonds, which Doolittle promptly turned over to Mrs. H. H. Arnold as Vice President of the Army Air Force Aid Society. Some money was sent to Mrs. Doolittle, who also forwarded it to the AAF Aid Society, United China Relief, Navy Relief and the American Red Cross. The largest single amount received was a check for $1,000 sent by Mr. Louis Pizitz of Birmingham, Alabama. Smallest amount was a 25 cent piece forwarded by 11-year-old Joe Rilkowski of Seattle, Washington who postscripted "I think your my hearo."

One of the telegrams was from Roscoe Turner, world famous racing and stunt pilot. Shortly after Doolittle had begun planning the raid, Turner had dropped him a note suggesting that the two of them should round up a group of long distance and racing pilots to bomb Tokyo in retaliation for the raid on Pearl Harbor. Turner reasoned that men with their experience were accustomed to the kind of precision navigation it would take to fly long distances and bomb the enemy in his homeland. Doolittle had replied that they were both too old for that kind of flying any more and that they should leave the combat flying to the younger generation. Turner's telegram said:

DEAR JIMMY,

YOU SON-OF-A-BITCH

ROSCOE

It has been a long-standing tradition among military pilots who bail out of a plane to save their lives that they should give a box of cigars to the man who packed the parachute they used. One of the first things Doolittle had done after his bail-out was to remove the inspection card from his chute which identified its packer. It showed that J. H. Patton of the Sacramento Air Depot had packed it two or three days before the *Hornet* had left the States. True to tradition, one of the first things Doolittle did was to buy a box of cigars and mail them anonymously to Patton. He could not identify himself because the details of the mission remained secret for a year. It was Doolittle's third parachute jump and he appreciated more than most pilots how valuable was that package of silk he always wore.

When the furor died down and the war moved into its next phase, Jimmy Doolittle and his raiders were off fighting the war around the globe. For Doolittle himself the Tokyo Raid was only the first of many narrow escapes and hair-raising experiences in combat.

NOTES TO CHAPTER 7

1. 12:30 Tokyo time.
2. Quentin Reynolds, *The Amazing Mr. Doolittle* (New York: Appleton-Century-Crofts, 1953), pp. 209-212.
3. One of the few officers ever to skip the rank of Colonel, Doolittle had also skipped the rank of Captain. He had resigned his regular commission as a First Lieutenant in 1930 and accepted a reserve commission as a Major. He was recalled to active duty in 1940 in his reserve rank. Retired in 1956 as a permanent Lieutenant General, he is the only Air Force Reserve officer ever to attain that rank.

Chapter 8

THE FIRST OF MANY

BY

CARL R. WILDNER

It was hard for me to believe that we were actually going on this mission, but here we were in take-off position. All of us held our breaths as Colonel Doolittle's plane roared down the deck. It seemed to me he was going too slow and wouldn't make it but about half-way down the deck his wheels lifted off and he was gone.

Looking back on those moments I know I was scared as our pilot, Travis Hoover, lined our plane up with the left wheel on the yellow line. We knew the odds were against us and it seemed to me we were doing things without thinking—like automatons. I guess we were and maybe that's the way it was supposed to be. Trav Hoover and "Foggy" Fitzhugh went through their pilots' checklist and I went through mine. I called Sergeant Doug Radney in the rear to see if he was all set and he answered with his characteristic "Roger, Sir, all set back here." Dick Miller, in the nose, checked in so we were ready.

Hoover looked back at me quizzically and I gave him the OK sign. He nodded and pushed the throttles forward all the way and

Crew No. 2 (Plane 40-2292): left to right, Lt. Carl N. Wildner (Navigator); Lt. Travis Hoover (Pilot); Lt. Richard E. Miller (Bombardier); Lt. William N. Fitzhugh (Co-Pilot); Sgt. Douglas V. Radney (Engineer-Gunner).

held the brakes. After what seemed an eternity to me, we started down the deck—much too slowly, I thought. I braced myself for the crash I felt was coming. I was sure we were going right off the end into the dirty green water splashing in big geysers over the bow. Halfway down the deck, though, we were airborne.

Instead of staggering into the air, we seemed to soar and the nose pointed higher and higher. I got a stall feeling in the pit of my stomach and the pilots must have, too. Both Hoover and Fitzhugh pushed forward on the controls at the same time. We were on our way. Gradually the tension in my stomach lessened and the flight settled down into a routine just like all the practice missions we had flown.

I stood between Hoover and Fitzhugh and saw Doolittle's plane up ahead. I told Hoover that if we would follow them, I would keep track of the course. Both planes had targets in Tokyo so it was easy to follow the leader.

Besides navigation, my job was to transfer gas from the auxiliary tanks into the main tanks. I did this every twenty minutes throughout the flight.

About ten minutes after take-off, Doolittle's plane, about three miles ahead, turned suddenly into a left bank and we followed. A ship the size of a freighter loomed out of the mist and we saw small patches of smoke appear as the lead plane went by. We figured it must have been small caliber gunfire. Apparently it didn't fire at us. That old tight feeling came back to me and I asked myself the question that I'm sure thousands of other navigators have asked: "Why am I here when it would have been so easy to be somewhere else?" I'll admit I was scared.

After what seemed a lifetime, we sighted the Japanese coast ahead. We also sighted several small boats and I fully expected to see them fire at us but they didn't. As navigator, I had other things to worry about. We had followed a course of 272° and landfall should have been made on a point of land on which sat Inubo Saki lighthouse. A white sandy beach appeared but no lighthouse and no point of land.

In all my life I have never felt so helpless. I was a navigator who had washed out of pilot training at Randolph Field and I had a little of the inferiority complex all navigators seem to have. I felt that all pilots looked down on us and doubted our ability to navigate. This mission was our big chance to prove our value. Over water, of course, there is no way to be sure of your position if you can't take radio or celestial bearings. You can only guess at the wind drift, hope your magnetic compass is right and that the pilot can fly the course you think he ought to fly. But now that we had sighted land, it was my responsibility to find out where we were and how to get to our target.

We zoomed over the beach and headed inland over pine trees and huts still trailing Doolittle's plane. Hoover asked what course to take up and I had to admit I didn't know. I told him to keep following Doolittle as I searched frantically on my maps to compare what I was seeing on the ground with what my maps showed. I couldn't see very far at 200 feet and I knew Hank Potter, the navigator in Doolittle's plane, must be having the same trouble.

We passed over rice paddies, streams and a few temples but I couldn't identify a single landmark on my maps. I knew the maps had been made up from very poor information but it seemed to me that the maps I was holding were of another part of the world. Nothing matched.

After heading inland for about twenty minutes, Hoover was getting worried. We were approaching some low hills which, again, I couldn't find on my maps. Doolittle turned south and I told Hoover to follow. I fully expected to see fighter planes boring in on us but none appeared. We did see some trainers doing loops and rolls but that was all.

As we headed southward, I began to see people on the ground going about their work unconcerned. We flew over a military camp and I could see a circle of officers standing around talking, their swords flashing in the sun.

Soon we saw rooftops and power lines ahead. Doolittle's plane had zigzagged a few times averaging a course of about 250° so I knew that Potter had figured we were north of Tokyo. As the landmarks increased, I knew he was right. We were approaching the Japanese capital from the northeast. I quickly picked out our checkpoints—a river and a canal—and after the second bend in the river, gave Hoover a course and advised him to start climbing. He leveled off at 900 feet and I figured we had about two minutes to go before we would be over our target. I had just picked up the interphone to tell Miller when I felt the bombs go off. The concussion lifted us up in the air noticeably. I was surprised and I was sure that Miller had bombed the wrong target. But not being in the nose, I didn't know for sure.

Later, I found out what had happened. Neither Miller nor Hoover could identify the target we were supposed to hit—a munitions plant and storage area. Miller saw what he thought looked reasonably like the target and let the bombs go on two factory buildings and storehouses. The only clue he had was three smoke stacks which were supposed to mark the target. He made a split second decision and it probably saved our lives. If we had found and bombed the munitions plant even at 1500 feet we probably would not have survived the blast.

As soon as the last bomb cleared the plane, Miller closed the bomb-bay doors and Hoover racked the plane up into a sharp left bank. None of us in the front could see where the bombs hit so we asked Radney if he could see.

"Yes, Sir," he reported to Hoover. "All four hit close together and there's smoke all over the area. We got it all right!"

"OK, gang, hold your hats," Hoover shouted over the interphone. "We're going down." I thought Hoover ought to slow down to save gas, but he wanted to get away from Tokyo as fast as possible.

Hoover shoved the wheel forward and everything that was loose floated upward, including my stomach. I glanced at the airspeed indicator and saw that it was close to the redline. Outside all I could see were rooftops—millions of them. With all due respect to Ted Lawson's book title "Thirty Seconds Over Tokyo," it seemed like we spent twenty minutes picking our way over rooftops before we reached Tokyo Bay. Hoover dropped down to wave top level and I was sure we were going to go in.

The whole bunch of us were looking out every window in the plane fully expecting the many ships in the harbor to open up on us but none of them did. To the west over the city we saw a large twin-engine bomber flying at 2500 feet. As we reached the mouth of Tokyo Bay both pilots and Miller in the nose saw a single-engine seaplane lifting off the water right into our flight path. He must have seen us a split second before we saw him because before Hoover could turn, he turned sharply away from us, almost digging his wing tips into the water.

Somebody shouted on the interphone to Radney about the plane we had almost collided with and he came back with the unwelcome news that his top turret had jammed. If we were attacked now, there was nothing we could do but rely on the pathetic .30 caliber gun in the nose—and pray.

Before heading out to sea, we saw Doolittle's plane ahead and Trav eased in toward him. Fitzhugh checked the gas gauges. I figured that with the winds as forecast before we left the carrier, we would reach the Chinese coast with fifty gallons. If they were any stiffer, we wouldn't reach it at all. We were using a little more gas than normal probably because our engines were not set for as lean a mixture as the other planes.

As we paralleled the south coast of Japan, we had lunch and relaxed. It had all seemed a little unreal to me and I don't think any of us really realized that we had just made our first real bombing run. However, it had almost been like a training mission. It was a beautiful day in Japan and I felt like a tourist wanting to land and see the sights on the ground.

One of the last islands we saw was a smoking volcano. High clouds appeared before we lost sight of land and as we started out across the China Sea, the thickening clouds became a solid overcast. The ceiling let down lower and lower and we hit occasional rain squalls. The water below us became muddier and a slow creeping realization that we might not make the coast began to sink into my brain.

I stood between Hoover and Fitzhugh and watched the gas gauge move steadily toward empty. All three of us were staring out the windshield when Hoover leaned forward and pointed. It was an island; as soon as I could ascertain its shape, I found it on the map. It was in the mouth of the Yangtze River and too close to the Japs. I told Hoover to head southwest. He tried to climb but the right engine coughed and quit. Fitzhugh turned on the fuel boost pumps and we all knew we had only a few minutes left in the air. The engine cut back in and Hoover tried again to pull up into the overcast. From what we could see ahead, the ceiling was right down on the ground. It was either climb and bail out or crash land. Hoover elected to climb and I knew what was going to come next.

As we started into the clouds again, the right engine cut out again and again Hoover jammed the nose down to make it cut back in. It wouldn't be long now. Hoover started to look for a place to land. Down below we saw a flat stretch of rice paddies along the edge of the water. Hoover buzzed the place twice, carefully avoiding getting the plane in such a position that would prevent landing on the mud flats of the bay if the engines quit cold. It was now drizzling and growing dark.

Hoover made his decision and turned on the approach. I stood behind Fitzhugh and put a seat cushion in front of my face to protect myself against the armor plate. It would be a controlled landing, wheels up. Everything depended on Trav's skill as a pilot.

I felt the plane level off, slow down and then hit. It was surprisingly easy. We slid to a halt in the mud and scrambled out. Damage to the plane was remarkably light. I noted that it was 2045 hours, a little over ten hours since we had left the *Hornet*. Our position was six miles east of Kiansian at longitude 121°50′, latitude 29°40′. We were down, safe and unhurt. Just as important, we were all together.

We took our guns, knives, flashlights, pocket compasses, canteens, emergency rations and a few items of clothing out of the plane. Sergeant Radney then ignited the incendiary bomb on the turret tank to set the plane on fire but it burned through and nothing happened. We went back and ignited the two landing flares but again the ship wouldn't burn. Radney got some engine covers out of the rear of the plane. Hoover then went back and set fire to the engine. The few gallons of gas and oil left finally caught and spread to the various parts of the plane. It was completely dark now and the fire reflected on the low hanging clouds enabling us to see. Getting rid of the plane by setting it on fire might be our downfall. We didn't know whether we were in friendly or enemy territory. We had to get away from the plane as quickly as possible.

The drizzle that had been falling when we landed turned into heavy rain. We climbed to the top of a hill by midnight and spent the remainder of that night in a trench, shivering and trying to sleep. We stayed hidden in an old pillbox on the top of the hill all the following day, April 19th, and started hiking westward at nightfall. Next day we slept about four hours and pushed farther westward into the hills, figuring that if there were any Japanese around, they would stick close to the shore of the bay. That night, the 20th, we built a lean-to.

We started at dawn again (the 21st) but made slow progress. In mid-afternoon, we came upon a house that seemed fairly neat and clean. We approached the house and found two women and a teenage boy. They were courteous and not at all surprised to see us. They gave us food and water and by means of sign language and our map found that we were in Chinese territory and that no Japanese were around. They seemed to know where our plane had landed.

We felt a little better after this and decided to walk along the main path paralleling the bay. Just at sunset we were suddenly surrounded by about 30 Chinese guerrillas who appeared out of nowhere. We were helpless and were sure we were going to be turned over to the Japanese when they searched us and took most of our remaining belongings. They marched us about 10 miles to Sungyao to meet their leader. He was a tough, dirty-looking individual but when he was convinced that we were Americans, he assured us through his one man who could speak a little English that he and his men were fighting the Japanese. He ordered his men to feed us and bed us down for the night. Some, but not all, of our belongings were returned.

Next morning, the 22nd, we walked to a secluded place on the bay and boarded a small river boat. We asked for our pistols back but were told we would receive them at Ning Hai, our next stop. That afternoon we landed near the south end of the bay, were fed and then escorted to a military camp by about eight of the guerrillas. We stayed there that night and the next day moved out again, this time in rickshas.

About noon we arrived as Sunchway and were met by Tung Sheng Liu, a Chinese aeronautical engineer who had just come from Shanghai disguised as a Chinese merchant. He had made his way through the Japanese lines and was on his way to a new aircraft factory that was being planned at Kweilin. Since he could speak a little English, General Yu Chi Ming, the ranking Chinese general in the area, whom he knew, had called him on the telephone and asked him to wait until we showed up and then act as interpreter until we reached Chuhsien. This act of friendship was to change his life and probably saved ours.[1]

With Liu's help, we managed to get splendid treatment. The Chinese fed us rice, green vegetables and dried fish. The guerrillas gave us back the rest of our belongings except our guns and knives and bent over backwards to be hospitable. We explained that we wanted to get to Chungking and were assured that Liu would get us there.

That night we all slept on boards laid across a pair of saw horses. Each bed had a quilt folded double. We slept in between the folds. It was smelly and full of lice and bugs.

The next day we traveled to Toon Kong where we met General Yu Chi Ming and then were taken by sedan chair to Ta Chiih by his men. Everywhere we went we were the center of attraction and everyone seemed to know all about us. How the word traveled so fast under those primitive conditions I'll never know. From their treatment of us, we were oddities as well as celebrities since most of them had probably never seen white men before. If they had, it could only have been a missionary and not men in uniform.

On the 25th we again traveled by sedan chair and ricksha to Cheng Sien. Each day we traveled by ricksha we had different men doing the pulling. They averaged about 115 pounds each and looked too frail for the job. They always seemed to make a grab for me when it came time to go since I was the lightest. The loser got Miller who weighed about 200 pounds.

As we jounced along from village to village, the going got rougher. The dirt or brick roads were half dug away leaving room for one ricksha to delay Japanese advances. We continually avoided collisions with farmers bearing their pair of "honey buckets."

When we arrived at Cheng Sien, we were met by the commissioner of the District, Fong Chi Chow. He gave us a guided tour of the city and showed us the damage done by Japanese bombs the year before. The next three days we went to Chang Loh, Tungying and Iwu.

During our whole trip under Liu's guidance, our treatment was superb. He was a gem. We could converse with him and could get what we wanted without a lot of sign language. We were wined and dined by every general and commissioner along our route. Liu told us that there was an edict that no grain would be used to make wine and no wine would be drunk for the duration—except when entertaining foreign guests. Consequently, foreign guests were very welcome as an excuse to dig into their hoard of aged wine. On one of our stops we had a banquet where we speared boiled pigeon eggs from a bowl of soup and drank toasts. At another stop we were entertained by a group of singing Chinese. A general gave us all Havana cigars. Where he got them nobody knew. At still another stop we had a turtle served to us—in the shell. We were also treated with aged eggs that had been dug out of the ground just to celebrate our arrival. I tried them, but the others did not share my curiosity.

We arrived at Iwu on the 28th where we were met by Governor Chang Soong Nien. Soon after we got there we experienced our first air raid warning and the gang of us hid in nearby fields until the all clear was sounded. About nine o'clock that night we boarded a train and arrived in Kingwa, a little after midnight. They put us up in a hotel and early the next morning we were hustled into a Ford station wagon and driven to the headquarters of General Chang Kai Shien, an Air Force general, which was about ten miles outside the city. That afternoon we again boarded a train and arrived at Chushien that evening.

We found "Davey" Jones and "Brick" Holstrom had arrived there before us and it was good to see them. We all wondered what had happened to the other crews and discussed every rumor that the Chinese gave us. We were told that one other crew had crashed near the coast and that two of the crew had been killed and the other three had been captured by the Japenese. We thought we knew what fate they had in store for them and thanked our lucky stars we had fallen into friendly hands. We all wondered who the unlucky ones were.

About nine o'clock on May 3rd, we boarded the train for Yeng Tan. On this leg of the trip, two white women missionaries gave us canned milk to drink. I have often wondered where they came from and where they went. At Yeng Tan we boarded a charcoal-burning bus and chugged our way in to Hengyang, arriving there on May 6th. Again we were taken to the local Chinese Air Force station and put up at their hostel in the care of John T. Yang, a pleasant-mannered man who also spoke a little English.

After fidgeting at this base for over a week, we were notified that we would soon be flown to Chungking. On May 14th a DC-3 piloted by an American crew dropped in on the dirt strip and picked us up. We wanted to take Liu with us but Army regulations forbade it. I had a lump in my throat as we shook hands with him and left him standing there on the dusty air strip. He had risked his neck for us and had seen to it that we had the best of care. We all vowed that we would help him if we could and in our official reports we recommended he be employed in some way by the AVG or the American forces in China. Although our

hearts ached for him, we all felt it would be the last we would
ever see or hear of him. Little did we know that he would later
come to America, become a citizen, and realize his dream of
working for the Air Force.

 Our arrival in Chungking that day was a day of rejoicing for
us. We were the third group to get in and that night, gracious
Madame Chiang Kai Shek put on her third party for our group.
We had a sumptuous banquet and she presented each of us with
the Chinese Army, Navy, and Air Force Medal. After our experiences of the previous month, we were glad we had finally arrived
at our original destination. For us as a crew this mission was
finally over. For most of us, however, it was just the first of many
combat missions to follow.

NOTE TO CHAPTER 8

 1. Liu later came to the United States in 1946 to further his engineering
education at the University of Minnesota. He is now a citizen of the U. S. and
working as a project engineer for the Air Force. He was made an honorary
member of the Tokyo Raiders for helping this crew.

Chapter 9

THE LAST FLIGHT OF "WHISKEY PETE"

BY

Jacob E. Manch

I was eating breakfast when the call to general quarters was sounded. When the call came "Army crews, man your planes" I rushed to my cabin (I was one of the 12 men who slept in the Captain's quarters) and hurriedly packed my B-4 bag. Besides my clothes, shaving kit and such, I stuffed in four boxes of Robert Burns cigars and two boxes of Baby Ruth candy bars. My phonograph and records would give us some American jazz in China so I decided to take it along. My records were in a cake tin and I asked Bob Clever to put them in his plane. Now that we were going I felt that the long hours of preparation were finally coming to an end. I had the fullest confidence in the B-25 and that we would make it off the deck safely.

Bob Gray wheeled "Whiskey Pete" (named after his pinto back in Texas) into position and we took off. After we got off and were level, we were constantly on the watch for enemy vessels and aircraft because we were sure that the task force had been detected. We did spot one vessel about fifteen minutes after take-off but since they didn't fire on us we kept right on course.

Crew No. 3 (Plane 40-2270): left to right, Lt. Charles J. Ozuk (Navigator); Lt. Robert M. Gray (Pilot); Sgt. Aden E. Jones (Bombardier); Lt. Jacob E. Manch (Co-Pilot); Cpl. Leland D. Faktor (Engineer-Gunner).

After we had settled down, Bob Gray turned to me with a grin and asked, "What are you doing up here?" I told him the same thing he was, "getting ready to get my fanny shot off." Although the cockpit was filled with fumes from the bladder tank lying on top of the bomb-bay, we broke open a box of Robert Burns and smoked them all the way in to the Japanese mainland. The sight of the Japanese coast was sort of awe-inspiring as it was the first land we had seen in five hours. We were happy to see it, but we knew the people there wouldn't be happy to see us. It was a bright and sunny day and I thought to myself that this was one country that looked exactly like I had pictured in my mind it would look.

We tried to home in with our radio compass on Japanese commercial radio stations. We thought we would know when the Boss dropped his bombs, as the Japanese would shut down their radio stations and our homing needle would stop pointing. (As it was, the Japanese never turned off the station we were tuned in on and we were tracking outbound on their station to China two hours after we dropped our bombs.) We figured that since we were the third ship in and that we were strung out 5 or 6 minutes apart, their fighters would be alerted and that their ack-ack would be waiting to pick us off, one by one.

Our target was in the Tokyo area on the east side of town, on the banks of a river. We had three 500-lb. HE bombs and one 500-lb. thermite cluster fire bomb. We dropped our bombs from 900 feet. The three explosive bombs were dumped on industrial type targets and the thermite cluster on the dock area. Anti-aircraft fire was light to moderate—it had the correct altitude but not our speed. We made an exceptionally slow bomb run, attempting to save fuel.

Before reaching the target, Bob Gray took a vote among the crew that if we were badly damaged by gun fire, what we wanted to do. All the members of the crew, with the exception of Gray, stated that if we had the chance, we would like to bail out. Bob said that if he had the chance, he would let us out, then he was going to pick out the biggest building in Tokyo and stick "Whiskey Pete" right in the middle of it.

As we dropped our last bomb, we were jumped by Japanese

fighters. Just prior to this, our gun turret went out of commission and we had to switch to the alternate source of power in order to get it operational. We had to increase our power settings in order to outrun these fighters. Sgt. Aden Jones, the bombardier, was strafing with the .30 caliber nose gun and the top turret was being fired by Corporal Faktor at the fighters. We suffered no damage and outran them.

As we passed through Tokyo Bay we could see the fires started by the bombs from the other crews ahead of us and noticed the barrage balloons up in the city of Tokyo. We passed by the Emperor's Palace and could easily have bombed it if we had wanted to.

Several destroyers and cruisers in the harbor were firing at us and had gotten underway. It looked like they were attempting to pick up our course heading so they could radio it on ahead. We picked up a heading of due south, hoping that they would think we were headed for the Philippines. We finally turned back, after about fifteen minutes, to our heading to China.

It was about this time that the Good Lord started giving us a hand. We had bucked a 15-knot headwind from the carrier to the target. As we left the target area, the wind shifted and gave us a tail wind, all the way into China. This is contrary to the winds in that country as they should have been blowing on our nose, from west to east. If we had not received this tail wind for about seven hours, we figured we would have landed about 200 miles out in the China Sea, out of fuel.

The only friendly aircraft we saw after leaving the target area was another B-25 about one hour before dusk. He was on a track of about 45 degrees different from ours. When I noticed this, I turned to our navigator, Lt. Ozuk, and said, "Ozuk, one of you two navigators is wrong. Who is it, you or him?" Ozuk replied confidently, "It's not me. Turn 2 more degrees off of his course."

It sure was a temptation to turn and follow the other aircraft so that at least two crews could have been together. I later found out that this was one of the two crews that was captured by the Japanese. Just after this we ran into weather and proceeded on instruments from there on.

If we had not gotten the tail wind that I mentioned, we had planned on ditching the plane in the China Sea, getting into the life raft and attempting to float to the China coast. After we went on instruments we knew that we wouldn't be intercepted by fighters so we decided to lighten the aircraft by throwing everything overboard that we could spare. We dumped half the ammunition that we had left in the guns and anything else that was not tied down.

Several times, after dark, we saw either fishing boats or people on islands blinking lights at us as if they were attempting to extract some signal from us. We flipped our landing lights on and off several times, hoping to give the proper signal if they were Japanese. We saw one large city all lit up through the overcast but could not determine where we were.

Since a ground station was supposed to have been established for us to contact on 4495 kilocycles, we called them for about an hour, but to no avail. We dropped two flares about an hour after we figured we had crossed the coast of China, hoping to see some flat land to land on but no luck.

We were still flying in a thin overcast when, about 10:00, with both tanks registering empty, we knew that we would have to bail out. Gray turned the plane due south and gave us the order to go. Sergeant Jones pulled the front hatch release and kicked the door out. I then called to Faktor in the rear to get his hatch off and bail out. I sent Jones out first and Lt. Ozuk after him. I flashed my light in the rear of the plane to see if Faktor had gone—saw no one and got no answer to my yell.

I grabbed a box of Robert Burns cigars and a bunch of Baby
Ruths and stuffed as many as I could inside my A-2 jacket. Then
I bundled up my private arsenal, a 44-40 Winchester rifle,
German Lueger, two .45 automatics, and .22 automatic and an
ax and a bowie knife and got ready to go. I told Bob Gray that I
would be walking west and that I would see him in Chungking.
I wished him luck and dropped through the escape hatch. Bob
had dropped the gear and flaps, slowing the plane to 140 mph in
order to give us a chance to bail out.

As I went out, I watched the two exhaust stacks go over my

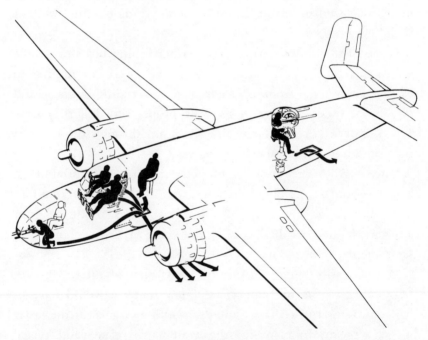

Eleven of the sixteen crews on the Doolittle mission elected to bail out
when they reached China. The artist's drawing above shows the escape route
most of them took when leaving their planes. The four men in the forward
section of the B-25 jumped from the main hatch located in the floor of the
navigator's compartment. The rear gunner went through the hatch in the
floor of the aft compartment. The four crews that crash-landed escaped
from hatches in the top portion of the aircraft above the pilot's seats and
in the rear section.

head, then reached for the D-ring on my 'chute but couldn't find it. Scrambling frantically, I finally found it dangling at my side and pulled. I was aware of the weirdest sound as I continued to fall. It was the rubber bands which held the shroud lines in my parachute pack twinging as they let go each bunch of lines.

Since I only had a 24-foot 'chute which was too small for my weight, the opening shock was something I wasn't ready for. I saw red and the impact jerked my bowie knife, axe, canteen and all my guns away, except the one in my holster. The box of cigars disappeared out of my jacket and the Baby Ruths were shucked, leaving nothing but the wrappers.

Coming down, I thought I heard waves breaking on a beach and the horrible thought came to me that I had sent the rest of the crew out without their Mae West life vests on. They would surely drown if we were over the ocean and not over land as we figured. Just as I struggled to release my leg straps to get away from the 'chute in case I landed in the water, I hit the ground with a thud. What I thought was waves slapping on a beach was wind blowing through pine trees.

After I hit the ground, I started to wander around but then thought better of it because I might fall off a cliff or into a ravine during my wanderings. Groping around, I found a fairly flat spot and rolled up in my parachute to attempt to keep dry and warm. It had begun to rain heavily and I was cold.

The next morning dawned bright and cheerful. I saw that I was in the mountains and had landed close to the top of one. If I had wandered around like I had started to do the night before, I probably would have killed myself or at least broken a leg. I searched awhile for my canteen and guns and other equipment but never found them. Knowing that I would have to have water sooner or later, I cut the back of my parachute open, pulled out the sponge rubber cushion and attempted to make a water bag out of it. While cutting holes in it, so that I could carry it on my back as a water bag, the pocket knife slipped and I cut my left index finger badly.

I got some water from a running stream and started down a little mountain trail. I had intended to walk the top of the mountains as we had been informed that there was only one railroad in that part of China and that if we could find it, it would take us into our destination. As I started down the trail, I ran into a Chinese man and woman who took one terrified look at me and took off running. I did not see another soul until much later that day when I came upon an old Chinese woman gathering firewood. The sight of me threw her into a panic and she threw her sticks down and hobbled off on her wrapped feet.

I wandered on for the rest of the day and that night slept on top of the seventh mountain I had crossed. My shoes were badly torn. It was still raining with a very stiff wind. On the third day, with nothing to eat, I became entangled in a thicket. My hands, legs and face were badly scratched and bleeding and I was dead tired. I just sat down in a creek, with water up to my waist, resting and trying to make up my mind what to do. About this time, the brush parted and a Chinese with a big smile on his face stuck out his hand to help me get out of the creek. Several more Chinese then came out of the brush and helped push and carry me up to a little trail on the mountain side. They were armed with old 17th century flint lock muskets. They evidently had never seen rubber before as they were very interested in the sponge rubber cushion from the back of my parachute. I had cut pieces of it to put under the heels of my shoes. They played with this rubber, felt it and bounced it around on the ground like a bunch of kids.

I was so tired about this time that I couldn't walk over 100 yards without rest. One of the Chinese, about 5'4" offered to carry me on his back. I laughed at him because I thought I would be too heavy for him. He insisted that I get on his back and when

I did, he threw it into high blower and went up and down those hills for two miles like a Billy goat and like I wasn't even on his back. As we approached his village at dark, I became embarrassed because he was carrying me, a supposedly great aviator. I tapped him on the head several times, indicating to let me off and that I could walk. I said to myself, "I'm going to walk into this damn village if it takes me all night. I won't come in with this little 5′4″ Chinaman carrying me."

I spent the night in that village and the next morning, my benefactors made signs and noises like airplanes hitting a mountain. I set out with them due south and then east and felt sure they were leading me the wrong way. We met some Chinese guerrillas about noon who were carrying parts of our plane. They led me to a village where I found pieces of baggage, clothes and navigation equipment. They were from our ship. They then led me to the wreckage and I found it had been stripped. Heading east again, they took me to a village where I found the body of Corporal Faktor, our engineer-gunner. Two Chinese soldiers gave me a note saying that Bob Gray and Sergeant Jones were one day ahead of me and had slept there the night before. There was nothing I could do for Faktor so I spent that night in the guerrilla headquarters.

The next morning we started out to catch up with the other two and reached them about 4 P.M. The three of us set out in a small boat down the river for Chuchow. Made twelve miles that afternoon but had to stop at dark because of bad rapids. Kept going for Chuchow the next morning at 6 A.M. and rode for 14 hours, reaching our destinatinon at 8 P.M.

We were well received at Chuchow and stayed there two days where we got food, shelter and medical attention. We experienced air raids both days. Twenty of us then set out for Kweilin but instead went to Hengyang after a three-day trip by train and bus. We were then taken to Chungking by C-47.

Chapter 10

A BOMBER PILOT'S DECISION

BY

Everett W. Holstrom

Take-off was at 0830 approximately 15 minutes after the preceding ship had taken off due to the difficulty in starting my right engine. No difficulty was experienced in the take-off, full flaps and 10° stabilizer was used. We circled the ship once to try and compensate our compass as we felt the island on the carrier had pulled it off. We flew close to the water to avoid detection, and cruised according to the fuel consumption chart we had. My gunner, Corporal Bert Jordan, kept trying to tell me something over the interphone but I could not understand him. We flew at about 75 feet over the water to avoid detection. Approximately at 0900 we saw a large freighter on our right. It made a sharp turn away from us which we did not understand because I did not believe they could see our airplane insignia. After our crawl-way tank was empty Jordan came forward and gave us the unwelcome news that our rear turret was out of commission leaving our fifty caliber guns useless. He also informed us that our left wing tank was leaking gas. From then on I did not fill the tank completely full when I transferred gas and most of

Crew No. 4 (Plane 40-2282): left to right, Lt. Harry C. McCool (Navigator); Cpl. Bert M. Jordan (Gunner); Lt. Everett W. Holstrom (Pilot); Sgt. Robert J. Stephens (Bombardier); Lt. Lucian N. Youngblood (Co-Pilot).

the leakage stopped as it came from around the cap. However, at the rate it was going out we must have lost considerable gas. I told the navigator, Lt. Harry McCool, to attempt to make a land fall just south of Tokyo going under the assumption that the three

planes ahead of me would make their land fall directly east of
Tokyo and bring interceptor airplanes out in that direction and
I could slip by them. We made our land fall south of Tokyo on
a small group of islands at approximately 1230. We were still
flying at 75 feet. The weather in had been broken clouds at 2,000
feet going to clear as we neared Japan.

Lucian Youngblood, my co-pilot, went back to transfer the last
bit of gas from the bomb-bay to the wing tanks which did not
quite fill the wing tanks up. He was still back there when I saw
two pursuits coming at us and I immediately turned under them.
One fired and I saw tracer bullets going over the pilots' compartment. I yelled to Youngblood to come back to his seat. The co-
pilot then pointed out two more fighters going across our bow at
about 1,500 feet and they looked as if they were ready to peel
off on us. I told the navigator to tell Corporal Bob Stephens in
the nose to try and use his nose guns. I had given him previous
instructions to have the bombardier salvo the bombs if we were
intercepted by pursuit, so the bombs were salvoed from about
75 feet. By this time we were indicating about 270 mph and I had
turned under the two pursuits that had come across our bow and
then turned due south. These pursuits all had non-retractable
landing gear and I presumed them to be of the "97" type. McCool
had come back to his compartment and said that he had seen
several pursuits that looked like British Spitfires and by looking
back through the navigator's side window I saw one of these
planes on our right rear completing a firing pass. It had an in-line
engine, retractable gear, and double tapered wings. I had no idea
what type this was but supposed it was a Zero with an in-line
engine. After running for about ten minutes nobody could see
another airplane so I turned and headed down the coast of Japan
towards China. We passed under two patrols of airplanes going
down the coast about one hour and thirty minutes from the

southern tip of Japan. They were heading in a generally northerly direction and flying at about 3,000 feet. Approximately 15 minutes separated each pair, so they were about forty miles apart. Apparently, none of them saw us since they never changed course.

After crossing the southern tip of Japan our right engine began to load up and cough. We corrected this by increasing the rpm every 20 or 30 minutes but later on this did not work and we had to run that engine in automatic rich. This, I believe, was due to faulty carburetion at low rpm.

At about 150 miles from the China Coast the weather got steadily worse and at about one hundred miles from the coast it began to rain heavily with the clouds going right down to the water. This, combined with the darkness, made it very difficult to keep contact with the water; however, we kept contact until we began seeing the small islands off the Chinese coast and then we went on instruments and climbed up into the clouds. This was approximately at 2150. We leveled out at 6,000 feet and after flying for 20 minutes, I realized we couldn't land and had everybody get ready to bail out as we were almost out of gas. We bailed out in the following order, the gunner, the bombardier, the navigator, then the co-pilot and myself. This was about 2230.

I landed on the side of a mountain and remained where I had fallen until the next morning. In the morning I started looking for my crew but as no one answered to my shouts and I had lost my gun in bailing out, I could not fire a shot. I gave this up around noon. I walked all that day along the mountain ridge and around four in the afternoon discovered three huts near the head of a stream in the mountains. I went down and was immediately surrounded by 7 or 8 Chinese men. After a few minutes of sign language, I came to the conclusion that they were more curious than unfriendly. I went into one of their homes and they wanted me to take off my clothes as they were all soaking wet.

I did this and they dried them out for me but they also took everything out of my pockets. I walked back out on the porch and everything was gone off my belt but my water canteen.

I slept in this small village all night. In the morning I tried to get my things back but I didn't have any luck. I had my identification card, web belt and canteen, leaving behind my watch, knife, gloves, silk scarf, first aid packet, billfold and pocket compass. One of the villagers walked most of the way down the trail with me passing many small settlements. Once I was stopped and searched for weapons but allowed to go on my way. That evening I came into a pretty good sized village called Ken Chi where a garrison of soldiers was stationed. Although nobody there could speak English they understood that I was an American.

They took very good care of me and the next day they took me down to the next garrison. We arrived there about 1400 hours but still there was no one who could talk English. I stayed there about an hour and they gave me a guide to lead me toward the railroad. I drew pictures of trains and a track to make him understand that I wanted to go that way.

A few miles down the trail we came to a "middle" school where I found a teacher who could speak English. He told me it was only 20 li to Shangjao. He got me a ricksha to take me into the city and that night I reached Shangjao. I was taken to the military headquarters immediately. I told them about the other four crew members and gave them the location of where we bailed out which was approximately forty miles south of Shangjao. That night I was put on the train and sent to Chuhsien, arriving there the next morning.

Major Hilger, Capt. Greening, Capt. Jones, Lt. Bower and their crews were already there. This was April 22. Lt. Youngblood arrived at Chuhsien on April 25 and on April 28 the other three members of my crew came out of Shangjao and were sent on to

Chungking. On April 26 General Doolittle came in and told Capt. Jones and myself to remain at Chuhsien to collect any information that we could and to gather all crews there.

That night, May 3, having done all we could in Chuhsien and being able to account for all crews definitely except the two reported captured, we got on the train and started for Chungking. The next morning at eight o'clock we arrived in Yan Tang and immediately got on a bus. We rode all that day and stayed that night in Ning To. The next day we arrived in Tai Ho at about 4:30 where we were entertained by Daniel Yang who had been in the U.S. for a short time. We left early the next morning around 0200 and arrived in Hengyang around 1600 in the afternoon. There was Lt. Watson and his crew. We stayed at a hostel in Heng Yang and they took very good care of us. On May 14 the plane arrived and took us to Chungking. Here most of the articles that had been taken from us were returned.

On the whole, I found that the Chinese were very kind to us and we received very good treatment in every case. Col. Wong and the station master did everything in their power to gather information for us about various crews and to make us comfortable while we were at Chuhsien. The military district at Shangjao also helped in this matter, giving us very good food and a wonderful banquet.

The report above was made on May 14, 1942 when I got to Chungking. It is interesting now to look back on that fateful day after more than twenty years have gone by. I see now that my report wasn't as complete as it might have been.

On the day before we took off from the *Hornet*, the upper gun turret was out of commission due to electrical and hydraulic problems. Corporal Jordan and the other armament men worked on it but their work was not completed before our unscheduled takeoff.

My co-pilot, Lt. Lucian Youngblood, and I discussed changing our approach to Tokyo while we were flying toward the Japanese coast. We thought it might be better not to follow the plane ahead of us on the theory that we would be less likely to run into fighters if we came into the target area on an entirely different heading. This change in course was made.

Apparently we were spotted from some small islands as we neared Tokyo Bay because as soon as we sighted land, four Japanese Zeros appeared heading directly for us. Jordan shouted over the interphone that he couldn't fire the turret guns even in a fixed position. We were pretty much sitting ducks for four fighters with nothing but a .30 caliber gun in the nose. All they would have to do would be bounce us from any direction *but* head-on and we wouldn't have a chance. I knew I'd better do something so I changed course immediately and the Zeros changed with us giving a positive indication that they had seen us.

Jordan then confirmed what we dreaded most. The four Zeros were peeling off at us, firing away. At the same time I spotted eight to ten more Zeros high above us and on an outbound course from Tokyo. By this time, of course, several bombs had already been dropped in the city by the previous planes. I made the decision that no bomber pilot ever wants to make, but sometimes must to save his plane and his crew from sure death. I ordered Sergeant Stephens to salvo the bombs and I turned out to sea to attempt to outrun the fighters.

After the bombs were gone and we headed southward at maximum speed, Jordan reported that the high planes had stayed high and were going on a steady course. I later figured that these airplanes were under some sort of fighter control and the four were considered adequate to shoot us down. They never caught us but it was only because they were not highly trained or they certainly could have. Never did a fighter pilot have a better chance.

Since the raid, people have asked me if I have any regrets. I can answer that this way. If I had had the experience that I gained in fighting the Japanese later in several real air scraps following the raid, I would not have jettisoned those bombs, or at least my decision to do so would have been delayed. Although we were in serious trouble, I had obviously over-estimated the capabilities of the enemy and could have at least retained the bombs to use on a target of opportunity.

Author's Note: Lieutenant Holstrom had already been in action against the Japanese before the Tokyo mission. On December 24, 1941, Holstrom and his crew consisting of Lt. Ross R. Wilder, co-pilot; Private John O. Van Marter, radio operator and Private First Class George R. Hammond, bombardier, had sunk a Japanese submarine off the mouth of the Columbia River while their group was stationed at Pendleton, Oregon. Wilder later flew the Tokyo mission as co-pilot for Captain David M. Jones. All received the Air Medal and are credited with sinking the first enemy submarine in American waters in World War II.

Chapter 11

NARRATIVE REPORT

BY

DAVID M. JONES

On the 17th of April when they started fueling the airplanes, it was discovered that the bomb-bay in my airplane was leaking. It was torn down and an attempt was made to patch it. A fair job was done and the tank was left empty all night to dry out.

Early on the morning of the 18th the bomb-bay tank was fueled and we started loading the bombs. All the airplanes were parked in place and all the others had been loaded. The order for Army personnel to man their airplanes for take-off was given just as we had finished loading the bombs, but we still had to fuel the crawl-way tank and top off the wing tanks in my airplane. During the ensuing confusion my engineer, Sergeant Joe Manske, fueled the crawl-way tank with the assistance of several Navy crewmen. He then climbed to the right wing of the airplane and topped off the two wing tanks. A Navy man was on the left wing topping the tanks there.

As soon as this operation was complete our crew entered the airplane. I immediately checked the gas gauge and noticed that the left rear tank registered about 30 gallons short. I called Manske

Crew No. 5 (Plane 40-2283): left to right, Lt. Eugene F. McGurl (Navigator); Capt. David M. Jones (Pilot); Lt. Denver V. Truelove (Bombardier); Lt. Rodney R. Wilder (Co-Pilot); Sgt. Joseph W. Manske (Engineer-Gunner).

and he got back on the wing to service the tank. A gas hose was passed up to him but the gas, for some reason, was not turned on. By this time the airplanes had started taking off and about a dozen people were shouting instructions so I told Manske to get back in the airplane and started the engines.

The take-off was not difficult and no trouble whatsoever was experienced in holding the airplane straight down the deck. As soon as we cleared the deck I throttled back to the desired settings and made a circle to the right passing back over the carrier at exactly 0845. I then turned on course and climbed very slowly to about 1,900 feet, which was close to the base of the clouds. About ¾ to one hour out we passed a boat painted dark grey which I believe was a tanker. Shortly after that a twin-engined land plane came out of a cloud ahead of us and passed us on the right. I maintained course while it turned to avoid us. The Japanese markings were plainly visible on it. It disappeared in the clouds behind us immediately.

Soon after this the weather cleared and I remained at 1,500 feet until after we sighted the coast line of Japan. As we approached the coast I dropped down to the water and crossed the coast line at about 50 feet altitude. There were many small boats near the coast and a few steamers. I increased my speed to about 200 mph but after a short time, since we had encountered no opposition, reduced it again to 180. After about 10 minutes flying we could not orient ourselves and I believed that we were too far north. Accordingly, I turned to a more southerly course. After about 15 minutes more we had not found Tokyo and I decided to drop our bombs on the first suitable target and get on our way. Just then we came on a bay and Gene McGurl, our navigator, discovered that it was the mouth of Tokyo Bay. I then turned north and approached Tokyo from the south. Since my gas was low and I had wasted time finding the area and there was a multitude of targets visible as I crossed the bay, I decided to bomb along the bay in S.W. Tokyo instead of turning east and flying around the city to get to my assigned area, which was just north of the business district of Tokyo. I informed my bombardier, Denver Truelove, of this and as I approached the docks pulled up rather sharply to 1,200 feet. Truelove coached me over the interphone in my direction. The first bomb dropped at approximately 1350 (ship time) and made a direct hit on an oil storage tank. He let the second bomb go and then I decided to turn left because the area there looked more profitable. I looked down in the town and could see the building, which I believe must have been a power plant, erupt in a great explosion. The next bomb was the incendiary and just ahead we saw a large 1 or 2 story building which covered two or more blocks. It was easy to hit and every one of the bombs in the cluster hit on the roof of this plant. By this time my speed had increased considerably due to the urge given us by intense A.A. fire, and the fourth bomb, which was aimed at another large building, hit a little over and probably only damaged one corner of said building. At the instant of release I again descended to minimum altitude and took up my course to the south for withdrawal.

I proceeded as planned and as soon as I reached the water again reduced power. We flew south until we passed the small islands and then took up a course to the southern tip of Honshu Island. I flew at about 1,000 feet during this stretch. During this time we saw a few small boats and about 200 miles from Yaka Shima Island we sighted three destroyers steaming N.E. We avoided them.

We passed the southern tip of Japan about 50 minutes ahead of our E.T.A. and took up a course which would put us on the 29th parallel just off the coast of China. As we passed into the China Sea the weather became increasingly worse. I remained contact. About one-half hour ahead of our E.T.A.[1] we sighted two small islands and decided we were far enough south to be out of occupied territory. I stayed low until we saw the coast line and since it was impossible to remain contact pulled up into the clouds. I climbed at about 500 feet per minute, and only increased my rpm to 1600. At 5,500 feet we broke out between layers. By this time it was completely dark and raining hard.

It was becoming more and more evident that the chances of a safe landing were very slim. I informed the crew of our situation and decided to remain on course and to jump out as close to Chuhsien as possible. I continued past our E.T.A. at Chuchow for 15 minutes in hopes of finding a break. This proved futile so I turned 180 degrees and flew back until I found a small hole in the clouds. We put out a landing flare which showed us that an attempted landing would be impossible. We then prepared to abandon ship. Manske and Truelove went out almost together, followed by McGurl. The co-pilot, "Hoss" Wilder, then went to the navigator's well and put on his gun belt. The airplane was on auto pilot so I climbed back in the navigator's compartment with Wilder. I put on my gun belt and wrapped the carrying strap of my musette bag around my left arm. Wilder eased himself down through the escape hatch and dropped out. I turned and started to go back into the cockpit to retard the throttle, but my foot slipped and since it was rather lonely in the airplane I gave up the idea and let myself out of the escape hatch.

I landed on the side of a hill and was uninjured. As soon as I got my breath I cut the shroud lines of the 'chute and climbed to the top of the hill. I draped the chute over a small tree and spent the night under it. At daybreak I started walking. I soon found some natives and after drawing a picture of a railroad train, finally got a general direction in which to walk. I reached the Shetsung station (18 miles east of Yushan) about 1100 where I found Wilder. The station master could write a little English and we conveyed to him our desire to go to Chuhsien. He called Yushan on the phone and a train came out and picked us up. When we reached Yushan a large crowd was assembled. We were given a royal reception. How they knew about us and our mission

I do not know, but certainly all the people knew about the "great deed of the brave American heroes." We were taken to the air station at Yushan, where they washed our feet, cleaned up our clothes, fed us and put us to bed. About 1700 we started for Chuhsien in a station wagon and arrived there about 1730. Upon arrival I found the rest of my crew all O.K.

The following day, the 20th, reports started coming in concerning the position of various crews and that night four complete crews came in. After about 20 members had assembled Major Jack Hilger sent them to Hengyang under command of Capt. Ross Greening. Col. Doolittle came in on the 26th and left with all the crew members except myself and Lt. Ozuk the following day.

I left Chuhsien on the evening of the 3rd with 12 other crew members. We got on the bus the next morning at Ying Tang. We stayed that night at Ning Too. The following day we traveled to Tai Ho and after a few hours rest started for Heng Yang, arriving there at 1600 May 6. We remained there until May 14 when an airplane picked us up and transported us to Chungking.

NOTE TO CHAPTER 11

1. Estimated time of arrival.

Chapter 12

TESTIMONY AT WAR CRIMES TRIAL [1]

BY

CHASE J. NIELSEN

Q. Tell the Commission in detail all you can remember relative to the briefing for the flight and the targets that should be attacked. You might have to take this in short sentences so they can translate it as you go along.

A. First we were given large target maps approximately that square (Indicating with his hands).

Q. Give the measurement in feet and inches.

A. I would say two and a half feet square.

Q. Continue.

A. These target maps only contained a target number; they only covered a small area, and they were detailed to a degree that showed all the highways, railroad tracks, the ground—a very descriptive view of the target and surroundings, even showed dwelling houses and all buildings. We had maps of a smaller scale to use to navigate to get into Tokyo. We also had maps of other targets in case we couldn't get in on our objective, and we would have two or three other targets that we could bomb.

Q. State specifically what conversation took place and what instructions were given as to bombing non-military targets.

A. We were definitely told not to bomb non-military objectives.

176

Crew No. 6 (Plane 40-2298): left to right, Lt. Chase J. Nielsen (Navigator); Lt. Dean E. Hallmark (Pilot); Sgt. Donald E. Fitzmaurice (Engineer-Gunner); Lt. Robert J. Meder (Co-Pilot); Sgt. William J. Dieter (Bombardier).

Q. What conversation took place either among the crews or with General Doolittle relative to bombing the Imperial Palace?

A. Well, when we found out we were going to bomb Tokyo, we cut a deck of cards to see who would get the Palace. We all wanted it.

Q. Why did the men each want to bomb the Imperial Palace?

A. Well, there wasn't any of us had any love for the Japs. Besides that, we figured the Emperor was at the bottom of the whole thing and we wanted to get at the bottom of it all.

Q. Did General Doolittle hear about this conversation you men had?

Q. Yes, and he told us definitely to leave the Imperial Palace alone, to bomb (military) objectives and nothing else.

Q. How much time each day was devoted to briefing on military targets?

A. Well, most all day.

Q. What target or targets were assigned to your crew?

A. The target we had was steel mills in the northeastern portion of Tokyo, around the edge of the bay.

Q. Tell the Commission briefly about the flight after you left the carrier until you sighted the islands of Japan.

A. Well, the three ships flew a wide formation until we sighted the island, and when we sighted the island we pulled our formation into close formation.

Q. At what elevation did you fly from the carrier to the island?

A. Approximately one hundred feet.

Q. Did you meet any Japanese planes after you left the carrier?

A. We passed one Japanese patrol plane when we were forty-two minutes from the *Hornet*.

Q. Did you sight any enemy aircraft after you came in over the islands?

A. After we came in over the islands we sighted six Jap planes but they were flying at approximately ten thousand feet. I don't think they saw us at all.

Q. Approximately at what elevation was the airplane when it came over the City of Tokyo?

A. We were at fifteen hundred feet.

Q. How intense was the anti-aircraft fire when you arrived over the City of Tokyo?

A. It was quite intense. They had our elevation but that was all.

Q. Tell the Commission what happened to the bombing of your target.

A. Well, as we came over the island we pulled our formation into a tight echelon. We were all to bomb this row of steel mills which was approximately six hundred feet in width and two thousand feet in length.

Q. At what point in the formation was your plane flying?

A. We were the last of the formation.

Q. Did you know who the pilots were on the other two planes?

A. Yes. Captain Jones was in the lead and Lt. Lawson was second and our ship third.

Q. Explain to the Commission what you saw and what happened in the bombing run.

A. Well, we levelled our formation off at 1,500 feet as we approached the target. We had already arranged before we left the *Hornet* that Captain Jones would give us a signal and we would alternate the bombs so our bombs would be scattered throughout the area. The bombs were dropped. I watched three or four of the first ones explode and the last three. We dropped our three and still had one bomb left and we turned to get out of the anti-aircraft fire because we were picking up all the fire that was turned on the lead ship. We made a second run on the target then.

Q. Did you observe where the bombs from the other two planes in that formation dropped?

A. They dropped down in the row of steel mills.

Q. Do you know whether or not the machine guns on your planes were fired while you were over Tokyo?

A. The machine guns on my plane were never fired.

Q. Do you mean to tell the Commission that the guns were never fired from the time you left the aircraft carrier until you landed later?

A. Yes, sir, they were never fired from the time we left the *Hornet* until we crashed.

Q. Tell the Commission about the crash in the ocean.

A. Both motors cut out about the same time although the left motor did cut out first. The left wing hit the water first and severed the wing off right up close to the fuselage, and as the fuselage hit, it split open all the way down to the bottom. The pilot was thrown from his chair right out through the windshield. The gunner was still in his turret, and went down. He said he thought he was about twenty fathoms deep but he finally got out. The bombardier was in the tunnel coming down to the bombardier section to the navigator's well. We all finally got out of the plane and got the life raft out. Our life raft wouldn't work and the bombardier and gunner were pretty badly beaten up.

Q. What were the names of the bombardier and gunner?

A. Dieter was the bombardier and Fitzmaurice the gunner.

Q. How many of you actually got to the coast after the plane crashed?

A. Three of us. Hallmark, Meder and myself.

Q. What happened to Fitzmaurice and Dieter?

A. They were still alive when they got out of the plane but we tried to stay together and swim in but it was raining and the ocean was rough and very dark and we finally got separated.

Q. Did you find out what happened to them?

A. Yes. The next morning when the three of us got together we went back to look for them and found their bodies on the shore. They had been so badly injured in the crash that they couldn't survive.

Q. Were you able to save anything from the aircraft?

A. Nothing other than the clothing we were wearing.

Q. Were any of you three survivors injured in the landing?

A. Well, Hallmark had some lacerations on his leg and Meder and I had a few lacerations.

Q. What happened to you the next day after the crash?

A. Well, after we finally got together there was a small Chinese guerrilla outfit garrisoned there. We went there.

Q. And were you later picked up by the Japs?

A. Well, we were with this garrison for about three days. We tried to get over all the mountain passes but the Japs had guards or sentries on all of them and we couldn't make it over.

Q. After the three day period what happened?

A. We were trying to get some sampans rigged up to go down the coast but evidently the Japs heard or picked up some word we were there. About three hundred Jap soldiers marched in and searched through the place until they found us.

Q. How serious were the injuries of Lt. Hallmark and Lt. Meder?

A. They were so bad they couldn't walk—that is, walk well. They were pretty badly crippled up.

Q. On what date were you captured, Captain?

A. We were taken over by the Japs on April 21st.

Q. What did the Japanese do with you after they captured you?

A. Well, we were loaded in coolie chairs and taken to the Japanese garrison.

Q. After that happened, what did the Japanese do?
A. We were transferred from there by boat to Shanghai.

Q. How were you treated when they took you to Shanghai?
A. Well, our trip up by boat, three of us were kept in one small room. We were handcuffed and tied by the elbows and tied tight enough to cut off the circulation.

Q. How long were you kept bound in that fashion?
A. We were that way while we were transferred from one place to another but while we were on the boat our arms weren't tied although we were handcuffed and at night the three of us had our legs cuffed together.

Q. How many days did it take you to arrive at your next destination?
A. We were about four days coming up the coast from where the Japs picked us up until we came to Shanghai.

Q. Where did the Japs take you when you came to Shanghai?
A. I think we were taken out to the airport.

Q. What happened after you got to the airport?
A. We arrived at the airport about four o'clock in the evening. We were put in individual cells and then I was taken out and questioned as to where I had been, where I had come from and what I was doing in China. I merely gave them my name, rank and serial number.

Q. Then what happened?
A. When I wouldn't tell them anything, they would kick me and slap me.

Q. Explain to the Commission where you were slapped.
A. I was slapped around the face and head very severely.

Q. You stated that you were kicked, where were you kicked—what part of your body?

A. I was kicked on the shins.

Q. How hard did they kick you?

A. Hard enough that I still have the scars today.

Witness showed scars on his legs to the Commission.

Q. What other physical treatment was administered to you at that time?

A. I was given what they call the water cure.

Q. Explain to the Commission what that was.

A. Well, I was put on my back on the floor with my arms and legs stretched out, one guard holding each limb. A towel was wrapped around my face and put across my face and water was poured on. They poured water on this towel until I was almost unconscious from strangulation, then they would let up until I'd get my breath, then they'd start all over again.

Q. How long did this treatment continue?

A. About twenty minutes.

Q. What was your sensation when they were pouring water on the towel? What did you physically feel?

A. I felt more or less like I was drowning, just gasping between life and death.

Q. What further mistreatment was administered to you while this questioning was going on?

A. The guards then brought in a large bamboo pole about three inches in diameter. This was placed directly behind my knees. I was then made to squat on the floor in this position (indicating squatting position) like a kneel. One guard had hold of each of my arms, one other guard then placed his foot on my thigh and would jump up and down causing severe pain in my knees.

Q. Explain to the Commission just the sensations you felt from this treatment.

A. It felt like my joints were coming apart but after about five minutes of that my knees were so numb I couldn't feel anything else.

Q. How long did this treatment last with the bamboo pole behind your knees?

A. About fifteen or twenty minutes.

Q. Do you know what happened to the other members of your crew who were with you?

A. I didn't know at the time but talking to them later I found out they were given similar treatment. Hallmark said they put him on a stretcher and stretched him out until he felt like his limbs were coming apart.

Q. Were any other threats made to you during the questioning?

A. By that time it was almost sundown. They said, well, if I won't talk they would take me out and I would be executed. I was then blindfolded and taken out.

Q. Then what happened?

A. The pain in my legs I could hardly walk so one guard took hold of me under each arm and we marched about three or four hundred feet down a gravel path. I could hear different groups of Japanese soldiers marching around in the area. They were drilling. After marching about 400 feet we stopped and as one of these squads marched up, they also stopped by us.

Q. What was said and done at that time?

A. As they stopped I could hear the rifle butts hit the ground and I thought this was execution.

Q. Then what happened?

A. After a short conference between several of the officers that was with me and whoever was marching the squad, the interpreter came back and he said, "We are Knights of the Bushido of the Order of the Rising Sun; we don't execute at sundown; we execute at sunrise."

Q. And then what happened?
A. I was taken back to my cell and the interpreter said unless I had decided to talk by morning I would be executed by sunrise.

NOTE TO CHAPTER 12

1. On February 16, 1946, a United States Military Commission was appointed in Shanghai, China "for the trial of persons, units and organizations accused as War Criminals in this theater." The trial of certain Japanese officers who had been involved in the imprisonment and execution of members of two of the B-25 crews was begun in February 27 and continued for two months. Lieutenant Chase J. Nielsen, navigator on the crew of Lieutenant Dean E. Hallmark, returned to China to appear as a witness since he was one of four survivors of forty months in Japanese military jails. Excerpts from his testimony, given on March 18, 1946, are repeated here. More on the story of the eight Doolittle raiders who fell into enemy hands is contained in Chapter 25.

Chapter 13

I WAS THE LUCKY ONE

BY

DAVID J. THATCHER

We were the seventh plane to take off the carrier at approximately 0900. From the time we left the ship until we got to Tokyo there were two of our planes ahead of us, but we never got close enough to see who they were. We saw a freighter off to our right and a lot of small boats as we sped in just off the wave tops. As we passed over the coast, people on the beach looked up and waved at us; people riding bicycles or walking along the roads stopped whatever they were doing and watched us go by. From the way they acted it seemed as though no Japanese planes ever flew that low.

We were apparently too far north of our course, because after going inland a little way, Lt. Lawson turned left and we flew parallel to the coast. About halfway down the coast toward Tokyo, while zigzagging among the mountains, we saw six pursuits flying approximately 5,000 feet above us and going in the exact opposite direction from which we had come. Two of them broke formation but I don't think they saw us or I'm sure they would have come after us.

Crew No. 7 (Plane 40-2261): left to right, Lt. Charles L. McClure (Navigator); Lt. Ted W. Lawson (Pilot); Lt. Robert S. Clever (Bombardier); Lt. Dean Davenport (Co-Pilot); Sgt. David J. Thatcher (Engineer-Gunner).

I had tested my guns just before reaching the coast but found I could only operate the turret when the emergency switch was on in the pilot's compartment. This meant the turret was operating directly from the battery, the 24-volt generator being out before we took off.

While flying over the bay just before reaching Tokyo we saw four or five barrage balloons off to our left but they weren't in our way. Just before we reached our target, which was a large factory on the waterfront, we climbed to 1,500 feet. When we leveled off, ack-ack began bursting on all sides of us. We dropped all four bombs (one of them had the Japanese medals attached) and I think I saw the first one explode. There was a large puff of black smoke coming up from the thickly congested building area. The ack-ack got awfully close just as we dropped the last one, one bursting just off the right wing. I could see the battery that fired that one off to our right. Lt. Lawson must have seen it too because he went into a steep dive to the left and we left Tokyo going 300 mph.

After leaving Tokyo we saw one of our planes ahead of us until we turned west and passed the southern tip of Japan. When we passed out of sight of land over the China Sea, I crawled up over the bomb-bay to the navigator's compartment and we talked over the experience we had just had in actual combat. We checked our gas and decided we had enough to reach the China coast. When we finally did, at about 9 P.M. it was getting dark. I had climbed back to the rear turret again just in case we should have some unexpected "friends" waiting for us.

Lawson found a bay after we reached the coast and circled it about three times trying to find a flat beach to land on. Lawson told us to remove our parachutes and said he was going to try a water landing so I sat next to the turret tank ready to release the life raft after we ditched. We hit the water with an extremely hard jolt and I was knocked out cold. When I came to about five minutes later I saw the water gushing in through the top of the turret which I thought was the rear escape hatch.

Still dazed, I pulled the strings to inflate my Mae West and tried to go out through the opening but I couldn't make it. I finally figured out that the plane was upside down so I found the rear escape hatch and got out there. I crawled up along the belly of the plane toward the nose and found that it was badly smashed.

Just at that time Lt. McClure called to me from the beach about a hundred yards away. The others were there, too. I swam to them and learned what had happened. Lt. Lawson had changed his mind and tried to make a wheels down landing on the beach but because of the rain hitting on the windshield and it being nearly dark, he had misjudged the distance and we hit just off the beach in about six feet of water doing about 140 mph.

I was lucky. The other four crew members up in front of the plane were all thrown out when we hit. The pilot, co-pilot and navigator were thrown up through the top of the cockpit and not straight forward. The bombardier, Lt. Bob Clever, was in the nose when we crashed and he was thrown through the plexiglass head first. The injuries he received were cuts around both eyes and the top of his head was so badly skinned that half his hair was gone but, strangely, there were no deep cuts in his head. His hips and back were sprained so that he was unable to stand up and walk; all he could do was crawl on his hands and knees. His eyes were soon swollen shut and he couldn't see. His face was covered with blood but I thought it would be better to leave it that way because of what Doc White had told us about infections. I knew infection would set in soon enough if we couldn't reach help; besides I had my hands full with the other members of the crew.

Lt. Lawson was, by far, the most seriously injured. The plane had landed with such force that both the pilot's and co-pilot's seats and armor plate had been uprooted and literally exploded out of the plane with them sitting in their seats. His worst injury was a long deep gash just above his left knee. He had another short deep cut on his left shin that left the bone exposed. His foot below the ankle was so badly bruised that it turned black within a few hours. He also had a deep gash on his left arm between elbow and shoulder. He had a few cuts on the top of his head and chin. Eight or nine of his front teeth were knocked out so that he was unable to bite or chew anything. He was so weak from loss of blood that I was afraid he would die if we didn't reach a hospital. He tried to sleep but it was almost impossible because he was in such intense pain. He was very good about it though and didn't complain very much. After I'd bandaged his injuries that first night I left them as they were and didn't try to wash them out or anything. Doc's lectures had really made an impression on me and I knew he was right.

Lt. Davenport, the co-pilot, received severe cuts on his right leg between knee and ankle. He walked a little just after the crash but not afterward. Lt. McClure, the navigator, only received a few scratches on his right foot in the way of cuts, these later being infected. The serious injury he had was in his shoulders. He said when we crashed that he was crouching between the pilot's and co-pilot's seats and hit the armor plate with both shoulders as he went out. His shoulders were swollen so badly clear down to his elbows that he could hardly move his hands. He was unable to lie down at all and had to try to sleep sitting up.

Both Lawson and Davenport said they were still fastened in their seats when they came to under water. With their injuries it's a wonder they weren't drowned. They both were able to unfasten their safety belts and float to the top, then swam or were washed ashore. It was only by the hand of God that any of us got out of there alive, let alone all of us. Luckily, out of all these injuries, there were no bones broken except Lawson losing those teeth.[1]

My injuries were all minor. I had a slight gash on the top of my head. If I hadn't had my flying helmet on it would have been much worse. My back was badly bruised and I had a few small cuts which later became infected, but I was in the best shape to take care of the others.

By the time I had reached the beach after Lt. McClure had called to me there were some Chinese fishermen there who had come down from a small village. We could tell almost immediately that they were friendly. The first thing they wanted to know by sign language was whether there were any more than five of us in the plane. When they found out there were no more they helped us to one of their huts which was about a half mile away. When we reached the hut I bandaged everybody's wounds as best I could. I was the only one to get out of the plane with a gun belt on so I used the bandage in my first air packet for the large wound on Lawson's knee. I used my handkerchief on the cut on his arm. For his other wounds and the wounds on Davenport and Clever I had to use old dirty rags that the fishermen gave us. I had no choice if I were going to stop their bleeding. Later that night I took a lantern and went out to try to get a large first aid kit out of the tail of the plane but it was impossible since the tide had come in and the plane was now under water.

Early the next morning I went out to the plane to get the first aid kit and morphine but couldn't find either. During the night the plane had washed up on the beach when the tide came in but the engines which had torn loose when we crashed were still out in the water. The nose of the plane was a mangled mess clear back to the bomb-bay. If the four men in the nose hadn't been thrown out, they'd never have gotten out of there alive. If I'd been sitting in the turret I'd never have gotten out alive either.

While I was looking at the plane and searching for things we could use, I spotted a Japanese gunboat out in the bay. Possibly I could have burned what was left of the plane because there was a little gasoline running out of one of the tanks but I didn't think of that at the time; all I was thinking of was trying to find the

first aid kit or morphine for the others and getting out of there
before the Japs came.

I learned that the name of the place where we crashed was
Nantien from a Chinese guerrilla who could speak a little English and had come with a group of them at the request of the
fishermen. We told him we wanted to get to a hospital as soon as
possible. That afternoon we left there with the four wounded
wrapped in blankets and carried on stretchers by coolies. All the
time Lawson was in terrific pain from the wound in his leg. We
had to climb up and over a high hill to get to the other side of
the island. By late afternoon we got to a river boat and headed
for the mainland.

We were on the river boat from about 6 P.M. April 19, until
about 3 P.M., April 20. There was a covering over the middle of
the boat which kept us dry while it was raining, which seemed
like all the time. I was kept busy going from one to the other
trying to make them as comfortable as possible. But they'd soon
get tired lying in one position so I would help them move into
another. I helped them as much as possible but there really
wasn't much I could do for them.

About midnight we stopped at one of the guerrilla hideouts to
get something to eat. I went up to the house with them and got a
bowl of what looked like noodle soup. I was pretty darned hungry
but whatever was in that bowl, I just couldn't swallow it. They
gave me some for the rest of the fellows in the boat but it only
added to their misery.

We didn't have any drinking water left by this time and I sure
didn't want to drink any of the dirty water from the streams or the
Chinese wells so I set my canteen cup to catch rain water. Lawson
was wanting water all the time because his throat was so dry from
the blood in his mouth where all his teeth had been knocked out.
I didn't think that night would ever end. I had understood the

guerrilla to say that it would only take two hours but it took almost twenty-four.

When we finally put in to shore, we were taken about five miles inland to a village called Hai Yu where two Chinese doctors and a nurse gave us our first medical aid. I sent a telegram to Col. Doolittle at Chungking telling him of our condition. The next day, after helping us as much as they could with the few medical supplies they had, they gave us a royal send-off with a band and everything. We then traveled 40 miles by sedan chair to Linhai where there was a hospital. A Chinese doctor and his son, with the aid of missionaries from the China Inland Mission immediately took care of the injured.

On April 23, I got a telegram from Lt. Travis Hoover saying that all of his crew was O.K. On the morning of the 24th, Lt. Don Smith and his crew arrived. They had heard of our predicament and Doc White knew he had to get to us as soon as possible. He took charge of the wounded from then on. The first thing he did was give Lawson a blood transfusion. He got blood from Lt. Griffith R. William, Smith's co-pilot, and had to use syringes to do it.

Since I was unhurt and couldn't help any more with the wounded, I left Linhai with Smith's crew on the morning of the 27th by sedan chair and traveled this way for three days. On the fourth, we started out in rickshas and at eleven that morning we came to a highway where much to our surprise, there was a 1938 Dodge sedan and a 1939 Ford sedan waiting for us. We went to Kinhwa in these cars and from there to Chuhsien by train.

At Chuhsien were Hoover's crew, Captain Jones, and Lts. Ozuk and Holstrom. There I learned that Faktor had been killed. Reverend John M. Birch, a missionary there, gave a funeral service for him in the air raid shelter the Sunday we were there, although the grave was not yet ready. Faktor was a good friend of mine and I certainly thought it was considerate of Reverend Birch to give that funeral service. I gave Birch as much information about Faktor as I could but I didn't know his exact age or his home town in Iowa.

We stayed at Chuhsien for several days and were helped considerably by a Mr. Liu, who had helped Hoover and his crew stay out of the hands of the Japanese. We had an air raid almost every day and always went to a bomb shelter in a hill nearby. Apparently, the Japanese were out looking for us and were going to retaliate against the Chinese for helping us. We left Chuhsien on May 3, and traveled by ancient bus for three days to Hengyang where we stayed until we were flown out to Chungking. I was worried all the time about the rest of my crew back in Linhai and hoped they were O.K. I was the lucky one. They had not only been badly injured but now were directly in the path of the advancing Japanese Army.

NOTE TO CHAPTER 13

1. The injuries suffered by Lieutenant McClure turned out to be much more serious than Thatcher thought. X-rays taken later showed bad breaks in both shoulders, which eventually caused him to be retired for disability in 1945.

Chapter 14

WE BECAME GUESTS OF THE KREMLIN

BY

ROBERT G. EMMENS

"Make darned sure those throttles don't slip back!" York said as he watched the navy flagman on the *Hornet*'s pitching deck, arm up and ready to give the "let-er-go" signal which sent each B-25 in its turn out across the gray North Pacific run to Tokyo and neighboring towns.

Our ship shuddered under the strain of both throttles being wide open. Flaps were full down, controls all the way back in our laps. Just at a point in the carrier's antics known to him alone, the flagman, that navy master of judgment, let his arms drop—the signal to roll.

York released his brakes and 2242 began to roll, left wheel on the white line, down the deck of the carrier, slowly at first—my God, how slowly! Then faster, faster—the island of the carrier was lost from sight as it passed a bare eight feet away from our right wing tip; and then like a big living thing, our plane seemed to leap into the air just as the deck of the ship disappeared under us and was replaced by the frothing sea. Now ease up a little on the controls—not too much—just enough to let her nose drop

Crew No. 8 (Plane 40-2242): left to right, Lt. Nolan A. Herndon (Navigator-Bombardier); Capt. Edward J. York (Pilot); S/Sgt. Theodore H. Laban (Engineer); Lt. Robert G. Emmens (Co-Pilot); Sgt. David W. Pohl (Gunner). Pohl, youngest man on the raid, was only twenty years of age.

and pick up flying speed. Wheels up. Now she's leveling out nicely. Air speed up within safe limits. Now start taking off flaps, throttles back to save that precious gasoline. We adjusted our power settings and checked our compass. And then we breathed again. There we were, off on a mission, being a member of which was more than any of us had ever dared hope for. The bombing of Tokyo.

We were number eight to get off the carrier, and somehow our own take-off didn't give me the thrill, actually doing it, that watching the seven ships take off ahead of us did, or that looking back on it now does. It's difficult to recapture now, the feelings—or mixture of feelings—we had as we settled down for our 780-mile run into Japan. I say "we" because I think the same feelings were surging through all of us. In my mind I removed, for a moment, all cause and reason from our situation and, looking at the instrument panel, the controls, the wings, and the engines, and closing out the "what" and "why" of the thing, it seemed to me like any of the hundreds of times I'd flown in a B-25; like any routine or cross-country flight back in the States. But looking down and out at the limitless expanse of water, reality was not long in coming to the front. Nor did recalling those "eggs" in our bomb bay, live ammunition—lots of it—in our guns, remind us of any routine cross-country flight back home.

I thought about the stack of razor blades, candy, and cartons of cigarettes I'd purchased aboard the *Hornet*. And then I laughed at myself for buying such things as if I would be gone a year, when actually here we were on our final mission, and it would be over that same day. And we would be starting back home, probably, in a few days.

Herndon gave us a corrected heading to fly to compensate for a pretty strong wind from our right front quarter, as we checked and rechecked power and propeller settings against air speed. Everything seemed to be running like clockwork. It was too early to check gas consumption, because our auxiliary tanks had no gauges in them. Pohl was operating the rear turret and fired a few bursts to be sure his guns were working. Laban was busy in the navigator's compartment checking the generators and rearranging our baggage load. "Take-off—0855," I wrote in the Form I.

Conversations were short and to the point. Every man was going over again in his mind each item for which he knew he was responsible. Of course, little black thoughts like an engine going out over that expanse of salt water, and the possibility of a reception committee of Jap Zeros, crept forward often enough to keep our minds well occupied with imaginary forced landings and combat tactics.

The sun was now fast burning away the low overcast which had prevailed during the early morning hours, and in its place was a clear blue sky broken only by the not too sharp line where it met the sea—north, south, east, and west. West—that was the only direction that mattered then, though.

Pohl called a little sooner than we expected, to tell us he had just dumped the last tin of gasoline into the auxiliary tail tank. York told him to be sure not to throw any of the tins away until we were much closer to Japan, and then to throw them out all in one bunch. This meant less chance of the cans being a telltale mark of our path of flight. There must be no clue as to our method and place of departure—the whereabouts of "Shangri-La."

As we reset the throttles and prop pitch controls to compensate for decrease in weight of gas consumed, the engines droned evenly on and the scenery remained unchanged. It reminded you of standing stationary on a treadmill with a watery flow passing underneath. Twice we spotted objects on the horizon ahead that might have been submarines, fishing craft, or even small ships out patrolling. We avoided these partly because of the probability of their radioing their base to expect us, and partly because of the danger of anti-aircraft fire. It was a temptation not to go over and see if the ship might be a sub, and lay an egg on it. But our bombs were earmarked for bigger and more important things. And little attention was paid to these small craft.

At ten-thirty the sky was clear and blue. Herndon gave us another correction for wind but it remained a head wind and continued from our right quarter. Where were the clouds we had hoped for to lend us the protection so vital to daylight raiding? Well, hell, we had a couple of hours to go and probably there would be clouds by then.

As our gasoline was used up we changed our power settings to compensate for the decrease in weight being carried. At about eleven o'clock we had been flying long enough to have a fairly definite check on the amount of gasoline we were burning. I flew while York did some figuring on paper.

"Hey, Bob, take a look at this. Am I screwy or are we burning this much gas?"

His figures showed we were burning more gas than we should have been at those power and RPM settings. York's figures were right. Maybe the gauge was inaccurate and would give the same reading after more time. Maybe we had developed a gas leak, letting pure gasoline spill into the Pacific Ocean. We should have flown out our reserve turret tank and part of our bomb bay tank by the time we hit Japan. But we were more than an hour from Japan and had been on our bomb bay tank then for quite some time. Maybe—but you can let your imagination run rampant at a time like that.

"Ski, if that's right we're not going to get near the Chinese coast."

Herndon, busy in the nose with his charts and sextant, came into the pilot's compartment now. He personally checked the reading on the bomb bay tank. Yes, there was no mistaking it. We were burning a hell of a lot of gasoline! Besides landing on

Japan, which, of course, was out of the question, we had one
alternative other than taking our originally planned course south
around the lower end of Japan and then west across the China
Sea. That was striking out across the North Japan Sea to Soviet
territory, to our allies, the Russians, who might or might not be
depended upon to give us gas so we could continue to China; who
might or might not recognize us as friendly, when and if we
approached their probably well-fortified eastern coast.

"Have you got a course from Tokyo to Russia plotted, Herndon?" asked York, voicing what we were all thinking.

"Yes, I've plotted all possibilities. Do you want it now?" Herndon had made Tokyo look like a rising sun, his course lines
representing sunrays emitting from the Japanese capital.

"No, I don't want it now. I guess you guys remember Doolittle
didn't exactly issue a direct order not to go to Russia, but he
made it plenty obvious that it wasn't a good idea."

Doolittle had told us more than once that Stalin had been asked
to cooperate on this mission and to allow us to fly to one of his
eastern airdromes for fuel. This would have made the mission.
The 600-mile run from Tokyo across the Japanese Sea would
have enabled each ship to expend a little extra gas for the actual
bombing and for outrunning any Jap pursuers. It would have
made returning via the Alaskan route a cinch within a few days
after the raid. It would have assured a safe landing for those sixteen B-25's which so dependably carried each crew over the miles
of Pacific Ocean, and it would have meant saving the lives of those
boys who afterward fell into Jap hands or who were killed bailing
out or crash-landing. And it would have broken the ice on
getting "Uncle Joe" to open his eastern seaboard for Allied use
against the Japanese. But Stalin had refused. Japan and Russia
were ostensibly at peace. Border skirmishes and disagreements
about fishing rights kept it from being an actual peace. Germany

was keeping the Soviets well occupied in the west though, and just now Joseph Stalin didn't feel he could afford to act as a shelter for Allied airplanes on so unbelievable a mission as bombing Tokyo.

And another thing—what if the Japs demanded that the Russians turn us over to them? Would they feel obligated to do so? Would they do it in order to wash their hands of the whole affair? Would it have such far-reaching repercussions as to strengthen—or weaken—the hands of trust existing between the United States and the USSR? Maybe there would be nothing to it; maybe several ships would turn to them as an only out.

"They'd probably give us gas and we'd be on our way across occupied Korea and China tomorrow morning," York said.

"We hope!" I answered.

A sudden jolt as York jerked the stick back to miss a startled sea gull brought all our eyes to the front. Sea gulls—that meant land was not so far now. It was nearly noon, and not a cloud appeared in the sky in any direction.

"We'll check the gas again as we're approaching the island before we make our decision to head toward Russia or not," Ski said.

It seemed as if we had been flying for a week. Check points are few and far between on an ocean. We wondered if the eight ships behind us had gotten off the carrier okay. We wondered how strong Jap resistance would be. Did you ever have that feeling of wishing you could see what you'd be doing in twelve hours or twenty-four hours—say, tomorrow at this same time—next week, next month, next year? That flashed through my mind. I wondered what Justine was doing at that minute. Gee, I wanted to be with her when the baby came. How we'd wanted a baby—since the day we were married over three years ago. And isn't that life for you—to have one on the way when the world exploded that

December 7? Ski was in the same boat on that score as I, although they weren't positive when he left the States.

The same twist of fate was at work there that seemed to be working for us now, it occurred to me. Getting off that morning early instead of having the advantage of a day's run at top carrier speed to put us nearer the target. And clear skies over a sea where clouds are so usual. And something making the gas go through our carburetor like—well, like water through a sieve.

I don't know who saw the speck of land appear on the horizon first. But there it was, unmistakable and growing.

"Let's take a final check on that bomb bay gauge," I said, starting to get out of my seat. But Sergeant Laban was already up on top of the bomb bay tank. The rubber extra tank which fitted on the top of the regular bomb bay was long since collapsed and rolled up ready to be dumped out with the cans. Laban's reading on the gas gauge was pretty discouraging. We wouldn't get closer than 300 miles to the Chinese coast.

York called Pohl and had him throw out the empty cans that had contained our reserve gas, and the collapsible rubber tank on top of the bomb bay followed. It didn't matter now. The Japs, finding them out there, wouldn't know from where we'd come.

By the time Pohl answered over the interphone system that the cans and rubber tank had been tossed clear and that he was again taking up his battle station in the rear turret, land was plainly visible. It stretched like any seacoast to the right and left out of sight. It was about ten minutes before noon then.

"Man, that sure looks like a carrier up ahead there!" said York.

And sure enough we could see what appeared to be a carrier paralleling the coast directly ahead of us. A carrier—they're dynamite at a time like that. What a reception we would be in for! We abruptly changed our course to the left to avoid her. But to our relief, as we approached a little nearer, we could see it was a freighter pretty heavily loaded, plowing slowly south along the Jap coast. We stayed out of her gun range and headed directly for the beach, now very plain in front of us.

"Where in the devil is Mount Fujiyama?" I said to Ski.

I'd seen lots of Jap laundry calendars and I thought old Fujiyama, snow-covered and pink, would be looming up to meet us long before now. But only a rugged mountainous sky line began appearing inland.

I must admit I was plenty tense about that time. I think we all were. We could see the breakers on the beach now, and in a matter of minutes we would not only be over dry land again, but Japanese dry land! Ski talked to each man to make sure each was in his assigned combat position and the interphone was working. Everything was in order.

Herndon called from his navigator's seat in the glass-encased nose, "Course from Tokyo to Vladivostok, three hundred degrees."

"Bob, I can't get over that gas consumption. Can you figure it out?" said Ski.

"No, unless we've got a gas leak—and there's no evidence of that. We sure must be burning a rich mixture, though."

"I guess Russia's our only out, then."

"I sure wish we could let them know we're coming so they'll know who we are when and if we get there," I said, aware of the impossibility of letting them know.

Now we were approaching the sandy beach. There seemed to be a part fenced off directly ahead of us. It looked as if there were a group of about two hundred people within the enclosure. In one corner away from the water, a tower about fifty feet high was erected supporting a little watch platform with a white roof. We zoomed right over the heads of the people on the beach and not very far from the watchman's cage itself. The people waved frantically and many of them jumped up and down. At that speed it was only a glimpse, really. But I'd swear those faces were the faces of white men, not Orientals. We both remarked about this and later we all, except Pohl, who couldn't see from his seat in the rear of the plane, spoke of it. Could they have been American and British prisoners? Looking back now it seems they were unusually excited. Lord, how I'd like to think they were Americans and British who looked up from their sordid surroundings and saw planes carrying the American emblem painted boldly on their wings. Maybe a ray of hope pierced their black existences for that brief moment. I hope so.

The interphone broke our radio silence with a garble of words from Herndon in the nose giving us course directions, and Pohl in the tail pointing out a formation of nine Jap planes high on our right, going in the opposite direction. Apparently they never saw us. They were in view such a short time and at such a distance that it was difficult to tell what kind of ships they were. They might have been trainers—or fighters.

Now we were in a more thickly populated area. A single tall radio transmitting pole rose ahead of us.

"There's the radio station JOAK right over there," came over the interphone from Herndon.

We had no time to investigate that, though. Suddenly from our right came a single small airplane. He was turning so that as he completed his turn we were well ahead of him. Pohl later told us we were well lined up on him with the rear guns, but he was lost behind us before he ever got into range for firing.

Suddenly Ski pulled up to about 1,500 feet. There was our target directly on our nose. It was a big factory installation with four puffing stacks; at least a three-story structure with a fair-sized river alongside and several railroad tracks entering its immediate area.

"Open your bomb bay doors, Herndon." And then to me, "That would be a fine thing at a time like this—to forget to open your bomb bay doors!"

The plane gave its characteristic shudder as the bomb bay doors underneath opened.

"PDI!" came the familiar voice from the nose.

Ski began ruddering the ship from right to left, keeping the needle on zero. Fifteen hundred feet was indicated on our altimeter and our air speed was well above 200 miles an hour now. It looked good to see that speed after the morning hours of riding along at a sluggish 165 to 170 indicated. The target disappeared under our nose.

"Bombs away!" A pause, and then, "Bomb bay doors closed," just as a slight jolt told us the "eggs" had landed, the repercussion making the ship rock.

We lost our altitude and the air speed climbed up yet higher as we made a turn to the right, then left, then right, searching the skies for pursuers.

Rat-tat-tat accompanied the acrid smell of burning gunpowder as it came up through the airplane from the nose.

In searching the skies, we had failed to notice as we came up over a little knoll, that we were practically over the edge of an airdrome. Tens of bi-winged trainers lined the field. Herndon told us this later. "I wasn't going through this thing without firing this gun, and, well, an airport—training field or otherwise—isn't a bad target!"

We were approaching the foothills now.

I called Pohl, "Keep your eyes peeled back there, Pohl."

"Yes, sir. All clear."

Our shadow, which I had watched jump about on the ground, continually changing shape and size as it passed over little hills and knolls on our approach to the target, was now becoming steadier and smaller under us as we started climbing to get over the six-to-eight-thousand-foot mountains which form the backbone of Japan. Here, away from the telltale structure of buildings and appearance of people, it looked like the mountains east of Seattle. Trees were scarce, however, unlike the wooded Cascades. Fujiyama reached skyward to our left and snow dotted the tops of all the mountains around us. We crossed the peak of the backbone only feet above the scrawny, leafless saplings, and land fell abruptly away under us. Ahead stretched a magnificent view of some fifty miles of flat green land, and on the horizon, the silver streak of the Sea of Japan.

Pohl gave us the "Okay—all clear" from his rear observation post as we started our descent down the western slopes of Japan's mountain ridge.

"I'll bet we're the first B-25 crew of five to bomb Tokyo and cross Japan at noon on a Saturday," I quipped, trying to say something funny to break the tension a little.

It did draw a smile from Ski as he answered, "And took off from an aircraft carrier called the *Hornet*."

It was approaching the five-hour mark in flying time since we'd left that floating palace, and I can remember opening another pack of cigarettes as we crossed that low, flat stretch with the mountains behind us now. Somehow, the candy bars we'd brought along—a carton of them—didn't appeal to us yet.

We could have used another load of bombs between the foothills and the sea. We passed low over a well-constructed railroad bridge, double-track. It would have looked good lying flat on the river bed. As we approached the coast, a low, sprawling city outlined itself against the sea beyond. We were turning right, left, right and left, slowly, keeping a watchful eye in all directions. Tall stacks reached up from the center of the town, obviously a metallurgical installation of some sort. The chimneys might have indicated the blast furnaces of a steel mill. What a target it would have been! A few minutes later we were again over water, our shadow, big and smooth now, chasing alongside of us.

For the second time, Herndon called us to give a drift correction to the right. We were favoring the right anyway. Our maps of the coast of Russia up there were not too accurate or detailed. We didn't want to take any chance of getting too far to the left. Any map will show you how much left drift you can safely allow on a course from Tokyo to Vladivostok. The border of Korea is not much over fifteen miles from Vladivostok itself. Korea would be, of course, as far as we were concerned, the same as Japan. So we were making plenty definite corrections to the right. Fifteen miles right or left is altogether too possible on a 600-mile overwater flight.

Now we were entering the murky area where we should have been getting a little turbulence. But we weren't. A faint blue tinge was growing brighter by the minute ahead of us, and suddenly, so suddenly it was almost unbelievable, we were out in the April sunshine again without a cloud to break the unending blue. Some freak air current must have pulled that funnel of haze and smoke from some place miles away to lie across the Sea of Japan.

"What do you think, Ski?" I asked.

The afternoon was waning. It was 4:00 P.M. on our watches. That old B-25—2242—was really showing her stuff. Not a murmur. Well, she shouldn't murmur! She'd been eating enough of our gas to satisfy any plane's appetite.

"I was just thinking—what do you think we ought to tell these people when we land? Think we ought to tell them who we are and what we've done?" said Ski.

"Let's wait till we see if they already know. Can you speak Russian?" I asked.

"No," said Ski. "I know a few Polish words. I come from a Polish family. You knew York wasn't my name until a year or two ago, didn't you?"

"Yes, I'd heard York was the name you had yours changed to legally after you got out of West Point, right?" I asked.

"Yes," he answered, "most people think my old name is a Russian name, but it isn't; it's Polish.

We were flying Herndon's given course and keeping a watchful eye out for land. Boy, how good dry, friendly land would look to us.

Herndon came up out of the nose and said, "Well, about another hour ought to do it!"

We split a candy bar three ways. Not until then did any of us realize our stomachs had been sadly neglected all day. But somehow that much candy was all I could take for the time being.

It was cool now. Herndon stayed in the navigator's compartment with Sergeant Laban.

"Hope they have 100-octane gas if we find an airdrome," said Ski.

"We could get away early in the morning and probably beat the rest of the guys to Chungking," I added.

"Or tonight," said Ski, and then, "We're probably not the only one flying this course."

We tried to get Pohl on the interphone, but he did not answer. We banked slightly right and left, peering behind us. No ships were in sight. We were alone with our ship, with the sky, and the Japanese Sea some fifty odd feet below us.

At about a quarter to five, land came slowly into view on the horizon—tall mountains looming dark out of the sea. Lord, what a welcome sight! They weren't really so high, they only seemed so to us, flying so low. We started climbing some and corrected our course slightly to the right where a point of land extended a little out into the sea.

About three miles out, we turned 90° right and flew north along the coastline. We thought if there was any possibility of having hit the coast south of the big jut of land where Vladivostok lies, we'd rather know about it now than after we crossed the shore line.

Ten minutes of flying convinced us, however, that we were actually flying along the Soviet coast line, not Korea's.

Herndon was up in the pilot's compartment behind us now with his coast-line map of that area.

"We're about here," he said, indicating a point about forty miles north of the peninsula end, and looking from map to coast line and back several times. Ski and I got the map up in front of us and verified our position by outstanding coast-line features. So we made a 180° turn and started down the coast again, this time closer to shore. The coast line was rugged, with very little beach; one little bay cut inland and a small group of houses could be seen at the head of the bay. We continued on and soon could see the end of the peninsula. There was no sign of anti-aircraft fire.

It didn't seem a good idea to round the end of the point and come sailing into the port of Vladivostok big as life. It was undoubtedly well defended. So we cut inland. As we turned, we could see, off to the left, the fingerlike projection of land extending seaward.

"Good Lord, look!" said Ski.

He turned the ship slightly so that we had an unobstructed

view of a huge airdrome with plenty of orange-winged aircraft, at least thirty to forty airplanes.

"Those must be navy," I said.

"Well, whatever they are, let's get the devil out of here," Ski answered.

And with that we turned slightly and lowered the nose to pick up speed, just in case some Russian "happened" to notice a two-engine bomber roaring over an aircraft base on that vulnerable east coast—and decided to shoot it down first and investigate later.

We were across the ridge of hills lining the coast now and we found ourselves approaching an inlet, or bay, at the head of which emptied a fair-sized river. The river flowed seaward through a wide, flat valley, bounded by the hills we had just crossed and another, higher ridge ahead of us.

"Let's find us a spot to sit down, what do you say?" said Ski.

"A good idea," I said.

We were both thinking the same thing. You can't fly around over the seaboard area of a country at war without someone in that country eventually doing something about it.

We were losing altitude now and turned right up the valley. Ahead of us, in the center of the valley, stretched a large square field with some dirty, white, tumbling, rather large buildings on one side.

"Here we are!" said Ski. "We'll fly over this field once and see what the ground looks like."

We were about 800 feet above the ground as we went across the field. On my side, I could see a couple of small buildings with a few men dressed in long black coats standing watching us. Just as I spotted a small airplane under a camouflage net not far from the building, Ski hit my arm and said, "It's an airport!"

The large dirty white buildings were on his side, as was a "T" made of white cloth strips on the ground, with black-coated men already arranging the strips to indicate the direction to land. This happened to be the same direction in which we were passing over the field.

Just as we started a turn to the left to begin our approach, a small fighter type bi-wing, single-seat plane came out of a dive on our right side, fairly close to us. We were pulling away from him as he lost his diving speed.

"For gosh sake, let's get our wheels down to let him know we're going to land and he won't have to shoot us down," I said, pointing him out to Ski and reaching for the gear control.

As our wheels came down our speed lowered, and our friend— we hoped—stayed on our tail.

We were turning now for our straightaway approach. Now the flaps were coming down—all the way down. Then the boundary of the field was behind us and Ski was breaking our glide.

A slight jolt and we were on the ground. Boy! Good old ground! From 8:35 A.M. till about a quarter to six, over 1,400 miles of water, over a hostile country—and now, at last, dry, good ground. It was a wonderful feeling.

The small ship had followed us in and sailed by over our heads.

"I'm going to taxi over here on the right near that camouflaged ship, Bob. Leave fifteen degrees of flaps down and let's take a look at these jokers to see if they've got slant eyes. If they have, we'll take off straight ahead!"

That would have been a fine thing after all that flying—to find slant eyes on the faces of our hosts. But no: as we taxied by a group of curious, staring, black-overcoated men, they smiled. And their eyes weren't slanted. We pulled around facing the open field, pulled the flaps the rest of the way up, and locked our brakes.

The sun was low on the horizon. It was clear, and the silence was deafening as our engines slowed and finally stopped. We cut the switches. For a moment no one spoke. I saw about twelve men, all dressed the same, in long black coats with tight black leather belts, blue tabs on their collars, and wearing perfectly round, flat black caps with ribbons in the back and blue lettering on the bands. They were gathering around just off the right wing, looking at our ship with curiosity—and they were grinning. We were in Russia!

Author's Note: The reason Ski York's crew landed in Russia could be traced back to the maintenance personnel at Sacramento. Both carburetors on York's plane had been removed without his knowledge and in spite of the fact that Doolittle had insisted no work be done without permission. No record of the change had been made on the plane's engine forms. Sergeant Ted Laban, the plane's crew chief, discovered on the carrier that the serial numbers on his records did not agree with those on the carburetors themselves. Doolittle had asked York how he felt about it and York said, "all right." He hoped that the new carburetors would at least have normal consumption and, with luck, would get them to China Coast but the early take-off and two carburetors set to burn at an excessively rich mixture caused York to make a command decision to set course for Vladivostok. His only other alternative was to ditch the Mitchell in the China Sea three hundred miles from land.

Relieved at being safe again on the ground, York and his crew got out of their plane and were approached by a Russian captain. York later described to intelligence officers what happened next:

"He took us into an office and we sat there for about two hours and a half at which time an interpreter came in and told us that they were fixing something for us to eat. They didn't question us about where we had come from—except that pilots would come in now and then and, out of curiosity, point to the map with an inquiring look. We pointed generally in the direction of Alaska. We didn't want to tell anyone the truth yet. That night a naval colonel, who was the C.O. there, told us through the interpreter that we had been a part of the raid on Japan. He accused us of it and I admitted we had. I asked him if he would fix us up with gasoline, and if he would that we would take off early the next morning and proceed to China. He agreed.

"When we went to bed that night we were fully confident we were going to leave the next morning. But the next morning a general showed up along with a divisional commissar—the equivalent ranking civilian town official. Evidently they had communications from higher headquarters and, after we finished eating, we were placed aboard a Russian DC-3 and flown to Khabarovsk, which is about 400 miles north of Vladivostok. When we arrived there we were interviewed for a short time by the Commander of the Far Eastern Red Army and he decided that we were to be interned.

"About three days later our personal belongs were sent to us. They had all been left at the station at Vladivostok. Anything that resembled airplane equipment had been removed, including our pistols. We were placed in a house about five miles out of town and very closely guarded. Five days later it was announced over the radio that we had landed in the country and had been interned. About five days after that we were taken aboard a train and sent to Penza in European Russia."

The trip to Penza took 21 days. Here the five men were shut up in a house. There was a fence around the house but they were never allowed outside of it. Three Soviet "companions," all captains, were assigned to them full time. The future looked grim since it appeared that they were not to enjoy the relative freedom of men who were interned in other countries during the war like Turkey, Sweden and Switzerland. They were prisoners for all practical purposes except that they were not in a prison. Their plight, unfortunately, had been caused by an over-eager American newspaperman in Moscow. During the five or six days after their arrival in Russia, a news conference had been held in Moscow at which the raid on Japan by the American airmen had been the main subject of discussion. The American newsman asked what the Russians would do if one of the planes involved in the raid landed in Russia. He insisted so much on an answer that the Russians thought he must have had some information on York's crew being there. Their presence was then announced for fear of Japanese retaliation since the two nations were not then at war. To remain legally neutral, they were obligated to retain the five Americans for the duration.

On April 22, four days after the raid, Ambassador William H. Standley had radioed Washington that a twin-engined North American bomber had made a forced landing in Primorskkrai and said, "The Soviet military authorities would like to have this information kept secret and especially do not wish that the press should know that a United States Army plane had landed in the Soviet Union."

It was over a month before any American representatives were allowed to visit the five internees. On May 24, Colonel Joseph A. Michela, military attache to Russia, flew to Penza to talk to the five men and report on their condition and morale. The next day he radioed the Ambassador from Kuibyshev:

> At this time crew members are lodged in a large, clean bungalow in a village approximately 10 miles outside of Penza. The bungalow is surrounded by lawns and gardens and adjoining a second house which contains the dining and recreation rooms and also houses three Soviet companions, one of whom is an interpreter. For recreation the Americans have been provided with books, billiards, athletic facilities and other distractions. All in all, the Soviet authorities have been extremely considerate in providing for the crew. The food which the men receive is superior to that obtainable by the diplomatic corps in Kuibyshev and the men are allowed the same freedom of movement permitted to chiefs of mission at Kuibyshev. All men seem to be in excellent mental and physical condition. It is stated that their only complaint is that they are urged to eat and drink too much . . .

York and his crew stayed at Penza for two and a half months and then were moved to the small village of Okhansk, eighty miles south of Molotov where they remained for the next eight months. About four months after their arrival in Okhansk, the "guards" were taken away and the five men lived by themselves, although visited by the Russians daily. On September 13th, Ambassador Standley wired the State Department that he and three others had visited York and his men and reported that "the crew is found to be comfortably housed, adequately fed, in good health and generally well cared for," and that their principal concern was the welfare of their families. The truth was that York and his men were bored from the inactivity and the uncertainty of their status. They pleaded for something useful to do.

On November 6, a formal request was sent by Major General Follet Bradley, on special assignment in Moscow, to the Pentagon recommending that the Secretary of War "direct Amembassy Moscow arrange with Soviet authorities permit Maj. York and crew . . . to participate in useful professional work. They have not been asked for nor have they given their paroles which would be necessary if they are permitted to fly. They are most anxious to work and I believe would give necessary paroles. If official request is made to Soviets I believe they would comply."

While waiting for word from Washington, the five airmen were allowed the free run of the village of Okhansk, which wasn't saying much. The people were poor; food was scarce and the luxuries of life were non-existent. They had no soap, tobacco, matches, or even the barest of "extras." Schools had been closed for the duration and there was only one newspaper for the entire population which was posted in the center of town. There was only one radio, which had loudspeakers attached so that everyone could hear the news from Radio Moscow. The only fringe benefit was a motion picture theater, an old barn, which showed occasional propaganda films, and, much to the delight of the raiders, good but old American films.

Time seemed to stand still for the Americans. Washington continued to ignore the November message request. The days and nights ran together with monotony. They talked, slept, read and re-read the letters they had received from the States, and studied the Russian language. It began to be an effort to study or take an interest in anything. They found themselves numbed as the days went by endlessly without any real contact with the outside world. After the New Year, they began to talk of escape as soon as the intense cold of winter subsided. On the off chance that they could make a dent in Soviet officialdom with a plea for release from their enforced idleness, they composed a letter to Premier Stalin and asked that they be allowed to leave Russia promising that their departure would be kept a secret. If this was not possible, they asked to be moved to a warmer climate and allowed to work where their training as a B-25 crew could be utilized. They really never expected to hear from the letter which they had given to their interpreter but anything was worth a try.

On March 25th, the unexpected *did* happen. On that day, two Russian officers arrived and told them that their letter had been received in Moscow in the headquarters of the Red Army and that they were to be granted the second and third parts of their requests; the first could not be granted. Within an hour they departed by automobile for Molotov, then by plane and train to Ashkhabad, not far from the Persian border.

True to the promise of the two officers, as soon as they arrived in their new surroundings they were given work passes, outfitted with working clothes, and assigned to an aircraft overhaul shop for bi-winged training planes. York and Emmens were given the job of dismantling fuselages and tearing away old fabric from the frames. Herndon and Pohl cleaned instruments while Laban worked on the small engines. After a few weeks of this, however, the urge to escape returned and, assisted by a friendly Russian named Kolya, they arranged with a Persian "border runner" by the name of Abdul Arram, to be smuggled into Iran. For the sum of $300 they were taken to the city of Meshhed by the crafty Persian. After several near-misses with Russian border guards, the quintet turned themselves in to the British Consul and returned to the United States on May 29, 1943. Both York and Emmens had become fathers while they were gone.

While their treatment could not be compared with that received by the eight men imprisoned by the Japanese, it had a lasting effect on York and his men. They were among the first Americans to realize that the Soviet Union had a population, as Bob Emmens expressed it, "controlled by terror and violence, nurtured on fear and suspicion." It was Bob Emmens who became one of the first Americans in uniform to warn what communism really meant. In the closing lines of his book, "Guests of the Kremlin" he wrote ". . . communism, like a malignant scab on the skin of the world, is spreading north, south, east, and west. FIGHT IT!"

Chapter 15

A BRIDGE BETWEEN FREE PEOPLES

BY

Eldred V. Scott

While I was loading our gear in the rear hatch of our plane, "The Whirling Dervish," I took one last look down the deck toward the bow. Colonel Doolittle had already taken off and the second plane was now revving up its engines. Man, I thought to myself, that deck sure does look short! But it was nice to know that it could be done. Before the Colonel did it, though, there was a little doubt in the minds of some of us.

I busied myself straightening up the rear compartment as Lt. Watson taxied into position. Before I could really worry about it, we were blasting down the deck and into the air. Takeoff was so simple that you would have thought we did that kind of thing every day.

My troubles as engineer started soon after the wheels were tucked up, however. The bottom tank where the lower turret had been taken out started to leak at the corner seams about fourteen inches from the top. I called Lt. Watson on the interphone and we transferred gas out of that tank as soon as we could burn it out of the mains. That done I turned my attention to my guns and

Crew No. 9 (Plane 40-2303): left to right, Lt. Thomas C. Griffin (Navigator); Lt. Harold F. Watson (Pilot); T/Sgt. Eldred V. Scott (Engineer-Gunner); Lt. James M. Parker, Jr. (Co-Pilot); Sgt. Wayne M. Bissell (Bombardier).

found that they wouldn't charge because of a malfunction of the hydraulic charger. I removed this mechanism as quickly as I could and found that I could charge them by hand.

About an hour away from the *Hornet* we passed a freighter

which surprised us all. It was about then that I started opening the five gallon cans of gas and poured them into the turret tanks. The gas was then immediately transferred to the wing tanks. After emptying all the cans, I cut holes in them and threw them overboard.

For a long time the flight was routine but then we began to see small fishing vessels and knew that the shoreline wasn't too far ahead. But before we saw a beach we could see the beautiful mountains of Japan and it looked exactly like the geography book pictures I remember in grammar school. It was hard to believe that this was enemy territory.

We made landfall over a long sweeping sandy beach and just below us as we flew in was an airfield with a line of silver planes parked wingtip to wingtip on the ground with their bright orange Rising Sun insignia painted on each wingtip. These looked like bombers and nearby some fighters were warming up as if on alert.

Since planes on the ground couldn't hurt us, I kept my eyes peeled for any that were in the air and off to the left I saw five of them. I turned my turret guns toward them but they were small bi-winged trainers and couldn't have caught us.

It was easy to see when we neared Tokyo because the flak started. I'll never forget the strange feeling I had watching the black puffs breaking ahead of us. That stuff could hurt us but it was hard to believe that anyone would shoot at us deliberately. Of course, this was the first enemy flak any of us had ever seen. Fortunately, it was very inaccurate, probably for the reason that we were the first enemy planes that the Japanese ack-ack gunners had ever fired on.

As we headed toward the city of Tokyo we flew over an airport that looked like it might have been the strip for an aircraft factory and the flak immediately got worse. At first, the bursts were below us but then started bursting above us. As soon as

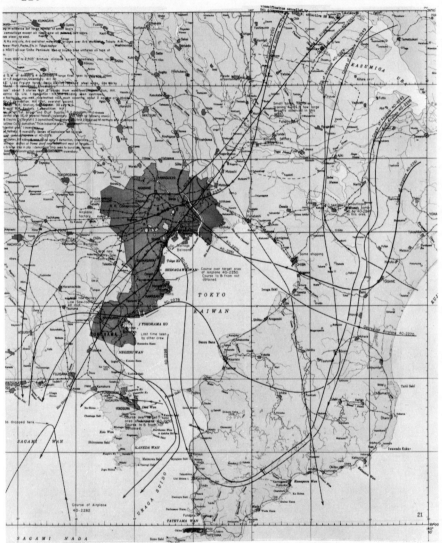

The map above shows the various routes used in the attack on the cities of Tokyo, Yokohama, and Yokosuka. The arrival of planes from so many directions led the Japanese to believe many more planes had been used. Other planes bombed Kobe, Osaka, and Nagoya.

they did, Lt. Watson dropped to rooftop level zig-zagging as he went. We continued toward our target and pulled upward so

Bissell could let go our bombs. When he called "Bombs away!" over the interphone, I looked backward to see where they would hit. The target was on a sand spit out in the water and appeared to be two saw-toothed roof buildings connected by a building running at right angles. I saw two of our bombs hit the building and spray debris everywhere. Out of the corner of my eye, though, I saw something else. Tracers were looping up at us from behind and below from a single fighter that was only a hundred yards away from us and pointing straight at me! I opened fire only to find that my sight fogged up. All I could do was keep my finger on the trigger and aim with my tracers. As my bullets came closer and closer, the enemy fighter fell off on the left wing and I never saw it again. I think I got him but I'll never be able to swear to it.

Lt. Watson dropped the plane down to the roof tops again and headed out over Tokyo Bay. I saw a large number of barges, a few tankers and, as we paralleled the coast, two cruisers and a battleship loomed out of the haze. The battleship opened fire with everything it had. Lt. Watson, by this time, had throttled way back to conserve gasoline and kept right on going. However, when he saw the shells hitting the water all around us, he shoved the throttles forward and got out of there. I could see the battleship still firing as we left it way behind and settled back down to maximum cruising power.

I saw several fishing boats during the next few hours and fired on them with the turret guns; however, I don't think I hit them. My purpose was merely to add to the confusion I hoped we had created back in Tokyo. I figured it might help us all if reports from scared Japanese fishermen would come pouring into their Navy Headquarters.

As we churned on hour after hour, I remember that the gasoline situation weighed on everyone's mind. We all knew it would be short because of the extra mileage we had to cover. Lt. Watson and Lt. Parker had talked it over and then talked it over with the rest of us. We would stay on our course for our destination in China as long as the gas held out. When it looked like we weren't going to make it, we would look for a fishing boat, strafe it, ditch beside it, take it over and sail toward the China coast.

Before we could take any action on our plan, however, the weather changed our ideas. We began to run into fog and as it got thicker we began to climb over it. We went higher and higher and then had to go into it. The fog became rain and the B-25 began to shudder and shake as we bored into updrafts and downdrafts. We all agreed that the best thing to do now was to head in a southerly direction, away from Japanese-held territory, and bail out when our gas was gone. Because of Lt. Watson's constant attention to conserving gas, we didn't know it then but we flew further inland than any of the other planes by a considerable distance.

After an amazing 15½ hours in the air, our engines started the sputtering we had been waiting to hear for about two hours. We were still in the soup and couldn't even see our wingtips. Lt. Watson told me to go first so I stuffed some cigarettes and a pint of whiskey in my jacket, removed the rear hatch, faced toward the rear and dropped out head first. I pulled the rip cord immediately; the 'chute opened and started to swing me back and forth. Before I could realize that I had actually bailed out of an airplane, I felt the 'chute snag in the top of a tree as I swung forward and dropped gently right into the fork of another.

Since I seemed solidly on a perch of some kind, I waited a few minutes collecting my thoughts and wondered how high up in the tree I was. I reached into my jacket and pulled out a cigarette and matches and took a few puffs. Then I flicked the ash off the cigarette and dropped it to see how far it would go. That little glow dropped down, down, down, and finally out of sight. For all I knew I was several hundred feet up in the air.

My predicament scared me more than a little and I decided that I was about as safe as anyone could be with my parachute harness on and the canopy hooked firmly in the branches. I remembered the pint of whiskey which was still intact so I sipped it slowly and gradually drifted off to sleep.

The next morning, I saw that I wasn't as bad off as I had feared. True, I was hanging in a tree on the edge of a cliff but it wasn't hard to climb down. Had I tried to climb down in the dark and slipped or gotten careless, though, it would have been curtains.

I climbed up the mountain as soon as I could see any distance but couldn't see anything that looked like civilization. I figured that if I headed due west, though, in a country as over-populated as China, I'd be bound to run into something. I walked most of the day and finally at three o'clock that afternoon came to a farm house where they gave me rice and peppers. By sign language I learned that two men had preceded me down the valley and in thirty minutes of walking I met Lts. Parker and Griffin. We decided to continue along the stream that ran along the valley and reasoned that eventually the stream would come to a village or city. By late afternoon we were tired and soaking wet from the drizzle that had been falling most of the day. We came upon a farmhouse and the farmer invited us inside and allowed us to take off our clothes and dry ourselves by his fire. We all put our guns on the table and were huddled around the fire when suddenly a Chinese officer appeared in the doorway holding a scroll in one hand and a pistol in the other! Turning around quickly we found that our own pistols had disappeared from the table and that other Chinese were covering us with rifles from every window and door. We were their prisoners.

You can imagine what we were thinking that night as we were marched about five miles, held captive by a Chinese Army unit, none of whom could speak English or would try to interpret our sign language. The words "Lishua Megwa" (I am an American) that Commander Jurika had taught us on board the carrier meant nothing in their district.

After a miserable night, the next morning two Catholic missionaries (Fathers Moore and Dunkir) from Ihwang, a nearby town, identified us as Americans and we suddenly became heroes! They wined and dined us and the priests furnished us with shoes and underclothes. For a week we stayed at the home of the local mandarin and ate our meals at the mission.

Two days after we arrived at the mission, our pilot Lt. "Doc" Watson was brought in with a badly injured shoulder. He was the last to bail out and had gotten his arm tangled up in the shroud lines. His right arm was badly dislocated and he couldn't get it back in place. (It was to be weeks before he would get any relief from the pain and he would have to have an operation at Walter Reed Hospital in the States before he could use that arm again.)

Sgt. Wayne Bissell, our bombardier, came in a day or two later, having also been held captive by Chinese bandits. He had escaped by simply running away when no one was looking. We didn't know about any of the other crews but at least ours was all safe and it made us feel good.

Before we left Ihwang we were taken to the wreckage of our plane which had plowed into a hillside several miles away. It had not burned and a lot of our equipment was still intact. Lt. Griffin's suitcase was in perfect shape and he got everything back, even his dress uniform which he has to this day.

We left Ihwang with Father Dunkir as guide and travelled for two days by sedan chair to Nanchang where we arrived on April

30th. We left there later that day by station wagon and arrived at Hengyang via Tahaw on May 3rd. We stayed there until May 14th before we were flown out to Chungking. While we waited in Hengyang we realized how close to the war we were. The Japanese were out looking for us in strength on the ground and in the air. Every day an observation plane came over. Two of those days it was followed by bombers that dropped their loads on the town. It was only the beginning of the war for us all but the Chinese were to pay a far greater price than we Americans.

Two years after I made my report in Chungking, I picked up a copy of the May, 1944 issue of the *Reader's Digest* and learned what happened to the kindly Chinese who helped me join my crew and get to safety. Reverend Charles L. Meeus, a Protestant missionary, had taken a trip to Ihwang in the fall of 1942 where he visited Wang Poo-fang, a barber friend, who invited him to occupy his brand-new makeshift chair: the bombardier's seat from our B-25. He learned from the 80-year old, English-speaking village school teacher that our crew had parachuted nearby and that he would show Reverend Meeus the scene of the crash. His letter to the *Reader's Digest* said:

"The mountain path we followed snaked in and out where high cliffs, hairy with pine and fern, overhung deep ravines split by white cascades. Suddenly the old teacher pointed. "There!" he said. On a green cushion of laurel bushes, shining in the light of the setting sun, glistened the silvery wings of the bomber. Yes, there was the pine tree in which Sergeant Scott had hung from his chute till daybreak . . . yonder the creek where Lieutenant Watson had fainted, to lie for hours in the icy water.

"We fed the Americans and carried them to safety," the little teacher said, "so that they could bomb Tokyo again. Then the dwarf-invaders came. They killed my three sons; they killed my wife, Angsing; they set fire to my school; they burned my books; they drowned my grandchildren in the well." His eyes shone fiercely. 'And I crawled out of the well at night, when they were drunk, and killed them with my own hands—one for every member of my family they had slaughtered.'

"He sat down on the wing of the plane. 'This is a symbol,' he told me patting the great black bold letters U.S., 'A bridge between our two peoples—and a token of the hopes of the peoples of all the world.' "

It was then that I knew that our raid on Japan had been truly successful.

Reverend Meeus took a fragment of our plane, "The Whirling Dervish," and brought it to Washington to give to the Vicar Apostolic of Nanking, Bishop Paul Yu Pin. Bishop Yu Pin sent it to Mrs. Franklin D. Roosevelt on July 2, 1944 saying, "I am presenting this fragment to you on the eve of the 'triple seven' anniversary, when seven years ago on the seventh day of the seventh month (July 7, 1937) the Japanese brought war to our land." This piece of our plane, a portion of the cowling of the right engine nacelle, was later mounted by the North American Aviation Co. and presented to the Tokyo Raiders for our archives. It is the only piece of any plane to return to the States.

Chapter 16

"THANKS FOR A SWELL RIDE"

BY

RICHARD O. JOYCE

As soon as Watson's plane blasted off the deck, I lined up and took off about five minutes later. I had been slightly delayed due to the continued misfiring of the right engine which finally smoothed out. The take-off was easy although I sweated out that right engine during those critical moments of the roll down the deck.

I circled the carrier once and flew parallel to its course and set my gyro compass and compared it with the magnetic compass. We picked up a true course of 270 degrees about 500 feet off the water. About an hour and a half out Sergeant Horton, on watch in the upper turret, shouted over the interphone.

"Gunner to pilot. Twin engine plane, twelve o'clock!"

Directly ahead and above us was a Japanese patrol plane and it must have seen us at the same time because it immediately dove out of the clouds directly at us. I increased the power on both engines and swept underneath it. We quickly outdistanced it and didn't attempt to fire on it because it never really got within range.

After that incident, I decided to fly the rest of the distance at

Crew No. 10 (Plane 40-2250): left to right, Lt. Horace E. Crouch (Navigator); Lt. Richard O. Joyce (Pilot); Unidentified; Lt. J. Royden Stork (Co-Pilot); Sgt. George E. Larkin, Jr. (Bombardier). Fifth member of this crew was the gunner, S/Sgt. Edwin W. Horton (in inset), who was substituted at the last moment because of his knowledge of gun turrets—a constant source of trouble. Surviving raiders are unable to identify the man in the center.

altitudes ranging from 1,000 to 4,000 feet in order to fly in the thin overcast and clouds to avoid detection. We hit Inubo Saki

right on the nose, thanks to our navigator, "Sally" Crouch. I
turned south for about ten miles and then turned west across
the neck of land to Tokyo Bay, then northwest at 3,500 feet in and
out of the scattered clouds. When I sighted my target, I dove
out of the clouds, and lined up with the target at 2,400 feet and
210 mph speed. I opened the bomb-bay doors and just as I did,
an aircraft carrier steaming toward the Yokosuka Naval Base
opened up on us with their ack-ack of presumably small caliber.
Fortunately, their fire was ineffective and inaccurate. However,
since we were toward the last of the bomber string, they were
waiting for us and I knew it would be no picnic the rest of the
way in.

We lined up on our primary target, the Japan Special Steel
Company and dropped two 500-lb. demos and got direct hits. One
bomb hit directly in the middle of a big building and the other
landed between two buildings, destroying the end sections of both.
The third demo and the incendiary cluster were dropped in the
heavy industrial section in the Shiba Ward.

The ack-ack fire became intense and since I had taken a long
straight run on the target, by the time the bombs were out we
found ourselves bracketed with the black puffs of smoke and
shrapnel coming very close, generally behind but catching up fast.

Just as the last bomb went out, a formation of nine Zeros came
in above us and a little to our right. I jammed the throttles forward and went into a steep diving turn to the left to escape both
the ack-ack fire and the fighters. The fighters had definitely seen
us and peeled off at us but I dove under them and eluded them
for the moment. We were doing 330 mph which was right on the
red line. I leveled out right on the ground and hedge-hopped all
the way back out to the bay. Three Nakajima 97's came out of
nowhere ahead and to our left. They tried to catch us but couldn't
keep up. The Zeros, however, had not been shaken. They had an

altitude advantage but didn't seem too eager to come in close. I could hear Horton firing at them from the turret from time to time to discourage them. We finally shook them as I turned west across the mountains. Shortly after, a single fighter appeared alongside and above us, just as I turned south again. We fired at him with both nose and turret guns and we think we hit him but none of us was sure we knocked him down. At any rate, he got extremely discouraged which was OK with us.

Just as we thought we had it made and I had begun to throttle back when three more enemy fighters bored in toward us. I pushed the throttles forward and climbed up into the clouds to elude them. I decided to turn out to sea for about thirty miles since it looked like they were really after us. Fortunately, that was the last enemy plane we ever saw.

When we passed through the Oshima Strait and headed west, I took inventory of our damage. We had sustained one anti-aircraft hit in the rear fuselage just ahead of the horizontal stabilizer. The hole was about 7 inches in diameter; luckily, no vital structural part was hit and about all it did was create quite a draft. We were also hit on the left wing tip by machine gun bullets but, again, the damage was slight. A few feet closer to the fuselage, however, and we would probably have lost gas to say the least.

As soon as we estimated we were nearing the China coast, the weather became foggy and rainy. I was forced to go on instruments about 100 miles out and stayed on them until we all bailed out. Our automatic pilot was inoperative so I had to "hand-fly" it all the way. Stork, of course, relieved me and shared the flying chore.

About the time Crouch estimated we should begin to climb to avoid the mountains along the coast we spotted an island and got a few glimpses of land as we came in over the coast. Those few glimpses gave us assurance that at least we were over land. It was now getting dark, still foggy and rainy and getting worse.

There was an overcast above us so I climbed up into it and continued on course. As we neared our ETA at Chuchow I realized positively that we could never expect to make a landing in that weather so I told the crew to get ready to bail out. I climbed to 9,000 feet with about 15 minutes of gas left. I had flown deliberately past Chuchow to be sure that we would come down in Chinese territory.

I had been talking back and forth to my crew from time to time and when I figured we had only about ten minutes of gas left, I asked Crouch to show us on the map where we were. I then gave them their instructions.

"Horton, you go first out the rear hatch," I said. "Then Larkin, then 'Sally' and Stork out the front. Larkin, you wait until Horton is gone before you release the forward escape door—you might hit him. OK, fellas, that's it. I'll see you all in Chuchow. Let me know when you're ready back there, Ed, and good luck to you."

"OK, Lieutenant," Horton answered over the interphone. "Here I go and thanks for a swell ride."

I couldn't help but laugh at that and it made me feel good. Here we had been flying for about 14 hours, had been in combat and hit, and now had to bail out and he thanked me for the ride! Horton's spirit of discipline was typical of my whole crew and I was thankful.

I was busy keeping the plane's speed at 120 mph on instruments and felt them go one by one. They were fine men. Not one was afraid but bitterly disappointed that we had to abandon our plane. It takes men like them to win a war and that's what we were trying to do.

When the last man was gone, I rolled the stabilizer back to keep the plane from gaining too much speed and then worked myself around to get out of the cockpit. I had some trouble squeezing in between the armor plate on the backs of the two seats and had to keep pushing the wheel forward to keep the plane from stalling. I had little time to do anything once I got to the escape hatch but I did manage to grab some food and equipment before I jumped.

I dropped clear of the ship and pulled the rip cord. The chute opened nicely but just as it did the metal on one of the leg straps broke and almost dropped me out of the chute harness. I slid down and the chest buckle socked me in the chin so hard I was stunned. At the same time my pistol was jerked out of its holster and flew into space. I swung wildly for about a minute and then straightened out. Just as I did, I heard the plane hit below me and explode. A few seconds later, I hit the ground which was quite a surprise. Luckily, I was uninjured even though I had landed on the side of a steep slope.

It was raining and foggy and I couldn't see a thing. I felt I had no choice but to wrap myself up in my parachute and try to stay dry and get some sleep.

The next morning it was still foggy but the rain had stopped. When it was clear enough for me to see, I started to look for our plane. When I saw how steep the hill was that I had landed on and saw how sharp the boulders were, I don't see how I missed getting badly hurt—or worse.

The plane turned out to be only a mile away but it took me four hours to get there over the rocks and cliffs. When I got to the site of the crash there were a number of Chinese there picking in the charred wreckage. I hailed them and made them understand that I was a friend.

There wasn't a single thing I could salvage out of the wreck; it was a total loss. There was nothing to do but start walking. The Chinese farmers took me to a town where I stayed that night. The next day I met some Chinese soldiers who escorted me to Tunki, Anhwei and, a week later, Chuhsien. My crew was safe and had no serious injuries. We had a lot to be thankful for.

Chapter 17

NOT AS BRIEFED

BY

FRANK A. KAPPELER

The trip aboard the *Hornet* had been thoroughly enjoyable. I never knew the Navy lived so plushly aboard ship. After what we had been through at Columbia living in tents and standing in chow lines, it was a pleasure to eat huge meals from plates and with ice cream yet! They also relaxed their rules about gambling aboard ship because we actually played a lot of poker right on board.

I'll never forget the morning of the 18th as I'm sure none of the other fellows will, either. We had been given mattresses to put on the floor (oops, I mean deck) and I was lying there in my undershirt and shorts, getting all the last minute rest I could. I had eaten an early breakfast and paid by check for the food that I had put away during the 18 days aboard the *Hornet*. I had already shaved, so decided to pack my bag. This included an electric razor, camera, a civilian coat and slacks and several boxes of candy bars. I had put my navigation equipment away in several briefcases. That loudspeaker announcement telling us to man our planes sounded convincingly like the real thing, especially when

Crew No. 11 (Plane 40-2249): left to right, Lt. Frank J. Kappeler (Navigator); Capt. C. Ross Greening (Pilot); Sgt. Melvin J. Gardner (Engineer-Gunner); Lt. Kenneth E. Reddy (Co-Pilot); S/Sgt. William L. Birch (Bombardier).

the ship's pom-pom guns started to fire, so I quickly dressed and headed to the flight deck with my belongings, loading them aboard our plane, the "Hari Carrier."

Captain Ross Greening, our pilot, had taken over our crew

half way through training at Eglin. Ross was from another squadron, and the crew and myself knew very little about him. However, after our first training flight together, we knew that we were lucky; we had one of the best. He was daring, but knew his airplane and his own limitations, and was well coordinated and exceptionally strong. If the others could do it we knew he could, too. The other ten planes had made it, so it was just a matter of getting on with it. Still, I'll have to admit that riding as a navigator and having to trust your life to the skill of another is not without its stomach-tightening moments. This was one of them.

Surprisingly, the take-off was easy. Since the *Hornet* could swing into the wind, there was no drift as we started to roll. If we did drift either way before we had flying speed, it would have been disastrous.

As soon as we were airborne, I dutifully noted our take-off heading and time off. In spite of what we hoped, the Navy had not given us any weather information so that we would have some idea as to the weather ahead of us. All we knew was that the wind was 27 knots from 310° when we left the *Hornet*.

From the *Hornet* into Japan, I practiced working out navigation problems from a navigation book called "Driesenstock."

A navigator buddy of mine who was not going, offered to help carry some of my equipment to the flight deck. I made my way through stacked planes with their props turning over and across the rolling deck, which was wet and slippery, to our plane. My friend followed behind with the rest of my gear. Occasionally it had been necessary to kneel down and wait for the rolling deck to temporarily come to a level position and then proceed for ten feet or so. I reached our plane, placed my equipment inside and then headed back to the ship's island for a final time check and ship's position. I passed my friend who was headed for the plane. Somehow he failed to get my equipment into the right plane. During this trip to the plane, a cruiser, the *Nashville,* crossed in front of the *Hornet,* as it was engaged in firing at a Japanese vessel. All I had in the way of equipment was my brief-case full of odds and ends. One of these items was a navigation book I had never used before. So, for some four hours en route to Japan, I practiced working celestial navigation problems at random to be able to navigate after nightfall.

Our target was a refinery in Yokohama. However, we decided on an alternate target—just in case. When we crossed the coast-line, I remember thinking that it looked like southern California but I knew I shouldn't be thinking about things like that. Shortly after I had pinpointed our position as being considerably north of course, we passed over a training field and noticed many bi-winged trainers in the air. People on the ground waved at us as we zoomed over their heads at 500 feet, and some ran to hide behind bushes.

About 30 miles out from our target, four fighters came out of nowhere. One of them made a pass at us while we were at cruising speed (166 mph). Greening pushed the throttles forward to the end of the quadrant and we indicated 260 mph. The fighter made another pass at us but our turret gunner, Sergeant Gardner, drove him off with a few bursts. At 260 mph, the fighters found it difficult to overtake us.

As we neared our primary target we noticed planes converging on us from all directions. Obviously being in the tail end of a bomber stream had its disadvantages. Greening decided to go after the alternate target which was an oil refinery and tank farm. The bombs, four incendiary clusters, were dropped from 600 feet instead of the planned 1500. We got a stiff jolt from below as they all went off. We immediately headed out into Tokyo Bay and the smoke and flames were visible for the next fifteen or twenty minutes.

Another enemy fighter had made a pass at us from the rear just as we dropped our bombs and Gardner scored a direct hit. It pulled up into a steep climb smoking heavily. We were sure it crashed, although we didn't see it go in. After executing the maneuver known as "getting the hell out" we turned on a heading of 250° to parallel the coast about 50 miles off shore. We occasionally climbed up into the clouds at about 3,000 feet to escape detection from surface vessels. When we reached the southern tip of Japan we turned and headed across the China Sea, as it became dark.

Half way across we ran into fog and under an overcast. We stayed on top of the fog which rose gradually and joined the clouds. When it got dark, we knew what the outcome of our mission would be. We were going to have to trade our B-25 for that oil refinery. But, it could have been worse. At least we were going down in friendly territory—or were we? After we went into the overcast, I could only compute our course by dead reckoning since no star shots could be made and the Chinese homing beacons we expected never came on the air.

It was approximately 11:30 P.M. ship's time when Greening gave us the order to jump. Our altimeter indicated 9,500 feet and we hoped that was high enough. We had briefly dropped below the clouds, and saw a few lights on the ground, as well as mountain peaks all around us. We could never land a plane here. Sgt. Mel Gardner was called up front from the rear compartment and he went first. Sergeant Bill Birch followed.

I went next and as soon as I got out my chute opened almost immediately. The candy bars I had so carefully stashed in my shirt and the flashlight, which I had stuck under my belt and left on, disappeared as if by magic. I watched the lighted flashlight falling for what seemed like several minutes. I guess it really took me about three minutes to reach the ground. My shroud lines were twisted and I was never sure that my main chute was fully open because it looked awfully small way up above me. Trying to get the lines untangled caused me to oscillate and go around in circles and I started to feel sick at my stomach. I thought my time had come.

Actually, I lucked out. My chute caught in the top of a pine tree on a steep slippery mountain side as I went by it. The tree was soft and broke my fall so nicely that I felt no shock at all as I touched the ground.

I came to rest facing the sky, with my Army "45" and canteen under my back. The parachute shroud lines prevented me from rolling over. Several times I tried to get to my feet, but all I accomplished was sliding several feet further down the slippery, pitch black mountainside. I decided to stay where I was until daylight. I pulled part of the parachute over me, which shortly became soaking wet. It was the longest night I've ever had, as I tried to sleep with rain beating in my face.

The next morning I loosened my chute, climbed up to a trail above me and followed it into a valley. In the valley, I approached some friendly Chinese farmers. After much refusal of unappetizing looking food and much good natured sign language, I was escorted up the mountain again after my chute. I recovered it, and with a couple of my newly-found friends, started walking through Chinese villages heading west. Before long, my caravan was some 200 strong. I felt like Lawrence of Arabia stalking ahead of my "Army," except I really didn't know where I was leading them.

A few hours later I noticed another caravan converging on us from another direction. Leading it were Sergeants Birch and Gardner. They were enjoying the attention they were receiving, although Gardner had sprained both ankles badly.

We united forces and I felt very much reassured. I had a little Chinese wine to drink and was feeling no pain. We kept on walking and I began to think we might spend the rest of our lives in

China. The Chinese started to guide us in a northerly direction after we ate something that seemed like noodle soup. We got a little concerned because we knew that Jap-occupied territory lay to the north but, after a mile or so, we came to a river and started westward again. We must have gone five or six miles up river when we reached a fair-sized village where a few Chinese soldiers were quartered. One of them spoke a little English and from him we learned that Ross Greening and Ken Reddy, our co-pilot, had been there a short time before and had continued on up stream to Chuhsien, another 30 miles.

We kept going and arrived in Chuhsien at about 10 that night where we were given hot tea, hot milk and crackers. After resting, we were taken to the only hotel in town where our two missing buddies were already ensconced and fast asleep. We found that Reddy had hit the ground head first and still had a piece of rock stuck in his scalp to prove what he said happened. He was slightly woozy but we bandaged him up and he had it removed later when we got to Chungking.

We had mixed feelings about the raid when we got together and talked about it. We knew we had accomplished our mission all right but we sure hated to have to report that we had to give up one perfectly good airplane. The "Hari Carrier" lived up to its name and committed hari kari all right—something we hadn't expected when we named her. Ross Greening summed it up for us when he said, "Well, I think they'll call the mission a success. But there's one thing you'll have to admit," he added.

"What's that?" we asked in unison.

"It was one of those that will have to go down as 'Not As Briefed.' "

We agreed with him.

Chapter 18

WE BOMBED "THE LAND OF THE DWARFS"

BY

WILLIAM R. POUND

I was sound asleep when the order was given for us to man our planes. Frankly, I thought it was a practice alert and didn't get too excited about it. Fact is, I went up on deck without my brief-case and had to hurry back down to my cabin to pack. Naval officers who were my roommates were making remarks as to how envious they were of me while I packed my bags. At that moment I was almost tempted to turn over my briefcase to them and let them have at it. I hadn't even had my breakfast yet and it didn't seem the way that we had planned it.

The extra stuff I packed was the same as most of the other fellows—cigarettes and candy bars—because we figured we'd never be able to get them in China, especially at Navy shipboard prices. As it turned out, I don't think a single man ever got his cigarettes or candy unless he had them in his inside pockets.

Our pilot, Lt. Bill Bower, was in the airplane by the time I had gotten back on deck. Bill is the most unruffled, unhurried man I know. It seemed like he was as unconcerned about this raid as he could possibly be. My impression was that it was just another

240

Crew No. 12 (Plane 40-2278): left to right, Lt. William R. Pound (Navigator); Lt. William M. Bower (Pilot); S/Sgt. Omer A. Duquette (Engineer-Gunner); Lt. Thadd H. Blanton (Co-Pilot); T/Sgt. Waldo J. Bither (Bombardier).

cross-country trip to him. Only difference was that the take-off strip was a little shorter than usual. Believe me, flying with a man like that is good for the nerves of a navigator and I wasn't a bit scared as we taxied onto the take-off line.

Take-off was more normal than some of the others, it seemed to me. Bill didn't snap the wheel back or let the plane ride up as fast.

We settled down on course quickly at about 500 feet. Being the navigator, I kept busy all the way in. We couldn't smoke because of the gasoline cans in the rear and the collapsible tank in the crawl-way so I just tried to figure our winddrift and estimate when and where we would make landfall. We were following the ship ahead of us in the distance and I was pretty sure that we were correcting a little too far to the north. We saw several small fishing craft just off the coast and they reminded me that we were just about to fly over hostile territory.

When we finally crossed the coast I was now sure we were north of course and we turned southwest toward our target in Yokohama. I searched all over the map I had to try to recognize something but I'll have to admit that I was lost. I suggested to Bill that we turn out to the coast again and follow it down until we hit our intended landfall point and go in to the target from there.

I began to locate check points on the ground that agreed with my map and we started in toward Yokohama a second time. As soon as we did, we saw quite a few aircraft both on the ground and in the air. Before we could do anything about it, we flew right through the traffic pattern of an air base and planes were all around us; none of them seemed to recognize us because no one came after us.

After crossing the bay we noted balloons ahead and saw that they were at 1,000 feet right over our target—the docks at Yokohama. They didn't bother Bill or Sergeant Bither, our bombardier. We just climbed up over them to 1,200 feet, opened the bomb doors and let all four bombs go in trail. I was watching through the driftmeter and saw them hit. There was no doubt but that a lot of work was stopped on the docks that day.

While I was watching through the driftmeter, we encountered flak but it was light and very inaccurate. Bill dove for the deck and we scooted away over the housetops. On the way back toward the water, Bither strafed a power station and some Japanese soldiers with the .30 caliber nose gun.

I recall that I was very tense at the time. Because we were not allowed to smoke, I was chewing gum. My mouth had become so dry that the gum got stuck all over the inside of my mouth and I felt I really had a mouth full of cotton. Funny how you can recall something like that many years later.

We saw a few aircraft after leaving the target area but none of them came after us. We continued south and then west as most of the other planes had done and as we passed away from Japan some naval craft turned broadside to us and started firing. Bill Bower took one look and calmly circled away from them out of the line of fire.

Bill did a double drift maneuver for me so that I could figure out what the wind was doing to us. Much to our surprise and pleasure we found that we had a tail wind. If it would stay with us, I figured we could just about make the China coast. We all felt a lot better then because we would never have made it with any kind of a headwind.

Fortunately, the wind stayed with us and now our only worry was whether or not we could make it from the coast to our intended destination. We were about three hours out from land when we ran into low ceilings and poor visibility. We stayed under the stuff at about 500 feet until I figured we were about an hour from land. At this point we decided to see if we could get above it, or at least between layers, at an altitude which would permit clearing the mountains. We felt this was the best decision, even if bail out became necessary, because it was getting dark and I didn't feel confident that we were exactly on course. I figured a "no wind" condition but made small southerly corrections periodically because we knew our chances of not being captured would be better if we were south of our destination.

We were cruising at about nine thousand feet when I figured our ETA was up. We had about twenty minutes of gas left so Bill had everyone assemble in the navigator's compartment.

Sergeant Bither grabbed his parachute in the dark of the nose of the plane and started to crawl rearward. It was a chest pack that is buckled on a harness before bailout and he grabbed the ripcord handle instead of the carry strap. His chute sprang open and there he was with an armful of white silk. There were no spare chutes aboard so Bither had no choice if he were going to bail out. He had to repack that chute in a few minutes right there.

Bither used my navigator's table and about five minutes later he had a reasonable facsimile of a packed chute. Bill looked back and asked him if he thought it would work, and Bither said he wasn't worried. So, clasping both arms around the pack fastened on his chest, he dropped through the hatch.[1]

Sergeant Williams, the engineer-gunner, was next, then me. I scraped my arm on something on the way out. When my chute opened, it knocked the wind out of me. When I got my wind back, I took my flashlight out and just as I did I hit the ground and the wind was knocked out of me again.

I recovered after a few seconds, gathered up my chute and then decided to stay put. I rolled up in the chute to stay dry and warm until daylight.

I slept like a log from exhaustion and woke up to the realization that I now had a survival problem on my hands. I remembered hearing the sound of running water when I was floating down the night before and thought it must have been the ocean and that I had bailed Bither and Williams out in the water. But it turned out to be a river, for which I was thankful. I had always been told to follow streams and rivers if lost and that's exactly what I decided to do now because I couldn't have been more lost than I was then.

I followed the stream for about an hour and ran into our co-pilot Thad Blanton. We crossed the river and made our way along a well-used path to a small village. We decided to take our chances and walk right in. We did this and didn't see a soul. We walked right through town without seeing a living thing. It gave us the creeps but we decided to keep on going. About a half hour later Sergeant Bither caught up with us. He told us he had made friends in a little village nearby by giving a child some candy and had been treated kindly. We turned around and went back. We found this time that the people had hidden because they were afraid of Blanton and me. I showed them my maps and they showed us where we were (about 40 miles northwest of our intended destination). We started walking in that direction.

That night we came to another small village and were welcomed to spend the night. They bedded us down all right—on wooden tables. The only advantage I could see was that it got us off the cold floor but what a way to sleep!

Bill Bower had arrived shortly before we did and was given a message, via sign language, by one of the Chinese that Sergeant Duquette was being brought in but that his foot was hurt. Next morning, sure enough, some Chinese coolies carried him in with a broken foot.

While we were pondering what to do, we got another message from "Sally" Crouch of Joyce's crew that they were in Siuan, the next town. The Chinese made sedan chairs for us out of our parachute harnesses and carried us all the next day to meet Joyce's crew. We went from there to Chuchow where we were well treated for the next six days, although we had to hide in a cave during the daylight hours because of Japanese air attacks. But when about twenty of us had collected, we started out for Chungking by bus, train, boat, and, eventually airplane. Every little town we came to insisted on giving "the glorious American airmen" a celebration. They were grateful that we had bombed the "land of the dwarfs" and were helping them in their war. We learned later that joy was turned to sorrow for many of them because the Japanese swept through the area and murdered hundreds of them for helping us.

NOTE TO CHAPTER 18

1. Sergeant Bither had helped around the parachute shops where he had repacked tow target sleeves many times before and felt sure the principle was the same. He told the author, "I *knew* it would work. In fact, I felt a lot better about it after I packed it myself than I had before."

Chapter 19

THE LUCKY THIRTEENTH

BY

RICHARD A. KNOBLOCH

Lt. Edgar E. McElroy of Ennis, Texas, was pilot of our crew. He was about 30 then, heavy set, with a rapidly receding hairline and a jovial face. Lt. Clayton J. Campbell of Oregon was navigator. He was about 28 at the time and very quiet, just the opposite of Master Sergeant Robert C. Bourgeois of New Orleans, our bombardier and the happiest-go-lucky fellow I've ever known. Sgt. Adam R. Williams, our engineer-gunner, was from Virginia, so we all called him "Hillbilly." I was co-pilot, just nine months out of flying school.

My last job on the *Hornet* before take-off was to pass out lunches to the 16 B-25s. I saw to it that our crew got double. We loaded quickly and were guided into position after the #12 crew took off. Mac gave the engine full throttle, watched the flagman give him the signal and we blasted off the deck. We joined up with planes piloted by Greening and Bower who had taken off just ahead of us.

Our three-ship formation flew on all morning, about 25 feet above the water. I hadn't gotten a full breakfast aboard the carrier

Crew No. 13 (Plane 40-2247): left to right, Lt. Clayton J. Campbell (Navigator); Lt. Edgar E. McElroy (Pilot); Sgt. Adam R. Williams (Engineer-Gunner); Lt. Richard A. Knobloch (Co-Pilot); Sgt. Robert C. Bourgeois (Bombardier).

so I snacked on sandwiches and oranges. Mac watched me eat but wouldn't join me.

About noon we saw the Japanese coastline. But what part of the coast was it? We all checked our maps, but nothing seemed to match what we saw on the ground.

"Think we're about 100 miles too far north," Campbell, our navigator, announced after long study. Mac immediately racked the Mitchell into a left turn. The navigators in the other planes must not have come to the same conclusion, although all three ships had the same target. Greening's ship turned right, while Bower continued straight ahead. We wondered who was right but since we had to maintain radio silence, we decided we were so continued down the coastline a few miles from shore.

The water was full of fishing boats—thousands of them. We skimmed over their masts and could see Jap fishermen going about their tasks. Some of them waved briefly. I took pictures with a little pocket camera.

About 1245 we came to a lighthouse which we identified on our maps as one east of Tokyo bay. We turned right and almost immediately saw the bay ahead. But we were a little south of our intended course and flew over an air field. Ack-ack blasted at us immediately so Mac hit the deck and dodged behind a hill. Campbell quickly checked his maps and said the ack-ack was a godsend because it enabled him to get a final accurate checkpoint before making our run over the target.

Mac pushed the throttles ahead and we roared up to 1500 feet straight out over the bay to the naval base. Bourgeois called for bomb doors open and then dropped a 500-pounder. Looking back I saw a big ship loading crane fly into the sky and then break into a thousand pieces.

Bourgeois dropped two more 500-pounders. A floating dry dock in which a merchant ship was being converted into an aircraft carrier suddenly toppled onto its side like a toy boat in a bath tub. Nearby workshops exploded. It seemed like there were hundreds of the close-packed machine shops so they also got our fourth and last bomb, a 500-pounder which broke apart into 120 incendiaries.

I didn't have much to do so I put aside a sandwich, got out my camera, and took pictures. These have been widely used. They

Although most crew members had cameras with them on the raid, only one man, Lt. Knobloch, returned with photographs taken in the air over Japan. Shown above is the naval base at Yokosuka just before "Bombs away!" The damage inflicted by this crew included an aircraft carrier in drydock.

were the only combat photos to come out of the Tokyo raid. Other cameras either didn't work, were forgotten, or got lost later. I guess that makes me the official Tokyo Raid combat cameraman.

When Bourgeois snapped the bomb doors shut, Mac made a sharp left turn and headed southeast back to sea to throw the

Japs off guard. Fifty miles out, we swung southwest. We followed the Japanese coastline, rounded the southern tip of the islands then headed due west for China. Because of head winds we never expected to make land. We figured we would run out of gas somewhere over the China Sea.

About 4 o'clock in the afternoon we ran into a heavy storm. It got dark early. We were lost in a fog and darkness. We kept flying straight ahead in and out of clouds, hoping it would soon clear up. I kept on eating. "Might as well die happy," I told Mac. He didn't think so. His mind was on the gas supply and the strong possibility of a night ditching at sea.

"I hope Columbus was right and if you go far west you get to the far east," Bourgeois said over the interphone.

"Maybe we'll come down in England," Williams said hopefully.

About 10 P.M. all four gas tanks registered empty. We went on for another ten minutes. Mac turned on the automatic pilot and called us amidships, over the escape hatch.

"We're at 6300 feet," Mac said. "If we jump quickly we may be able to land together."

Or drown together, I thought.

Williams was to go first. We all said goodbye. I wish I had a picture of us. We had five long, long faces.

Williams eased through the hatch. His head vanished. Then popped up again. "Well, goodbye," he said. Again his head vanished. Then up again. He grinned. "Well, goodbye," he said.

"Goodbye for the last time," I said. I pretended I was going to step on his head. This time he went for good.

Mac and I helped Bourgeois through the hatch, then Campbell. I squeezed into the hole. As I shoved downward I could see Mac's feet coming after me. I let go and fell. Out into the fog and rain. Somewhere below was China or the China Sea, none of us knew which.

"One thousand and one," I said after I dropped.

I pulled the "D" ring on the 'chute. Nothing seemed to happen and then there was a tremendous jerk. "I pulled too soon and snagged the plane's tail," I thought. I was scared.

But it was all over in a few seconds. I felt myself swinging back and forth in the rain. The 'chute was free after all. I was so happy to be alive I forgot about where I might land.

I drifted down silently through the clouds. I looked for the 'chutes of the other four men in the blackness but couldn't see them. I shouted. Only the occasional swish of the silk canopy above me answered.

The clouds parted. Below was the most welcome sight a man ever saw—two silver ribbons. They meant land! We had made China after all. A river and a wide highway, I thought. I reached up to spill the air from my canopy and then, bang, I hit the ground.

I must have been only 50 feet or so above the ground when I saw the silver ribbons. Instead of being a wide river and a highway they were two small creeks running along a rice paddy. I was in the field in six inches of mud and water. I couldn't complain, though. If I ever have to jump again, I'll be grateful to have a rice paddy for a landing.

I unsnapped my 'chute and hid it along a creek bank. It probably made its finder a rich man. My gun and belt had slipped off my hips when my 'chute snapped open. But over my shoulder I still had a bag with flashlight, extra ammunition, and first aid kit. I was wearing my flying coveralls and jacket.

I dug out the light and flashed it, hoping to get an answer from my buddies. Seven lights answered. It didn't take much of a mathematician to figure out that the five of us weren't alone so I put the light away.

I started across the rice fields, stumbling through the mud. Every few feet there would be a little dirt ridge, and each time

I came on one I would fall flat on my face in the muck. Within an hour I came to a river. I was tired and cold. I decided to try to sleep but I was shivering so violently my head bounced up and down against the ground.

Lying there trying to keep myself from shaking apart, I saw a streak of light flash across the sky. Somebody signalling, I thought. I answered. The light came again, from down river. I walked that way and saw a man walking on the other bank about 150 feet away. "Hey!" I shouted. The figure halted. "Hey!" I repeated a little louder. No answer. I tried a new turn. "Mac!" I shouted.

"That you, Dick?" The answer was low, but was it ever welcome. It *was* McElroy.

I started across the river, but the water was icy cold and waist deep, so I turned back. "Have to wait until morning," I told him. "Let's get some sleep."

I found a stack of rice straw nearby, crawled into it, and pulled it over me. Fortunately, it was warm. I could hear Mac's teeth chattering clear across the river. Soon I was asleep. Mac said I snored something terrible.

I woke up about dawn. A boat about 25 feet long, loaded with hay, was coming upstream. A man sat at the rudder. A boy about 10 years old was walking along the bank pulling the heavy craft by a rope over his tiny shoulder.

Boldly I went toward them. I smiled. We had been told that if we landed in China we should smile when we met inhabitants. If they grinned back they were Japanese. If they smiled and bowed they were Chinese.

These two did neither. The man turned the boat out into the stream. The boy just bent over closer to the ground and pulled harder.

I found a small boat under some weeds, kicked out a seat board to use for an oar, and paddled over to Mac.

A mile or two down the river we saw a village. We had no idea where the Japs were so Mac stayed a short distance from the cluster of huts while I approached. Thirty or 40 men, women and children ganged around me, feeling my clothes and face. "Chiang Kai Shek," I said. It was the only thing I could think of. They all smiled and bowed. At least they are Chinese, I thought.

Our instructions were to be calm, so I pulled out a cigarette lighter. As soon as I snapped it, the Chinese vanished, as though they had been blasted away. I waited and one by one they came out of their huts. I kept flicking the lighter on and off.

One man, bolder than the rest, came up. I gave him the lighter. It was our key to China. The man took me to his house with the village following. From a big teakfood chest he took out a map and studied it carefully. The room was packed with people.

"Do you speak English or American?" a voice said. "Who said that?" I asked, startled. Everyone smiled and bowed. I went back to the map, thinking I was mistaken. Again came the voice. "Do you speak English or American?" I looked around quickly. Those in the room smiled. I thought maybe I was going out of my mind.

Then I saw one little old man open his mouth and say, "Do you speak English or American?" I pushed through to him. "I'm American," I said. "Say, am I glad you speak English!" He smiled and bowed. "Do you speak English or American?" he said again. Right then I realized that was all the English he knew.

The man with the map wasn't much help, either. I tried to ask him to locate the village on the map. Every time I'd point to a spot, he would nod and bow and smile. It was my introduction to the land of the perpetual yes. I don't believe I ever heard a Chinese say no all the time I was in China.

I gave up hope of getting any information from my host when I discovered he was looking at the map upside down. Nobody in the village could show me where we were or where the Japs were.

I walked out of the hut and back to Mac. We headed down river. Then a youth, whom I shall always remember gratefully, ran out and grabbed my arm. He shook his head violently and pointed downstream. He imitated guns with his hands just as we did when we were kids playing cops and robbers. "Bang, bang," he said. He put his hands over his heart, made an awful face, and fell over backward in a heap.

"Must mean Japs are that way," Mac said. Later we learned Jap soldiers were only two miles downstream. That boy probably saved our lives.

We followed when the boy started off across a field. After a mile or so we came upon a hut. A man in ragged coat and armed with a rifle jumped out and stood squarely in the path. On his lapel was a button which identified him as a soldier of China.

He pointed his rifle at us and snapped the bolt into place. The boy shouted to him. He let us advance. I didn't want to take any chances so when I got close enough I grabbed the sentry's rifle.

The weapon almost came apart in my hands. The barrel was tied to the stock with a piece of string. I pulled the bolt open. The breech was empty.

Mac and I still didn't have the least idea where we were or where the Japs were. The tattered soldier called a sergeant. The sergeant called a captain whom we could have hugged. He talked a little English and could read and write expertly.

Capt. Wong Nin was his name. He was commander of a nearby detachment and told us we were some 40 miles out of Poyang, which is about 100 miles northeast of Nanchang and 100 miles west of Chuchow—the base for which we were headed. Despite our early morning take-off from the carrier, we had not only flown to our intended landing field but had actually overshot it. And for hours we had worried about coming down in the China Sea!

We didn't realize how lucky we were, however, until Captain Wong told us we had come down by parachute only two or three miles from Japanese lines. The two of us wondered what had become of our three buddies who jumped just before we did.

Captain Wong led us to a village. He picked out the best house, which wasn't much of a place, and took over. He stripped off the doors and laid them on sawhorses for our beds. He went through the village seizing blankets from beds and jammed them to his nose. Usually he would make a wry face and throw them down again. It took him quite a while to get an armload of blankets that didn't smell too pungent for his American guests. Similarly, he went through the houses tasting soup. When he found some that suited him, Mac and I turned it down. I asked for some eggs. He brought me three, and I boiled some water over a charcoal fire and cooked the eggs in it.

We had tea to drink. It was by far the foulest stuff I have ever swallowed. I'm sure the Chinese make tea once a year, then add dirty water the rest of the year.

A man of 40 or so, whom I thought of as a boy, because all the Chinese were so small, coming only to my chest (and I'm only an even six feet)—took a shine to me. The captain said he wanted to wash my feet. I let him. Then I suggested he wash my shoes. He scrubbed them hard and placed them before the fire. Captain Wong and I sat up three hours talking while Mac dozed off. Before turning in on my door bed I tested my shoes to see if they were dry. The outsides were nice and dry, but the insides were small lakes. My energetic bootblack had set them before the fire filled to the top with water.

We were eager to leave the next morning but Captain Wong said to wait; two men were coming. A half hour later Sgt. Robert C. Bourgeois, our bombardier, and Sgt. Adam R. Williams, our engineer-gunner walked in. Only Lt. Clayton J. Campbell, the navigator, was still missing but the Chinese brought him in before the day was over.

The five of us set out on small shaggy ponies for Poyang, the nearest free China city. The ponies were so small our feet dragged on the ground so I walked most of the way. We covered 10 miles that way, then stayed in another village. All the way a hundred or more Chinese farmers followed us day and night.

The following day we were promised "big horses" which turned out to be sedan chairs. Captain Wong had a detachment of 100

The crew of Lt. McElroy traveled by boat, donkey, ricksha, sedan chair, bus, and train to escape the searching Japanese troops. This picture, taken by Lt. Knobloch, shows, left to right, Lt. Campbell, Sgt. Williams, Lt. McElroy, and Sgt. Bourgeois being escorted to safety by friendly Chinese. Thousands of Chinese were slaughtered by the Japanese for helping the American flyers.

soldiers who patrolled ridges on both sides of the route and also provided locomotion for the sedan chairs. When a carrier grew tired the soldiers would run into the fields and impress farmers. Soon the grapevine spread the news and the farmers vanished so the patrol would surround a village along the route and line up the men. Our captain would pick out the strongest and make them carry the chairs to the next village. I weighed twice as much as the Chinese and didn't like to be carried by men no bigger than boys, so again I walked most of the way.

We arrived outside Poyang late in the afternoon. There we were stopped and for an hour or more we had to wait. Wong gave us no explanation.

We could hear strange noises ahead growing louder. A procession wound out from the houses of Poyang, a city of some 300,000. At the head was a man in the first decent army uniform we had seen in China. He turned out to be "Brigadier Joe," a general. Behind him was an eight-piece band, the creator of the strange noises that had been bothering us. Behind were two men in American clothes, Pu Ching Hu, master of arts from Michigan University and clerk of the Poyang mass meetings, and a Mr. Chu, a graduate of Harvard extension in Shanghai.

The general welcomed us and told us to fall in behind. The procession moved back into the city. Then we could see why the delay. From virtually every house fluttered a banner saying in English:

"Welcome Brave American Flyers. First to Bomb Tokyo. United States and China Rule the Pacific."

Under the words were Chinese characters which Mr. Chu said repeated the message in Chinese.

The streets were lined with stolid Chinese who threw firecrackers at us as we marched up and down the streets for miles and miles. It grew dark, but still we marched. After a couple of hours we finally recognized the noises the band was making—they were the band's idea of the Canadian national anthem. Over and over again the band played it.

At last we crossed a river to Mr. Chu's house. The Poyang Catholic mission, which cared for some 200 Chinese girl orphans, sent over a supper. And what a feast! Chicken and mashed potatoes and pie. Of course there was rice wine. We must have drunk a hundred toasts during the evening. That was quite a night. I don't remember how we got to bed.

The next morning we went over to the mission to thank the sisters and get another treat—a warm bath in a real tub that belonged to a Father Meyer. Coolies heated water and filled the tub for me. I had just climbed in when an air raid siren sounded. We were told that the Japs were looking for us and were making retaliatory raids against our intended landing fields.

But the water was warm. The tub looked strong. Why should I run to a shelter? I didn't. So I spent my first air raid alert in a tub. It was very pleasant.

Later that day our two American-speaking Chinese friends put us aboard a bullet-spattered launch on Poyang Lake. The lake, 250 miles inland from Shanghai, or about half way to Chungking from the coast, was Jap-controlled except around the city of Poyang.

The launch sneaked through a slough bordering the lake. Once two Jap planes circled overhead. "Looking for you and your friends," Mr. Hu shouted.

The Chinese crew ran into the bank, jumped, and flopped into the weeds. They wouldn't come back until the planes vanished. We stayed aboard and watched from below decks.

The launch took us to Ying Tan and another Catholic mission. It was operated by Father William J. Glynn. This mission was also very good to us. Their help was to prove fatal to thousands

of Chinese, because we heard just before we left China that the
Japs had wiped out the city for assisting American flyers.

We were put aboard a train that carried us east to Chuchow,
our original destination, 100 miles away. The trip took a night
and a day. I could have run faster than the train moved at night.
Much of the day the train was under air attack, and we hid in
the fields between attacks. Machine gun bullets killed one man
and injured a woman.

We came into Chuchow eight days after the bombing. General
Doolittle, his crew, and eight other crews were already there
ahead of us.

After a week at Chuchow we rode evil-smelling charcoal-burning buses to Hengyang.

The Chinese there seemed genuinely grateful and tried to cheer
us by putting on a play. It lasted for hours. Of course, it was in
Chinese so an officer told us the plot concerned a man, wife and
another woman—old stuff that must be the same 'round the world.
The Chinese use no settings, and for us the play would have been
a flop except for an old stage hand. He wandered around on the
stage, breaking into actors' speeches to bring them tea, which
they would sip, roll around in their mouths, and spit.

An American ferry plane picked us up in Hengyang and
whisked us to Chungking. The Chiang Kai Sheks had us to dinner.
Madame Chiang served preserves made from something she called
flower of the moon. It was very good. Chiang made a speech, but
we didn't understand it, since he doesn't speak English. The
beautiful Madame gave us Chinese inscriptions saying we were
members of the Chinese Order of the Clouds.

General Bissell gave us Distinguished Flying Crosses, except
there weren't any crosses, since they had been captured by Jap-

anese who seized the truck that was bringing them up the Burma Road.

But medals weren't all that was missing in Chungking. Headquarters said the Chinese had only enough ammunition for two months. General Bissell kept a plane ready to evacuate on a moment's notice. Flyers were scarce. The Army asked if we Tokyo veterans would stay and help fight. I did and flew more than 50 missions in B-25's before returning to the States.

Chapter 20

TARGET: NAGOYA

FROM THE DIARY OF

JOHN A. HILGER

Saturday, April 18, 1942.

I will never forget this day as long as I live. At 4:15 A.M. we were called to battle stations and knew that we would not be released before take-off. We loaded all baggage aboard the planes, had breakfast and were waiting for developments when the cruiser on our port side opened fire on a small boat which had intercepted us. Word was passed over the speaker for all crews to man the planes for take-off since it was feared that the small boat had reported our position prior to being sunk.

Colonel Doolittle, flying the No. 1 plane, got off nicely at 8:20 in spite of the rough weather which threw sea water over the flight deck. The sea was the roughest we have had and when an aircraft carrier takes water over the flight deck as we did it is really rough. The other planes followed quickly in order. The sailors and men on deck cheered lustily when the colonel got off and I think they really thought it couldn't be done. Our mission was based on a take-off not farther than 400 miles from Tokyo

Crew No. 14 (Plane 40-2297): left to right, Lt. James H. Macia (Navigator-Bombardier); Major John A. Hilger (Pilot); S/Sgt. Jacob Eierman (Engineer); Lt. Jack A. Sims (Co-Pilot); S/Sgt. Edwin V. Bain (Gunner).

and our present position of Lat. 35°10′N, Long. 153°23′E places us 670 nautical miles from the point of land just east of Tokyo. Everyone knows that it will be a miracle if we reach the China coast because we have a total distance of 2,200 miles to the coast itself, not to mention the additional 170 miles from the coast to our destination.

Our plane was the fourteenth to take off and I was leading the final flight. My three planes were to go to Nagoya, Kobe and Osaka. My plane was to go to Nagoya. The take-off was not particularly difficult even though the gross load of the plane was 31,000 pounds and the deck run available was 460 feet. The wind over the deck was 45 to 50 m.p.h. Full flap was used and all of us had room left over. Take-off was 9:15.

The run into the coast of Japan was uneventful except for the sighting of one long-range patrol plane. He did not see us, however, as we continued on in and made our landfall at noon. We continued on a westerly course along the southern coast of the Empire until we reached a point just south of Nagoya. We passed many fishing boats and the crews always stood and waved at us. It was apparent that they weren't expecting us and that our raid was a complete surprise. Smith (Don G.) was flying on my wing but I had not seen Farrow who should have been on my other wing. He apparently lost us soon after take-off when we passed through a rainstorm. When about 70 miles due south of Nagoya we separated and I turned for Nagoya. All of our flight had been at 100 feet and we continued on up the east side of Nagoya Bay at this altitude. On the outskirts of the city we passed over a ball park where a large crowd was witnessing a baseball game. They still did not suspect an air raid. It was a beautiful spring day with not a cloud in the sky. The Japanese country is beautiful and their towns look like children's play gardens. It is a shame to bomb them but they asked for it.

As we started our climb to our bombing altitude of 1,500 feet, the antiaircraft opened up on us. I will never forget the hurt and indignant tone in Sergeant Bain's voice as he called over the interphone and said, "Major, those guys are shooting at us!"

The antiaircraft fire was moderately heavy in volume but very inaccurate. Only two or three shots were too close. The size of the bursts indicated it was from medium caliber (about 40 mm) guns.

We swung around to our left onto a southerly course and picked up our first target, the military barracks which surrounded Nagoya Castle, the military headquarters of that district. The first bomb dropped and nicely bracketed the barracks buildings, of which there were about 20. Sergeant Eierman saw many intense fires start among them. I quickly turned toward our second target, an oil and gasoline storage warehouse. We saw the bombs hit that target but because it was a large building with a high roof and the bombs went on through, we did not see any fire immediately.

Our third target was an arsenal, a tremendous building with a high, arched roof. Macia could have hit it with his eyes shut. By this time the air was thick with black puffs of smoke from anti-aircraft and fires were starting on the ground behind us.

Our fourth and last target was one that I had been waiting to take a crack at ever since this war started. It was the Mitsubishi Aircraft Works. It turns out a bi-motored medium bomber very similar to the B-25. The main building was about 250 yds. square. Macia hit it dead center and if there is anything in that building that is inflammable, it is probably still burning.

After dropping our last bomb, we dropped down almost to the water and flew due south. When we were 30 miles from Nagoya and just before we cleared the headland which marks the end of the bay, we looked back and saw a huge column of oily black smoke standing over the city. Our bombs had started their work.

The flight from Nagoya to the China Coast was made out of sight of land and was uneventful with the exception of sighting six Jap cruisers and having our left engine start acting up. The

low rpm cooled the engines excessively, and unless they were
speeded up occasionally, they would backfire through the intake
and scare you out of a year's growth.

Just at dark and about one hour off the China Coast we ran
into zero-zero weather and went on instruments. I had a little
premonition then as to what was waiting for us and I was right.
As we crossed the coast and continued inland the weather got
worse with heavy driving rain and zero visibility. I passed the
word for everyone to prepare to bail out and got ready myself.
At 1920 (Chungking time) Macia estimated that we were over
our objective in unoccupied China, Chuchow Chuhsien, and I
gave the order to bail out. Everyone went out promptly and with
no excitement. I've never been as lonesome in my life as I was
when I looked back and found I was all alone in the plane. I
trimmed the plane for level flight and slid my seat back to get out.
I had a little trouble getting between the armor plate but finally
managed it and picked up my musette bag which the other fellows had laid out for me. I sat down on the edge of the escape
hatch, leaned over and let go.

At the time I left the airplane it was still running like a clock
and we had some 40 gallons of our original 1150 gallons of gasoline left. We had been in the air 13 hours and 5 minutes and
flown a distance of 2,300 statute miles. When I pulled the rip
cord I thought someone had dropped the ceiling on me. My breath
was knocked out of me and I saw enough stars to keep the movie
industry running for ten years. I fought to recover consciousness
and when I did I found I had lost my musette bag with all my
rations, matches and whiskey but still had my gun and canteen
full of water. I had a terrific pain in my left groin and soon found
that in crawling between the armor plate I had unfastened my
right leg strap. As a result I had slipped down in my harness and
the breast strap had socked me under the chin and then hit me in

the nose so that I had a bleeding nose along with my other worries.

We had jumped at 8,500 feet, and it must have taken me a minute and a half before I saw what I thought was a hole in the overcast. I steered for it and hit it but instead of a hole it turned out to be a mountain peak. I hit with a terrific wallop and was again knocked colder than a turkey. When I recovered I found I had torn down two pine trees about two inches in diameter and was lying on a 45° slope with my chute hung in the trees. It was very dark and the rain was pouring down. The wind was blowing quite hard and since I had lost my flashlight, I decided to stay right where I was for the night.

Although my left wrist and hand were badly sprained and my back was wrenched, I managed to cut my chute down and crawl to a small shelf above me on the slope. I made a tent of part of my 'chute by spreading it over two bushes and rolled up the rest of it and went to sleep. My last thought before sleeping was that I was very lucky to hit such rough terrain and not break or sprain an ankle in landing.

Sunday, April 19, 1942.

I spent a horrible night last night. I awakened when the wind died down and could hear what sounded like surf on three sides of me. That meant the other four fellows were out in the ocean. The last thing I had seen on leaving the plane was two life jackets near the hatch. This thought kept me awake all night and it was not until more than an hour after daylight when the fog cleared that I discovered a beautiful flat valley below me and a tumbling mountain stream on either side, that had given me the illusion of surf. Columbus was never happier with a discovery than I was at that moment.

There was a small Chinese village in the valley just at the foot of the peak on which I had landed and as I started toward it the villagers saw my parachute and started up the mountain. I did not know exactly where I was but hoped that I was not in occupied territory. When I met the villagers, I found myself among the people Pearl Buck writes about. The leader of the villagers was a story-book character with long black robe, stringy beard and mustache and a black skull cap. They did not know who I was but their smiles told me that I was among friends and welcome. I found out that afternoon that I was the only white man they had ever seen.

I had landed in the China of a thousand years ago and the farmers in the valley were plowing their fields with wooden plows drawn by water buffalo. They wore the same cone-shaped straw hats and palm-fiber raincoats which their ancestors have worn for hundreds of years. They offered me food but I refused as politely as I could and tried to let them know I wanted to get a train or to a telephone. After much picture drawing and sign language and sound effects, one Chinese boy got the idea and set out with me to get to a telephone. Every mile or so we would pass a small village and he would proudly exhibit me to his friends. At every stop they offered me tea and food and their hot tea kept me going.

We hit a road about ten feet wide by this time and I was just about all in when an antiquated truck, loaded with soldiers, came around a bend in the road. They were out looking for Jap parachutists and jumped out of the truck when they saw us, with their machine guns aimed straight at me. My poor guide jumped in front of me and started jabbering excitedly trying to tell them who I was but all the time the whole truck load of soldiers were jabbering for us to get out of the way. I'm sure he felt he didn't have long to live but was going to try to save me nevertheless.

Finally one of the officers recognized my insignia and my troubles were over. I told them by pictures and signs where the rest of my crew should be and they organized searching parties and then started me toward their barracks. The barracks were twelve miles from where I had landed.

After resting at the barracks for a while and eating some of their native pastry (which I discovered later was made of dog meat and fat) we started for a walled village about ten miles distant Kuang Feng. Because I was injured they insisted that I ride in a ricksha. The streets were of rough cobblestone and at every jolt I felt as if I were about to shake a lung loose.

Kuang Feng was the kind of Chinese city I had read about but never really believed existed. More than 1,500 years old, it has a high wall about the entire city with towering pagodas at the entry gates. The streets were about 8 feet wide and paved with cobblestones worn smooth by centuries of bare feet. Just outside the city I met Sims, my co-pilot, Macia and Sergeant Eierman, and the officials now proceeded to have an impromptu parade. They regarded us as heroes and word had spread via the grapevine so that the entire town had turned out. We ended up at the mayor's quarters, and after cleaning up they took us to our sleeping quarters. The bed was made of woven rope springs with a straw mat for a mattress, but I think it was the best I have ever slept on. About 6 that evening they waked us and brought us the evening meal. It was fried eggs, a meat-and-vegetable dish similar to chow mein and rice. We had constantly at hand drinks made of boiling water, canned milk and sugar. My back and hand were giving me a lot of trouble and even though I couldn't sit up or lie down unassisted I still got a good night's sleep on the straw pad. All of us went to sleep that night with a lot of respect for the Chinese people. Their honesty, willingness to help and hospitality were unequaled by anything we have ever seen.

Everywhere the Tokyo raiders went, they were greeted by friendly Chinese who proudly escorted them to the next village along their escape routes. The Americans shown here are, left to right, Lt. Macia, Lt. Sims, S/Sgt. Eierman, and Major Hilger. The photo was taken by the fifth member of the crew, Sgt. Bain.

Monday, April 20, 1942.

Sergeant Bain came in during the night and we all felt better now because our crew is complete. We had eggs again for breakfast and then another parade through the streets. We started by motor to Shangjao to call on the Commanding General of the 3rd War Zone at about 10 in the morning.

After spending a day at the military headquarters and having many good meals and meeting many fine Chinese officers we finally got aboard a train for Chuchow where we were scheduled to meet the rest of our outfit. The train was slow and rattled and jerked but we all agreed it was the finest night's sleep we had ever had.

We arrived at Chuchow about daybreak and were immediately whisked out to the quarters near the airport where our gang was to stay. I was never so glad to see anyone in my life as I was to see Jones, Greening, Bower and all their crew members. It was like a homecoming and we were all as happy as kids. There's nothing like a familiar face in a foreign country.

Tuesday, April 21, 1942.

Promptly at 6:00 the air raid siren just outside our window screamed its warning and we were all loaded aboard cars and hustled to a new air raid shelter just out of town. It is near the air station quarters and is a big cave cut into solid sandstone. Since this is my first air raid I want to stand outside and watch the planes but I am promptly pulled inside by the interpreter.

The Japanese knew that we have landed somewhere in the vicinity and they are frantically searching for our planes. We hear the bombs go on the airdrome and learn later that of 40 bombs dropped, 22 were duds.

While we were in the shelter the interpreter read the news to us. The Japs admitted that our raid did great damage. The Chinese press has played up our flight and all of us have suddenly become heroes to the Chinese people. The editorials in the papers say such good things about us that we wonder if they really mean us.

The raid continued most of the day and we had lunch in the shelter. Later in the afternoon I called on the Station C.O., Major Chen, and told him the technical details of our foray. As usual that straw pad felt mighty good at night, even to my sore back.

Wednesday, April 21 to Monday, April 27.

Things have moved so fast that I must consolidate a few days to catch up. Every day but Sunday, which had very bad weather, the Japs kept us in the air raid shelter practically all day.

On Wednesday some of us inspected the local grammar school. The children were clean, intelligent, and well disciplined. They are not much different from our own children except that they are better behaved. They make us feel like heels because every time we pass them on the street they stop and stand at rigid attention until we are past. The papers have written us up as such great heroes that we are almost believing we are.

On Saturday the Station C.O. gave us a dinner in our honor. My friend from Shangjao, Lt. General Tang, chief of artillery, was the principal speaker. He paid us high compliment and really made us welcome.

The Colonel and his gang arrived Sunday. They landed near Hangchow Bay and it's five days travel from there. They were all in good shape and were as glad to see us as we were to see them. They make 56 men unaccounted for.

The first pilots and crews accounted for thus far are Col. Doolittle, myself, Greening, Jones, Bower, McElroy, Holstrom, Gray, Joyce, Smith, Watson and Lawson. We have definite word of three dead and six captured by the Japs. However, not one plane was shot down in Japan and all were flown to their approximate destination except one which went to Siberia. We hear that the crew has been interned.

The incoming crews bring stories of successful attacks against the targets. Great damage has been done to their manufacturing plants and oil-storage depots. McElroy, single-handed, made a shambles of the Yokosuka Naval Yard. That will hurt them. All our bombs worked perfectly and we understand that the five principal cities of Japan—Tokyo, Yokohama, Nagoya, Osaka and Kobe—burned for two days. As a result of our bombing we hear they relieved all the high ranking officers of the aircraft warning service and demanded a reorganization of the air force.

On Monday, Col. Doolittle and I went to Shangjao to inspect the airfield and call on the commander-in-chief of the 3rd War Zone, General Kou. He had us, along with four Russian military advisors, to dinner that evening. It was an excellent dinner and was well lubricated by brandy which we all agreed was the best we had ever had. If you don't think it is difficult to carry on a conversation through two interpreters, just try it some time.

Twenty of our gang left on Saturday for Kweilin where they are to wait for us and then we will all fly to Chungking.

After the dinner at General Kou's house Monday night he quietly gave Col. Doolittle $20,000 Chinese money. He explained that it was to replace a few of the things we had lost in our ships. They cannot do enough for us and I haven't spent a cent since I have been in China. They are fine people and we all agree that we want to fight for them.

Tuesday, April 28.

The Chinese rainy season has started and all this morning was a constant downpour.

At 3 in the afternoon, Col. Doolittle and I went to Gen. Tang's home for tea. He had a guard on honor for us and we felt quite important. His wife was the first Chinese lady to whom we have been introduced. She was very charming and very beautiful.

After tea we witnessed a demonstration of one of the general's anti-tank units. They delivered very accurate fire at 900 meters with a 37 mm gun.

At midnight we boarded a train for Yintan and this is being written as we jerk along. The rest of our gang was aboard the train for Chuchow and we feel that we are now well on our way.

Wednesday, April 29.

We got little sleep on the train last night and the 350 kilometers we traveled by bus after reaching Yintan was a nightmare of bad roads and hard seats. The Catholic mission at Yintan had all of us to breakfast this morning and it was really good. Real coffee and butter that melted in your mouth. They also had the best drinking water we have had in China.

We reached Ning Lee, an ancient city in the very heart of China at 7:40 P.M. We are in the only hotel in town and it is pretty nice. The court yard outside is without a doubt the most beautiful sight I've seen in China. There is a small lake with a pavilion and bridge and the entire courtyard is shaded by an immense camphor tree which must have a spread of 200 feet.

The B-25 crews used every means of transportation possible to reach their destinations after bailing out or crash landing in China. This photo, taken by Lt. Sims, shows the crew of Major Hilger being transported by sedan chairs.

The full moon shining through completes the effect and makes all of us lonesome.

I am writing by the light of a lamp which is nothing more than a wick in a bowl of oil. You may give China oil for her lamps but you can't change the lamps.

Thursday, April 30, 1942.

Today we traveled by bus from Yintan to Taiho, a distance of 200 km. This part of China presents a rugged, wild scenery which really equals or surpasses our own Rockies. The mountains are covered with scrub pine. There are lots of wild roses and azaleas. Most of the country around Chuchow has oranges and grapefruit and they are also in bloom. The odor of orange blossoms took me right back to Riverside, California. The ride today was a dusty nightmare. We ended up by being delayed by a flood. A large river near here was flooded and we had to leave our bus on the other side and cross the river in an ancient motor launch driven by a charcoal engine. That was the most dangerous thing we had to do. We had to walk about three miles after we crossed the river but the officials at Taiho had a big banquet waiting for us and that made everything O.K. After the banquet we all had a bath in a real bath tub—the first I've had in China and it was really good.

Friday, May 1, 1942.

A ride from Taiho to Hengyang today was a repetition of past bus rides except that the bus today had padded seats. It makes quite a difference. We are staying at the air station at Shangjao. They have real mattresses on the beds and we have real shower baths and a sewerage disposal system. We feel that we are really beginning to live again. The plane arrives from Chungking to-morrow to take us back there. Ross Greening and his gang arrived there two days ago so things are probably well started by now. We have heard from all the crews but two now. They all had much the same experience as our crew. Only one man, Lt. Ozuk, suffered a severe cut on his leg. Lawson's crew was forced down at sea and suffered from exposure but they are OK now. Bob Emmens and Ski York are dead or captured at Heng-chang. That is bad.

China is beautiful tonight under a full moon. The night is

full of sounds. There are thousands of frogs and crickets and birds all making their own sounds at once. The only unpleasant sound is from the large mosquitoes and they will cease to bother us soon for our beds are covered with large mosquito netting.

So far we have ridden every form of transportation China has to offer and tomorrow we ride the most modern one, the airplane.

Saturday, May 2, 1942.

The weather was bad all day and we are still at Hengyang. All the civil and military officials turned out tonight and gave a reception for us. Before the reception they presented us with five of the most beautiful pieces of Chinese embroidery I have ever seen. They are all community property so I guess they will end up in a museum somewhere.

After the reception we witnessed a Chinese opera and once was enough to convince me. To our ears it was a symphony of discord but the Chinese seemed to like it.

Sunday, May 3, 1942.

We got word early this morning that our plane had left Chungking and at 10 o'clock it circled our field. That star in the circle certainly looked good to us. We had an uneventful flight to Chungking and arrived at 12:40. Waiting for us at the field were General Bissell and Colonel E. H. Alexander, the same Alex from March Field. We were taken to the quarters of the U.S. Military Mission. After eating the best lunch we've had in China, General Bissell read congratulatory messages to us from the President, General Marshall and General Arnold. He then read a citation from the President and presented each of us with the Distinguished Flying Cross. That was certainly something we didn't expect. Chungking is just another overcrowded city. Razor blades are 25c gold and Scotch whiskey is $50 gold a fifth, when you can get it, which is seldom. Cigarettes are 3c each so I'm glad I don't smoke.

Monday, May 4, 1942.

Today was an exciting day. At noon we went to the residence of the Generalissimo and Madame Chiang Kai Shek. Madame Chiang welcomed us and then decorated us in the name of the Chinese Government. She is very gracious and charming and as beautiful as her pictures. After the presentation ceremony, we had lunch and it was really a good one. All of us left for home impressed by Madame Chiang's graciousness.

The afternoon was spent making out numerous reports and we are still only half through. General Doolittle was promoted yesterday and leaves for home tomorrow then we will be here on our own. I think we are going to India and take up their fight there. I will like that.

Tuesday, May 5, 1942.

I saw the General off today so I'm now the head of the family here. It seems that I have done nothing but write all day long. It has taken us longer to write the reports on this mission than to fly it. The Army and Navy enlisted men of the mission are giving a party tonight for the men of our gang and it's in full swing downstairs now. It may not be good singing but it's loud.

After arrival in Chungking, the Tokyo raiders were decorated by Madame Chiang Kai Chek, shown here reading the citations. Earlier that day, April 29, 1942, Doolittle had just been promoted from Lieutenant Colonel to Brigadier General. Doolittle received the Order of Yung-Hui, 3rd Class; Major Hilger, at right received the Order of Yung-Hui, 4th Class.

We are due to take off for Calcutta tomorrow. Everyone is anxious to get going so we can get back in the fight in Burma. Things look pretty gloomy down there for the Allies but we can help change that.

Wednesday, May 6, 1942.

Spent most of today waiting for orders to take off. None came because of the weather. We hope to get out tomorrow.

Thursday, May 7, 1942.

Rained most of the day and we are still in Chungking. The Japs took Bhamo today so if they don't hurry and get us out of here it's going to be too late.

Got the best news of the war today when I found out that Bob Emmens and Ski York were in Russia instead of captured.

Saturday, May 9, 1942.

Finally got off for Calcutta today. Stopped off at Kunming and had lunch with the AVG [1] and then on to Dinjan in the heart of the Indian big game country. Elephants, rhinos and tigers can be hunted within twenty miles of the field. Our flight from Kunming was made across Jap territory in an unarmed transport which was probably the most dangerous thing we have had to do.

Sunday, May 10, 1942.

Arrived Calcutta about noon. It is the best city we have hit so far. We are all staying at the Great Eastern Hotel and are having a hard time getting used to having a servant at our elbow at all times. We saw our first movie since leaving the States today.

Tuesday, May 12, 1942.

When we arrived at Calcutta we had just what we were wearing. We have all been outfitted with British shorts and jacket and all looked like British colonials. We left Calcutta and arrived at Allahabad, the base of the 9th Bomb Squadron at 6 P.M. They were returning from a mission to Burma and we came up with them. They are doing a fine job here. The temperature here goes to 108°F but it is still the best climate we have been in.

Thursday, May 14, 1942.

We have had two nice days with the 9th Bomb Squadron and they're a nice bunch of fellows and have a nice setup here. They have regular GI food and it's surely good. We leave by air tomorrow for Delhi where we are to report for orders. I hope the place they send us is somewhere other than India.

Friday, May 15, 1942.

We arrived at Delhi aboard a B-17 at noon today. Met Clyde Box who is General Naiden's aide and he immediately took us in hand and showed us around. There will be no more entries in this diary because Ross Greening, Dave Jones and I are going back to Chungking on a special detail. Diaries are quite a burden when you move from one country to another because they cannot be covered along with diplomatic mail and the diplomatic mail is too uncertain between here and China.

NOTE TO CHAPTER 20

1. American Volunteer Group (Flying Tigers).

Chapter 21

AS WE SAW IT

BY

DONALD G. SMITH AND THOMAS R. WHITE

We started our engines just after Major Hilger, our flight leader, started his. He cleared the deck, and I was given the signal to ease forward and turned it up to 44 inches, but the ship failed to move. I checked again to make sure brakes were off, which they were, and looking out, noticed the men had not removed the blocks from the wheels, so we called the signaler's attention to it. They removed them, and it took about three more minutes to taxi from my parking position to the takeoff position. The ship was rolling heavily, and I could only advance as the bow dipped down and the waves broke over it.

I reached the position for takeoff, locked the brakes and checked the flaps, which were full. I was given the signal to start increasing the throttle, and after reaching 44 inches had to bring them back as the ship was listing too heavily, but on the second try, I received the signal to go. We gathered speed down the deck, and about 50 feet from the end of the deck the carrier dropped away, leaving the ship in the air, doing about 90 m.p.h. It was 0915 ship time when we cleared the deck. The wheels came up

Crew No. 15 (Plane 40-2267): left to right, Lt. Howard A. Sessler (Navigator-Bombardier); Lt. Donald G. Smith (Pilot); Lt. (Dr.) Thomas R. White (Gunner); Lt. Griffith P. Williams (Co-Pilot); Sgt. Edward J. Saylor (Engineer).

as soon as we were clear the deck, and Lt. Williams started easing back on the throttle and propeller control. The flaps came up, and soon we had a speed of 150, so we throttled back to long range cruising settings plus a little more so we could catch the leader of our flight who was disappearing into the haze off to our left.

Lt. Farrow, the last ship to take off, was supposed to be on the left wing, but we never saw him or at any time did he join the formation.

We were able to hold our speed with 1425 r.p.m. and less than the required 29 inches by almost an inch. Half an hour from the ship the weather became CAVU (ceiling and visibility unlimited), and for the first transfer of gas we put 15 gallons from the catwalk into the right wing, and 15 gallons from the bomb-bay to the left wing, as we were losing a little gas out the overflow. This stopped all overflow, and we continued to transfer from the cat-walk tank until it was completely used. After that we finished the bomb-bay tank, and in checking our gas consumption found that we were using the correct amount per hour according to the chart.

We emptied the turret-tank, and Sgt. Saylor poured the 7½ gal. cans into the tank, and we transferred it to the front tanks and the cans were thrown overboard at about 1245.

About 300 miles from the Japanese Coast, we picked up a Japanese Radio Station at about 1400 kcs. A normal program seemed to be in progress, and I listened to it at intervals for over an hour. As we approached closer I checked the position of the station by the compass indicators and found it swung slightly to the right, indicating the station was probably at Tokyo.

At approximately 1325, the station cut in on the regular program and an alarm bell sounded. After 45 seconds of ringing a voice shouted 3 words, and the alarm sounded again, this took place about 10 times and then the station became silent. The bell was sounding when it went off the air, indicating the power was out or else it was shut off in a hurry. That was the last we heard of the station, and although I listened on the frequency many times later I failed to pick it up again.

We sighted land at about 1350, and as we were north of our course we swung south and cleared the land at the entrance to Tokyo Bay. We were about 10 miles to sea, and saw a plane coming out from the Bay, and swung to a southwest course and continue on in front of us. About this time we sighted our first fishing boats, and as they were very small with only 4 or 5 men on board, we paid no heed. We continued on, within a hundred feet of the water, paralleling the southern coast of Japan. We turned into Nagoya Bay and stayed there until Major Hilger turned northward toward Nagoya a few minutes later. We continued on the same heading alone, staying close to the water. On passing an island, marked on the map as fortified, we failed to see any anti-aircraft defenses, and could not see any naval batteries. We passed 5 miles north of an airfield, but saw no airplanes on the ground, and one small plane flying at about 5,000 feet, on the other side of the field. It gave no evidence of having seen us, and we remained at 1400 r.p.m. and 28 inches throttle setting until we left the coast. Nagoya Bay was rather crowded with small fishing boats, none of which we fired on.

Upon reaching the shore we increased to 1800 r.p.m. and 29 inches and started climbing slowly so we could clear the mountains some 15 miles ahead. We crossed the mountains at 3,000 feet, held the same throttle settings, and passed just north of Osaka. We found a heavy haze over Osaka and the northeastern part of Kobe, so planned to stay at 2,000 feet for the bombing. We noted that the two cities were continuous and joined together on the north end of the bay. We passed a half mile north of the large patrol bomber factory, and from the altitude at which we were flying it looked like a very good target. We decided to continue on to our planned targets. This patrol bomber factory was a rectangular building, 900 feet long and 700 feet wide. It looked to be a rather old building, or was camouflaged in a dark color. The roof was saw-tooth and we could not tell if it was made of wood, or tile. No finished planes were noticed outside. We continued on, flying over congested railroad and highway areas.

We turned to a heading of 230 degrees, aligned ourselves with the steel works in the northeast part of town and started our run. We were flying as I stated before at 2000 feet and 240 m.p.h. Everything looked very much as the objective folder had shown, and we had no trouble in finding our targets. No anti-aircraft fire was encountered, and nothing hindered us from completing the mission. The bomb-release light was not working, and didn't light until the fourth bomb was dropped, so I could not tell from the pilot's compartment when the bombs were released. After Lt. Sessler called and said "door closed," a gun on the south edge of the town opened fire at us, and we dove for the water, pulling out just above it, indicating 325 m.p.h.

After reaching the water, we flew directly south, out of the bay and 10 minutes after passing the last point of land we turned southwest, paralleling the coast. An hour after turning southwest we saw a surfaced submarine a mile off the left of our ship, and there were two "97" pursuits diving on the craft. We stayed low to the water and tried sneaking past, but as we pulled opposite them they saw us and gave chase. We went to 31 inches and 2100 r.p.m. and in 5 minutes at 245 m.p.h. they gave up the chase and disappeared from sight. A few minutes later we saw 3 objects on the horizon, and on approaching closer found they were warships, the exact type unknown, but believed to be cruisers due to the amount of super-structure showing. We passed between the north ship and land, and the ship nearest us turned and tried heading us off, but we soon passed.

We passed through the strait north of Yakashima and changed our course toward the China coast, planning to hit the coast at

San Men Bay. The weather was steadily getting worse, ceiling lowering, visibility decreasing and scattered showers. We stayed in contact with the water, hoping to pass through the front before reaching the coast. Lt. Sessler noticed we were drifting to the right, so we flew between 5° and 10° left to correct for it, the first hour after going through the strait, and then we changed back to the original heading.

We hit the coast 25 minutes earlier than expected, and only 10 miles north of our planned point. The visibility was almost zero, and the ceiling about 300 feet and it was almost dark, being 2055, when we caught the outline of a mountain sticking out of the sea directly ahead. I immediately started a bank to the right, increased the throttles so we could climb and turned due east and headed back out to sea. The right engine was giving very little power, and the left one was back-firing, and as it was evident we could not remain in the air, we prepared for a water landing. We landed 400 to 500 yards off shore, south of the Island of Tantowshan Tao at 29°10′ north latitude and 122°02′ east latitude. The plane landed satisfactorily and remained afloat for about 8 minutes, giving us time to remove parachutes, gun belts, rations, Lt. White's medical supplies, and his A-2 bag containing surgical kit. These articles were placed in the inflated life-raft. The raft was on the left wing inboard of the engine nacelle, and a wave caused the raft to hit against the edges of the flap, puncturing and deflating one-half of the raft. The equipment remained aboard, and the crew, less Lt. Sessler who left the raft and swam ashore, boarded the raft and started paddling to shore. We had been underway about a half hour when a large wave upset the raft, all the salvaged equipment falling out and only one bag of emergency rations coming to the surface, which I was able to hang on to until reaching shore. We landed, after an hour and a half in the water, made our way up the 80-foot rock cliff and huddled together in the dusk for an hour before seeing a light across the valley, toward which we made our way. Lt. White hid his film, and as soon as possible inside the hut we burned all papers and notes we had on us. All personal records went down with the ship, which sank in about 100 foot of water, and we are sure it never fell into enemy hands.

Lt. White showed extreme coolness in the landing. By careful work and thoughtfulness, he was able to gather his medical equipment together and stayed in the ship until he had everything he could salvage and had safely passed them out of the ship.

After reaching Nandian, and Lt. White learned of the injured men, he seemed to have only one desire, which was to reach them as soon as possible and do what he could for them. After we reached Linhai, with what little equipment was available he set to work doing what he could for the injured men. He gave a blood transfusion with a syringe; crude as it was it proved to be very effective in an attempt to save Lt. Lawson's leg as well as his life. He remained there when we left, and has had at this time three hard weeks of work.

We remained inside the fisherman's hut until the night of the 19th and at that time we were rowed to the island of Nandian, and Jai Foo Chang, the guerilla leader, took us over and assigned 5 guards to accompany us to Hiahu, San Men province. On the night of the 20th we started across the island, night travel being mandatory as we were very close to Shipu, Japanese occupied territory. We hid in a Buddhist Temple on the 21st while 65 Japanese soldiers searched the island for us. The night of the 21st we embarked in a junk and sailed across to Paiki, south of Hiahu, this detour being necessary as two Japanese gunboats were lying in wait for us at the entrance to Hiahu Bay.

Lt. Lawson's plane had crashed on Nandian, and the same guerrillas had brought them to Hiahu on the night of the 19th. As all the crew were injured, Lt. White wanted to catch them and administer what medical attention he could, but the Japanese had found his plane and were causing us to use extreme caution and slowing us down to keep from being caught. As a result of this we headed for Hiahu on the morning of the 22nd, arriving there about 1600, when we were received by the Chinese Army. We learned that Lt. Lawson's crew had been given first aid, and sent on to Linhai where there was a hospital.

We remained overnight, had a bath and general cleaning, and on the morning of the 23rd headed for Linhai with an English-speaking guide and a military escort. We reached Linhai about 1000 on the 24th, went to the hospital, and Dr. White began work on his patients that we had finally overtaken. That after-noon we received a telegram from Major Hilger, telling us to go to San Men and pick up two bodies. We had left Hiahu, the district headquarters and felt there was an error in this statement. We conferred with the magistrate of Linhai and he called the magistrate at Hiahu and asked about the bodies. The reply was to the effect that the two bodies, along with the three living members of the crew, were at Siangshan, south of Ningpo, in enemy hands.

On the 25th Lt. Williams gave Lt. Lawson two transfusions, and we decided to remain over the 26th, Sunday, and leave on Monday for Chuchow. Dr. White remained behind and Corporal Thatcher joined our crew, as he was fit to travel. The night of the 27th we stayed in Sienku, 28th in Pantan, 29th in Huchen. On the 30th we were picked up at 1300 by two cars, 10 miles south of Yunghang. We had a big dinner and were taken on to Kinhwa and boarded the train for Chuchow. We arrived in Chu-chow at 2130 and made our way to the air station.

We stayed in Chuchow until 1930 on May 3rd and then caught a westbound train. We changed from train to bus at

Yingtan on the morning of the 4th and at 1630 arrived in Hengyang.

On the 14th of May at 1020 we took off in an army transport for Chungking, arriving there at 1300.

After landing in China many Chinese helped us in our journey inland, the following is a list of some of those people:

The fisherman on the island of Tantowshan Tao, who first took us in and gave us food.

Jai Foo Chang, on the island of Nandien, who took us from the fisherman and assigned 5 guards to accompany us to Hiahu and turn us over to the Chinese Army. These 5 men outsmarted the Japanese soldiers twice. Once by hiding us in the Buddhist Temple cave and the second time by taking us, not to Hiahu, but to another bay south of it. Two Japanese gunboats were blocking the route to Hiahu.

Capt. Chen Chieh at Hiahu, and the interpreter and guards he sent with us to Linhai.

It was mainly through the efforts of these people that we reached our destination safely.

Dr. Thomas R. White, turret gunner on Lieutenant Don Smith's crew, modestly documented his providential join-up with the badly injured crew of the "Ruptured Duck," piloted by Ted Lawson. Staying one jump ahead of the searching Japanese, White reached Linhai on April 24 with the other members of Smith's crew and began the task of taking care of their injuries and ultimately saving Lawson's life. His candid diary records not only his narrow escape but the unselfish help given him by both the Chinese and American missionaries who refused to flee in the face of the Japanese onslaught:

April 24

Went to hospital to stay and take care of Lawson's crew. Lawson in very poor shape with compound fracture of left knee and badly infected leg, right front teeth knocked out and cuts about the chin and face. Davenport not too good—badly infected cuts on right leg. McClure suffering sprained or possibly fractured right shoulder and nerve injury to left arm, small infected cuts. Clever has infected cuts above left eye, scalp and right leg, sprained right ankle and cuts on right hand. Thatcher, one small cut on head. The Drs. Ching, a father and son are looking after them. This hospital once belonged to a Britisher, a Dr. Bevington, who built up such a reputation for cures that even though he left 20 years ago, the place still shines in his reflected glory. It later belonged to the Church Mission Society and now to the Drs. Ching. The hospital is on a hill called "Hill to View the Heavens." We call it "Hill of Difficulty."

Went to work on the boys. Wired Chungking to fly some supplies down. Found some sulfanilamide and put Lawson and Davenport on it. Dressed wounds, wearing gloves.

The Chinese newspapers came out with news of our raid, causing much excitement. Deputations from the town, schools and all sorts of organizations came and brought eggs, cookies and oranges.

Wire from Major Hilger to pick up two bodies at San Men. None there but two or three in the hands of the Japs and Ningpo. Worse luck. Lishui and Chuhsien bombed.

April 25 (One Week in China)

Lawson had a bad night. Gave him two transfusions of 150 and 200cc by two-syringe method. The co-pilot, Lt. Williams was donor. Syringes clogged! He was better afterward.

All of us given Chinese names. I'm "Way Esong" meaning "great and powerful doctor!" It rained. We had several air raid alarms. Planes apparently on way to bomb Lishui, a nearby town.

April 26

Made a splint for Lawson's leg at Mr. England's and installed it. Very painful. Had a table made for McClure to get his arms up. Put a splint on his left hand to prevent contraction.

April 27

Gave Lawson an intravenous and he had a very sharp reaction. Running out of sulfanilimide.

Smith, Williams, Sessler, Saylor and Thatcher left via chair for the next town. Sent letters with them.

April 28

Cold and rainy. Lawson no better so gave him chloroform and operated to improve drainage. He nearly went out under the anesthetic.

May 1

Our gang reached Chuhsien last night. Heard one of our ships
went to Russia.

Lawson's wounds don't look so good. Put in sulfa powder. Dr.
Ching got us some more, thank goodness.

May 2

Rainy. Met Dr. Ding from Plague Prevention Unit. He brought
a little morphine and sulfa and a blood transfusion set. Dressed
the boys' wounds. I'm feeling better today but still very rheu-
matic. Lawson no better. Gave him another blood transfusion—
Clever and McClure, donors.

May 3

A Chinese professor, a Dr. Seng, arrived from Provincial Medical School. Deputations from Chinese Air Force at Chuhsien, girl
guides. Hwangyen Youth Movement, and a neighboring village
with about 400 eggs, cakes, sugar, oranges, etc., arrived. We've
had several thousand eggs given us already.

Checked on the river for possible seaplane landing. Lawson no
better. Afraid he'll lose that leg. Rainy. Wired for a seaplane to
pick up Lawson.[1]

Lawson much worse. Decided to amputate. Did a high mid-
thigh under spinal. Gave him 1500cc. blood for transfusion. A

Jap plane flew over. Changed dressings. Lawson not reacting very well so far.

May 5

Lawson much better. Very little drainage so far.

May 6

News of Corregidor's surrender! Drs. Seng and Ding left this morning. Lawson definitely more lucid. Changed dressings.

May 7

Lawson better but still running some temperature. Gave him a second pint of my blood. Felt this one a bit. Other boys doing well.

Air raid warning is old temple bell on hill beside pagoda. 1 - 2 early warning. Rapid notes means planes overhead. Slow, all clear.

May 8

Lawson looking somewhat better in the A.M. but bloody stump is infected. Changed dressings. Feeling somewhat shaky from the transfusions. Lawson much worse in the evening. Not eating. Gave him an intravenous and some morphine.

Had a big Chinese feast at Dr. Chen's—16 courses and 6 extras! Dr. Chen apologized for not having anything worth eating ! ! ! Got mildly lit and carried Davenport home on a stretcher.

May 9

Lawson some better but stump plenty infected. Did some dentistry and put in two fillings for Mr. Sharmon, a Welshman visiting the Englands. There have been several patients who wanted me to look at them but I've explained that I'm a military doctor. I can't take them except on consultation with Dr. Ching. They seem to understand and honor me for it. There is no other hospital nearby.

Had three more dentistry patients and three eye patients. Opthalmoscopy and retinoscopy by candlelight!

May 10

Lawson better. Took stitches out. Sulfathiazole arrived, started same.

The guide, Mr. Liu, who took Smith and bunch to Chuhsien returned with letters from Smith and Jones. 13 ships now accounted for. Heard York and Farrow in hands of Japs. Hallmark went to Russia, they say.[2] Col. Jimmy safe, thank goodness.

May 12

Busy A.M. Changed dressings. Lawson much better. Filled six teeth and pulled two on two patients.

May 13

Changed dressings. Lawson still improving. McClure having trouble with his arms. Checked General Du's son over for TB. The Tsingfu (city government) man is here every day to get us anything we need. The Tsingfu is furnishing everything, food and clothing and paying for the hospital!

May 14

McClure and Lawson both have temperatures. Poor Mac has boils. Lawson's temperature going up. Starting sulfanilimide on both of them.

May 15

Did some dressings. Lawson somewhat better but still shaky.
Looked over bombed area. Had news of the bombing of Tien Tai and got a scare the Japs were coming. News just a rumor apparently. Still planning to leave as soon as possible. The Japs are attacking along the Burma Road in Yunan Province and have 30,000 men in Hangchow. May have to leave soon. Plane flew over this evening.

May 16

Changed dressings. Lawson about the same but very upset from the sulfa. Stopped same. Mac's boils some better but still very uncomfortable.

Opened a boil for McClure. He's pretty severely knocked out.

May 17

Had news that the Japs were moving up fast. Plan to get out tomorrow, to be on the safe side. Wrote letters to Dr. Chen and the magistrate. Dr. Chen won't take any money for his services or expenses.

News not so good. The Army and the banks have already left town. Have to leave tomorrow, rain or shine.

Whatever people say about the unsanitary conditions of the Chinese, no one can ever complain about their hospitality.

May 18 (Written in sedan chair)

One month after take-off. Still raining but left anyhow.

Arrived Sien Ku late on account of wet weather. Porters spilled Clever out but fortunately no one else. Met by officials. Chief magistrate is down with malaria so we were entertained at the hospital by the Maritime Customs Officer and the magistrate's representative. Swell meal. Some of the officials left the feast early. Said they had an emergency telegram from Tien Tai. Looks as though the Japs are making time and gaining on us. The boatmen refused to take our escorts back to Linhai because they are afraid of Japs.

Wired the Commanding Officer at Chungking: ENROUTE CHUHSIEN WITH FOUR INJURED OFFICERS. EXPECTED TIME OF ARRIVAL MAY 22. REQUEST PLANE MEET US.

May 19

Up at 5. News that Japs have taken Tien Tai and one other town. Wire from Provincial Government to bypass Kinhwa. May have to go via Lishui.

At first rest stop Lawson's chair was 15 minutes late. One of his bearer's was sick or drunk. Walked the last 15 li. to Wonchi. Arrived 4:45 P.M. Met by officials, non-English speaking. Supper, dressings and to bed.

May 20

Up at 5 and off by 7:05. Dr. Chen telephoned around. We have to detour and go by Lishui which takes a couple of extra days. Hwen Tsing tonight over the mountain. May have car tomorrow.

Lovely scenery. Hills terraced nearly to the tops. Trail wound up and down through lots of villages. The trail makers had a fine disregard for the ease of travel for the wayfarers. Stones shiny by the feet of travelers. All travel goes over this trail. The only other way is ½ li from the Jap lines. Arrived Hwo Tsing at 4 P.M. Met by officials with banners saying "Welcome to American Air heroes." Boy Scouts and Girl Guides lined up with more banners. Taken to local party hqtrs. for a feast and the night. Very good food (and a very hard bed).

May 21

Up at 4 A.M. Four in rickshas: Clever, Davenport, McClure and I. Dr. Chen and Lawson in chairs. The ricksha coolies very lazy and always stopping for a bite. We stopped for tea about 40 li from Hwo Tsing and Ted bought some firecrackers. Had three breakdowns out of four rickshas. Mac's broke a rim 20 li from Tsing Yung (Lishui). I walked the rest of the way. 10 li later Mac's ricksha broke a spring and Dean's had a flat. Put the luggage in the one with a broken rim and Davenport rode in Clever's. Met another ricksha and commandeered it for Mac. Met many refugees. One plane passed over. Met outside of Tsing Yung at 1:30 P.M. by officials and conducted through the city to a house on other side for fear of bombings. Three trucks and a station wagon there, one a charcoal burner.

Clever and I dosed mosquito, flea, and bug bites until we spilled the iodine. Had pictures taken, then loaded Ted and Dr. Chen into a truck and we got into a station wagon ('41 Ford with bullet holes) and drove to Lishui. Ted had a pretty rough ride. Bed at 10:20, very tired. Dressed Ted's leg.

May 22

Up at 3 A.M. Can't go to Chuhsien because the Japs have taken Yungkong and Kinhwa. Going to skip Chuhsien and go south-west to Puchin. Off at 4:15 A.M. after breakfast. Got out just as the air raid was sounded, all riding in a bus which smelled strongly of camphor. Ferried a river to Lungtwang.

Long day. 260 k. to Puchong. Checked one hotel. No good. Spent night at Bank of Commerce . . . feast.

Wired Chungking change of plans.

May 23

Up at four, breakfast of cookies and hot water. Loaded and off by 5:10. Stopped outside the city for gas, quite a delay. Raining pretty hard. Several stops to clean carburetor. Arrived Chung-yanks 11:15 (118 k). Ferried river twice. Once it was very swift and full and we had a wild ride. Almost didn't make it. Another place the bridge was nearly under water. Rainy season starting. Long day—had lunch in the car—supper at Quong Sah, a small but quite modern town. They had German missionaries there soon to be sent to concentration camps. Also a USC graduate, a widow.

Finally arrived Nanchang 1:30 A.M. Put up at army hqtrs. outside city.

May 24

Slept 'till 9:30 A.M. Bath, shave and breakfast. Raining hard. Station wagon coming from Kian. Wrote letters. Bed bugs bad. Fixed machine gun left from Watson's ship—got one .50 cal. and the .30 cal. operating.

Late news! Colonel Doolittle made Brigadier General and got Congressional Medal of Honor. Hurrah! We all will get Distinguished Flying Cross!

May 25

Up at 4:30 A.M. Said goodbye to Fong and Beep Beep No. 1 (the
driver) and took off at 6 for Kian. Smooth road and new car,
averaged 60 km per hour. What a change! Beep Beep No. 2 is a
wild one. Takes lots of chances.

Stopped at Ling Tse for "lunch" at 9:30 A.M. Some confusion
as to destination. On through Curco and to the river. Charcoal
burning tug broke down in midstream. A second one put out to
take over but it didn't have sufficient power. Finally got both
tugs running and made some headway. Had a blowout and nearly
went into creek. Clever took a bath while we changed tires.
Passed a British colonel on his way to a battle who said, "Cheerio,
I must be off."

Arrived Kian at 6. Taken to hostel. Had a "foreign" dinner and
met the "station master" or "Field Marshal." The hostel manager
T. M. Wang, and several others speak English.

May 26

Slept late. Had an air raid alarm. The Chinese know from
their spies what type and how many planes are coming before
they take off! Also, sometimes their objective. A single ship came
over, an old slow attack bomber. Flew around over the city and
airfield for a while and then went back.

May 27

Crossed the Mi Kiang River by pontoon bridge and had another flat but no patches. Limped into Chaling and spent four
hours getting two tires patched.

Had tea, shot firecrackers and chased beggars. Bandits between us and Hengyang so picked up a soldier and two Mausers which Davenport and I appropriated. Finally got off and after crossing another pontoon bridge and a ferry, arrived at a hostel at Hengyang about 9. Plane due in a couple of days.

May 28

Slept late. We have to go to Kweilin for the plane. Airport bombed two days ago with over 100 bombs. Take a week to fix. Plane to meet us tomorrow. Thought for awhile we'd be here two days and then go. Take train tonight.

Had our pictures taken. Did dressings. Davenport developed another superficial skin infection and isn't feeling so spry. Had early supper and left for station via Japanese horse captured for use of guests.

To station—American locomotive and English cars. Toilet facilities are open window.

May 29

Arrived Kweilin at 8 A.M. Loaded us into a station wagon and luggage into ambulance and drove to hostel, 5 km from field. Scenery was rugged—vertical peaks and pinnacles. Air raid shelter is a natural cave—very cool. Plane coming tomorrow, we hope. Was supposed to come today.

May 30

Had an air raid. Twelve Japs ships circled overhead at 15-20,000 feet above overcast. Dropped some bombs north of city. I borrowed a sub-machine gun belonging to a AVG man in case any came low.

Called Chungking. Spoke to some American officer who said he'd speak to Gen. Bissell about getting us a plane. Rumors of a plane this P.M. Rode a '35 Ford burning alcohol. AVG man, Sasser, has a Ford jeep looted from Rangoon.

Saw a DC-3 come floating in to the wrong airport. CNAC and did not have room for us.

June 1

Feeling better. Cool day. No reply from wire yet and no plane. Local air corps chief called and stayed to dinner. Brought news we may get a plane tomorrow afternoon.

Linhai has fallen.

June 3

Worked on medical histories. Plane arrived—Army DC-3 with McElroy co-pilot. Davy Jones came along. Gave him my sword cane. Pilot named Carlton.

NOTES TO CHAPTER 21

1. A PBY amphibian was requested from the Philippines but the request was impossible to fulfill. Corregidor surrendered on May 6.
2. York and Hallmark's crew were mixed in reports received until the American ambassador to Russia reported York's crew interned.

Chapter 22

DESTINATION: FORTY MONTHS OF HELL

GEORGE BARR

The idea of a top secret mission had appealed to me but until it was announced on board ship, I thought we were going to Hawaii. It didn't bother me, though, when we got the word. Whatever happened, it would come out all right with Jimmy Doolittle as commander.

I was in the mess hall eating breakfast when the call came and was as unprepared as anyone else. The running around, the bag packing and the rushing to board our planes was real enough but, somehow, I couldn't make myself believe we were really going. Being the last plane on the deck and watching the others go one by one soon convinced me that the action we had anxiously been awaiting had already commenced. Little did I realize that of the eighty raiders I would be the last to make it back to the States alive.

Bill Farrow started the engines and Bob Hite crawled in beside him. Our rear compartment was sticking out over the end of the deck so Sergeant Harold Spatz, our top turret gunner couldn't load until we were pulled forward a little bit. Corporal Jake

Crew No. 16 (Plane 40-2268): left to right, Lt. George Barr (Navigator); Lt. William G. Farrow (Pilot); Sgt. Harold A. Spatz (Engineer-Gunner); Lt. Robert L. Hite (Co-Pilot); Cpl. Jacob DeShazer (Bombardier).

DeShazer loaded his stuff in the nose, I closed the belly hatch, and we pulled up behind Lt. Don Smith in No. 15 airplane.

Out in front of our plane, the Navy deck hands were swarming around pushing and pulling and it seemed to me that it wouldn't take much for someone to get hurt in all the confusion. Sure enough, before we could do anything about it, a sailor slipped in front of our left prop and the blast from Don Smith's plane blew him right into it.

It was an unfortunate accident and there was nothing we could do about it. The seaman's arm was practically cut off and he was carried away by his buddies. This accident unnerved me and it was all I could think about as we lined up for our take-off. I hoped it wasn't going to be a taste of worse to come. Little did I realize how tragic our mission was to become.

I spent much of my time taking notes, reading charts and watching while enroute to Japan. Approximately twenty minutes after leaving the *Hornet*'s deck, we spotted a Japanese aircraft carrier anchored in an area of heavy sea smoke. We had a great desire to bomb her, but we realized the incendiaries we carried could be put to better use on the Japanese mainland. Our course gave us a landfall south of Tokyo as planned and we changed course slightly for a straight run into Nagoya, our target city. Over the mainland we were cruising only about 100 feet off the deck. Up above us were scattered clouds at about 2,500 feet. I was scanning upward when I spotted three Japanese fighters above us and to our right. I pointed to them and Farrow poured the coal to the engines and climbed rapidly to get into the clouds.

A short time later we let down again to the deck and hedge-hopped into Nagoya. We had four incendiaries in our bomb-bay because of the nature of our targets. Up ahead we spotted anti-aircraft fire. Being last off the carrier, we knew the whole island was looking for us and ready with everything they had.

We spotted our first target, a battery of oil storage tanks and let go our first incendiary cluster. We had three more to go. To the north (on our right side) I could see smoke and fire coming from two different places. This meant that Jack Hilger and Don

Smith had found their targets. The air around their targets was speckled with ack-ack bursts. I saw Hilger's plane flying in a southerly direction and at a lower altitude than ours. (We were at 1,500 feet.) Then we realized the Japs were firing at him and coming close to us, since we were crossing his line of flight.

But our job wasn't finished yet. Up ahead I saw a nice long aircraft factory loom up a little bit to our left. Bill saw it, too, and without any direction from me, he changed course, lined the building up and we made a run on it end to end, dropping our remaining incendiaries.

I hastily got a course worked out as we headed across the bay and down the valley toward Osaka. All was peaceful in the valley. We were back down to 100 feet altitude and men, women and children waved to us all the way. We couldn't help but laugh at their innocence but I kept wondering what would happen if we had an engine conk out now.

We came in over Osaka and changed course to a more southerly direction, heading for the southern tip of Kyushu. As we went through the narrow strait we spotted two other of our planes. We presumed them to be Hilger and Smith.

So far, all had gone well. I gave the pilot a new heading and we started on our last leg of the trip. What had me guessing, though, was that one of the two planes we sighted was headed on a more northerly heading than ours, while the other had a more southerly course. We decided to keep on our own course and split the difference since we had had no trouble navigating so far.

We kept our altitude to a minimum while the Jap mainland was visible and one time struck a wave with our prop. It was then that we thought we'd climb a little so we could gauge our wind direction. Off and on during that last leg, we took wind drift readings and compensated accordingly. Then the weather started to get bad midway over the China Sea. We saw several water spouts which could only come from cumulus buildups and knew we would be in for something we hadn't planned on.

Bill Farrow had throttled the engines way back and I recall that our estimated ground speed was only 125 miles per hour as near as I could figure it over the water. We had dropped far behind the other two planes. At that speed I was visualizing us as making our landfall over the coast at dark. Should we speed up and eat up precious gas in order to get a visual fix when we crossed the coast? Or should we keep our airspeed as it was along with our good gas consumption and try for Chuchow by dead reckoning in the dark?

The decision to keep our airspeed and conserve our gas was made. As a result we made our landfall just as night fell. Partial identification of several lighthouse beacons was made which served to indicate we were on course. Bill Farrow, Bob Hite, the co-pilot, and I held a consultation and we decided to climb into the weather to clear the coastal mountains. We climbed to 11,000 feet and took up a heading for Chuchow.

Bill and Bob both tried to make radio contact with the ground on the frequencies we had been assigned but to no avail. We were on top of an overcast and when our time was up for Chuchow, we started to circle the area hoping we could rouse somebody below to turn on their radio beacons. There was nothing on the radio except static. We couldn't let down for fear of hitting the mountains so we held another confab to decide our next move. The pilot and co-pilot overruled my recommendation to fly west for 15 minutes and then change course to a southerly direction, which I felt sure would put us over unoccupied territory. This had been the unanimously agreed plan we had made aboard the *Hornet*. Bill, however, wanted to take a long chance of breaking through the overcast for a possible forced landing farther west, at the same time getting us that much closer to Nanking. I know how he felt. He wanted to keep the plane in one piece if he could and we had the gas to try so we flew west until our gas exhausted.

Just as the fuel warning light indicator came on we spotted a break in the overcast to our right. Lights of Nanchang verified my dead reckoning position. However, we had been told before we left the *Hornet* that the surrounding area was presumed to be Jap-held. Now we had no choice left. The pilot ordered us to bail out. Spatz went out the rear, DeShazer out the hatch in the navigator's compartment and I followed. Bob Hite was right behind me and Farrow last.

I landed easily in a rice paddy up to my waist in water. Except for a slight back sprain and a bruised ankle I was all right. The time was 12:55 A.M.

I wandered around in the maze of rice paddies in the dark trying to find a path. I finally found one and followed it until I reached a position that was guarded by wild jackals that the Japs used as sentries. To attempt to avoid them I headed out into the flooded rice paddies again but I couldn't by-pass the area where they were being kept.

Unable to make any headway I decided to go back to the path and head in the opposite direction which would take me toward the town. I followed this path for about half a mile to a river. The bridge that spanned the river had been completely bombed out, but I managed to get to the opposite bank by jumping from one piling to the next. In the dark, this was no easy task. Directly in front of me was a dirt barricade with an entrance. I walked through it. Just as I did, a soldier shouted something at me and shoved a rifle in my back. My heart stood still. Was he Japanese or Chinese? Was he going to shoot me in the back or what?

He didn't shoot but prodded me to a dugout in the side of a small embankment where he woke up some other soldiers sleeping on the ground. They searched me and then tied my hands in front and my elbows behind me and proceeded to march me into a nearby town. I was still hoping they were Chinese just doing their duty but when we got to the town I was brought into a room where there were about 10 or 15 Japanese officers in full military dress, sitting around a table overloaded with a variety of wines, whiskies, cigarettes and delicacies.

Lt. Hite is shown being led blindfolded from a Japanese transport plane after being flown from China to Tokyo. Along with four other Tokyo raiders he was sentenced to life imprisonment in a mock trial on October 15, 1942. He survived 40 months of imprisonment, most of it in solitary confinement, and he is now manager of a hotel in Camden, Arkansas. Three other raiders were executed by the enemy for their part in the bombing.

Needless to say, they were delighted with their captive. I was a rare prize. They immediately interrogated me through an interpreter. After refusing the food and drink and giving them only my name, rank and serial number, they directed me to a room where I could sleep. During the night, Bob Hite was brought in and the following day we learned that Farrow, Spatz and DeShazer were also captured. There were forty months of hell waiting for Hite, DeShazer and me. Spatz and Farrow were spared that. They were executed.

Author's Note: The aftermath for this crew is fully covered in Chapter 25.

Part III

AFTERMATH

The fortunes of war are always difficult to assess or justify and can never be fully explained to the satisfaction of everyone. On the one hand the Tokyo Raid might be termed a failure because all airplanes, including the one interned by the Russians, were lost to the American Army Air Forces. One C-47 transport and two Chinese fighter planes crashed while attempting to make preliminary arrangements to receive the group in China. Of the eighty men who went on the raid, three were killed in a crash landing or bailout. Four men were seriously injured—one so seriously that his leg had to be amputated to save his life. Five men were lost to the fighting forces because of their internment in the U.S.S.R. Eight others were taken prisoner by the enemy, three of whom were to die by execution and one of starvation. But the mission was not conceived merely as a raid to inflict material damage on the enemy, with the majority of planes returning safely home. The risks were great and the losses high, yet the psychological effect of the raid was to force a major revision in the overall strategy of the Japanese High Command.

For those who survived a crash landing or bailout and made their uncertain way to safety, the war was not over. A number of them volunteered to remain in the China-Burma-India Theater and continue fighting the Japanese; several died there. Others, including Jimmy Doolittle, were ordered home to new assignments which, for most of these, meant returning to combat in Europe, North Africa, or the South Pacific. A few of these did not return, and four of them became prisoners of war of the Germans. All of the men who could fly again did. For them the Tokyo Raid was only the first of many more combat missions to come.

The raid on Japan marked the end of five lean months when the American public had been starving for news of a single outright offensive blow against the enemy in the Pacific. It marked the beginning of the resurgence of Allied power in the Far East. Although New Guinea and the Aleutians would still yield the Japanese limited successes of a temporary nature, there would be no more big victories. After the Doolittle attack came the Coral Sea victory, then Midway, then the landings on Guadalcanal. From April 18, 1942 onward, the Allied view of the war in the Far East was never again so cheerless.

To the people of the United States, the news of the raid was immediately stimulating and heartening. The Allied press and radio reflected unrestrained enthusiasm for the daring and boldness exhibited by the 80 men who willingly risked their lives to carry the fight to the enemy. But the spotlight of war was soon directed to other scenes of action, and the raid seemed destined to be remembered as an interesting and courageous incident which had only passing propaganda significance and value.

But the Japanese would not permit it to rest there. A minor note of discontent in the United States because the story of the raid was not fully told, and some expressions of doubt that the operation had been a success, were suddenly swept away by the announcement that the Japanese had executed some of the captured airmen. A wave of rage swept over the country. What had been merely an incident suddenly became a symbol. One year after the operation its values were reassessed and reaffirmed and the American people were stirred as they had not been since Pearl Harbor.

Seven of Doolittle's raiders lost their lives as the result of their participation in the operation and several hundred Japanese were killed in the attack. But the greatest price in human lives was paid by the Chinese peasants who helped the American airmen escape the Japanese troops sent out to find them. Untold hundreds of humble and innocent Chinese were murdered in retribution for their acts of kindness; ironically, very few of them ever actually saw the Americans or even knew that Japan had been bombed.

When the war was over, four Japanese were brought to trial and made to pay for their parts in the execution of three of the prisoners. For all practical purposes, this trial closed the chapter on the Doolittle mission.

While the story of the raid itself has been told in brief by many writers, its aftermath has never been fully described. Over a fifth of a century has passed and classified files have now been opened. The truth can now be revealed and the many myths connected with the raid can be dispelled. But the aftermath includes more than revenge and retribution. The surviving Tokyo Raiders harbor no rancor and no regrets. They know they not only influenced the past but are determined to influence the future by their unselfish efforts to help promising young scientists of tomorrow. This part of their story also deserves to be told.

Chapter 23

THE CHINESE HELP . . . AND SUFFER
THE CONSEQUENCES

In the days immediately preceding the raid, Chiang Kai Shek had received reports in Chungking that the Japanese were concentrating their forces at Hangchow preparatory for a march south against Chuchow. This impending threat to his supply lines, especially the Chekiang-Kiangsi Railroad, was of vital concern to the Generalissimo. He objected violently to the use of the Chuchow airfield by the Americans because he predicted a violent Japanese reaction to an attack against their homeland.

The Japanese did react with all the fury and fanaticism of which they were capable. A three-month ground campaign was begun which was preceded by more than six hundred air raids to cover the advancing army.

As Chiang had feared, 53 Japanese battalions slashed their way through Chekiang Province where most of the raiders had landed. On April 30, the China Expeditionary Forces were given orders to "thwart the enemy's plans to carry out air raids on the homeland of Japan from the Chekiang Province area." To accomplish the task, the Commander-in-Chief of the Expeditionary Forces was ordered to annihilate enemy forces in the area and destroy the principal air bases. Thus was it plainly evident how extremely sensitive were the Japanese to American bombing of Japan proper.

317

Chiang was furious at the Japanese onslaught and reported in a cable to the United States Government: "After they had been caught unawares by the falling of American bombs on Tokyo, Japanese troops attacked the coastal areas of China where many of the American flyers had landed. These Japanese troops slaughtered every man, woman, and child in those areas—let me repeat—these Japanese troops slaughtered every man, woman, and child in those areas, reproducing on a wholesale scale the horrors which the world had seen at Lidice, but about which the people have been uninformed in these instances." [1]

Chiang was not exaggerating his claims. In describing the campaign of retaliation in his memoirs, General Claire Chennault recalled that the Japanese drove two hundred miles into the heart of East China to wreak revenge. Twenty thousand square miles of Chinese territory were searched; landing fields were plowed up; hundreds of villagers were murdered who were even remotely suspected of having aided the Doolittle crews. "Entire villages through which the raiders had passed were slaughtered to the last child and burned to the ground," he said. "One sizable city was razed for no other reason than the sentiment displayed by its citizens in filling up Jap bomb craters on the nearby airfield. . . . A quarter million Chinese soldiers and civilians were killed in the three-month campaign."

Typical of the reports that filtered into Chungking was one that was forwarded to General Joseph Stilwell by General C. J. Chow, Director, Commission on Aeronautical Affairs. Written by a member of the Magistrate's office in Hsiangshan, it documented the revenge committed against the innocent Chinese who attempted to help Lieutenant Dean Hallmark and his crew:

At about 6 P.M. on April 18, 1942, a plane force-landed on the sea off Numeachiae (2 li from the coast of Chiachsi), Chiachsi,[2] Hsiangshan. Yang Shib-diao, the village Alderman, heard it and went out to see when he saw three foreigners trudging on the road wet with water and in great distress. He knew at once that they had swam in the sea and tried to find out their trouble. But owing to the language barrier Yang could not get anything that would help. Thereupon, both tried to draw pictures of flags in the sand with their fingers from which Alderman Yang understood that the survivors were American Pilots who after bombing Tokyo had dropped on the sea. He found out also that two other members of the crew who could not swim were drowned in the sea. Seeing the importance of the matter Alderman Yang led the American members to his home where he gave them such comforts as were available. On the following morning Yang led by a secret path the American Pilots to the Magistrate's Office under an escort of some ten inhabitants hoping to save them out of danger. But unfortunately the puppet troops (one company of puppet troops were at Chiachsi when the town fell in 1942) heard it and told the enemy about it. On arriving at Paishawan some forty to fifty enemy troops suddenly came and took them all up. The American Pilots were sent to Macyang but the Chinese inhabitants were ordered to stand in a row when all of them were machine-gunned by the enemy. After killing the local inhabitants the enemy then went into Chiachsi in search for more. Whilst in Chiachsi Village they committed many atrocities killing and robbing the inhabitants. Alderman Yang though escaped death at first died of shock afterwards when his home and those of many other local inhabitants were robbed and destroyed by the enemy. On the morning of May 1, however, an enemy vessel arrived covered by an airplane which hovered above Numenchiao. The enemy then picked up the wrecked plane from the sea and carried it away. The bodies of the two American Pilots who had been drowned floated for sometime on the sea but were afterwards picked up by Alderman Yang and buried at Shatow, Chiachsi. Stone tablets were set up at the tombs.

We are sorry that what we had done toward saving the American Pilots was very little and at the same time our hearts burn with rage for the cruel deeds of the enemy who killed our inhabitants.

Further testimony of the brutal retaliation was furnished by Reverend Charles L. Meeus, a missionary who escaped to America in November, 1943. According to Father Meeus, the Japanese high command punished the entire populations of towns and villages along the trails taken by Doolittle's men, throughout Kiangsi and Chekiang provinces. A naturalized Chinese citizen of Belgian ancestry, the minister followed the trail of revenge across both provinces. He estimated that the dead numbered twenty-five thousand in the towns he visited.

All Chinese citizens had been given strict instructions to surrender any American fliers found in their territory, he told American intelligence officers, with a warning that "the very stones of your towns and villages will be crushed into dust," if they disobeyed.

"Little did the Doolittle men realize," Father Meeus said, "that those same little gifts, which they gave their rescuers in grateful acknowledgment of their hospitality—the parachutes, gloves, nickels and dimes—would, a few weeks later, become the telltale evidence of their presence and lead to the torture and death of their friends."

The irony of the vengeance-seeking was that hundreds of those massacred never even heard of the Tokyo bombing. Meeus had found the wreckage of Lieutenant Harold F. "Doc" Watson's plane, "The Whirling Dervish," near Ihwang in Kiangsi Province and learned the horrible acts committed there. "They found the man who had given shelter to Lieutenant Watson," he wrote Bishop Paul Yu Pin, Vicar Apostolic of Nanking in the fall of 1942. "They wrapped him up in some blankets, poured the oil of the lamp on him and obliged his wife to set fire to the human torch. They threw hundreds of people to the bottom of their wells to drown there. They destroyed all the American missions in the vicinity (29 out of 31), they desecrated the graves of all these missionaries, they destroyed the ancestor tablets in the various villages they went through. Cannibalism is the only terror they spared the Chinese people of Kiangsi."

The Japanese began their large-scale advance on Chuchow from the Hangchow area on May 15. Chiang marshalled his forces and initiated an elaborate "elastic defense" whereby light forces within the city walls were to engage the enemy and draw him on while heavier forces were deployed north and south of the city. When the Japanese were fully committed to an attack on the city, the defending troops would swoop down the mountain passes at the enemy flanks and rear. Aerial reconnaissance by the Japanese, however, revealed the concentrations outside the city and Chuchow was lost.

The Chuchow airfield, destination toward which most of the Doolittle raiders headed, was thoroughly destroyed. Using four thousand Chinese coolies, the Japanese forced them to work for almost three months digging trenches 3 feet deep and 8 feet wide at right angles to the runway at 120-foot intervals over the entire surface. It was this thoroughness, also carried out at Yushan and Lishui, which prompted Chennault to say that "it was easier to build new fields than to restore the damage." [3]

When the destruction and carnage was deemed complete, the Japanese army withdrew toward Hangchow and allowed the Chinese to reoccupy the area. An estimated fifty thousand soldier casualties were suffered by the Chinese in this campaign. Except to capture the airfields and demolish them, the entire operation seemed to have no other clear purpose. The Chinese people were to be taught a permanent lesson about the consequences of helping the Americans. To their eternal credit, they spurned both the lesson and its teacher. Hundreds of American airmen are alive today who owe their lives to the aid given them by humble Chinese peasants in the next three years of war.

In the closing days of April, while the Japanese were leaving no stone unturned to find Doolittle's crews, a tall, gaunt, dark-eyed American missionary was wending his way unobtrusively through the villages of Chekiang Province. He was trying to organize a new chain of Baptist missions to replace those lost when the Japanese interned Americans in Hangchow. Cut off from his church through the severance of communications with the outside world, this dedicated man of God was determined to carry on his missionary work, war or no war. Paradoxically, this devotion to his calling was eventually to lead to his name becoming synonymous with ultra-conservatism. A highly vocal anti-communist organization was to bear his name. He would be called "the first casualty of World War III" because he fell victim to Chinese Communist brutality and died in August, 1945 from bayonet wounds—ten days after World War II was officially over. His name: John M. Birch.

Birch, the son of Baptist lay missionaries, had been born in Landaur, India, graduated from Mercer University in 1939 and the Bible Baptist Seminary in 1940 and sent to Shanghai, China to begin his missionary work. After six months of intensive study learning the language, Birch went to Hangchow which he used as a base of operations for his missionary work.

Soon after December 7, when the Japanese began to round up all Americans they could find, Birch fled to Shangjao, two hundred and fifty miles to the southwest.

Three or four days after the Tokyo Raid, Birch was returning to Shangjao from a trip down river. En route, tired and hungry, he stopped at a crowded Chinese inn in a small village and had just seated himself at a crude wooden table to begin a typical meal of boiled rice bamboo shoots and meat scraps. From a corner of the room a Chinese came over and sat down silently across from him. When he felt he wouldn't be overhead, the Chinese whispered, "You American?"

Birch, startled to hear someone speak English, looked up and nodded.

The Chinese went back to his meal. A few minutes later, the Chinese said, "You finish. You follow me."

Again Birch nodded. A few minutes after the Chinese left and made his way to the river, Birch followed at a distance and saw the man climb aboard a river boat tied to the dock. Hesitating at first, Birch swung aboard after him.

"Americans," the Chinese said, pointing toward a closed cabin door.

Birch banged on the door and shouted in his best Georgia drawl "Are there any Americans in there?"

Behind the closed door five Americans tensed. It was Jimmy Doolittle and his crew consisting of Dick Cole, Hank Potter, Fred Braemer and Paul Leonard. They looked at each other and finally Leonard said, "Hell, no Japanese can talk American like that," and opened the door.

Birch was as delighted to see his fellow Americans as they were to see him. Doolittle quickly briefed him on their predicament and Birch agreed to join the group, help them as a translator and accompany them to Lanchi on the Chientang River, about halfway between Hangchow and Shangjao.

"John Birch was a fine young man," Doolittle recalled, "who was living 'off-the-cuff' and having a rough go of it. He wanted to join the American military forces in some capacity, preferably as a chaplain, and do his part to drive the Japanese invaders out. I promised to put in a word for him and get in touch if we needed him to help round up our men."

When Birch left the Doolittle crew he did not know whether he would ever hear from his offer to serve in uniform or not. A few days later he was to embark on a military career as an intelligence agent for Chennault's Flying Tigers. John Birch wrote in his own words what happened next. The following report has been recently declassified and can now be released:

REPORT ON ACTIVITIES IN CH'U HSIEN (ALSO CALLED CHUCHOW), CHEKIANG

On Monday, April 27, 1942, I received a telegram from the Chinese Air Base at Ch'u Hsien, Chekiang, calling me to go there immediately, and to await orders from the American Military Mission in China. I took the train to Ch'u Hsien arriving early in the morning of April 28, and went to the village of Wan Tsuen, headquarters of the Chinese Air Force at Ch'u Hsien.

At Wan Tsuen I met Captain D. F. Jones and many other men of the U.S. Army Air Corps group which had bombed objectives in Japan on April 18, 1942. I was told that Colonel Doolittle and Major Hilger had already left for Shangjao, Kiangsi, where they intended to contact, among others, a man supposed to have been appointed by the Military Mission as chaplain and secretary to the group of American fliers in Ch'u Hsien. Some of the Chinese officers then told me that Colonel Doolittle had already contacted my Canadian friend, Rev. C. T. Paulson, of Yang Kou, (near Shangjao). I offered to leave immediately, but decided to wait for a day at the invitation of Captain Jones and the Chinese officers. I stayed overnight at the headquarters, after acting as interpreter for a group of the aviators who entrained that evening for points west.

The following morning, April 29, Paulson told me by telephone that Colonel Doolittle had left with him two thousand dollars (Chinese) and instructions for me; he also invited me to meet him at his home the following day. I took the train that night, and received the following from him on April 30: (1) Two thousand dollars Chinese; and (2) instructions (verbal) to buy a burial plot at or near Ch'u Hsien, bury Corporal Leland D. Faktor and any others who might be brought in for burial, obtain all information possible on the dead and missing aviators, act in any helpful way as secretary to the aviators stopping over, accompany the last group to Chungking, and report to the Military Mission there.

I returned to Ch'u Hsien accompanied by a Colonel Huang from the Third War Zone headquarters, arriving on the morning of May 1. Until their departure on the night of May 3, I did my best to serve as chaplain-interpreter to the thirteen men who left Ch'u Hsien with Captain Jones.

The Chinese officials at Ch'u Hsien told me that outright purchase of a burial plot was prohibited by existing international law, but that Major Y. C. Chen, representing the Chinese Air Force, would like to present to the U.S. Army Air Corps the free use of a plot for one hundred years or so long as the Air Corps wanted it. I thanked them for their kind expressions, and asked them to wait until May 5; meanwhile (May 2) I sent the following telegram to the Military Mission: "Colonel Doolittle's instructions to buy plot received. Major Chen Ch'u Hsien air station offering plot not for sale but for free American use. Shall accept if not otherwise instructed before May 5. Birch."

The reason for my sending this message instead of immediately accepting the offer of Major Chen was my reluctance to arbitrarily change the instructions relayed to me from Colonel Doolittle. As to the international law aspect of the situation, I thought that the Military Mission would be completely informed, whereas I was personally ignorant, save for the remarks of the Chinese officers.

No contrary instructions came, so I accepted Major Chen's offer on May 5. He offered to supply the labor connected with the burial, and asked me to instruct the workmen. Hindered by constant air-raid alarms and air raids, the workmen failed to have the grave and stone ready until May 19, on which date Faktor's body was buried. The burial plot is located about one thousand meters southeast of the main group of buildings at the Wan Tsuen headquarters, approximately eight hundred meters south-southeast of the center of the village of Wan Tsuen, and is just south of the motor road from Ch'u Hsien.

As to information gathered: For what I could learn regarding Faktor, see Report on Death and Burial enclosed. Concerning those who came down outside of free China—unofficial and uncertain reports locate them as follows: In Siberia, five men, condition and identity unknown here; near Nanchang, five men, probably those in Captain York's plane, two reported dead, two captured, and one rumored to be safe in free China; in Hsiang San Bay, five men, two reported dead and three captured, identity unknown to me.

On May 18 a telegram came to Ch'u Hsien from Doctor White at Ling Hai, just as his party was leaving there for Ch'u Chou (Ch'u Hsien). He expected to reach us at Ch'u Hsien by May 22.

On May 20 I wired the Military Mission, asking whether or not I should accompany him to Chungking; at that time I could not anticipate the subsequent change of his route which kept him from coming by way of Ch'u Hsien. The reply calling me to Chungking reached me May 23. Also on that date the Chinese Air Force officers at Wan Tsuen turned over to me a number of personal articles salvaged from the B-25 which crashed near Shuei Chang, Chekiang, these articles to be carried to the Military Mission at Chungking.

The funds I received from Paulson are untouched; as regards board and lodging, I was the guest of the Chinese Air Force from April 28 to May 26, 1942.

Respectfully submitted,
(signed)   John M. Birch

Report on Death and Burial of Corporal Leland D. Faktor, United States Army Air Corps

TIME AND PLACE OF DEATH: April 18, 1942, approximately 7:30 P.M. in rural district near Shuei Chang, Chekiang, China.

CAUSE OF DEATH: Failure to make successful parachute jump from United States Army bomber lost in Chekiang under impossible landing conditions.

IDENTIFICATION: Identifying papers and metal identification tags either destroyed in plane crash or missing through activities of relic hunters after the crash. Body reliably identified through combined testimony of fellow crew members and Chinese officials at Shuei Chang who took the body in charge following the crash. Information lacking regarding exact age, home address, and relatives.

INTERMENT: Body removed from Shuei, Chang to Ch'u Hsien (also called Chuchow), Chekiang, April 30, 1942. Memorial service held at Wan Tsuen, near Ch'u Hsien, May 3, 1942, with thirteen members of U.S. Army Air Corps group attending. Body interred at Wan Tsuen, 5:00 P.M., May 19, 1942; military honors accorded by Chinese Air Force, represented at the graveside by Major Y. C. Chen, commandant at the Ch'u Hsien Air Base, and two hundred of the air base personnel. The free use of the burial plot was given to the United States Army Air Corps by Major Chen in behalf of the Chinese Air Force. The coffin was donated by the county magistrate at Shuei Chang.

Both the memorial service and the burial service were conducted by Reverend J. M. Birch.
                          Respectfully submitted,
               (signed) John M. Birch
                          Secretary to the U.S. Army Air Corps
                          group located temporarily at Ch'u
                          Hsien, Chekiang, China.

Jimmy Doolittle never saw John Birch again but he was grateful for the assistance he had given and relayed Birch's request to serve to the American Military Mission in Chungking. Birch was commissioned a second lieutenant in the Army Air Forces on July 4, 1942, the official birthday of the Fourteenth Air Force. Chennault already had a chaplain but to run his intelligence net he desperately needed old China hands who knew the Chinese people, spoke their language, were aware of their intricate social customs and could live in the field on Chinese food; consequently Birch never became a chaplain. However, for his entire period of service with the Fourteenth, Birch never lost sight of his original calling. Without fail, wherever he found himself on a Sunday, he conducted religious services, often at the risk of his life when behind Japanese lines. He served honorably and with fanatical dedication. Chennault, fearful that he would crack under the constant strain and tension of his clandestine operations, tried to persuade him to take a leave or temporary duty back to the United States. His only comment was, "Thank you, General, but I'll leave China only when the last Jap is gone."

NOTES TO CHAPTER 23

1. Cable to United States Government, April 28, 1942.
2. Chueh-shi, village on the coast south of Nimrod Bay, about 37 miles southeast of Ningpo.
3. *Way of a Fighter: The Memoirs of Claire Lee Chennault*, ed. Robert Hotz (New York: G. P. Putnam's Sons, 1949), p. 168.

Chapter 24

A DIRECT HIT ON ENEMY MORALE

Vice Admiral Matoi Ugaki, chief of staff of the Combined Fleet headquarters in Tokyo, was at lunch when the call came over his special military telephone announcing an enemy attack.

The bad news confused Ugaki. "At 1300 (1 P.M.) I heard various reports from headquarters that Japan had been attacked," he wrote in his diary, "but I doubted their validity, and had difficulty in making any plans or decisions."

It was the responsibility of the Combined Fleet to attack the enemy task force that launched the planes but he could do nothing now about the planes themselves. Ugaki recorded:

> I repeatedly ordered the 3rd Submarine Fleet, which was located 200 miles west of the enemy aircraft carriers to attack but no units came in contact with the enemy, and in spite of the fact that our primary purpose was to catch the enemy, the enemy's position was unknown. I did not know what was happening, and all I could do was order a pursuit to the east. Today I was very irritated when the sun went down at 1700; at 1600 I received a message from the Kirarazu unit that had departed to attack. It stated that the unit had gone 700 nautical miles without finding a trace of the enemy. According to later reports the attack planes were twin-engine long distance bombers, which took off from aircraft carriers, bombed 9 places in Tokyo, and dropped incendiary

bombs. Casualties were 12 dead and more than 100 wounded. Fifty houses were burned down, 50 were half destroyed. Kobe, Wakayama, and Nagoya were bombed and it is reported that one plane bombed the Nitsu oil wells in Niigata. The bow of a large whaling vessel which was at anchor at Yokosuka sustained some damage. Apparently there were more than a few planes, and it is not clear whether they returned to their mother ship, headed toward Siberia or China, or contacted a Soviet vessel which was sailing 20 nautical miles south of Ashizurizaki. However, the enemy aircraft carrier seems to have pulled back to the east and it is very regrettable that I missed my chance three or four times. It had always been my motto not to allow Tokyo or the homeland to be attacked from the air, but today my pride has been deeply hurt and my spirits are low as today I gave the enemy his glory.

The next day, April 19, Ugaki had more information and wrote:

One enemy plane was captured in Nanchang. It is reported that it took off from Baiel Island south of Midway. There is no such island on the map. The intelligence reports come from low-ranking Army officers who do not know English, have no knowledge of the sea and are unreliable, so I have dispatched an intelligence officer from the Navy. Anyway, it is clear that 13 B-25's landed in Chung-shui. Those planes might return from China and attack our homeland again. Since sufficient measures had to be taken, after lunch I ordered my staff to solve the riddle of the American planes.

Ugaki further wrote that day that he had ordered the Second and Fifth Fleets and all the planes he could muster to pursue the carrier task force but no trace was ever found. Exhausted and weary from two days of pacing the floor hoping for some news that the Americans had been sighted, he was moved to note that, "I am at the end of my resources. The enemy casts an eye of contempt at the clamoring Japanese. Thus we were invaded, but missed our chance to fight back; this is most regrettable." [1]

The reaction of the Japanese public to the raid was relatively mild on the surface in the first few hours after the raid. Reverend Bruno Bitter, a Catholic priest and educator, reported to Army Air Forces Intelligence after he was allowed to leave Japan that the air raid seemed to have little effect on the population when it happened. "It was just 12 o'clock noon when the alarm was given." he recalled. "Most of the people did not believe it, thinking it was just another drill. But when they learned it was a real raid, nobody could hold them back to go outside, to climb the roofs or the chimneys to get a better view. In other words, it was a thrill rather than a frightening event."

The chief editorial writer for the *Nippon Times,* an English language newspaper, confirmed this viewpoint. "The people looked upon the Doolittle raid as a curiosity," he said, "and they did not even bother to go to the shelters. The sirens did not even go off until the planes were over the city and the sky was full of anti-aircraft fire. I was out and saw the firing, but thought it was just practice, although it seemed strange to be practicing with what appeared to be live shells. Then I saw the planes and realized it was a raid."

The U.S. Ambassador to Japan, Joseph C. Grew, kept a diary during his ten years in Japan. His entry for April 18, 1942, reads: [2]

> The Swiss Minister came again, and just as he was leaving before lunch we heard a lot of planes overhead and saw five or six large fires burning in different directions with great volumes of smoke. At first we thought that it was only maneuvers but soon became aware that it was the first big raid on Japan by American bombers which are reported to have attacked first in Hokkaido and then, in turn, Tokyo, Yokosuka, Nagoya and Kobe. We saw one of them, apparently losing altitude and flying very low, just over the tops of the buildings to the west, and at first we feared that it had crashed but then realized that it was intentionally following these tactics in order to avoid the dives

of pursuit planes and the antiaircraft fire. To the east we saw a plane with a whole line of black puffs of smoke, indicating anti-aircraft explosions, just on its tail; it didn't look like a bomber and we are inclined to believe that the Japanese batteries lost their heads and fired on their own pursuit planes.

All this was very exciting, but at the time it was hard to believe that it was more than a realistic practice by Japanese planes. The Japanese press claimed that nine enemy planes had crashed, but we doubt if any were lost since, if even one had crashed on land, the papers would have been full of triumphant pictures of the wreck. They appeared too large to have come from an aircraft carrier, and they may have been flying from the Aleutian Islands to the new air bases in China. We were all very happy and proud in the Embassy, and the British told us later that they drank toasts all day to the American fliers."

While Grew was under loose restrictions in the American Embassy, Otto D. Tolischus, a reporter for the *New York Times*, viewed the raid from a different vantage point—solitary confinement in a Tokyo jail. Interned at the beginning of the war, he was interrogated continually for six months before being released in June 25, 1942 and returned home on the *Gripsholm*. In his book *Tokyo Record* he recalled: [3]

This afternoon, the air raid sirens began to scream, and the guards came rushing through the corridors to double-lock the cell doors. During the day, the cell door could be opened from the outside by just turning a handle. But during the night, during earthquakes, and during air-raid drills, it was locked with a key and could be opened only with a key. My friendly floor guard opened my door long enough to indicate to me this was no drill, but the real thing. He made a long face and shook his head. An air raid—a real honest-to-goodness air raid—was apparently something the Japanese had not counted upon. I felt like cheering. I had heard sirens during the first few nights in prison and had rushed to the window to listen, filled with the hope that this was an American air armada come to smash the whole town into smithereens, and the whole blasted prison with it. But every time

I had realized that what I heard was merely the siren of fire engines going by. Now there was no mistake. Soon I heard gunfire, some close by. It was an air raid! I listened for the bomb explosions, but could hear none. After about half an hour, the doors were unlocked. It was all over. But I felt much, much better.

It took some time for the significance of the raid to sink into the minds of the Japanese. The psychological effect was a creeping, insidious realization that, in spite of propaganda to the contrary, the confidence of the people was severely shaken. Toshiko Matsumura, only 13 years old at the time, lived in the southern suburbs of Tokyo toward Yokohama.[4] She recalled that she did not even know there had been a raid until she overheard her elders discussing it anxiously a few days later. "My people had always placed emphasis on spiritual strength and the medieval belief that Japan would never be attacked," she said. "As children we had been taught to believe what the Emperor and his advisors told us. It was a severe psychological shock to even the most ardent believer when it was announced that we had been attacked. The eventual effect was great but was not immediately evident. We finally began to realize that all we were told was not true— that the Government had lied when it said we were invulnerable. We then started to doubt that we were also invincible."

Within an hour and a half after Jimmy Doolittle dropped his first bomb, the Japanese Eastern Army Headquarters propaganda machine issued its first communiques for home consumption which were broadcast over the radio that day and appeared in newspapers on the next: "At 12:30 hours, several enemy planes came from (direction censored) and attacked the Tokyo-Yokohama area. However, they were attacked by air units of our ground and air forces and are now in retreat. The number of known enemy planes downed at present is nine. Damage to our side appears to be slight. The Imperial Household is safe."

Premier Hideki Tojo, furious over the raid, summoned Home Minister Michio Yuzawa to his residence for a hurried consultation. Yuzawa then reported to the Emperor and that evening issued a statement intended to allay the fears of the citizenry quickly. "The damage was fortunately very slight," he said, "and the people on the whole were not perturbed." The first hint that the people should expect more attacks was given when he said, "I believe that since the outbreak of the East Asian War everyone has recognized the difficulty of avoiding air attacks . . . (but) there was little to fear." [5]

Noting in its April 19 edition the "triumphant" actions of the Civil Defense Corps and the Neighborhood Association Air Defense Groups (five fighting organizations), *Asahi Shimbun*, Tokyo's leading newspaper, became the first to arouse national indignation for the raid. "While fleeing helter skelter to avoid the curtain of shells which burst forth from our antiaircraft batteries," it said, "the enemy planes chose innocent people and city streets as their targets. They did not go near military installations. They carried out an inhuman, insatiable, indiscriminate bombing attack on the sly, and the fact that they schemed to strafe civilians and non-combatants demonstrates their fiendish behavior."

A martyr to the "inhuman" bombing was needed and quickly found. On the front page of the April 19 issue of *Asahi Shimbun* appeared the following story to prove the bestiality of the American airmen. Naturally, no parallel was ever drawn between the Doolittle raid and the surprise carrier-launched attacks on Pearl Harbor. The story follows:

ENEMY DEVILS STRAFE SCHOOLYARD

One Fleeing Pupil Strafed and Killed.

The fact that one of the enemy planes that attacked the capital appeared in the sky above the (xx) national school around 1:40 P.M., strafed innocent young scholars who were on their way home, and killed one of them, is an act which cannot be disregarded as far as human morality is concerned. This action has aroused the indignation of everyone.

At that time, 40 first-year secondary school students had just finished cleaning their classroom and were about to leave the

Photographs of the crew of Lt. Farrow taken after their capture were used for propaganda purposes. The circular shown above, published and distributed by the Japanese, was spread throughout China. The text, translated from the Chinese, reads: "The cruel, inhuman, and beastlike American pilots who, in a bold intrusion of the holy territory of the Empire on April 18, 1942, dropped incendiaries and bombs on non-military hospitals, schools, and private houses and even dive-strafed playing school children, were captured, court-martialed, and severely punished according to military law." Front row: Cpl. DeShazer and Sgt. Spatz; rear row: Lts. Farrow, Barr, and Hite. Farrow and Spatz were executed by firing squad on October 15, 1942 after a mock trial. The other three men survived forty months of imprisonment, most of which was in solitary confinement.

school gates and return home when an enemy plane flew over at terrific speed. As soon as the workers (instructors) saw it, they guided the students to shelter. At that time Hinosuke Ishibe (age 14) rushed back from the gate and just as he was about to enter his classroom, the enemy plane which had descended to an altitude of 50 meters fired about ten rounds of ammunition at the schoolyard. One of them went through the corridor window glass and struck Ishibe in the right thigh. At 2 P.M. the same day he breathed his last in the arms of his teachers. School principal Ichikawa made the following statement:

"I feel deep sympathy for the bereaved family of Mr. Ishibe and can only be indignant towards the villainous actions of the enemy. All we can, and must, do is to vow to move forward on the road to smashing and annihilating England and America."

The attempts at reassurance continued in the Japanese press in order to minimize the effects of the raid and convince the people they had nothing to fear. The air raid alert warning was officially lifted on the morning of the 20th. The announcement was not made in the papers until the next day, however, with the caution that "we must imagine that, as the enemy did not achieve his objectives in the first air attack, he will make several more vain attempts." [6]

The Japanese propagandists knew they had to counter the visible effects of the bombs in the target cities. Thousands of people saw what damage the American bombs had done. Proof that the bombers had been destroyed was needed. Since no planes had actually been shot down in Japan, the orders went out to Japanese occupation troops in China to obtain wreckage of American planes at all costs.

On April 25th, the next Saturday following the raid, an extra attraction was announced for the second day of the Yasukuni Shrine Provisional Festival. It was an exhibit consisting of a twisted wing and landing gear tubing from an American B-25 and a parachute draped over a gingko tree in full bloom. [7] The authenticity of the display could not be doubted. The words "North American" could be seen stamped on the torn metal of the wings and "U.S. Army Air Forces" was stencilled on the parachute harness. The canvas covering showed that the parachute had been manufactured in June, 1941, by the Switlick Company.

Over two million Japanese passed by the display as they paid homage to their war dead during the Festival. At last, here was proof that the people need not worry about defense from air attacks. After all, the Government had said at least nine planes were shot down and here was one of them. What more proof was needed?

One last attempt to minimize the raid was made in *Shashin Shuho,* an illustrated Japanese weekly, dated April 29, 1942. The following story is a classic illustration of the propaganda efforts of an authoritarian government forced to rationalize its failures and prepare its people for uncertainties in the future:

PLANE OF ENEMY AIR RAID ENDS IN COMPLETE FAILURE

On the afternoon of 18 April, enemy planes suddenly appeared in the skies over our home islands and insolently bombed and strafed the Tokyo-Yokohama area, Nagoya, Kobe and Wakayama. This was the first attack by enemy planes since the Great Asian War began. Of course, the common sense of modern warfare led us to anticipate at the beginning of the war that enemy planes would attack us. When we received the Imperial Rescript on the declaration of war on 8 December, we were firmly resolved to protect our country from enemy air attack and in our mind we were already prepared to fight resolutely to the death in the same way as our officers and men on the front lines. Indeed, we had trained ourselves thoroughly, and when confronted with the first air raid we acted against that which we already anticipated, and fully displayed our true strength. Those of us who worked bravely to extinguish fires while the bombs were still falling were keenly aware of the fact that we were the "front behind the lines," that each one of us was "a warrior defending his country."

The enemy planes did not attack military installations. Instead, they focused their attack on innocent people and ordinary city streets, and dropped incendiaries and other bombs. While it has been the policy of our army and navy air forces since the war began to make military installations their targets, the enemy, who pretends to be always just and righteous has committed unpardonable crimes first by bombing our hospital ship and now by his present atrocities. The fact that the enemy has gone so far as to strafe our schools and fire upon and kill helpless children particularly reveals his true diabolical character, and we will not be satisfied even to smash him to bits. With deep sympathy we must also bury those noble ones who fell victims to our inhuman enemies. In order to repay the spirits of these noble victims who died serving their country, we must put into practice as completely as possible the training we have received from our war experience. Since before the war our enemies have boasted that in order to reduce Japan to a shambles it would merely be necessary to scatter incendiary bombs everywhere. They said this because their attention was focused solely on the fact that Japanese houses are made of wood. We must say that these are careless remarks, for our enemies have neglected the world-famous Japanese spirit of the people living in those houses. Proof speaks louder than theory. During the air raid the Civilian Defense Corps and Neighborhood Association Air Defense Groups, either individually or in groups, bravely defied the incendiary bombs that were dropped, put out fires, worked hard to prevent them from spreading, and prevented an increase in the number of victims while that number was extremely slight. We gained confidence from our regular training. We learned that when voluntarily fighting a fire *we have nothing to fear from incendiary bombs.* We also experienced personally that *bombs also should not be feared.* The loss of human life from bomb explosions was extremely small and instantaneous, and the number of victims of the blast effect was not as great as reported. Consequently, the number of people who fell victims to bombs was very slight. It is only natural that there be loss of human lives during a war, for to have no victims at all would be unusual indeed. We have learned from the blood of the noble victims that those who were felled by direct hits were just unlucky.

There is no country which has been defeated only by air raids, regardless of how many it sustained. Moreover, our country will not be reduced to ashes by incendiary bombs, as the enemy has schemed. Judging from the *modus operandi* of this first enemy air raid, the enemy did not live up to his threats and war cries and, acting as if he acknowledges this fact, he used only a few planes and gained little success even though he conducted a broad-scale attack. Also, the fact that the bombing targets were streets and towns rather than military installations means that he was not aiming to destroy completely all facilities, but had schemed to rally the public opinion of his own country since his people have suffered defeat after defeat. His attack was intended as effective propaganda to be broadcast to other countries and to produce the psychological warfare effect of disturbing the spirit of the Japanese people on the home front. This plan of the enemy met with failure in his first attack. The enemy will probably repeat persistent guerrilla-type raids. However, we must be firmly resolved not to become disturbed, regardless of how many times we are attacked from the air. To become disturbed is to fall victims to the enemy's intended scheme of psychological warfare. We must respond to the brilliant battle achievements of our officers and men on the front lines and in order to win the Great Asian War, we must rouse our warrior spirit and vow to defend our homeland to the death.

Saburo Sakai, Japan's leading air ace, was stationed on Lae at the time of the raid. He recalled in his book *Samurai!* that "officially, the government disclaimed any heavy damage, which seemed reasonable in view of the limited number of attacking planes. But the raid unnerved almost every pilot at Lae. The knowledge that the enemy was strong enough to smash at our homeland, even in what might be a punitive raid, was cause for serious apprehension of future and heavier attacks." [8]

From the very day that the raid had been conceived, its objective had been to lower morale of the Japanese people as well

Ryozo Asano, left, owner of a steel plant in Tokyo, looks through the wreckage caused by the Doolittle raid. After the war, Asano testified to occupation officials that he was opposed to the war and had told the Emperor that Japan could not win, but only "in conversations, never in writing." (Photograph courtesy of *Life* magazine; copyright, 1945, by Time, Inc.)

as inflict some material damage to the war effort. When measured in terms of later raids on Japan by B-29 Superfortresses which ended the war with the single-plane attacks on Nagasaki and

Hiroshima, material damage was not great. But the impact on Japanese morale, the primary objective of the raid, was considerable. Public confidence was shaken to the core. For the first time the Japanese people began to take a cynical view of government propaganda.

Americans allowed to return from Japan on the *Gripsholm* in June, 1942, were almost unanimous in their belief that the B-25's had scored direct hits on the national morale and that from this standpoint alone, the operation had magnificently justified itself. "I did not know one American in Japan," said Otto Tolischus, interned *New York Times* correspondent, "who would even question that fact."

To bolster morale and as part of the air defense program, Japanese propagandists composed a song which the people heard over and over again on the radio:

> Why should we be afraid of air raids?
> The big sky is protected with iron defenses.
> For young and old it is time to stand up;
> We are loaded with the honor of defending the homeland.
> Come on, enemy planes! Come on many times!

American planes would have indeed "come on many times" if the planes, the men to fly them and the bases had been available. The Japanese homeland had a recess from bombing which lasted more than two years. On June 16, 1944, China-based B-29's bombed the Yawata steel plant in northern Kyushu. Fourteen months after that a single plane dropped a single bomb on a city called Hiroshima and the course of history was forever altered.

NOTES TO CHAPTER 24

1. Typically, in the manner of many cultured Japanese, Ugaki composed two poems in his diary in the verse form known as *haiku* to express his feelings. There is almost always in it the name of a season, or key words giving the season by inference. He wrote:
Spring is departing.
While the enemy slips away to the east.

Our planes have proceeded west.
And yellow rose petals have fluttered down over
the bomb craters.

2. Joseph C. Grew, *Ten Years in Japan* (New York: Simon and Schuster, 1944), p. 526.

3. Otto D. Tolischus, *Tokyo Record* (New York: Harcourt, Brace & World, 1943), p. 268.

4. Now Mrs. John Toland, wife of writer John Toland, noted for his excellent book *But Not in Shame.*

5. *Asahi Shimbun,* April 19, 1942.

6. *Asahi Shimbun,* April 21, 1942.

7. This was probably Farrow's plane and a parachute belonging to one of his crew.

8. Saburo Sakai, with Martin Caidin and Fred Saito, *Samurai!* (New York: E. P. Dutton & Co. Inc., 1957), p. 148.

Chapter 25

FOUR DIE—FOUR SURVIVE

Jimmy Doolittle received the Medal of Honor at the White House on May 19. Though he was immediately put to work on other projects for Arnold, he felt an obligation to the men he had led on the Tokyo Raid to know of their physical condition and their whereabouts. He wrote letters to the next-of-kin of every man and told what he knew about their loved ones. He sent many messages to Chungking inquiring about the injured and seeking the latest information on those captured.

When the majority of the men who were returning to the States had arrived in Washington, an awards ceremony was held at Bolling Field, where the men were formally presented with their Distinguished Flying Crosses. The injured—Lieutenants McClure, Lawson and Watson—received theirs at nearby Walter Reed Hospital.

The fate of the crews of Hallmark and Farrow worried Doolittle; he did not know who had been captured and who had been killed. Although he had arranged for ransom to be paid to the Japanese or a reward to Chinese guerrillas for the return of any of the crewmen, the gesture was fruitless. Eight men were captured and the Japanese were not going to let them go.[1] Nevertheless, Doolittle persisted in his efforts to find out what had happened and on August 15, learned from the Swiss Con-

sulate General in Shanghai that eight American aviators had
been kept as prisoners at Police Headquarters, Bridge House,
Shanghai. The communique stated that the men were in good
health but the only name that could be learned was "Farrow."
Although the Swiss endeavored to obtain further information,
they were not successful.

On October 19, 1942, the Japanese Government broadcast
over the radio that it had tried the members of two of Doolittle's
crews and sentenced them to death. After commutation of the
sentence to life imprisonment for the larger number of them, it
was also announced that the death sentence had already been
carried out for certain of the accused. No names or other facts
were given.

Secretary of State Cordell Hull contacted the Swiss Minister
to the United States and asked that his Government inquire
through their minister in Tokyo if the reports were true. On
February 17, 1943, the Japanese verified that they intended to try
all American prisoners of war before military tribunals and im-
pose severe penalties upon them including the death penalty.
Hull conveyed this information to President Roosevelt along
with information received later that an unspecified number of
the Doolittle crewmen had been put to death. Hull proposed
a long message to be sent to Tokyo via the American Legation
in Bern and a recommended public announcement to be issued
shortly thereafter.

Roosevelt was profoundly shocked upon receiving this information and penned a reply to Hull on April 8, saying, "I
am deeply stirred and horrified by the execution of American
aviators by the Japanese Government." He approved the proposed message to the Japanese and added, "In view of the severe
tone of this note and especially of the warning in the last paragraph that we propose to retaliate on Japanese prisoners in our

hands I can see no reason for delaying a public announcement on my part."

The "severe" paragraph Roosevelt referred to was unprecedented in American history and presaged a new concept of international justice to be invoked at the close of the war. The paragraph stated:

"The American Government also solemnly warns the Japanese Government that for any other violations of its undertakings as regards American prisoners of war or for any other acts of criminal barbarity inflicted upon American prisoners in violation of the rules of warfare accepted and practiced by civilized nations as military operations now in progress draw to their inexorable and inevitable conclusion, the American Government will visit upon the officers of the Japanese Government responsible for such uncivilized and inhuman acts the punishment they deserve."

On April 21, 1943, the President made his announcement to the press which confirmed what the newspapers had been speculating on for weeks:

It is with a feeling of deepest horror, which I know will be shared by all civilized peoples, that I have to announce the barbarous execution by the Japanese Government of some of the members of this country's armed forces who fell into Japanese hands as an incident of warfare.

The press has just carried the details of the American bombing of Japan a year ago. The crews of two of the American bombers were captured by the Japanese. On October 19, 1942, this Government learned from Japanese radio broadcasts of the capture, trial, and severe punishment of those Americans. Continued endeavor was made to obtain confirmation of those reports from Tokyo. It was not until March 12, 1943, that the American Government received the communication given by the Japanese Government stating that these Americans had in fact been tried and that the death penalty had been pronounced against them. It was further stated that the death penalty was commuted for some but that the sentence of death had been applied to others.

This Government has vigorously condemned this act of barbarity in a formal communication sent to the Japanese Government. In that communication this Goverent has informed the Japanese Goverent that the American Government will hold personally and officially responsible for these diabolical crimes all of those officers of the Japanese Government who have participated therein and will in due course bring those officers to justice.

This recourse by our enemies to frightfulness is barbarous. The effort of the Japanese war lords thus to intimidate us will utterly fail. It will make the American people more determined than ever to blot out the shameless militarism of Japan.

On many occasions after this announcement Roosevelt reiterated his determination that all Axis war criminals would be brought to trial after the war. Accordingly, as soon as the Germans and Japanese surrendered, one of the first follow-up tasks for American troops was to search for evidence of war crimes committed and find those responsible. Top priority was given to finding any survivors of the Doolittle Raid and accumulating evidence against those responsible for the execution of the others.

It was precisely 10 o'clock in the morning of February 27, 1946 when Colonel Edwin R. McReynolds, called the Court to order. Eleven days before, Special Order No. 42 had been issued by the Headquarters, United States Air Forces, China Theater in Shanghai to try "persons, units and organizations accused as War Criminals in this theater." It was McReynolds' task, and that of four other Army officers, to try four Japanese accused of "violation of the laws and customs of war." Specifically the charges were leveled at the quartet for their mistreatment of the eight survivors of the crews of Lieutenants Dean Hallmark and Bill Farrow.

The trial actually began on March 18, 1946 after the arraign-
ment on February 27, to allow the defense counsel time to visit
Japan to procure evidence, secure witnesses and prepare its case.
Every request for aid for the defense, such as air transportation
to and from Japan, was readily granted by the court. All proceedings were interpreted in the Japanese language and verbatim
records were made in both languages. In short, the trial was a
model of American justice in action and its effect was not lost on
the Japanese.

The trial lasted until April 15, 1946. Over six hundred pages
of testimony, argument and documentary evidence record the
aftermath of the raid for the eight luckless men who were captured. As the trial proceeded, a drama of human cruelty and
misery unfolded which proved the effect the Doolittle raid had
on the Japanese military mind. An example had to be made of
the eight captives to prove Japanese superiority and "save face"
for having allowed the homeland to be raided. In addition, the
American people had to be taught that there would be dire
consequences for any American airman caught after daring to
carry out attacks against Japanese territory. The retaliation taken
against the Hallmark and Farrow crews was proof of the deep
Japanese fear of American airpower.

The fate suffered by the eight imprisoned raiders has never
been told before. The results of the trial, although published in
newspapers around the world at the time, were overshadowed by
the proceedings and results of the International War Crimes trials
of higher Japanese and German officials held in Tokyo and
Nuremberg. In the following pages, the facts concerning the death
of four of the eight captives and the forty months of torture and
imprisonment of the others are revealed in narrative form for
the first time.

Dean Hallmark, pilot of the sixth plane off the *Hornet,* was a big man whose nickname "Jungle Jim" had been given to him by his squadron mates because of his husky, well-distributed two-hundred-pound physique. He walked with a peculiar swagger that seemed to go with his loud laugh and aggressive personality. His co-pilot, Bob Meder, was also sturdily built and was Hallmark's opposite number, quiet, reserved and conscientious.

Chase Nielsen, tall, dark, part-Indian navigator on Hallmark's crew, was the third survivor. Corporal William J. Dieter, the bombardier and Corporal Donald E. Fitzmaurice, engineer-gunner, were injured in the crash water landing and died before they could reach shore. Their bodies were found washed up on the beach the next morning.

Nielsen swam for four hours after he found his life raft would not work. When he reached shore he staggered out of the water and collapsed. Next morning he made his way to a small Chinese fishing village where he found Hallmark and Meder badly shaken from the crash of the night before but not too seriously injured. They had met a Chinese guerrilla officer accompanied by an English-speaking soldier who advised the trio to go to a larger Chinese garrison nearby and ask to be taken to Chuchow. It was the intention of the three to commandeer a sampan then and search for other crews.

"We went over to this garrison," Nielsen said in a deposition taken after the war, "and they were trying to get some junks rigged to take us down the coast. We were there until the afternoon of April 21 when one of the Chinese soldiers came running in yelling 'Japanese come!'

"We went out to take a look and saw about 300 Japanese soldiers fully armed come marching down to the camp. We were going to make a run for it but decided to hide instead."

The guerrillas, on speaking terms with the Japanese, stood their ground. The Japanese commandant approached the guerrilla leader and demanded that the Americans be turned over to him. After a heated argument, the guerrilla chieftain, hopelessly outnumbered and outgunned, gave in. Hallmark, Meder and Nielsen were turned over to the Japanese and marched away. "It is my opinion," Nielsen said, "that the Japanese who stayed behind slaughtered the Chinese for protecting us."

As they moved away, one Japanese officer began to push and shove the three prisoners unnecessarily. It was more than Nielsen's hair-trigger temper could take.

"I was a little agitated to find we were in the hands of the Japanese," he said, "and, quite naturally, did not think we had much longer to live." He lashed out in fury at the officer but missed. His reward was a vicious kick on the shins which opened wounds on his left leg. Shin-kicking, the prisoners were to discover, was the favorite counter-blow administered to all prisoners.

The three men were moved to a jail near the airport in Shanghai and placed in solitary confinement. "The Japanese took me out of my cell about 3 o'clock in the afternoon of April 24," Nielsen recalled, "and started questioning me. I gave them my name, rank and serial number and told them that was all the information I had.

"The first thing they did was to put pencils between my fingers, squeezing my hands and forcing the pencils up and down causing the skin to break." When he wouldn't talk, he was then stretched out on the floor and given the infamous "water cure." Four soldiers sat on arms and legs while a fifth placed a wet towel over his face and poured water on it. Every time he gasped for breath, more water was poured on the towel which had the same effect on the helpless victim as drowning.

The more they tortured, the more Nielsen was determined he

was not going to talk. The tough, sinewy Utahan was then given another standard Oriental torture. A bamboo stick about three feet long and two inches in diameter was placed behind his knees and he was forced to kneel and sit back as far as he could. One of the soldiers held him in this position while another jumped up and down on his thighs. But Nielsen didn't give in and the Japanese finally gave up.

The same treatment was given to Hallmark and Meder but to no avail. The three officers were then moved to another Shanghai jail on April 24 and again tortured throughout the night. On the 25th, handcuffed and tied to individual seats in a transport plane, they were flown to Tokyo.

Meanwhile, Lieutenant Bill Farrow, tall, lanky pilot of the last plane, and his crew consisting of Lieutenant Bob Hite and George Barr, Sergeant Harold Spatz and Corporal Jake DeShazer had already been captured near Nanchang, given the same crippling tortures as the others—water cure, stretching rack and knee beating—and flown to Tokyo on the 20th.

The eight fliers were held in Tokyo for about forty-six days— all but the last four days in solitary confinement. The Japanese Gendarmerie, experts in torture methods, questioned them day and night for hours at a time trying to force information as to their mission out of them. They were beaten, kicked, slapped, not fed properly, not permitted to wash, shave or remove their clothing and kept in leg irons all this time. For the first eighteen days all eight of the men successfully resisted answering vital questions and only made replies concerning their personal lives. This was not enough for their captors and questions continued about where their mission originated from, the targets they bombed, and their training. Later, exhausted, weak and sick, they were shown maps and charts that the Japanese had recovered from one of the crashed planes. It was then that they knew the

tortures had been needless. The enemy had known all the important details since shortly after their capture.

On May 22, the eight prisoners were forced to sign papers
written in Japanese which they were led to believe contained only
statements about their personal lives. What they signed were
actually statements confessing their "crimes" and admissions that
they had bombed and strafed schools and hospitals instead of
military targets. Following are excerpts from 7330 Noboro Unit
Military Police Report No. 352 which alleged to be the interroga-
tion transcript for each prisoner: [2]

> *Q.* Did you do any strafing while getting away from Nagoya?
> *Hite:* Heretofore, I haven't revealed any information on this
> point, but the truth is that about five to six minutes after leaving
> the city we saw in the distance what looked like an elementary
> school with many children at play. The pilot steadily dropped
> altitude and ordered the gunmen to their stations. When the
> plane was at an oblique angle, the skipper gave firing orders, and
> bursts of machine gun fire sprayed the ground.

> *Q.* While heading out to sea from Nagoya, didn't you strafe
> children of an elementary school?
> *Farrow:* There is truly no excuse for this. I have made no men-
> tion of this before, but after leaving Nagoya, I do not quite re-
> member the place—there was a place which looked like a school,
> with many people there. As parting shot, with a feeling of "damn
> these Japs," I made a power dive and carried out some strafing.
> There was absolutely no defensive fire from below.

> *Q.* What are you thinking of after killing and wounding so
> many innocent people?
> *Hallmark:* Since it was our intention to bomb Tokyo and es-
> cape to China quickly, we also dropped bombs over objectives
> other than those targets specified, and made a hasty escape.
> Therefore, we also bombed residential homes, killing and wound-
> ing many people.

> *Q.* After the bombing of Nagoya, did you not actually carry out
> strafing?

Spatz: It was an extremely inexcusable deed. Shortly after leaving Nagoya, while flying southward along the coast, the pilot immediately upon perceiving a school, steadily reduced altitude and ordered us to our stations. I aimed at the children in the school yard and fired only one burst before we headed out to sea. My feelings at that time were "damn these Japs" and I wanted to give them a burst of fire. Now I clearly see that this was truly unpardonable and in all decency should not have been committed.

Q. Even if you were instructed by the pilot to drop the bomb properly, didn't you as the bombardier, think that in the name of humanity you shouldn't have bombed innocent civilians?
DeShazer: With our technique and methods used in that air attack such things, even if we thought about them, would have been impossible.

Q. State the conditions at the time of the bombing.
Nielsen: At that time I was mainly observing the situation outside from the windows. At an altitude of 1,500 meters, as soon as we crossed the Noka River in the northeast part of Tokyo, the pilot frantically ordered the bombing. In general the main objective was the factories but with such a bombing method, I believed we missed it completely.

Q. You not only bombed the factories, but you also bombed homes of innocent civilians and killed many people. What are your reactions in that respect?
Meder: It is natural that dropping bombs on a crowded place like Tokyo will cause damage in the vicinity of the target. All the more so with our technique of dropping bombs while making a hit-and-run attack, so I believe it was strictly unavoidable. Moreover, Colonel Doolittle never did order us to avoid such bombings and neither were we particularly worried about the possible damages.

Q. Did you not strafe an elementary school while headed out to sea after the Nagoya raid?
Barr: I am quite sure that was done. Only when the pilot steadily dropped altitude and the strafing was executed was I aware of it.

On June 18, the eight fliers were handcuffed in pairs and sent by train to Nagasaki; from there they were returned by ship to Shanghai and placed in the Bridge House, a small apartment building made into a jail by the Japanese, and put in a cell along with fourteen Chinese.

"We remained in the Bridge House for seventy days," Bob Hite said in a deposition after his release in 1945. "The Chinese in our cell were removed a few days after we arrived, and for the rest of the time the eight of us were in the cell together. Here we were particularly troubled by the conditions of our imprisonment. We were bothered by bugs, rats, and lice which bit us continually until finally our faces and hands swelled out of proportion from the bites. We slept on the floor with one blanket to each man. Our only sanitary facilities were a small bucket in the corner of the cell called a 'benjo' which was emptied periodically, usually only after we had complained because it was overflowing.

"We were not allowed to bathe or wash, and for the first 120 days after we were captured none of us was given the opportunity to shave or bathe. We received three meals daily. For breakfast we received about one-half pint of wormy, watery rice. For lunch and dinner we were generally given some bread which usually amounted to about five ounces. We were given one-half cup of water per man per day.

"While we were in Bridge House we were not permitted to leave the cell for exercise. Usually we were forced to sit cross-legged and motionless on the floor facing the door of the cell. We were not permitted to talk or move during the whole day. There was a light in the ceiling which was left burning 24 hours a day and made it difficult for us to sleep."

On August 28, the eight weakened men were transferred to the Kiangwan Military Prison, on the northern outskirts of Shanghai. Ironically, this prison was sometimes called the "Civic Center," but was really a top security prison reserved for the most important prisoners and, as such, was under the direct command of the supreme commander of the Japanese Expeditionary Army in China whose headquarters was at Nanking. By this time, all eight had dysentery and were in the first stages of beri-beri. Hallmark was by far the sickest of all. He was so weak that he could not stand by himself and had to be carried to Kiangwan on a stretcher.

When they arrived at Kiangwan, the eight prisoners were stood before an assembly of Japanese officers. Hallmark, still on his stretcher, was placed on the floor beside the others. Five Japanese officers, all in uniform, sat on a raised platform. There was the solemn atmosphere of a trial in the room as the five men stared stonily at the Americans. Behind them stood an audience of about ten other Japanese officers.

After a few seconds of silence, the Japanese in the center of the five nodded to a man standing at the side of the room. His name was Caesar Luis dos Remedios, a half Portuguese-half Japanese, who had been sentenced to seven years imprisonment as a spy. Since he could speak Chinese and English as well as Portuguese and Japanese, he was used by his captors as an interpreter.

Remedios stepped toward the men and began questioning them about their life histories. "This was translated to the Court after which some conversation ensued in Japanese," Hite recalled. "When we realized that this was a trial of some sort which had taken about an hour, we asked for a translation of what had taken place, but this was refused. We were not told what the charge against us was or what our sentence was. No interpretation was made to us of any part of the proceedings."

When the "trial" was over, one of the Japanese stood up and read from a manuscript in Japanese which was not translated for the benefit of the prisoners. The seven standing prisoners were then led off to solitary confinement in five-by-nine feet cells.

Hallmark, delirious and too weak to take any interest in what was going on, was carried out and taken back to Bridge House to be put in a cell with about twenty Chinese prisoners, one Japanese and a Russian by the name of Alexander Hindrava. Hindrava could speak a little English and had been sentenced to prison for three years, presumably as a spy. He wasn't sure what his "crime" was since he could speak no Japanese and he, too, had not been allowed a translation of the proceedings. At the War Crimes Trial, Hindrava testified as to Hallmark's condition:

> Q. Please describe to the Commission Lt. Hallmark's condition.
> A. He was laying on the floor with a big growth of beard and very thin and starving.

> Q. Did he have any blankets?
> A. He had two, one underneath and one over.

> Q. Can you state to the Commission whether or not Lt. Hallmark was suffering from dysentery?
> A. Yes. Lt. Hallmark was suffering from dysentery. His bowels would just move themselves.

> Q. Please state to the Commission the daily food ration that the prisoners in Cell No. 6 received.
> A. One cup of punch in the morning. About four ounces cup. One ounce of rice and three ounces water.

> Q. At noon?
> A. At noon the foreigners were getting four ounces of bread or rice and a little fish. You had to choose from them.

> Q. At night?
> A. The same as at noon.

> Q. Did Lt. Hallmark receive this same ration also?
> A. Yes, he did.

Q. Any more?
A. Three times a week he used to get a soup made out of water in which the vegetables were washed.

Q. Can you state to the Commission whether or not during this period that you observed him, Lt. Hallmark received any medical attention?
A. I didn't see him get any medical attention.

Q. What were the latrine facilities in the cell?
A. It was just a wooden bucket back in the corner next to Lt. Hallmark.

Q. Did he use it?
A. Yes. He had to be helped to put him on and take him off. Mostly he was lying on the floor.

Q. Mr. Hindrava, would you be able to tell the court approximately how much Lt. Hallmark weighed at the time?
A. That is very hard to say from as much as he lost already. Only as much as his bones weighed. He was all skin and bones.

Q. Will you please describe Lt. Hallmark's condition when he left the cell?
A. His dysentery had passed but he was too weak to walk by himself. He could only walk a few steps but not more.

Q. Did he seem to know that he was in Bridge House as punishment?
A. No, he thought that just because he had dysentery they left him there.

Q. What were the lighting conditions in the cell?
A. We could get a little of daylight from the window in the side and then there were two electric lights going twenty-four hours.

Back at Kiangwan, the seven others were kept in solitary confinement for twenty days and then permitted to leave their cells

individually for exercise a few minutes each day. They were fed
a bowl of rice and some soup three times a day. It was the monot-
onous diet and the deadly routine that soon began to tell on the
prisoners. But worse than that was the nothingness of solitary
confinement. Lieutenant Chase Nielsen described their days as:
"Get up at 6 A.M. Breakfast at 8. Exercise with a guard between
10:30 and 11. Lunch at 12. Supper at 5 P.M. Bed at 9:30. The rest
of the time we had nothing to do and nothing is the hardest thing
in the world to do."

Prior to their trial on August 28, a curious rationalization had
taken place to decide the fate of the eight Americans. A draft of
a Japanese law concerning the punishment of captured enemy
airmen had been sent from the War Ministry in Tokyo to Headquarters of the China Expeditionary Forces in Nanking in July
with instructions for the latter to "establish" the law. At the same
time Tokyo requested the Thirteenth Japanese Army Headquarters to defer its trial of the eight American fliers until the
new military law had been enacted. The supreme commander at
Nanking, General Shunroku Hata "established" the Enemy Airmen's Act on August 13, 1942, following the outline received
from Tokyo and then issued it to the Thirteenth Army.

This law stated in substance that it would take effect immediately, be applicable to all acts committed prior to the date of its
approval, and apply to all enemy airmen raiding Japanese terri-
tories. It also explained that anyone who participated in the
bombing or strafing of non-military targets or any other violation
of international law would be sentenced to death. "Should the
circumstances warrant," the Act stated, "this sentence may be
commuted to life imprisonment, or a term of imprisonment for
not less than ten years."

As soon as the Act was published, a staff officer from Tokyo was
sent to China to give instructions regarding the trial of the eight

Doolittle raiders and demand that General Hata have the prosecutor require the death sentence and report the Court's decision to Tokyo. Thus, the mock trial was held on August 28 but the death penalty had already been prescribed.

A record of the trial was made which concluded that the eight defendants "have been found guilty as charged, and are hereby sentenced to death." Under the "reasons for the sentence" the defendants were said to have arrived over their respective targets and "suddenly exhibited cowardice when confronted with opposition in the air and on the ground, and with the intent of cowing, killing and wounding innocent civilians, and wreaking havoc on residences and other living quarters of no military significance whatsoever . . . did carry on indiscriminate bombing and strafing . . ." This record was signed by Lieutenant Colonel Toyama Nakajo, chief judge, Lieutenant Yusei Wako, and Lieutenant Ryuhei Okada of the 7330 Noboro Unit Military Tribunal on August 28 and forwarded to Tokyo. However, they had been told that executions were not to be carried out until Tokyo had approved the sentence.

The fate of the eight airmen was sealed in Tokyo by October 10. On that day, chief of staff of the Grand Imperial Headquarters, General Sugiyama, put his chop on a message to Hata in China which approved the sentence of death for Hallmark, Farrow and Spatz but reduced the death sentences to life imprisonment for the other five, adding that "as war criminals, their treatment shall not be that accorded ordinary prisoners of war (and) even in the event of an exchange of war prisoners they may not be repatriated to the United States forces." Date of execution of the three men was set for October 15. In passing on the decision to spare the lives of the five men to General Sadamu Shimomura, commanding the Thirteenth Army, General Hata instructed that "in making this announcement to the convicted

men, special mention must be made of the Emperor's leniency."
No reasons were ever given for the death sentences imposed on
the two pilots and one engineer-gunner.

On the afternoon of October 14, Dean Hallmark was brought to
Kiangwan and placed in a cell by himself. That evening Hallmark, Farrow and Spatz were informed that they had been sentenced to death and would be executed the next day. They were
given paper and pencils and told through interpreter Remedios
that they could write letters to their friends and relatives.
Remedios described what happened:

> On 14 October 1942 I was instructed by Sergeant Sotojiro
> Tatsuta (later Captain) to have Lt. Farrow, Lt. Hallmark, and
> Sgt. Spatz sign their names on two blank sheets of white paper.
> One page was signed by each of them in the middle of the sheet,
> and the other page was signed by each at the bottom. They asked
> me why they were made to sign these papers. Tatsuta told me
> that they were signing these as a receipt for their belongings and
> that he would fill the rest in Japanese later on.
> Later Tatsuta gave each two sheets of paper, one on which to
> write a letter to their family, which he said he would send
> through the Red Cross; and the other sheet was to be used to
> describe the treatment they received by the Japanese while they
> were confined. At that time I didn't know what the Japanese were
> going to do to these three airmen. The fliers asked me what they
> should write. My opinion was to give a little 'top hat' for the
> Japanese, so that they would be given good treatment later on.
> I didn't read the letters, but gave them to Sgt. Tatsuta early the
> next morning.

The letters, later introduced as evidence for the prosecution
in the 1946 trials, were poignant farewell messages to their loved
ones. In a letter to his mother, father and sister in Dallas, Texas,
Dean Hallmark wrote:

"I hardly know what to say. They have just told me that I am liable to execution. I can hardly believe it . . . I am a prisoner of war and I thought I would be taken care of until the end of the war . . . I did everything that the Japanese have asked me to do and tried to cooperate with them because I knew that my part in the war was over." He added that "I wanted to be a commercial pilot and would have been if it hadn't been for this war," and asked his mother to "try and stand up under this and pray."

Harold Spatz wrote to his widower father in Lebo, Kansas saying that he had nothing to leave him but his clothes. "If I have inherited anything since I became of age," he wrote, "I will give it to you, and Dad, I want you to know that I love you and may God bless you." Then he added: "I want you to know that I died fighting for my country like a soldier."

Lieutenant Bill Farrow, sensitive, tall, blue-eyed 23-year old pilot from Darlington, South Carolina, wrote to his widowed mother:

"Don't let this get you down. Just remember that God will make everything right, and that I will see you again in the hereafter."

Farrow had a number of personal words for his sister Margaret, several aunts and uncles and service friends, Helen and Ivan Ferguson. He thanked his fiancee "for bringing to my life a deep, rich love for a fine girl." In a separate letter to her he wrote that "you are, to me, the only girl that would have meant the completion of my life . . ." He added, "Please write and comfort Mom, because she will need you—she loves you, and thinks you are a fine girl . . ."

Farrow added a postscript to his mother's letter:

"Read 'Thanatopsis' by Bryan if you want to know how I am taking this. My faith in God is complete, so I am unafraid." [3]

The orders to execute Hallmark, Farrow and Spatz were clear.

They were to be shot on the afternoon of October 15 with proper military ceremony. That morning, at Public Cemetery No. 1 outside Shanghai, Tomoicha Yoneya headed a detail to erect three small crosses made of new lumber at the regimental carpenter shop the night before. Shigeji Mayama, one of the detail, cut the grass in the vicinity of the execution ground and helped erect the crosses. Nearby a small table was placed to serve as a ceremonial altar.

At half past four in the afternoon the three Americans were brought to the cemetery in three separate trucks under guard. They were led to the crosses, turned around and placed on their knees; their arms were tied in two places to each cross. White blindfolds were placed over the eyes of each man and a mark of black ink was put on the white cloth directly over the center of their foreheads.

While the preparations were being made, a firing squad of six men marched into position in a double rank about twenty feet away. Two riflemen were assigned to each man—one primary who would fire first, and a secondary in case the first missed or had a dud cartridge.

Other Japanese arrived. According to military custom, Colonel Akinobu Ito, the prosecutor of the district in which the trial was held, Major Itsuro Hata who was the prosecutor for the case against the accused, Sergeant Sotojiro Tatsuta, the warden of the military prison, and Chosei Fujita, clerk of the court that tried the raiders, were present. Three medical officers, three members of the Shanghai Military Police Headquarters and an interpreter were witnesses. First Lieutenant Goro Tashida, commander of the firing squad, posted a non-commissioned officer and three enlisted men as security guards around the cemetery. An incense burner was lighted on the altar-like table. All was now in readiness. The 55-year-old Tatsuta, in his trial testimony, described what happened when he arrived at the cemetery:

I arrived at the execution grounds and there I saw the American fliers. Major Hata was looking after the execution preparations and I read, at the time, the statement which was prepared by the prosecutor—which was prepared by Hata but which was actually issued by Colonel Ito and this statement was in accordance with the orders given by the Commander of the 13th Army and was signed in the name of Ooka Takijiro, the Chief Warden at Nanking.

Then I told the fliers, "I do not know what relation I had with you in the previous life but we have been living together under the same roof and on this day you are going to be executed, but I feel sorry for you. My sympathies are with you. Men must die sooner or later. Your lives were very short but your names will remain everlastingly. I do not remember if this was Lieutenant Farrow but one of them said, "Thank you very much for all the trouble you have taken while we were in your confinement, but please tell the folks at home that we died very bravely." And I told them that "your ashes will be sent through the International Red Cross to your homes."

I told them that Christ was born and died on the cross and you on your part must die on the cross but when you are executed— when you die on the cross you will be honored as Gods, and I told them to pray and they made a sign which resembled the sign of the cross and they prayed. I told them "you will soon be bound to the crosses and when this is done it is a fact that it is a form that man's faith and cross shall be united. Therefore, have faith." Then they smiled and said they understood very well. Then I asked them if they had any more to say and they said they had nothing more to say. That was all that was said.

Q. When you got to the cemetery what did you do with the fliers?

A. First the medical officer spoke to them and then the prosecutor spoke to them and then I had a few words with them as I mentioned before.

Q. Which prosecutor spoke?

A. Prosecutor Hata.

Q. Tell the Commission what Hata said.

A. I do not remember exactly but I believe that he said something to make them feel more easy about their coming death.

Q. Was Hata very sorry?
A. I believe so because he gave them the deepest bow at the end of his speech.

When Hata finished his speech, Tatsuta, the official executioner, nodded to Lieutenant Tashido. Tashido clicked his boots and turned to his firing squad.

"Attention! Face the target!" The six men faced toward the helpless men tied to the crosses.

"Prepare!"

The three soldiers in the front rank raised their rifles and aimed at the black marks on the blindfolds only thirty feet away. Tashida raised his arm.

"Fire!" he shouted as he snapped his arm down. Three shots broke the afternoon stillness. Each of three bullets found their marks. Death was mercifully instantaneous; no second shots were necessary.

Tashida, seeing that his marksmen had done their work well, about-faced the squad, marched them a few steps away and ordered them to extract their cartridges. The three medical officers each checked one man and feeling no pulse bandaged the wounds. Three coffins, freshly made the night before, were brought up, the bodies untied and placed inside by the guards. The three coffins were then silently carried to the altar where the incense was burning and carefully laid side by side on the ground. Acting according to the Code of the Knight of the Bushido, the entire assemblage stood on the other side of the table and after a brief period of meditation, saluted and "paid their last respects to their spirits."

The three coffins were quickly loaded into a truck and taken to the Japanese Resident's Association Crematorium where the

Three crosses mark the location where Lts. Hallmark and Farrow and Sgt. Spatz were executed by a Japanese firing squad on October 15, 1942. Five other crew members were sentenced to life imprisonment; one, Lt. Meder, died of beri-beri and malnutrition in December, 1943.

bodies were promptly cremated. The ashes were placed in small boxes and brought back to the waiting room of the branch office of Kiangwan Prison. There they were placed on an altar and incense burners placed in front of them. About a month later the boxes were removed and taken to the International Funeral Home in Shanghai where they remained until the end of the war. Hallmark, Farrow and Spatz had, like Faktor, Dieter and Fitzmaurice, paid with their lives for participating in the raid.

In Kiangwan Prison, the remaining five prisoners were unaware that their buddies had been led away and would be seen no more. Still in solitary confinement, each was trying to maintain his reason against the loneliness and uncertainty. Almost at the same moment that Hallmark, Farrow and Spatz were being readied for the ride to the cemetery, the other five were roused out of their cells and marched to the same room where they had had their mock trial in August. Standing solemnly in a row, they were told in English that they had been sentenced to death but because of the mercy of His Imperial Majesty, the Emperor, their sentences had been commuted to life imprisonment "with special treatment." No mention of the other three Americans was made and no explanation of the "special treatment" was ever given. They were to learn, however, that it meant continuation of the solitary confinement and the starvation diet.

The days of boredom continued and each man's health was deteriorating rapidly. All were suffering from dysentery and malnutrition and developing dropsy and beri-beri because of the complete lack of fruit and vegetables. On April 18, 1943, exactly one year from the day of the raid, the quintet was transferred to a military prison in Nanking. Neither the food nor the treatment improved.

While their strength ebbed, their spirits surprisingly did not. At Nanking they were allowed to exercise 30 minutes a day together which helped their morale considerably. Although the exercise in the sunlight helped, each was still getting progressively weaker and Bob Meder was now weakest of the five survivors. Normally weighing about 175 pounds he was now only about 110. Although he always came out each day to exercise it was obvious he had to have medical attention. As the spring passed into summer and then into late autumn, Meder showed no improvement. Finally on December 1, 1943, the once sturdily-built Meder, now only a walking skeleton, died quietly in his cell.

The following deposition was taken from Lieutenant George Barr after the war which described Meder's death:

Q. Do you know the cause of his (Meder's) death?
A. Dysentery, beri-beri.

Q. Was he given medical care?
A. I can't say that he got very much.

Q. Were you in the same cell with Lt. Meder?
A. No, sir. We were in solitary confinement.

Q. When did you learn of Lt. Meder's illness?
A. He was ill for seventy days before he died.

Q. Was he in the same cell at Nanking, China for the whole seventy days?
A. Yes, sir.

Q. Do you have any knowledge as to how much medical treatment was given to him?
A. Very little was given to him. A medical orderly came around with pills, approximately every three days.

Q. What is the source of your information as to the medical care that he received?
A. You could hear the cell doors open, and the medical orderly would stop at our cells when he came by.

Q. Did the men talk back and forth?
A. No, sir.

Q. Did you have tapping signals?
A. Yes, sir.

Q. Were you able to talk (by Morse code signal) to Lt. Meder?
A. No, sir. Lt. Chase J. Nielsen could talk to Lt. Robert J. Meder and I could talk to Lt. Chase J. Nielsen, and Lt. Robert J. Meder told Lt. Chase J. Nielsen that he wasn't being given medical care.

Q. Did Lt. Robert J. Meder continue to exercise with the rest of you?

A. Yes, sir. He even exercised the last day—the day of his death.

Q. Describe Lt. Meder's physical condition as you remember when he went out and took exercise on the day that he died.

A. I would say that he was extremely thin. He was very weak but would not admit it.

Q. What exercise did Lt. Meder take that day?

A. Just light exercise. Arm exercises and body bending exercises.

Q. Did Lt. Meder take all the exercises that the rest of you took that day?

A. No, sir. We used to run around for about five or ten minutes, but Lt. Meder would stand over in the corner of the yard and do arm exercises.

Q. When did you learn of his death?

A. At approximately 4:30 the day he died.

Q. Do you know the approximate time of his death?

A. Between two and four o'clock P.M.

Q. Who informed you of the death of Lt. Meder?

A. I happened to be out serving meals and when he didn't answer when I passed his meal in, the guard opened the door and there was no response from Lt. Meder and that was when we found out he was dead.

After two days, Meder's body was removed from the cell and cremated. His ashes were placed in a jar which in turn was put in a cardboard box tied with string. The box was then placed on a table in a cell across from Barr and was there until the remaining four men were later transferred to Peiping. The medical report required by Japanese military regulations was filled out by First Lieutenant Soshi Yasuharu who certified that Meder's death was due to "heart failure resulting from beri-beri and inflammation of the intestines."

Meder's death caused a slight improvement in the diet of the four survivors. Their daily ration increased to two and a half cups of rice and soup for breakfast, with occasional hot tea; lunch consisted of more rice with occasional greens and half a fish; supper included tea with rice curry spiced with occasional pieces of unidentified chopped meat.

The day's routine, however, was the same dismal boredom of complete inactivity in their cells alone punctuated only with the short daily exercise periods and a once-a-week bath. There was no heat in the cells and clothing was inadequate. They had to sleep on straw mats on the floor with only one blanket each. However, after Meder died, a second blanket was issued. Strangely, none of them caught any serious respiratory diseases even though their resistance was low and it was cold enough to freeze water in the bowls of the wash stand outside.

Weeks became months and the seasons came and went endlessly. No reading material had been allowed, although they asked for something to read whenever a sympathetic guard who could speak English was on duty. Finally, probably because of Meder's death, a few English language books were provided. One of these was a Bible and its messages provided the link to sanity they each needed so desperately because, as Nielsen said, they suffered from "gnawing hunger in our heads and stomachs."

Up to this time, each man had resorted to different things to pass the hundreds of lonely hours away. Nielsen tried, by mental pictures, to build a home. Barr worked mentally on an elaborate neon sign while Hite planned a model farm down to the last fence post. DeShazer, the son of an Oregon minister-farmer, recalled his childhood and composed poetry. While these mental exercises

helped, it was the acquisition of the Bible which they unanimously admitted later had a profound effect upon their respective
outlooks. Each one of them read it every hour of daylight he had
it, and then passed it on to the next man.

None of the surviving four men would have called himself
religious and none had ever read the Bible through before.
Between turns, they thought about the passages they had read
and memorized them. The words, only vaguely familiar from
their childhood churchgoing, now took a deep meaning and
significance. The words conveyed a new hope which was almost
gone after Meder died.

The summer of 1944 turned out to be the hottest in Nanking's
history. The prison cells were almost unbearable in the daytime
because there was no circulation of air. The cell doors were of
solid wood and there was only one small window in each cell.
At night it was difficult to sleep for the same reason. Bob Hite
became ill with a very high fever and was dangerously close to
death. When the guards recognized that his life was in jeopardy,
they removed the solid wood door from his cell and replaced it
with a screen door.

Apparently, someone in the prison administration had been
severely chastised after Meder's death for when it was found that
Hite was near death, a medical assistant was ordered to live in
the prison and nurse him back to health. Under this kind of constant attention and the advent of cooler weather, Hite recovered.
The Bible's message of hope was indeed encouraging. At least the
Japanese seemed to want them to stay alive.

While the summer of 1944 was the worst, the winter of 1944-45
shared the same dubious honor. Snow fell on December 1, and
stayed on the ground until March 1. Heavier clothes were issued
and, as the winter became more severe, they even got their own

American uniforms back which they put on over their prison garb. This also proved a small but important morale factor.

A high point in the long months of imprisonment was reached on Christmas Day, 1944. Without warning, some strange fighter planes the prisoners could not identify roared over the prison straight for the oil refineries and storage tanks nearby. The roar of engines was followed by explosions and machine gun fire. Black smoke billowed slowly up into the sky. Those were American planes and Nanking had just been successfully bombed!

The four Americans were so elated they leaped toward the windows to catch a glimpse of what was going on. The fighters followed their bomb runs with strafing attacks. Japanese anti-aircraft batteries opened up but they had missed their chance. Within a few minutes the raid was over and the skies were silent again.

The prisoners were beside themselves with joy. It couldn't be long now before they would be released, they reasoned. But weeks went by and no more planes came. On June 15, 1945, for some reason unknown to them, they were transferred hurriedly to Peiping by train. Enroute they had their hands and legs tied with belts. Each man had a guard who hung on to a rope tied to their waists. A large green raincoat was thrown over each man and a hat placed on their heads, with a mask attached, which fell down over their faces.

After nearly three days of train traveling, they arrived in Peiping and were placed in an inner section of the Japanese military prison in solitary cells. Immediately, they found their treatment was not as good as it had gotten to be in Nanking. They were made to sit all day in their cells on little stools made out of a piece of two-by-four about eight inches long and required to face the wall three feet away. The hope they all had felt in

Nanking turned to deep despair again as they stared at nothing for hours on end all day long and lay on their straw mats staring at nothing at night.

DeShazer now became the weakest of the four. Huge boils—he counted seventy-five at one time—broke out all over his body. He became delirious and couldn't sit on the stool. Since he was apparently near death from malnutrition, a Japanese medical officer finally gave him shots and his health improved. He had been praying silently for months and was now convinced that his prayers had been answered. On August 9, 1945, DeShazer describes a remarkable experience which determined his future. As soon as he awakened that morning, he heard a voice tell him to "start praying":

I asked, "What shall I pray about?" Pray for peace and pray without ceasing, I was told. I had prayed about peace but very little, if at all, before that time, as it seemed useless. I thought God could stop the war any time with the power which he had manifested.

But God was now teaching me the lesson of cooperation. It was God's joy for me to be willing to let Him use me. God does use human instruments to accomplish His will here on earth. It will be a great joy to us through all eternity if we can cooperate with Him. I started to pray for peace although I had a very poor idea of what was taking place in the world at that time.

About seven o'clock in the morning I began to pray. It seemed very easy to pray on the subject of peace. I prayed that God would put a great desire in the hearts of the Japanese leaders for peace. I thought about the days of peace that would follow. Japanese people would no doubt be discouraged, and I felt sympathetic toward them. I prayed that God would not allow them to fall into persecution by the victorious armies.

At two o'clock in the afternoon the Holy Spirit told me, "You don't need to pray any more. The victory is won." I was amazed. I thought this was quicker and better than the regular method of receiving world news. Probably this news broadcast had not come over the radio to America as yet. I thought I would just wait and see what was to happen.[4]

It was several days before DeShazer was to know that August 9, 1945 was the day that the second atomic bomb had been dropped on Nagasaki and that the Japanese were considering complete surrender. The guards did not mention anything but a few days later they appeared on duty all wearing new uniforms and began breaking into their supply rooms. DeShazer somehow knew that it would not be long before they would be free men again. He was certain now that Japan had been defeated.

"I could not help wondering what would happen to Japan now," he said. "Their hopes had been set on victory. It would be an awful blow to suffer defeat. But, if the Japanese found out about Jesus, the military defeat to them would in reality be a great victory."

It was then that DeShazer heard the same voice he had heard before tell him, "You are called to go and teach the Japanese people and to go wherever I send you."

Just ten days after DeShazer had heard the prediction of peace without benefit of radio or outside reports, a Japanese prison official opened the cell doors of the four Americans and said, simply, "The war is over. You can go home now."

The four dazed men were led from their cells, given their three-year old clothes back, offered haircuts and shaves and taken to the Peking Hotel. While Hite, Nielsen and DeShazer were able to walk, George Barr had to be helped by the now friendly, solicitous Japanese. It was then they were told about the atomic bomb and that the war had actually ended on August 15.

The Japanese were not proud of the prison treatment they had given the four Doolittle raiders. When American parachute teams

Three of the four Tokyo raiders who survived Japanese prisons are shown
as they arrived at Chungking after release from 40 months of imprisonment. Left to right are Cpl. DeShazer, Lt. Hite, and Lt. Nielsen. The
fourth survivor, Lt. Barr, was too ill to be moved and was returned to
the United States several weeks later. DeShazer returned to Japan as a
missionary after the war and is there today.

dropped into the Peiping area to accept their surrender, they
asked about the whereabouts of the Doolittle flyers. The Japanese said that they had been executed but Chinese intelligence

had informed otherwise. Within a few hours, Hite, DeShazer, Barr and Nielsen were being interviewed by newsmen and soon brought back to the United States. For them, the forty months of hell were over, but its aftermath would be with them for the rest of their lives. They were all suffering from dysentery and beri-beri and required several months of treatment before they were pronounced fit again. Today, all four men are still living and in fair health; however, they are changed men from the carefree, devil-may-care "flyboys" they were when captured. Jake DeShazer answered his call to the ministry and after separation attended Seattle Pacific College where he graduated on June 7, 1948. Today, he is a missionary in Japan where he lives the sincere, dedicated life of a man who is certain that his life was spared by a revelation and faith in his God. Today, this quiet, soft-spoken man is the best known American missionary in Japan.

George Barr, who probably would not have survived another month in prison, was unable to return to the United States immediately upon release. His health shattered, he spent several weeks in China under close medical care and more weeks in Walter Reed Hospital in Washington when he was able to travel. He was subsequently given a medical discharge and is now employed as a Weapons Analyst for the U.S. Army.

Bob Hite, alert, quick-witted Oklahoman, recovered quickly and was separated from the Air Force in 1946. He returned to active duty during the Korean War and is now the manager of a hotel in Camden, Arkansas.

Chase Nielsen, tough part-Indian from Utah, decided to remain in uniform. He retired from the Air Force in 1962, and is now employed as an engineer for a nationally known firm engaged in missile production.

Each man paid a price of some kind for his part in the raid on Japan. For most it was a few hours of nerve-shattering apprehension. For seven of them it was death. For these four men it was more than three irreplaceable years out of their lives.

As soon as hostilities ceased, American agents fanned out all over Japan proper and Japanese-occupied territory seeking information and evidence for the trial of individuals who had violated international law and the laws of war in the treatment of prisoners. In a short time, hundreds of Japanese were located who had been named by ex-prisoners of war as being particularly cruel or had caused the death of their comrades. Those concerned with the execution of the Doolittle crews must have known they would be sought because a few days after the surrender was signed on the *Missouri,* some unnamed Japanese came to the office of the International Funeral Directors in Shanghai to search for the urns containing the ashes of Lieutenants Hallmark and Farrow and Sergeant Spatz. They directed the names on the boxes be changed to "J. Smith" for Hallmark, "H.E. Gande" for Farrow and "E. L. Brister" for Spatz to confuse anyone attempting to learn the fate of these three. American investigators, however, soon uncovered the facts from the original Japanese records and the urns were properly identified.

Between August 1945 and the following February, it was found that a number of Japanese should be brought to trial for the unlawful treatment of the Doolittle fliers but because many were then dead or accused of more serious war crimes, the list to be brought to trial in China narrowed down to four: Lieutenant General Shigeru Sawada, commanding general of the Japanese Imperial Thirteenth Expeditionary Army in China; Captain Ryuhei Okada, a member of the "Court" that tried the fliers; Lieutenant Yusei Wako, prosecutor during the mock trial, and Captain Sotojiro Tatsuta, the warden of Kiangwan Military

Prison and official executioner. Major Itsuro Hata, the prosecutor at the mock trial and Lieutenant Colonel Toyama Nakajo, the chief judge, had died. General Skunroku Hata, commanding general of all Japanese forces in China and Sawada's superior, and Lieutenant General Sadamu Shimomura, who succeeded Sawada as Commander of the Thirteenth Army and actually signed the order of execution for the three airmen, were both held in Tokyo in connection with the prosecution of the International War Crimes cases. Their release to the Military commission for this trial had been refused.

The four accused were tried under separate and different charges of violations of the laws and customs of war. Sawada, as commanding general of the Thirteenth Army, was charged with causing the eight captured fliers to be tried and sentenced to death by a Japanese military tribunal on false and fraudulent charges and that he had the power to commute or revoke the sentences but failed to do so. He was also charged with responsibility for the cruel and brutal atrocities and other offenses including the denial of proper food, clothing, medical care and shelter for the prisoners.

Tatsuta was charged as having commanded and executed an unlawful order of a Japanese military tribunal which caused the death of three of the fliers and as warden of Kiangwan Military Prison was blamed for denying the prisoners adequate food, shelter, sanitary facilities and medical care.

Okada and Wako were accused of unlawfully trying and judging the eight airmen under false and fraudulent charges without affording them a fair trial, interpretation of the proceedings, counsel, or an opportunity to defend, and sentenced them to death.

The charges against all four men were deemed adequate and proper by the legal advisors to General Albert C. Wedemeyer,

Commander of American forces in China. "Here the test is international law," Colonel Edward H. Young, his staff judge advocate noted, "not the national law, civil or military of any one nation, not the law of the United States nor of Japan, but the law of nations. Japan and the United States both were parties to the Hague Convention, and Japan agreed to abide by the provisions of the Geneva Prisoner of War Convention."

When all the testimony was completed, the Commission deliberated for two days and arrived at its findings and sentences. The Commission concluded:

> The offenses of each of the accused resulted largely from obedience to the laws and instructions of their Government and their Military Superiors. They exercised no initiative to any marked degree. The preponderance of evidence shows beyond reasonable doubt that other officers, including high governmental and military officials, were responsible for the enactment of the Ex Post Facto 'Enemy Airman's Law' and the issuance of special instructions as to how these American Prisoners were to be treated, tried, sentenced and punished.

Sawada, Wako, Okada and Tatsuta were all found guilty to the charges made against them. Sawada, Okada and Tatsuta were sentenced to confinement at hard labor for five years and Wako, the only man with prior legal training serving on the mock trial court, was sentenced to nine years, presumably because he was a lawyer and knew that the "Enemy Airmen's Act" was *ex post facto* and had been enacted specifically for the detriment of the eight fliers.

Colonel Young disagreed with the leniency of the sentences when he reviewed the case for General Wedemeyer. The maximum penalty for all four could have been death and Young wrote in his review that the Commission "by awarding such extremely lenient and inadequate penalties committed a serious error of judgment." He added that "it is clear that when they found the accused guilty of the capital offenses of mistreatment and murder under the laws of war, the penalties should have been commensurate with the findings. On the other hand, as the principle issues of the very case it was adjudging involved the illegal performance of judicial functions under the laws of war by the accused, and with few recorded precedents available, the Commission membership no doubt was particularly conscious of its own obligations in this regard. Accordingly, it is then pertinent to note that if an error of judgment was made, then contrary to the Japanese ideas of justice and humanity, the Commission favored the accused with all the benefits thereof."

Under the American concept of legal justice, no sentence can be increased by a reviewing authority, no matter how lenient it might seem. Colonel Young recommended that the sentences against the accused stand and General Wedemeyer agreed. The four began serving their sentences immediately.

When the news of the sentences was released to the world's press, reaction in the States was immediate. Parents and relatives of the executed men wrote indignant letters to the President and their Congressmen. Veterans' organizations protested vigorously the "soft-hearted leniency" expressed by the Military Commission. But the protests were academic. A fair trial had been held, the accused judged and sentences meted out. The sentences could not be increased according to the American system of law. Hallmark, Farrow, Meder and Spatz had given their lives to help preserve that system.

NOTES TO CHAPTER 25

1. Corporals Donald E. Fitzmaurice and William J. Dieter of Lieutenant Hallmark's crew died as a result of the crash landing.

2. The falsification is obvious from the odd, stilted sentence structure and strange colloquialisms used. Since the statements they signed had been in Japanese and none of the eight could speak, read, or write the language, no assumption can be made other than that their fate had already been decided. This transcript was used as evidence at the 1946 War Crimes Trial.

3. The Japanese never turned these letters over to the International Red Cross. They were translated into Japanese and the originals lost or destroyed. After the war, however, these translations were discovered in the files of the War Ministry in Tokyo. Actually, the condemned men wrote a total of twelve letters but only three were introduced as evidence.

4. C. Hoyt Watson, *The Amazing Story of Sergeant Jacob DeShazer* (Winona Lake, Indiana: Light and Life Press, 1950), p. 120-121.

Chapter 26

SHANGRI-LA TO MIDWAY TO VICTORY

On the afternoon of April 18, 1942, the first good news of the war appeared in "war extras" all over the country. It had its beginning in the Roosevelt mansion located in Hyde Park. The President had gone there to rest over the weekend and prepare his seven-point anti-inflation message to the Congress and the fireside chat which was to follow it. He was working quietly in his study with Mrs. Grace Tully, his trusted secretary, and Samuel I. Rosenman, a speech writer, when the call came from Washington announcing the raid. Rosenman later described the President's reaction: [1]

> The President was, of course, overjoyed by the news. He knew the heartening effect it would have on American morale and the morale of our Allies, and the blow to the prestige of the Japanese, to have American bombers over Tokyo even for a short fleeting time . . .
>
> After receiving the news, the President was on the telephone several times with people in Washington, and in the course of one conversation he was asked to be prepared to answer questions on where the bombers had been launched. We were talking about it over a cup of tea. I said, "Mr. President, do you remember the novel of James Hilton, *Lost Horizon,* telling of that wonderful, timeless place known as Shangri-La? It was located in the track-less wastes of Tibet. Why not tell them that that's where the planes came from? If you use a fictional place like that, it's a

polite way of saying that you do not intend to tell the enemy or
anybody else where the planes really came from."

The President put in a call for Steve Early and told him that if
anyone wanted to know where the bombers originated, he was
going to say "Shangri-La!" [2]

Upon his return to Washington, the President held a press
conference on April 21. The headlines in the 'war extras' that
evening had the effect the President wanted. There was an air

On May 19, 1942, Jimmy Doolittle, previously promoted to Brigadier General,
was presented the Congressional Medal of Honor by President Franklin D.
Roosevelt. Looking on are General H. Arnold, Mrs. Doolittle, and General
George C. Marshall.

of mystery surrounding the launching point that confounded the Japanese and delighted the Allies. The sneak raid on Pearl Harbor had been avenged in kind by American bombers led by the most famous of American airmen. "DOOLITTLE DO'OD IT" one paper's front page had announced. The "Shangri-La" remark added the exact psychological chord that the country had been waiting so long to hear. The United States *could* strike back after all. Revenge had at last been taken for that day "which will live in infamy" and the boast made by Premier Hideki Tojo that "Japan has never lost a war in all the 2,600 years of her glorious history" was not going to be continued.[3]

American newspapers were jubilant over the news, and speculated on every possible angle of the Doolittle raid. Japanese reports and radio broadcasts were analyzed and editorial imaginations roamed over the whole spectrum of possibilities about the attack. The Japanese radio had announced on the 19th that the planes which flew over the Japanese mainland "numbered about 10, consisting of North American B-25 type bombers," and added that "at dawn Saturday an enemy force consisting of three (sic) aircraft carriers appeared on the high seas far off the Japanese mainland but fled away without approaching the Japanese soil in fear of the Japanese counterattacks."

Newspaper editors tried to put these facts together but were not convinced that the B-25's could have departed from carriers. One wire service cautioned its editors that "either the Japanese identification of the raiding planes or the implication that they were carrier-launched seemed in error." The advisory noted that the B-25 medium bomber "is too heavy for carrier use" and therefore tended to discourage speculation on this point. Reports from the British press suggested that the B-25's had flown from bases in the Aleutians and then flew on to Chinese bases, thus requiring a range of 4,000 miles.

The War and Navy Departments would neither confirm nor

deny any of these speculations. In spite of the fact that over ten thousand Navy and about two hundred Army Air Forces personnel knew the details, the secret of the raid proved to be one of the best kept of the war. The only instructions given to the crew of the *Hornet* appeared on the bulletin board just before she docked at Pearl Harbor on April 25. Commander George R. Henderson, executive officer, wrote:

> The mission of this force or work in any way with it, movements of ships involved or action taken by any unit of the force should not be mentioned or discussed ashore with *anyone*. The term anyone includes all members of the armed forces of this country as well as civilians, including the members of your immediate family. Remember that the success of a future mission similar to the one we have just completed depends to a great extent on your ability to keep this one secret.

It is a tribute to all the men who knew the secret of Shangri-La that not one of them let it out until it was officially released a year later.[4]

Between the initial announcement of the raid and the President's press conference, there was much confusion as to what had really happened. While Doolittle and his planes were winging their way toward Japan, General Stilwell wired the War Department saying that the Generalissimo requested further details about the forthcoming mission and stated that Chiang was violently opposed to diversion of these aircraft to the Indian theater. No messages concerning the raid passed between Chungking and Washington on the 19th but on the 20th, Colonel Clayton Bissell, Stilwell's air officer, sent a "most urgent" message to the War Department:

CHINESE AIR FORCE HAS CONFUSED MESSAGE IN
SUBSTANCE AS FOLLOWS: 3 REPEAT 3 CREW MEMBERS
OF B-25 AIRPLANE ARE AT CHUCHOW. CREW MEM-
BERS REPORT THEY FLEW 21 HOURS, THAT 16 AIR-
PLANES STARTED, THAT BAD WEATHER DISPERSED
THE FORMATION. WEATHER STILL PRECLUDES FLY-
ING IN ENTIRE AREA. FURTHER INFORMATION WILL
BE FORWARDED WHEN RECEIVED. BISSELL.

Later, on the 21st, another message was sent saying that Stilwell's headquarters had received many conflicting reports and
could not verify the number of crew members killed or injured.
A report from the Chinese at Chuchow said 19 crew members had
now been found.

Stilwell's headquarters was still confused about the project and
requested information on the number of planes and crew members involved in the project "in order to facilitate rescue and
evacuation of B-25 crews dispersed over 100,000 square miles of
eastern China."

Arnold reported in a memorandum to the President on the
21st, that "for the past few days we have had very little positive
information as to what happened to Colonel Doolittle's Squadron
after it took off for its attack on Japan" but added, ". . . it is quite
evident that his Squadron attacked with a considerable amount
of success the targets located in the Tokyo-Osaka area" and that
"the attack came as a complete surprise." He further noted that
"the Japanese, in retaliation, bombed Yushan yesterday morning."

Arnold concluded his memorandum by saying:

"From the viewpoint of damage to enemy installations and
property, and the tremendous effect it had upon our Allies, as
well as the demoralizing effect upon our enemies, the raid was
undoubtedly highly successful. However, from the viewpoint of
an Air Force operation the raid was not a success, for no raid is

a success in which losses exceed ten per cent and it now appears that probably all of the airplanes were lost."

In Washington later that same day, T. V. Soong, the Chinese Minister for Foreign Affairs to the United States, sent a note to General Arnold stating that he had just received a message from Chungking:

> PLEASE TRANSMIT FOLLOWING MESSAGE TO LIEU-
> TENANT GENERAL ARNOLD COMMANDING U. S. AIR
> CORPS
> MISSION TO BOMB TOKYO HAS BEEN ACCOM-
> PLISHED. ON ENTERING CHINA WE RAN INTO BAD
> WEATHER AND IT IS FEARED THAT ALL PLANES
> CRASHED. UP TO THE PRESENT ALREADY FIVE
> CREWS ARE SAFE.
>   COLONEL DOOLITTLE

This was the first news Hap Arnold had received that Doolittle himself was safe. He dispatched a congratulatory message to Doolittle through Chungking, then informed the President by memorandum of what information he had available and added, "Everything points to Doolittle having accomplished a most remarkable flight. He knowingly and willingly took off twelve hours ahead of time, which put him over Japan at the worst possible time of day. He also knew that this would put him over China at night where, if the weather broke against him the chances of getting in safely were very, very poor. Thus, he had the breaks against him on the take-off, at the time he did his bombing, and also at the time of landing in China."

As the hours went by, news of the whereabouts of the crews came in slowly to Stilwell's headquarters in Chungking. Just before midnight on the 21st, Bissell reported to Arnold that "8 airplanes and about 40 crewmen have been located—3 of them are dead." He listed the known survivors and added:

CHINESE AIR WARNING SERVICE PLOTTED MOVE-
MENTS OF 10 AIRCRAFT FROM SEACOAST (OF) OCCU-
PIED CHINA WHICH INDICATED GENERALLY EXCEL-
LENT NAVIGATION TO VICINITY OF AIRDROMES AND
THEREAFTER ERRATIC NAVIGATION.
VERIFIED WEATHER REPORTS INDICATE LATE
AFTERNOON AND EARLY EVENING WEATHER ENTIRE
AIRDROME AREA VERY LOW CLOUDS, MIST, RAIN
AND SOME FOG WITH CEILINGS AND VISIBILITY AT
SOME AIRDROMES UNDER 500 METERS.

At 2:20 P.M. on Wednesday, April 22, the War Department received word from Ambassador William H. Standley in Moscow
that the American Consul in Vladivostok had been notified that
a B-25 had made a forced landing on the 18th at an airfield in
Primovskkrai after their raid on Japan. "Soviet military authorities," he said, "are conducting an investigation for the purpose
of verifying the foregoing information and in the meantime they
have seized the plane and interned the crew at Khaborovsk."

This was Captain Ski York's plane and his crew was reported in
good health. Standley further advised the War Department that
"the Soviet military authorities would like to have this information kept secret and especially do not wish that the press should
know that a United States Army plane had landed in the Soviet
Union." It was this neutralist plea that caused York's crew to be
treated almost as prisoners for the next thirteen months.

It took many days for the story to unravel as Bissell's reports
came in listing survivors and the circumstances as reported to
him by the Chinese. On the 22nd, Arnold wired Bissell to "confer
Distinguished Flying Cross upon all members of Doolittle's flight"
and directed Stilwell to "make this a private ceremony with no
publicity whatsoever attached." This was accomplished and by
May 6, Bissell reported "General Doolittle and all crewmen who

arrived Chungking by May 3 have been decorated by Madame Chiang for Chinese government."

There was an irony about the situation in Chungking of which Arnold and Doolittle were unaware and was not to be known for another seven years. General Claire L. Chennault, leader of the Flying Tigers, was disgusted when he learned of the outcome of Doolittle's mission. Bissell had not once asked him for advice and his bitterness toward the powers in Washington who ignored his experience in fighting the Japanese alongside the Chinese was carried to his grave. Chennault had prepared target folders on Japanese industries four years before and noted in his memoirs that ". . . our notebooks and pictures contained more information on Japanese targets than the War Department intelligence files. Washington intelligence on Japan was so poor that even after Pearl Harbor most of the pages in its secret manuals dealing with Japanese army and navy aircraft were blank. When Jimmy Doolittle wanted pinpoint targets for his first Tokyo raid in the spring of 1942, he found War Department files useless. He had to get his information by personally visiting American business firms with prewar branches in Japan . . ." [5]

Chennault had personally disliked Bissell since his days as a student at the Air Corps Tactical School in 1931. He complained that Bissell was so secretive about the Doolittle raid preparations that he never once informed Chennault what he was planning.

"As a result," Chennault wrote, "when the Doolittle raiders were forced to change their plans and arrived over China in darkness and bad weather the vast warning net of East China had no way of communicating with the American bombers and guiding them over the unfamiliar terrain. If I had been notified, a single A.V.G. command ground radio station plugged into the East China net would have talked most of the raiders into a friendly field . . . My bitterness over that bit of bungling has not eased with the passing years." [6]

Behind the scenes in the newly-occupied Pentagon building in Washington, Major General Dwight D. Eisenhower, Assistant Chief of Staff to General Marshall, reviewed the scanty Chungking reports on April 20. He asked that an analysis of Japanese capability to retaliate for the Doolittle raid be made immediately by the military intelligence staff. The report, written later that day, affirmed what Eisenhower had feared: "Japan can make an air attack on lucrative military objectives in southern California and elsewhere on the west coast," it said, "by using aircraft carriers . . . From the information available as to Japanese naval dispositions, it appears that a carrier-borne attack can hardly be made before the first week in May. It can readily be made at any time after May 10, 1942. . . . It seems obvious that the Japanese would be willing to take long risks in order to achieve the objectives of causing destruction of or serious damage to important military objectives on the west coast of the United States."

Military intelligence analysts studied the effect of the raid on the Japanese and reported to Eisenhower that the Japanese believed "saving face" was all important to an Oriental. "A gift must be properly and promptly recognized by giving to the donor a gift of equal or greater value," Eisenhower was told, "otherwise you will be deemed inferior to the first donor, both in his mind, and also in the minds of all who know or may know of the transaction."

The report left with Eisenhower further pointed out:

. . . in the samurai (warrior) class and among those who, while not samurai, emulate their deeds and glorify their traditions, an injury received or a wrong done must be repaid in kind or in greater measure. Failure to do so would again make the recipient of the injury feel that he was untrue to the ideals of "Bushido"

Major General Millard F. Harmon, Chief of the Air Staff under General Arnold, decorated the most seriously injured Tokyo raiders at Walter Reed Hospital, Washington, D.C. Left to right are General Harmon, Brig. Gen. Doolittle, Lt. McClure, Secretary of the Treasury Henry Morgenthau, Lt. Watson, and Lt. Lawson. Lawson's leg was amputated by Lt. White, the only physician on the raid, in China.

(way of the warrior) and inferior to the one who dealt the injury or wrong. The offender would know he was superior to the offended and all who knew about the circumstances would know who was the superior individual.[7]

The successes enjoyed by the Japanese had, beyond doubt, solidified their national war effort and American slowness to return the injury received, to the Japanese mind, was "a sign of cowardice and national apathy to the war."

The report continued:

> Japanese airmen have become national heroes and are naturally regarded as wholly superior to all other airmen. A raid on the west coast of America would maintain their prestige. Failure to make such a raid would impair it.
>
> The military clique in Japan has acquired a semi-sacred status. In order to maintain this status, it is obviously necessary to keep the people convinced of the infallibility of the clique and the invulnerability of Japan.
>
> A repetition of the attack on the Hawaiian Islands would hardly be considered sufficient as retaliation for the attack on Japan. A direct Axis attack on Washington would be the only type to be considered in full retaliation. Short of that only an attack on the west coast of the United States or on the Panama Canal would suffice.

Eisenhower, ever-mindful of the lack of preparedness at Pearl Harbor, composed a message in the name of General Marshall and dispatched it to the Commanding General, Western Defense Command. The message warned of the possibility of a Japanese air raid and promised that if an attack were imminent, additional planes and antiaircraft batteries would be provided.

The carrier-borne attack against the continent of the United States never materialized but if it had plans had been promptly laid to strengthen air defenses along the west coastal regions. As planes and trained personnel became available, fear of the attack lessened.

The precaution taken by Eisenhower to protect the mainland from attack was the least of the after-effects of the raid. After the surrender of Japan, United States Strategic Bombing Survey teams interviewed hundreds of Japanese Army and Navy personnel to determine the total effects of the Doolittle and subsequent Allied raids on the enemy. Not only the physical effects of aerial bombardment but the psychological effects on the minds and actions of the Japanese were also studied. After a careful analysis it was found that the Doolittle raid had a far greater impact on Japanese strategy and morale in the Pacific than anyone had realized. Postwar histories, memoirs, and interrogations reveal some surprising changes caused by this operation that took place in Japanese planning.

Early in 1941, Admiral Isoroku Yamamoto, Commander-in-Chief of the Japanese Combined Fleet, followed the steady deterioration in Japanese-United States relations closely. In the planning sessions when the possibility of war was openly discussed, Yamamoto argued that Japan had no hope of winning a war against America unless the Hawaii-based U.S. Pacific Fleet were destroyed. This could be done, he said, at Pearl Harbor with a surprise air raid of Navy carrier planes. It was this concept of Yamamoto's which led to the Combined Fleet's Secret Operation Order No. 1—the Pearl Harbor attack—and almost accomplished his objective.[8]

The subsequent conquest of the Philippines, Netherlands, East Indies, Burma, and Malaya, completed by the end of March, 1942, had required only about half the time the Japanese had anticipated. In the entire campaign they had lost no naval vessel larger than a destroyer.

The speed of attainment of these objectives so surprised Japanese planners that a basic decision as to future strategy had to be made. The gains already made would naturally have to be consolidated, but what next? Should they move westward against Ceylon and India, southward against Australia or eastward against Midway, Hawaii, the Aleutians, and eventually the United States?

The first two possibilities were advocated by some officers of the Naval General Staff, while Yamamoto and his Combined Fleet planners believed the third course was essential to complete the destruction of the American fleet. There were also serious objections from Japanese Army officers to the first two strategies because of the necessity for committing large numbers of troops to cover such vast territory. To satisfy these opposing viewpoints, a compromise strategy was developed. Australia was to be isolated by moving from Rabaul into Eastern New Guinea then through the Solomons and the New Hebrides to New Caledonia, the Fijis, and Samoa.

The Japanese landings at Lae and Salamaua in early March, 1942, were in support of this compromise plan and preparations were underway in early April to capture Port Moresby and Tulagi. But Yamamoto, a strong advocate of carrier-based air power, was concerned about the American carriers still afloat which had been missed at Pearl Harbor. He argued that destruction of these carriers was absolutely essential to Japanese security in the Pacific and persisted in the view that Midway Island should be seized and operations against the Aleutians begun at the earliest possible moment to draw out the remnants of the American naval forces, especially the carriers.[9]

The debate in Japanese military circles was in full swing while the Halsey task force was steaming toward Japan. Although Yamamoto had finally convinced the reluctant Japanese Naval General

Staff of the merits of his argument, the details had not been worked out and no date had been set if the strategy were approved by the Imperial General Headquarters.

Yamamoto was deeply shocked when he heard the news of the Doolittle attack. He spurred his staff into frantic activity to locate the carriers and, at the same time, determine the launching point of the bombers since he did not believe the B-25's had departed from a carrier. At first, his staff was divided in their estimates. One group believed that the Americans had intended to make an attack combining land-based medium bombers with the shorter-range carrier planes. The bombers were thought by some to have come from Midway, 2,300 miles east of Tokyo. Others, estimating that not enough gas and bombs could be carried on the B-25 to make that distance and still fly to China, felt that somehow the clever Americans had devised a method for launching heavy land bombers from the incredibly short length of a carrier's deck. It was several days before his staff was completely convinced that the latter estimate was correct.

Yamamoto's shock was not exaggerated. He was sharply sensitive to his responsibility and had the deep-rooted devotion to his Emperor which had long characterized the Japanese national psychology. The Army and Navy had been thoroughly imbued with the idea that it was their individual and collective duty to protect the Emperor and his family from danger. It was considered a grave dereliction of duty for anyone in a responsible position to allow the Emperor's life to be placed in jeopardy by even a single enemy raid on the capital city.

Although the primary responsibility for air defense of the home islands rested with the Army, the fact that the bombers had come from an enemy naval task force made it a naval responsibility. Yamamoto, as supreme commander of the Japanese Fleet, considered the Doolittle attack a personal affront to his military judgment and blamed himself for allowing the Americans to carry out a surprise attack from the sea precisely as his forces had done at Pearl Harbor. Some retaliatory action had to be taken as soon as possible.[10]

The debate about Yamamoto's strategy ended when it was deduced that the raid had indeed been launched by an American task force. Reluctantly, it was agreed that Yamamoto should be allowed to pursue his original master plan.

Within two weeks after Doolittle's B-25's swooped down over Tokyo, Yamamoto officially approved and forwarded the details for "Operation MI" which had as its objective the occupancy of Midway and the capture of certain positions along the Aleutian chain. He was confident that Nimitz would commit all his available forces to prevent this possibility and an overwhelming Japanese victory would be inevitable. On May 5, Navy Order No. 18 was issued by Imperial General Headquarters directing Yamamoto to:

Invade and occupy Midway Island and key points in the western Aleutians in cooperation with the Army, in order to prevent enemy task forces from making attacks against the homeland.

Destroy all enemy forces that may oppose the invasion.

This was to be the most ambitious undertaking in the ten-year history of the modern Japanese navy. Just as with the attack on Pearl Harbor, Yamamoto had his way in how it was to be carried out. Unlike the operation at Pearl Harbor, however, the outcome was disastrous for the Japanese. Well over 150 Japanese ships, including 11 battleships, 10 heavy cruisers, and 5 aircraft carriers with full complements of planes aboard, sailed into battle. Arrayed against this formidable force was the woefully inferior

American fleet built around the carriers *Hornet, Enterprise* and *Yorktown*. Eight cruisers, 14 destroyers, 25 submarines and a number of tankers were mustered. With the Army Air Forces B-17's based on Midway, it was to be a duel to the death. When the battle was over, however, American losses were only 1 aircraft carrier and 1 destroyer sunk and 147 planes destroyed. The Japanese lost 4 carriers, a heavy cruiser and suffered major damage to 6 other large warships. In addition, the amazing total of 332 Japanese planes were destroyed or failed to return from their missions.

Captain Y. Watanabe, commander-in-chief of the Second Fleet at the Battle of Midway, was a gunnery officer on Yamamoto's staff when the operation was being planned. Watanabe was interrogated soon after the war and confirmed the significance of the Doolittle raid in connection with the Midway operation. The following transcript, long buried in naval intelligence files, was made on October 15, 1945 in Tokyo:

Q. What were the plans leading up to the attack?
A. We intended to capture Midway because on 18 April we were attacked in Tokyo for the first time. We thought the planes came from Midway.

Q. Did you believe that by taking Midway there would be no more raids on Tokyo?
A. Yes.

Q. Did you intend to go beyond Midway?
A. If we could, we wanted to go to Pearl Harbor; but it was not authorized because it was too far. We intended to capture small islands between Midway and Pearl Harbor. If we captured these islands, the land-based planes could attack Pearl Harbor. We wanted to capture Pearl Harbor later.

Both American and Japanese historians now concur that the war was lost for Japan beginning at the Battle of Midway. Yamamoto's crippled forces limped home to lick their wounds, never again to make such a bold offensive toward American shores. The Imperial Navy General Staff recognized the disaster for what it was but the truth remained hidden as a Navy secret, even from Premier Tojo, until the war was almost over. The historic action was a joint Army Air Forces-Navy victory for the Americans and marked the exact moment when the Rising Sun reached its zenith in the sky. From that time on, it became a setting sun, in large part because of the seemingly inconsequential raid of Doolittle's bombers six weeks before.[11]

Another curious evidence of the impact of the Doolittle raid came to light after the war. It is known that during the final stages of the Pacific war the Japanese made a futile effort to attack the western portion of the United States by means of bomb-carrying free balloons launched from the home islands and carried across the Pacific at high altitudes by the prevailing westerly winds. At least six people were killed by these bombs in the U.S. A total of 285 balloons were identified as having landed in the U.S., Alaska, and Canada between November 4, 1944 and August 8, 1945.[12]

After the defeat of Japan, newspapermen queried Japanese military authorities as to the reasons for the balloon attacks and learned that "the balloon bomb was Japan's V-1 weapon in efforts to get revenge for the Doolittle raid on Tokyo in April, 1942." According to the news reports, the Tokyo raid so angered Japanese military authorities that they were determined to find a means of attacking the United States in retaliation. Because of the poverty of Japan and the effects of the war, the balloons were made of large sheets of paper which were glued together in small family workshops; they were then launched from three sites near Tokyo. Two years were required to complete the experiments and more than nine million yen (over two million dollars at prewar exchange) was spent on the project.

It has never been possible to determine exactly how much physical damage the bombs dropped from the B-25's actually caused. After the raid, the Japanese moved almost immediately to screen the effects of the attack from public view. In the first few hours after the attack, control over the news releases was partly lost and there were some highly exaggerated statements such as the one heard on the radio aboard the *Hornet,* which reported large fleets of bombers and several thousand casualties. Thereafter, the official statements were all vague and misleading. The propaganda line eventually became that there was little or no damage to military targets and that the Americans had bombed only schools and hospitals. Thus, the average Japanese knew very little or nothing about damage done or the casualties.

In the months following the raid, many Japanese prisoners were interrogated with reference to the Tokyo bombing and it was found that they repeated largely the words the government had put in their mouths. Few had seen anything of consequence even though they may have been in Tokyo at the time.[13] The policy of covering up the effects of the raid was so effective that no records of physical damage were ever found after the war. However, the psychological after-effects and the fact that the Battle of Midway might not have been fought except for the Doolittle raid are the real reasons this single air raid has become a legend and deserves to be remembered.

NOTES TO CHAPTER 26

1. Samuel I. Rosenman, *The Public Papers and Addresses of Franklin D. Roosevelt,* 1942 Volume (New York: Harper & Row, 1950), p. 216.

2. The President accepted the name "Shangri-La" for his retreat in the Catoctin Mountains of Maryland when newsmen and others called it that later. Toward the end of the war, the Navy also named an aircraft carrier the *Shangri-La.*

3. Tokyo Radio, December 8, 1941.

4. An Army officer, in discussing the raid with a civilian member of the motion picture industry in Los Angeles, speculated that the raid had been carried out from a carrier. The civilian was "shocked that an Army officer was giving out such information" and turned his name in to Army intelligence. An investigation was ordered immediately by General Arnold but it was concluded that the officer had no definite information on the raid and that all comments had been based on rumor or hearsay. He was, however, given an official admonition by Arnold "for loose talk about military matters," and "enjoined henceforth to comply strictly with existing regulations regarding discussion of military subjects in the presence of unauthorized persons."

5. *Way of a Fighter: The Memoirs of Claire Lee Chennault,* pp. 32-33.

6. *Ibid.,* p. 168.

7. Memorandum for the Assistant Chief of Staff, OPD, Subject: Increased Probability of a Japanese Air Raid on the West Coast as the Result of the Air Attack on Japan, April 20, 1942.

8. See Thaddeus V. Tuleja, *Climax at Midway* (New York: Berkley Books, 1960) for an excellent account of the preliminaries leading to the Midway action.

9. It was largely through Yamamoto's efforts that the Japanese Imperial Navy had ten aircraft carriers in commission by December, 1941, while the United States had only half that number. All U. S. carriers were still afloat although the *Saratoga* had been damaged by a Japanese submarine torpedo on January 11 and the *Enterprise* by a Japanese plane crashing on its deck on February. 1.

10. Mitsuo Fuchida and Masatake Okumiya, *Midway: The Battle That Doomed Japan* (Annapolis: United States Naval Institute, 1955), pp. 68-69.

11. Ironically, Yamamoto was killed on the first anniversary of the raid, April 18, 1943, when the transport in which he was a passenger was shot down by an Air Force fighter plane near Bougainville.

12. Fourth Air Force Historical Study No. III-2.

13. Colonel S. L. A. Marshall, "Report of Tokyo Raid," Manuscript No. 2-3.7, Office of the Chief of Military History, Special Staff, U. S. Army, undated.

EPILOGUE

On board the *Hornet* the day before the take-off, Jimmy Doo-little promised, "If we get to Chungking, I'll throw you fellas the biggest party you ever had." He was unable to keep that promise because he was ordered to return to the States before his crews were collected in Chungking. But he never forgot this vow be-cause the comradeship and the sharing of a common fate with his men meant more to him than anything else in his military life. He had faced danger and death with them; more than that, he had worked and trained beside them and then led them into battle. He loved them for their bravery and their bravado. He respected them for their ingenuity and their individualism. He wanted them to stick together and keep in touch with him and one another.

April 18, 1943, the first anniversary of the raid, found Doolittle, by then a major general, and a few other officer veterans of the Tokyo Raid in North Africa. A party was held in a small farm-house to celebrate the first anniversary of their mission but it was not what Doolittle had in mind. He wanted all of his Raiders to come and they were spread all over the globe fighting the enemy on a dozen fronts.

Although war correspondents played up the event in North Africa, the Raiders themselves did not. Reporters asked Hank Potter, Doolittle's navigator, about the raid and he told them he was more concerned about the war in North Africa than the single mission they had flown a year before. The others felt the

General Doolittle and veterans of the raid held an informal reunion on the first anniversary of their historic mission. Meeting in a North African farmhouse, they drank a toast to those who could not join them. Not all of those pictured actually flew on the mission; some were available on the carrier as spare crew members. On this same day, April 18, 1943, Admiral Isoroku Yamamoto, the Japanese who masterminded the attack on Pearl Harbor, was shot down by Army Air Force planes off Bougainville.

same way. While informal reunions were held in 1944 and 1945 whenever several Raiders found themselves near each other and could spare time from their duties, it was not until the war was over that Doolittle was able to keep his promise.

In the fall of 1945, Doolittle passed the word to all living members of his group who could make it to meet him in Miami at the MacFadden Deauville Hotel. It cost Jimmy Doolittle over $2,000 out of his own pocket to make good on the vow he had made on the *Hornet*. The Raiders had a rousing good time and enjoyed themselves so much that someone suggested, "Let's do this every year!" Doolittle replied, "I'd like that fellas, but I'm afraid I couldn't afford it. From here on, it's up to you to carry the ball."

No reunion was held in 1946 but Miami again echoed to the laughter and toasts of Jimmy Doolittle and his men in 1947. With two years of post-war adjustment behind them, they relaxed completely, much to the chagrin of Tom Willemstyn, the hotel's night watchman. He reported to his boss:

> The Doolittle boys added some gray hairs to my head. This has been the worst night since I worked here. They were completely out of my control.
>
> I let them make a lot of noise but when about fifteen of them went in the pool at 1:00 A.M. (including Doolittle) I told them there was no swimming allowed at night. They were in the pool until 2:30 A.M.
>
> I went up twice more without results. They were running around in the halls in their bathing suits and were noisy up until 5:00 A. M. Yes, it was a rough night.

The hotel manager was not upset when he read Willemstyn's report. He turned the memo over to Doolittle saying that his boys had earned the right to make all the noise they wanted in his hotel. He asked if they would honor the occasion by autographing the report, which they did.

Every year since 1947, (except 1951 because of the Korean War), the group has met in various cities from coast to coast as the guests of prominent members of the community, civic organizations, and industry. Gifts have been given to the Raiders by a grateful citizenry; for example, the beautiful display case and the silver goblets used by the men in their annual toast to their departed comrades was presented to them by the City of Tucson in 1959. The year before, the North American Aviation Co. presented a B-25 Mitchell bomber to the group similar to the model they had all flown from the *Hornet*. Completely reconditioned, it was flown to Las Vegas, site of the sixteenth reunion and then to Wright-Patterson Air Force Base, Ohio for permanent display in the Air Force Museum—where it can be seen today.

The reunions are mostly lighthearted affairs consisting of three days of reminiscing for the Raiders. A press conference is held and a formal banquet is planned to which the public is invited. The entertainment for the banquet is usually a celebrity who donates his time and talent in grateful appreciation to Jimmy Doolittle's boys. Bob Hope, Arthur Godfrey, Joe E. Brown, Bob Cummings, Alex Drier, Chester Louck (of Lum and Abner) and George Jessel have been among those who have appeared. Many Congressmen and high-ranking Army, Navy, and Air Force personnel have attended.

The thirteenth reunion held in Los Angeles in April 1955 was one that three of the Raiders will never forget. Colonel Bill Bower, then commander of Dobbins Air Force Base, Georgia, Ed Horton and Adam R. Williams were passengers on a C-47 that was going to take them to the West Coast. The plane took off from Atlanta, where it had stopped for more passengers, and headed for Barksdale Air Force Base, Louisiana. A few minutes after take-off, the left propeller started to surge and then "ran away." The pilot, Capt. John England and co-pilot Capt. W. E. Brown, turned back toward their home base but the overspeeding propeller could not be controlled and the plane rapidly began to lose speed and altitude.

The co-pilot ordered all baggage thrown overboard and told the passengers they would have to bail out. One by one in orderly fashion, ten men bailed out, the last about one thousand feet above the ground. Bill Bower, calm and unruffled as usual, elected to stay with the plane.

After the jump, the plane gained a little speed, just managed to clear a ridge near the Fulton County Airport, Georgia and landed on its short runway. When the crippled C-47 stopped, Bill Bower leaped out and saw a helicopter warming up on the parking ramp. He quickly told its pilot what had happened and was immediately back in the air searching for the ten men who had parachuted only minutes before. Fortunately, all ten were found safe and only two were slightly injured. Ed Horton, the calm, efficient gunner on Dick Joyce's plane suffered laceration of an ear in this, his second jump. It was Adam Williams' fourth bail-out, his first being the night he jumped from the plane in China.

Undaunted, the three Tokyo Raiders proceeded to the reunion, the only irksome development being that they were without their luggage which had been strewn over the Georgia countryside and was not all found until after their return.

The tone of the annual meetings has changed over the years since Jimmy Doolittle carried out his promise in 1945. The Raiders frankly admit they met at first solely for fun and fellowship. But as the years passed and their personal responsibilities grew, the Raiders' original purpose enlarged and matured with them. Now they meet for three purposes: to renew old friendships, to honor the memory of those who have passed on and to participate in some activity which is of benefit to the nation, to the Air Force and the community in which they meet.

Each year the Tokyo Raiders present two trophies to the units of the Air Force with the best traffic safety and ground safety records. These annual awards were decided upon to encourage safety consciousness on the ground, since more people in the Air Force are killed in ground activities than in any other kind of accident. Since the awards have been made, the Air Force has reported that there has been a 40 percent reduction in fatalities occurring on the ground, due in large measure to the safety consciousness created by the awards. Not only the Air Force but the Nation has benefitted.

On the twentieth anniversary of their day of glory, the Raiders decided to chip in for an annual scholarship to be awarded to a deserving young man enrolled in an accredited university in the city in which they meet each year. The candidate for the award must be a top student enrolled as a senior in science and engineering who intends to seek a career in aerospace science. Established in the name of General Doolittle because of deep respect and affection for his inspirational leadership, the first scholarship, in the amount of $1,500, was proudly awarded by the Raiders to Robert P. Wilcke of Santa Monica, California, a student at the University of California at Los Angeles.

Much as they would like to, the Raiders cannot always make the $1,500 needed each year to maintain the scholarship. Whatever deficiency there is each year is made up by anonymous donors and private industry. In 1963, the group incorporated itself as the Doolittle Tokyo Raiders Association, a non-profit organization.

Congressman George P. Miller of Alameda, California, chairman of the House Committee on Science and Astronautics and a guest of the Raiders in 1962, expressed his appreciation in behalf of the Nation for their unselfish act in establishing the Doolittle scholarship. He said, "you are awarding a scholarship to a young man who is representative of the next generation to assume responsibility for the future growth of America. You have by this award recognized both tacitly and specifically that the growth of the United States is so very dependent upon the knowledge and capabilities of the people who will contribute to it.

"It is particularly significant that this scholarship is directed toward scientific and technical training, for this highlights a very serious problem confronting the United States, the solution of which can have direct and material effects upon the future progress and survival of our country as a community of free people."

Congressman Miller concluded by congratulating the Raiders on establishing the scholarship because "it manifests your deep desire to contribute in a material way to the betterment of our Nation," and then added "you men who are on the roster of great 'firsts' in peace and war, have risen to meet the greatest challenges asked by you and your country and by yourselves. There can be no higher accolade than that."

Brigadier General John A. Hilger, chairman of the 1963 reunion in Seattle, gave a short introductory speech at the banquet given in the Raiders' honor. He reminded the audience that at that very moment, there were hundreds of officers and men of the Air Force and the other armed services standing lonely vigils so that they might have such a meeting in safety.

> The names of many of these places where our men are standing watch are quite familiar to you: Berlin—Viet Nam—South Korea—the straits of Florida. There are many other places, too,

which we in our existence here in the United States don't hear much about and have a tendency to forget. These are such places as the lonely radar sites in the Arctic, the closer, but sometimes just as lonely, radar sites along our eastern and western coasts and along our northern boundary—missile sites, scattered from Seattle to Sioux City with underground control rooms where men sit for endless hours watching control boards to be certain that we will be able and ready to strike back if we are attacked— the air defense alert rooms where fighter crews stand ready on the alert in all areas where the enemy could approach by air— aboard silent submarines, cruising below the oceans of the world—our carrier task forces at sea and alert—our airborne Strategic Air Command alert force in the air in order that they will not be surprised on the ground—pacing sentries watchfully waiting in Guam and Guantanamo—our alert Tactical Air Command and Strike Command forces waiting to be deployed to Turkey or Taiwan; to Cuba or the Congo, or wherever trouble rears its head.

These men of all services all over the world are our comrades in arms but none of these men can be effective without the support of our nation. There must be reassurance that never again shall our country be caught unprepared or not ready to fight when fighting is the only course of action left open.

Hilger concluded by saying, "Tonight our prayers are for peace. We all know full well that an effective armed force is our best guarantee of this peace. Our heartfelt hope is that the vigil will remain a vigil; that our forces will never need to be called into action. But, if we must fight, may God grant us the foresight to be prepared."

Jimmy Doolittle and his men, now all past the threshold of middle age, plan to meet each year as long as they live. Each year they will continue to drink a toast to their fellow crew members who can no longer join them. The last two surviving members will open a bottle of brandy contained in the display case where their silver goblets are kept and drink a final toast. When that inevitable day comes, a glorious chapter in aviation history will close forever. But the deed the original 80 men performed that eventful day in 1942 will never be forgotten. Our nation has been fortunate that it has always had men like Jimmy Doolittle and his intrepid airmen who have risen to the challenge of death when our nation's life has been threatened. May it always be so.

APPENDICES

THE DEED . . . 1. Chart of Results of the Mission

Pilot	Target City	Interception	Anti-aircraft	Results	Landing
Doolittle	Tokyo	Nine	Intense	Factory area	Bailed out near Tien Mu Shen, 70 miles north of Chuchow.
Hoover	Tokyo	None	None	Two factories and warehouse	Crash landed near Ningpo.
Gray	Tokyo	Several	Moderate	Gas and Chemical plant Dock area	Bailed out southeast of Chuchow. Cpl. Leland Faktor killed after bailout.
Holstrom	Tokyo	Large number	None	Guns inoperative; bombs jettisoned	Bailed out southeast of Shangjao.
Jones	Tokyo	None	Intense	Oil storage tanks, power station and factory	Bailed out southeast of Chuchow.
Hallmark	Tokyo	None	Intense	Steel mills	Crash-landed in Nanchang area near Poyang Lake. Sgt. W. J. Dieter and Cpl. D. E. Fitzmaurice died of injuries. Rest of crew captured.
Lawson	Tokyo	None	Moderate	Direct hits on factory, steel mill	Crash landed in water off coast near Shangchow.
York	Tokyo	One	None	Large factory	Landed 40 miles north of Vladivostok; crew interned.

Pilot	Target	Enemy Aircraft	Anti-Aircraft Fire	Targets Bombed	Remarks
Watson	Tokyo	One (believed shot down)	Intense	Gas plant, power station and tank factory	Bailed out 100 miles south of Poyang Lake.
Joyce	Tokyo	Sixteen (two believed shot down)	Heavy (hole in aircraft)	Steel works and factory area	Bailed out 30 miles north of Chuchow.
Greening	Yokohama	Five (two believed shot down)	Light	Refinery and oil storage tanks; patrol boat burned	Bailed out 50 miles northwest of Chuchow.
Bower	Yokohama	None	Light	Dock area	Bailed out at Suien, northwest of Chuchow.
McElroy	Yokosuka	None	Heavy	Dock area; aircraft carrier in dry dock	Bailed out near Hsihsien.
Hilger	Nagoya	None	Heavy	Aircraft factory, barracks, oil tanks, arsenal	Bailed out southeast of Shangjao near Kwangfeng.
Smith	Kobe	Two	Light	Steel works	Crash landed in water near Shangchow.
Farrow	Nagoya *	Three	Heavy	Oil tanks, aircraft factory	Bailed out near coast at Shipu south of Hanchung. Crew captured.

* Primary target assigned was Osaka; Nagoya was secondary.

409

THE MEN . . . 2. Biographical Sketches of the Raiders

There were only eighty men on the raid that bombed Japan on April 18, 1942. Through the years, however, many imposters have represented themselves as having "flown with Doolittle on the Tokyo Raid." For the record, biographical sketches of each man are provided the reader. Ranks shown are the highest ranks held while in either active duty or reserve status with the Air Force.

The Tokyo Raiders have honored two other men by making them "Honorary Tokyo Raiders" for the parts they have played in assisting the Raiders. No other persons can claim membership in this exclusive fraternity.

BAIN, EDWIN V., Master Sergeant
        Born September 23, 1917 at Greensboro, North Carolina. Attended Garfield High School, Los Angeles, California. Entered service August 20, 1936. Graduated Radio Repair and Operator School, Chanute Field, Illinois. Served in North Africa after Tokyo Raid. Killed in action July 19, 1943 when plane crashed in Tyrrhenean Sea while returning from combat mission over Italy. Decorations include Distinguished Flying Cross, Soldier's Medal, Air Medal with two Oak Leaf Cluster, Purple Heart, and Chinese Army, Navy, Air Corps Medal, Class A, 1st Grade.

BARR, GEORGE, Captain
        Born April 6, 1917 at Brooklyn, New York. Graduated Yonders High School, Yonkers, New York. Entered service on February 10, 1941. Completed training as a navigator and commissioned a Second Lieutenant at Pendleton, Oregon on December 6, 1941. Earned BA degree from Northland College, Ashland, Wisconsin and MA from Columbia University, New York, N.Y. Was prisoner of war of Japanese from April, 1942 until August, 1945. Retired for physical disability on September 16, 1947. Decorations: Distinguished Flying Cross, Chinese Breast Order of Pao Ting. Employed as a management analyst for the U.S. Army until his death on July 12, 1967.

BIRCH, WILLIAM L., Second Lieutenant
Born September 7, 1917 at Galexico, California. Graduated from Kern County Union High School, California. Entered service on September 14, 1939 at March Field, California. Graduted from Bombsight Maintenance School, Lowry Field, Colorado. After raid attended Pilot Training Schools and graduated from Advanced Flying School, Lubbock, Texas in June, 1943. Separated from service after various Stateside assignments on December 7, 1945. Decorations include Distinguished Flying Cross and Chinese Army, Navy, and Air Corps Medal, Class A, 1st Grade.

BISSELL, WAYNE MAX, First Lieutenant
Born October 22, 1921 at Walker, Minnesota. Graduated from Vancouver High School, Vancouver, Washington in 1939. Enlisted U.S. Army September 14, 1939 and completed enlisted bombardier training. After Doolittle Raid, attended pilot training and received wings and commission on July 28, 1943. Served as B-25 pilot in Soutwest Pacific. Separated from service July, 1945. Decorations incude Distinguished Flying Cross, Air Medal with 2 Oak Leaf Clusters, and Chinese Army, Navy, and Air Corps Medal, Class A, 1st Grade.

BITHER, WALDO J., Major
Born October 31, 1906 in Linnew, Maine. Graduated from Ricker Classical Institute. Entered service January 27, 1925. Served in Coast Artillery in Philippines from 1925 until 1928. Enlisted Army Air Corps and completed armorer and bombardier-navigator training. After Tokyo Raid was commissioned and served as Aircraft Maintenance Officer in European Theater of Operations and Japan, in addition to Stateside service. Retired January 31, 1954 with over 28 years of service. Employed by General Services Administration; retired from Civil Service January 31, 1971. Decorations include Distinguised Flying Cross, Bronze Star, and Chinese Army, Navy, and Air Corps Medal, Class A, 1st Grade.

BLANTON, THADD HARRISON, Lieutenant Colonel
Born February 25, 1919 at Archer City, Texas. Attended Texas State Teachers College. Entered service on November 25, 1940 at Dallas, Texas. Completed flight training in July, 1941. Remained in China-Burma-India Theater after Tokyo Raid until July, 1943. Escaped from enemy territory after plane crash in Burma. Stationed in Alaska, British West Indies, and the Philippines after World War II.

412Appendices

Retired for physical disability on November 15, 1960. Died at Orlando, Florida September 27, 1961. Decorations include Distinguished Flying Cross, Air Medal, Chinese Army, Navy, and Air Corps Medal, Class A, 1st Grade, and Chinese Order of the Cloud Banner, 5th Class.

BOURGEOIS, ROBERT C., Flight Officer
Born September 28, 1917 at Lecompte, Louisiana. Graduated from high school and attended Delgado Trade School, New Orleans, Louisiana. Entered service October 14, 1939 at New Orleans. Graduated Bombsight Maintenance School, Lowry Air Force Base, Colorado. Remained in China, Burma-India-Theater after Tokyo Raid until July 15, 1943. Separated from active duty March 9, 1946. Decorations include Distinguished Flying Cross, Air Medal, and Chinese Army, Navy, and Air Corps Medal, Class A, 1st Grade.

BOWER, WILLIAM M., Colonel
Born February 13, 1917 in Ravenna, Ohio. Attended Hiram College and Kent State University, Ohio. Commissioned and rated Pilot October 4, 1940. After Tokyo Raid served with Mediterranean Air Force and 12th Air Force in England, Africa, and Italy. Joined Regular Air Force after WWII. Retired 1966. Decorations include Distinguished Flying Cross, Bronze Star, Air Medal and Clusters, Army and Air Force Commendation Ribbon, Chinese Army, Navy, and Air Corps Medal, Class A, and French Croix de Guerre.

BRAEMER, FRED ANTHONY, Captain
Born January 31, 1917 at Seattle, Washington. Graduated Ballard High School, Seattle in 1935. Enlisted at Fort Jay, New York on September 16, 1935. Attended Military Intelligence, Bombardier and Navigator Schools before Tokyo Raid. Remained In China-Burma-India Theater after raid until July 15, 1943. Commissioned as Second Lieutenant and attended Bombardier, Radar, and Observer Training Schools and became "triple rated." Released from active duty as an officer on November 1, 1945. Re-entered service in enlisted status during Korean War. Retired 1968. Decorations include Distinguished Flying Cross, Air Medal with 1 Oak Leaf Cluster, and Chinese Army, Navy, and Air Corps Medal, Class A, 1st Grade.

CAMPBELL, CLAYTON J., Lieutenant Colonel
Born March 14, 1917 at St. Maries, Idaho. Graduated from University of Idaho, with B.S. degree, 1940. Entered service June, 1940 at Fort Wright, Spokane, Washington. Commissioned and rated

as navigator, June, 1941. Remained in China-Burma-India Theater after Tokyo Raid and flew 250 combat hours. Released from active duty, December, 1945. Decorations include Distinguished Flying Cross, Silver Star, Air Medal and Chinese Army, Navy and Air Corps Medal, Class A, 1st Grade.

CLEVER, ROBERT STEVENSON, First Lieutenant
Born May 22, 1914 at Portland, Oregon. Enlisted as Aviation Cadet at Vancouver Barracks, Washington on March 15, 1941. Commissioned as Second Lieutenant with rating of bombardier on December 16, 1941 at Pendleton Field, Oregon. Injured on Tokyo Raid. Stationed at Baer Field, Fort Wayne, Indiana when he was killed in an airplane crash near Versailles, Ohio on November 20, 1942. Decorations include Distinguished Flying Cross and Chinese Army, Navy, and Air Corps Medal, Class A, 1st Grade.

COLE, RICHARD E., Colonel
Born September 7, 1915 at Dayton, Ohio. Graduated Steele High School, Dayton and completed two years college at Ohio University. Enlisted November 22, 1940. Completed pilot training and commissioned as Second Lieutenant, July, 1941. Remained in CBI after Tokyo Raid until June, 1943, and served again in CBI from October, 1943 until June, 1944. Relieved from active duty in January, 1947 but returned to active duty in August 1947. Was Operations Advisor to Venezuelan Air Force from 1959 to 1962. Peacetime service in Ohio, North Carolina, and California. Rated as command pilot. Decorations include Distinguished Flying Cross with 2 Oak Leaf Clusters, Air Medal with 1 Oak Leaf Cluster, Bronze Star Medal, Air Force Commendation Medal, and Chinese Army, Navy, and Air Corps Medal, Class A, 1st Grade. Retired January 1, 1967.

CROUCH, HORACE ELLIS, Lieutenant Colonel
Born October 29, 1918 at Columbia, South Carolina. Graduated from Columbia High School in 1936. Graduated with B.S. in civil engineering from The Citadel in 1940. Served in South Carolina National Guard from 1937 until 1940. Accepted commission as Second Lieutenant July 11, 1940. Attended Bombardier, Navigator and Radar Training and became "triple rated." Remained in China-Burma-India Theater after Tokyo Raid until June 13, 1943. After World War II, served three tours in the Pacific and one tour each in England, North Africa, and Germany. Retired as Lieutenant Colonel on April 30, 1962. Decorations include the Silver Star, Distinguished Flying Cross, Air Medal with 1 Oak Leaf Cluster, and the Chinese

Army, Navy, and Air Corps Medal, Class A, 1st Grade. Received Master of Industrial Education degree from Clemson University, 1973. Teaches mathematics and drafting at Columbia High School, Columbia, S.C.

DAVENPORT, DEAN, Colonel
        Born June 29, 1918 at Spokane, Washington. Graduated from Portland High School, Portland, Oregon in 1937. Studied law at Albany and Northwestern Colleges in Portland until he enlisted as a Flying Cadet on February 7, 1941. Graduated from Advanced Flying School and commissioned as a Second Lieutenant on September 27, 1941. Returned from India in October, 1942. Was later technical advisor for film "Thirty Seconds Over Tokyo" which was story of his pilot, Ted Lawson. Served in Alaska flying P-40, P-38 and P-51 aircraft from 1944 until 1947. Has been commanding officer of several fighter units and is now commanding an Air Defense Command unit flying F-106 interceptors. Served in Korea and flew 86 combat missions. Decorations include the Silver Star, Legion of Merit with 1 Oak Leaf Cluster, Distinguished Flying Cross, Air Medal, Commendation Medal with one Oak Leaf Cluster, and the Chinese Army, Navy, and Air Corps Medal, Class A, 1st Grade. Retired September 1, 1967.

DeSHAZER, JACOB DANIEL, Staff Sergeant
        Born November 15, 1912 at West Stayton, Oregon. Graduated from Madras High School, Madras, Oregon in 1931. Enlisted on February 26, 1940 at Fort McDowell, California. Attended Bombardier and Airplane Mechanics Schools. Was captured by the Japanese after the Tokyo Raid and spent forty months as a prisoner of war. Released on August 20, 1945 and separated from the service on October 15, 1945. Graduated Seattle Pacific College, Seattle, Washington, on June 7, 1948 with Bachelor of Arts degree in preparation for a life as a missionary. After completion of his missionary training, he returned to Japan on December 28, 1948 to fulfill the vision he had while a prisoner, Graduated Asbury Theological Seminary with Master of Divinity degree June 1958 during sabbatical leave. Decorations include Distinguished Flying Cross, Purple Heart, and Chinese Breast Order of Yung Hui.

DIETER, WILLIAM J., Staff Sergeant
        Born October 5, 1912 at Vail, Iowa. Completed one year of high school. Enlisted October 29, 1936 at Vancouver Barracks, Washington. Graduated from Coast Artillery Motor School, Fort Lewis,

Washington, 1938. Re-enlisted December 12, 1940 with 95th Bombardment Squadron, McChord Field, Washington on December 12, 1940. Was killed on April 18, 1942 in crash landing after Tokyo Raid. Interred by Chinese at Shatow, China. Decorations awarded posthumously include Distinguished Flying Cross, Purple Heart, and the Chinese Breast Order of Yung Hui.

DOOLITTLE, JAMES HAROLD, Lieutenant General
Born Decmber 14, 1896 at Alameda, California. Educated in Nome, Alaska; Los Angeles Junior College and spent a year at the University of California of Mines. Enlisted as a Flying Cadet in the Signal Corps Reserve on October 6, 1917. Completed flight training and commissioned second lieutenant on March 11, 1918. Received BA degree from University of California in 1922, MS from Massachusetts Institute of Technology in 1924 and his Doctor of Science degree from M.I.T. in 1925.

Flew demonstration and experimental flights in South America in 1926 and 1928 while on leave. In 1928 assisted in the development of blind flying equipment at Mitchell Field, New York and accomplished the first flight completely dependent upon instruments.

Resigning from the Army in 1930, Doolittle was named manager of the Aviation Department of the Shell Oil Company. In 1932, while on temporary active duty, set a world's high speed record for land aircraft. Named President of the Institute of Aeronautical Sciences in 1940.

Recalled to active duty in July, 1940. In September 1942, after Tokyo Raid, assumed command of the 12th Air Force in North Africa and in March 1943 became commanding general of the 15th Air Force in the Mediterranean Theatre. From January 1944 to September 1945 Doolittle commanded the Eighth Air Force.

He returned to Shell Oil Company as a vice-president and later as a director following the war when he reverted to inactive reserve status. He was Chairman of the Board, Space Technology Laboratories, Redondo Beach, California, until 1962 and then a consultant. In 1963 he became a trustee on the board of the Aerospace Corporation and from 1965 to 1969 served as Vice Chairman of the executive committee. Currently he is a director on the board and a consultant to the Mutual of Omaha Insurance Company and its affiliate.

Doolittle's honors include the Schneider and Mackay Trophies awarded in 1925, the Harmon Trophy in 1930, the Bendix Trophy in 1931, and the Thompson Trophy in 1932.

His decorations include the Medal of Honor, Distinguished Service

Medal with 1 Oak Leaf Cluster, Silver Star, Distinguished Flying
Cross with two Oak Leaf Clusters, Bronze Star, Air Medal with 3 Oak
Leaf Clusters, the Chinese Order of Yung Hui, 3rd Class and eight
other foreign decorations.

DUQUETTE, OMER ADELARD, Staff Sergeant
        Born on January 25, 1916 at West Warnick, Rhode Island.
Attended high school for two years. Entered service on February 2,
1938 at Providence, Rhode Island and served at Fort Slocum, New
York and Albrook Field, Canal Zone before joining the 37th Bomb
Squadron at Pendleton, Oregon. Remained in China-Burma-India
Theater after Tokyo Raid. Was killed on June 3, 1942 when plane
crashed into mountain after bombing Lashio, Burma while en route
to Kunming, China. Decorations include the Distinguished Flying
Cross, Purple Heart, and the Chinese Army, Navy, and Air Corps
Medal, Class A, 1st Grade.

EIERMAN, JACOB, Major
        Born February 2, 1913 at Baltimore, Maryland. Enlisted
December 4, 1935 at Baltimore, Maryland and served at bases in New
York, Hawaii, California, and Illinois before joining the 89th Recon-
naissance Squadron at McChord Field, Washington in June, 1940.
After the Tokyo Raid, was assigned to Anti-Submarine Wings on the
East Coast until February, 1945. Qualified for Officer's Candidate
School and was commissioned a Second Lieutenant in June, 1945.
Post-war assignments included service in Germany and Japan. Re-
tired from the service on June 30, 1957. Decorations include the Dis-
tinguished Flying Cross and the Chinese Army, Navy, and Air Corps
Medal, Class A, 1st Grade.

EMMENS, ROBERT G., Colonel
        Born July 22, 1914 at Medford, Oregon. Entered service
on February 23, 1937 at Vancouver Barracks, Washington. Graduated from Medford High School, Medford, Oregon in 1931. Attended University of Oregon, 1931–1934. Graduated from Flying
Training School with rating of pilot, February, 1938. Assigned to
17th Bomb Group at March Field, California. Joined the Tokyo mission just before boarding carrier without training at Eglin. Was co-pilot on crew interned for thirteen months in Russia. Author of *Guests of
the Kremlin*, published by Macmillan in 1949. Graduate of Army Command and Staff School, Fort Leavenworth, Kansas. Served in Europe

and Japan on Intelligence assignments. Decorations include Distinguished Flying Cross, Chinese Army, Navy, and Air Corps Medal, Class A, 1st Grade, and the Japanese Order of the Sacred Treasure. Retired December 7, 1965.

FAKTOR, LELAND D., Corporal
   Born May 17, 1921 at Plymouth, Iowa. Completed high school and enlisted in the service at Fort Des Moines, Iowa on August 9, 1940. Completed Airplane Mechanic's School at Chanute Field, Illinois in April 1941. Assigned to 95th Bomb Squadron, 17th Bomb Group at McChord Field, Washington. Was killed at Sui-chang, Chekiang Province, China on bail-out from plane after the Tokyo Raid on April 18, 1942. Interred at Wan Tsuen, China and returned to Plymouth, Iowa for reburial April 1949. Decorations include the Distinguished Flying Cross, Purple Heart, and Chinese Breast Order of Yung Hui, awarded posthumously. Dormitory named Faktor Hall dedicated in his memory at Chanute Air Force Base May 20, 1978.

FARROW, WILLIAM G., First Lieutenant
   Born September 24, 1918 at Darlington, South Carolina. Completed high school and attended two years at University of South Carolina. Entered service on November 23, 1940 at Fort Jackson, South Carolina. Completed flight training at Kelly Field, Texas and commissioned as Second Lieutenant July, 1941. Was captured by Japanese after Tokyo Raid and executed on October 15, 1942 at Kiangwan Cemetery, Shanghai, China. Decorations awarded posthumously include the Distinguished Flying Cross, Purple Heart, and Chinese Breast Order of Pao Ting.

FITZHUGH, WILLIAM N., Major
   Born February 18, 1915 at Temple Texas. Graduated from University of Texas with Bachelor of Business Administration degree. Entered service November, 1940 at Houston, Texas. Graduated from Advanced Flying School, Stockton, California as Pilot and commissioned as Second Lieutenant, July 1941. After Tokyo Raid remained in China-Burma-India Theater until June, 1943. Served as test pilot and maintenance officer at Brookley Field, Alabama until release from active duty in July, 1946. Decorations include the Distinguished Flying Cross and the Chinese Army, Navy, and Air Corps Medal, Class A, 1st Grade.

FITZMAURICE, DONALD E., Sergeant
      Born March 13, 1919 at Lincoln, Nebraska. Graduated
from high school in 1937 and attended one year of college. Enlisted
August 13, 1940 at Chanute Field, Illinois and attended Airplane Mechanic's School there. Graduated in March 1941 and assigned to the
95th Bomb Squadron, 17th Bomb Group, McChord Field, Washington. Killed on April 18, 1942 in crash landing of B-25 after raid on
Japan. Interred at Shatow, China by Chinese. Decorations include
Distinguished Flying Cross, Purple Heart, and Chinese Breast Order
of Yung Hui awarded posthumously.

GARDNER, MELVIN J., Staff Sergeant
      Born April 6, 1920 at Mesa, Arizona. Graduated from high
school and enlisted in the service at Fort Bliss, Texas on October 5,
1939. Attended Airplane Mechanic's Course at Chanute Field, Illinois. Assigned to 34th Bomb Squadron at March Field, California.
Remained in China-Burma-India Theater after Tokyo Raid. Was
killed in action on June 3, 1942 while en route to Kunming, China
after bombing mission on Lashio, Burma. Decorations include the
Distinguished Flying Cross, Purple Heart (posthumous) and the Chinese Army, Navy, and Air Corps Medal, Class A, 1st Grade.

GRAY, ROBERT MANNING, Captain
      Born May 24, 1919 at Killeen, Texas. Completed two years
of college. Enlisted as Flying Cadet on June 29, 1940 at Dallas, Texas.
Graduated with rating of pilot and commissioned as Second Lieutenant at Kelly Field, Texas on February 8, 1941. Assigned 34th Bomb
Squadron and then 95th Bomb Squadron of 17th Bomb Group at
McChord Field, Washington. Remained in China-Burma-India Theater after Tokyo Raid. Killed while on combat mission on October 18,
1942 near Assam, India. Gray Air Force Base, Texas, named in his
honor. Decorations include the Distinguished Flying Cross and the
Chinese Army, Navy, and Air Corps Medal, Class A, 1st Grade.

GREENING, CHARLES ROSS, Colonel
      Born November 12, 1914 at Carroll, Iowa. Received BA
degree from Washington State College in Fine Arts in 1936. Entered
military service on June 23, 1936 at Fort Lewis, Washington. Graduated from Advanced Flying School at Kelly Field, Texas, June 9,
1937. Served at bases in Louisiana and California before joining 17th
Bomb Group at Pendleton, Oregon in June, 1940. After Tokyo Raid
was assigned to B-26 Group in North Africa and was shot down on
July 17. 1943 while on a raid against Naples, Italy. He was captured
by the Germans and after two months imprisonment escaped. After

evading capture for six months, he was recaptured and spent the rest of the war in Stalag Luft I at Barth, Germany. After the war, had Stateside assignments until 1955 at which time he was assigned for a brief period as Air Attache to Australia and New Zealand. Died March 29, 1957 at Bethesda Navy Hospital, Bethesda, MD. Decorations include Distinguished Flying Cross, Silver Star, Air Medal with 4 Oak Leaf Clusters, Purple Heart, and Chinese Order of Yung Hui, 5th Class.

GRIFFIN, THOMAS CARSON, Major

Born July 10, 1917 at Green Bay, Wisconsin. Graduated from University of Alabama wih BA in Political Science in 1939. Entered service on July 5, 1939 as Second Lieutenant, Coast Artillery, but requested relief from active duty in 1940 to enlist as a Flying Cadet. Was rated as a navigator and recommissioned on July 1, 1940. After Tokyo Raid, served as navigator in North Africa until shot down and captured by the Germans on July 3, 1943. Remained a POW until release in April, 1945. Decorations include the Distinguished Flying Cross, Air Medal with 3 Oak Leaf Clusters, and the Chinese Army, Navy, and Air Corps Medal, Class A, 1st Grade.

HALLMARK, DEAN EDWARD, First Lieutenant

Born January 20, 1914 at Robert Lee, Texas. Graduated Greenville High School, Greenville, Texas and attended Paris Junior College, Texas and Alabama Polytechnic Institute, Alabama for two years. Entered service on November 21, 1940 at Houston, Texas. Graduated as pilot and commissioned as Second Lieutenant from Advanced Bomb Squadron at Pendleton, Oregon. Was captured by the Japanese and executed on October 15, 1942 at Kiangwan Prison, Shanghai, China. Decorations include Distinguished Flying Cross, Purple Heart (posthumous), and the Chinese Breast Order of Pao Ting.

HERNDON, NOLAN ANDERSON, Major

Born December 12, 1918 at Greenville, Texas. Attended college for two years and entered service on July 27, 1940 at Dallas, Texas. Graduated from navigator training and commissioned as Second Lieutenant June 24, 1941. Completed bombardier training. Was interned in Russia after Tokyo Raid for thirteen months until returned to the United States on May 29, 1943. Held various Stateside assignments until end of World War II. Relieved from active duty on November 4, 1945. Decorations include Distinguished Flying Cross and Chinese Army, Navy, and Air Corps Medal, Class A, 1st Grade.

HILGER, JOHN A., Brigadier General
Born January 11, 1909 at Sherman, Texas. Graduated from Sherman High School in June, 1926 and attended Texas A&M College, College Station, Texas, graduating with a B.S. degree in Mechanical Engineering in 1932. Commissioned as a Second Lieutenant in the Infantry, he resigned the commission to enter the Army Air Corps as a Flying Cadet in February, 1933. Received wings and was placed on active duty as a Flying Cadet in February, 1934. Was commissioned as a Second Lieutenant in February, 1935. Was commanding officer of the 89th Reconnaissance Squadron when the Tokyo Raid was planned. After the raid, he returned to the China-Burma-India Theater as a commander of a Bomb Group. During the last eighteen months of the war, he served on the staff of Admiral Chester A. Nimitz, Commander-in-Chief, Pacific Area. Attended Air War College and National War College and has served in various operational and staff assignments. During Korean War was commander of 307th Bomb Wing located on Okinawa. Also served in Turkey and Norway. Presently assigned as Chief of Staff, Air Training Command, Randolph Air Force Base, Texas. Retired August, 1966. Decorations include Silver Star, Legion of Merit with 1 Oak Leaf Cluster, Distinguished Flying Cross with 1 Oak Leaf Cluster, Bronze Star, Air Medal with 2 Oak Leaf Clusters, and the Chinese Order of Yung Hui, 4th Class.

HITE, ROBERT L., Lieutenant Colonel
Born March 3, 1920 at Odell, Texas, graduated from High School in 1937; completed three years of college and enlisted as an Aviation Cadet on September 9, 1940 at Lubbock, Texas. Commissioned as Second Lieutenant and rated as pilot on May 29, 1941. Was captured after Tokyo Raid and imprisoned by the Japanese for forty months. Liberated by American troops on August 20, 1945, he remained on active duty until September 30, 1947. Returned to active duty during Korean War on March 9, 1951 and served overseas before relief from active duty again in November, 1955. Decorations include Distinguished Flying Cross, Purple Heart with 1 Oak Leaf Cluster, and Chinese Breast Order of Pao Ting.

HOLSTROM, EVERETT W., Brigadier General
Born May 4, 1916 at Cottage Grove, Oregon. Graduated from Pleasant Hill High School, Pleasant Hill, Oregon in 1934 and attended Oregon State College until he entered military service at Fort Lewis, Washington in December, 1939. Commissioned as Second Lieutenant and rated as pilot upon graduation from Kelly Field in 1940. Destroyed first enemy submarine sunk off West Coast of the

U.S. on December 24, 1941 while a member of the 95th Bomb Squadron. Remained in China-Burma-India Theater after Tokyo Raid as 11th Bomb Squadron Commander until the end of 1943. Following World War II, was assigned to Strategic Air Command where he has held various operational assignments and is one of the few men who has commanded wings and flown all the multi-engine jet bombers in the SAC inventory—B-45, B-47, B-52 and B-58. Commanded SAC's first supersonic Bombardment Wing at Carswell Air Force Base, Texas. Retired July, 1969. Decorations include Silver Star, Legion of Merit, Distinguished Flying Cross with 1 Oak Leaf Cluster, Air Medal with 4 Oak Leaf Clusters, Commendation Ribbon with 1 Oak Leaf Cluster, and Chinese Army, Navy, and Air Corps Medal, Class A, 1st Grade. Holds aeronautical rating of command pilot and is entitled to wear the Air Force's Missile Badge. Retired October 1, 1969.

HOOVER, TRAVIS, Colonel
        Born September 21, 1917 at Melrose, New Mexico. Graduated from Polytechnic High School, Riverside, California, 1936. Received AA degree from Riverside Junior College in 1938 and BA degree from University of California in 1949. Enlisted in National Guard November 9, 1938 and Regular Army in August, 1939. Completed pilot training and commissioned Second Lieutenant, May, 1940. Remained in China-Burma-India Theater after Tokyo Raid until June, 1942. Served as bomber pilot in England, North Africa, and Italy from July, 1942 until September, 1944. Peacetime overseas service has been on Okinawa. Stateside assignments have been in Washington, D.C., Texas, California, Mississippi, and Kansas. Rated as command pilot. Decorations include Silver Star, Distinguished Flying Cross, Air Medal with 9 Oak Leaf Clusters, Army Commendation Medal, and Chinese Army, Navy, and Air Corps Medal, Class A, 1st Grade.

HORTON, EDWIN WESTON, JR., Master Sergeant
        Born March 28, 1916 at North Eastham, Massachusetts. Graduated from high school in 1934 and entered service on September 30, 1935 at Providence, Rhode Island. Served overseas with Field Artillery at Schofield Barracks, Hawaii from 1935 to 1938 before re-enlisting and serving with 95th Bomb Squadron at March Field, California. Completed Gun Turret-Maintenance School, Aircraft Armorer and Aircraft Mechanics Schools. Remained in China-Burma-India Theater after Tokyo Raid until July, 1943. Held various Stateside assignments in Oklahoma and Florida. Served overseas at Wheelus Field, Tripoli, Libya and retired from the service in 1960. Decorations include Distinguished Flying Cross and the Chinese Army, Navy, and Air Corps Medal, Class A, 1st Grade.

JONES, ADEN EARL, Second Lieutenant
    Born September 7, 1920 at Flint, Michigan. Graduated from high school and entered service on September 19, 1939 at Fort MacArthur, California. Stationed at March and McChord Fields with 95th Bomb Squadron. Remained in China-Burma-India Theater after Tokyo Raid until July 15, 1943. Graduated as bombardier. Held various Stateside assignments at bases in South Carolina, Louisiana, and California. Served briefly in Japan after the war and was discharged December 17, 1948. Decorations include Distinguished Flying Cross, with 1 Oak Leaf Cluster, Air Medal, and the Chinese Army, Navy, and Air Corps Medal, Class A, 1st Grade.

JONES, DAVID M., Major General
    Born December 18, 1913 at Marshfield, Oregon. Graduated Tucson High School, Tucson, Arizona, 1932; University of Arizona, 1936, commissioned as second lieutenant, Cavalry. Began pilot training June 1937. Gained rating as pilot June 1938 and served with 17th Bomb Group at March and McChord Fields. After Tokyo Raid, served in North Africa and was shot down over Bizerte on December 4, 1942. Spend 2½ years as POW in Germany. Graduated from Command and General Staff School, Armed Forces Staff College and National War College. Had varied operational assignments after World War II at bases in Louisiana, Virginia, North Carolina, Texas, and Ohio. Served overseas as 47th Bomb Wing Commander at Sculthorpe, England. He was the Commander of the Air Force Eastern Test Range and Department of Defense Manager for Support of the Apollo Program. Decorations include Distinguished Service Medal, Legion of Merit, Distinguished Flying Cross with 1 Oak Leaf Cluster, Air Medal, Purple Heart, Commendation Ribbon, NASA Distinguished Service Medal, NASA Exceptional Service Medal, and Chinese Order of Yung Hui, 5th Class. Retired June 1973.

JORDAN, BERT M., Chief Master Sergeant
    Born September 3, 1919 at Covington, Oklahoma. Entered service November, 1939. Completed aircraft and engine mechanic's course, April, 1941. Rated as engineer-gunner, February, 1942. After Tokyo Raid, remained in China-Burma-India Theater until 1943 and in 1945 served in Asiatic Pacific Theater. Has served overseas since World War II in Germany, England, Japan, Guam, Canada, Vietnam, and Thailand as an aircraft-maintenance technician. Decorations include Distinguished Flying Cross and Chinese Army, Navy, and Air Corps Medal, Class A, 1st Grade. Retired August 1, 1971.

JOYCE, RICHARD OUTCALT, Lieutenant Colonel

Born September 29, 1919 at Lincoln, Nebraska. Graduated from high school in 1937 and attended the University of Nebraska. Entered service on July 26, 1940 and received pilot wings and commission at Kelly Field, Texas, March, 1941 and assigned 89th Reconnaissance Squadron at McChord Field, Washington. Remained in China-Burma-India Theater until December, 1942. Held various Stateside assignments until relieved from active duty on March 10, 1946. Decorations include Distinguished Flying Cross and Chinese Army, Navy, and Air Corps Medal, Class A, 1st Grade.

KAPPELER, FRANK ALBERT, Lieutenant Colonel

Born January 2, 1914 at San Francisco, California. Graduated high school in 1932 and Polytechnic College of Engineering, Oakland, California with a BS degree in Aeronautical Engineering. Enlisted May 9, 1936 in U.S. Navy and assigned VS-15R Squadron, Oakland, California. Transferred to Aviation Cadet training in December, 1939 and was commissioned a second lieutenant, June, 1941 at McChord Field, Washington with rating as navigator. Later received training as bombardier. Remained in China-Burma-India Theater after Tokyo Raid until August, 1942. Served in European Theater of Operations from November, 1943 until June, 1945. Stateside assignments after the war included bases in Texas, Ohio, California before returning overseas to Japan where he served from May, 1951 until February, 1952. Assigned as Deputy Commander, Minuteman Site Activation Task Force and then as Executive Officer, 810th Air Division, Minot Air Force Base, North Dakota. Decorations include Distinguished Flying Cross, Air Medal with 2 Silver Oak Leaf Clusters, Bronze Star Medal, and Chinese Army, Navy, and Air Corps Medal, Class A, 1st Grade.

KNOBLOCH, RICHARD A., Brigadier General

Born May 27, 1918 at Milwaukee, Wisconsin. Graduated from Kansas State University with BS degree. Entered military service November, 1940 at Randolph Field, Texas. Graduated from pilot training and commissioned as a Second Lieutenant, July, 1941. After raid on Tokyo, remained in China-Burma-India Theater and completed more than 50 bombing missions before returning to the States in 1943. After various assignments in the U.S. he reported to England for duty with the Royal Air Force. Served as deputy commander of a Tactical Reconnaissance Wing, then as Air Attache to Italy, deputy commander, AF Personnel Center and Wing Commander, Andrews

424

AFB, Md. Graduate of Industrial College of the Armed Forces. Decorations include Distinguished Service Medal, Legion of Merit with 1 Oak Leaf Cluster, Distinguished Flying Cross with 1 Oak Leaf Cluster, and Chinese, Italian, and Thai decorations. Retired January 31, 1970. Became Vice President of United Technologies Corporation and now is a member of the Board of Directors of Barclay's Bank of New York.

LABAN, THEODORE H., Master Sergeant
Born July 13, 1914 at Kenosha, Wisconsin. Graduated from Kenosha High School; entered military service October 12, 1935. Completed aircraft maintenance courses on B-25, B-26 and B-29 aircraft. Was interned by Russian Government after Tokyo Raid for thirteen months. Subsequently served overseas in England, Philippines and Guam. Retired November 30, 1956. After retirement, received Bachelor of Science degree in Electrical Engineering and is presently a research engineer. Decorations include the Distinguished Flying Cross, Air Medal with 3 Oak Leaf Clusters, Purple Heart, and Chinese Army, Navy, and Air Corps Medal, Class A, 1st Grade. Died September 16, 1978.

LARKIN, GEORGE ELMER, JR., Staff Sergeant
Born November 26, 1918 at New Haven, Kentucky. Graduated from New Haven High School and entered military service on November 27, 1939 at Fort Knox, Kentucky. Graduated from Airplane Mechanic's School and assigned to 89th Reconnaissance Squadron, McChord Field. Remained in China-Burma-India Theater after the Tokyo Raid. Killed on October 18, 1942 in airplane crash near Assam, India while assigned to 11th Bomb Squadron and on Detached Service with the 26th Fighter Squadron. Decorations include Distinguished Flying Cross and Chinese Army, Navy, and Air Corps Medal, Class A, 1st Grade.

LAWSON, TED W., Major
Born March 7, 1917 at Fresno, California. Received degree in Aero Engineering from Los Angeles City College. Worked at Douglas Aircraft as design engineer. Joined Army Air Corps March 1940 and received wings and commission November 15, 1940. In April 1942 was seriously injured and had leg amputated in China as result of crash landing after Tokyo Raid. Author of *Thirty Seconds Over Tokyo*, story of his crew. Served as Liaison Officer, U.S. Air Mission, Santiago, Chile May 1943 to April 1944, then assigned to March Field as Assistant Technical Inspector. Retired from Service February

1945; subsequently owned C & L Tooling Machine Shop, served as technical writer for North American Aviation, and was employed as technical advisor for Reynolds Metal Company. Decorations include Distinguished Flying Cross, Purple Heart, and Chinese Army, Navy, and Air Corps Medal, Class A, 1st Grade.

LEONARD, PAUL JOHN, Master Sergeant
Born June 19, 1912 at Roswell, New Mexico. Attended high school for two years and enlisted July 13, 1931 at Fort Bliss, Texas. Received training as airplane mechanic and after assignments to units at Kelly Field, Texas, Chanute Field, Illinois and Lowry Field, Colorado was assigned to 37th Bomb Squadron in May, 1941. Remained in China-Burma-India Theater after Tokyo Raid until June, 1942 after which he returned to States to become crew chief for General Doolittle. Served in England and North Africa from September, 1942 until January, 1943. Killed by enemy aircraft on January 5, 1943 at Youks-Les-Bains, Algeria. Decorations include Distinguished Flying Cross, Purple Heart (posthumous), and the Chinese Army, Navy, and Air Corps Medal, Class A, 1st Grade.

MACIA, JAMES HERBERT, Colonel
Born April 10, 1916 at Tombstone, Arizona. Graduated from Tombstone High School; attended University of Arizona prior to entering military service on June 24, 1940. Completed navigator training and commissioned Second Lieutenant in June, 1941. Subsequent to Tokyo Raid, served in European Theater of Operations from December 1942 until April 1945. Relieved from active duty February 1946 and recalled in March, 1951. Decorations include Legion of Merit with 3 Oak Leaf Clusters, Silver Star, Distinguished Flying Cross with 1 Oak Leaf Cluster, Air Medal with 8 Oak Leaf Clusters, Croix de Guerre avec Palme, and Chinese Army, Navy, and Air Corps Medal, Class A, 1st Grade. Retired October 1, 1973.

MANCH, JACOB EARLE, Lieutenant Colonel
Born December 26, 1918 at Staunton, Virginia. Appointed Second Lieutenant Infantry Reserve, May 10, 1940. Enlisted as Flying Cadet on February 10, 1941 and graduated from Advanced Flying School, Stockton, California, with rating as pilot in September, 1941. Assigned to 17th Bomb Group at Pendleton Field, Oregon. Remained in China-Burma-India Theater after Tokyo Raid until June, 1943. Assigned to Stateside bases in California, Utah and New Jersey during the rest of the war. Served in Japan and Korea as Air Liaison Officer with 7th U.S. Infantry Division during Korean War. Re-

turned to the United States in September, 1953 and stationed at Nellis Air Force Base, Nevada. Killed in aircraft accident near Las Vegas, Nevada on March 24, 1958. Decorations include Distinguished Flying Cross, Soldier's Medal, and Chinese Army, Navy, and Air Corps Medal, Class A, 1st Grade.

MANSKE, JOSEPH W., Colonel

Born April 13, 1921 at Gowanda, New York. Graduated Gowanda High School and entered service September 30, 1939 at Chanute Field, Illinois. Completed aircraft mechanics course. After Tokyo Raid, attended OCS and was commissioned a second lieutenant in December 1942. Served in various Materiel assignments with B-25 units in Europe 1943–1945. Relieved of active duty 1946, joined Air Reserve program. In 1948 activated Air National Guard Base, Niagara Falls, NY and served as full-time Maintenance and Supply Group Commander. In 1957 rejoined Air Force and served in Logistics Command Depot System and Air Staff until retirement February 1973. Decorations include Distinguished Flying Cross, Meritorious Service Medal, Air Force Commendation Medal with 1 Oak Leaf Cluster, and Chinese Army, Navy, and Air Corps Medal, Class A, 1st Grade.

McCLURE, CHARLES L., Captain

Born October 4, 1916 at St. Louis, Missouri. Graduated University High School, University, Missouri and attended University of Missouri. Enlisted as Flying Cadet on October 12, 1940 at Jefferson Barracks, Missouri. Graduated from navigator training and commissioned as Second Lieutenant on December 5, 1941. Was injured on Tokyo Raid and hospitalized until January, 1943. Assigned duties as navigator instructor and again hospitalized from February, 1945 to April, 1945. Retired for physical disability April, 1945. Decorations include Distinguished Flying Cross, Purple Heart, and Chinese Army, Navy, and Air Corps Medal, Class A, 1st Grade.

McCOOL, HARRY C., Lieutenant Colonel

Born April 19, 1918 at La Junta, Colorado. Graduated Beaver High School, Beaver, Oklahoma and received BS degree from Institute of Technology. Weatherford, Oklahoma, January, 1940. Entered military service March 26, 1940 at Oklahoma City, Oklahoma. Completed navigator training and commissioned as Second Lieutenant June 1941. After Tokyo Raid served in China-Burma-India Theater until September 1942. Assigned to European Theater as B-26 and B-17 navigator January 1944 to September 1945. Also served in

North Africa with Strategic Air Command. Later rated as bombadier. Received MS degree in systems management from University of Southern California. Retired from active duty September 1, 1966. Joined civil service as logistics analyst for U.S. Navy at Pearl Harbor; retired April 18, 1980. Decorations include Distinguished Flying Cross, Purple Heart with 1 Oak Cluster, Air Medal with 5 Oak Leaf Clusters, and Chinese Army, Navy, and Air Corps Medal, Class A, 1st Grade.

McELROY, EDGAR E., Lieutenant Colonel
Born March 24, 1912 at Ennis, Texas. Graduated Ennis High School and attended Trinity University for three years. Entered military service November 28, 1940. Completed pilot training and commissioned as Second Lieutenant, July, 1941. Remained in China-Burma-India Command after Tokyo Raid until June, 1943. Subsequently served in many operational assignments as squadron, group and wing level, including service with 6th Bomb Group flying B-29s from Tinian Island. Rated as command pilot. Postwar service in Japan, Korea, England, Germany, and Laos. Retired June 30, 1962. Decorations include Distinguished Flying Cross, Silver Star, Air Medal, Army and Air Force Commendation Medals, and Chinese Army, Navy, and Air Corps Medal, Class A, 1st Grade.

McGURL, EUGENE FRANCIS, First Lieutenant
Born February 8, 1917 at Belmont, Massachusetts. Three years college before enlisting on February 11, 1941 at Boston, Mass. Completed navigation training and commissioned as Second Lieutenant, December 6, 1941. Remained in China-Burma-India Theater after Tokyo mission. Killed in action on June 3, 1942 when plane crashed into mountain after bombing Lashio, Burma enroute to Kunming, China. Decorations include Distinguished Flying Cross, Purple Heart (posthumous) and Chinese Army, Navy, Air Corps Medal, Class A, 1st Grade.

MEDER, ROBERT JOHN, First Lieutenant
Born August 23, 1917 at Cleveland, Ohio. Graduated college with BS degree. Entered service on November 22, 1940 at Fort Hayes, Ohio. Rated as pilot and commissioned Second Lieutenant, July 12, 1941. Assigned 95th Bomb Squadron. Was captured after Tokyo Raid and remained a Prisoner of War from April, 1942 until his death due to beri-beri and dysentery in prison camp on December 1, 1943. Decorations include Distinguished Flying Cross and Chinese Breast Order of Pao Ting.

MILLER, RICHARD EWING, Captain
Born March 2, 1916 at Fort Wayne, Indiana. Two years college. Enlisted as Flying Cadet, February 25, 1939 at Fort Benjamin Harrison, Indiana. Eliminated from pilot training, April, 1939. Reenlisted as Flying Cadet for Bombardier training, May 29, 1941. Rated as bombardier and commissioned as Second Lieutenant, December 16, 1941. After Tokyo Raid was assigned to 319th Bomb Group and served in North Africa. Died January 22, 1943 of wounds received in action while on a bombing mission. Decorations include Silver Star, Distinguished Flying Cross, Purple Heart, Air Medal with 1 Oak Leaf Cluster, and the Chinese Army, Navy, and Air Corps Medal, Class A, 1st Grade.

NIELSEN, CHASE JAY, Lieutenant Colonel
Born January 14, 1917 at Hyrum, Utah. Graduated South Cache High School, Hyrum, Utah, 1935. Attended Utah State University from 1935 to 1938; majored in Civil Engineering. Enlisted as Flying Cadet at Fort Douglas, Utah on August 18, 1939. Commissioned and rated as Navigator, June, 1941. Later earned ratings as Senior Aircraft Observer and Master Navigator. Was Prisoner of War, Japanese, after Tokyo raid from April, 1942 until release in August, 1945. Was only Tokyo Raider who returned to testify at Japanese War Crimes Trials and is only living survivor of his crew. Remained in service with various units of the Strategic Air Command until retirement in November, 1961. Decorations include Distinguished Flying Cross, Purple Heart with 1 Oak Leaf Cluster, and Chinese Breast Order of Pao Ting.

OZUK, CHARLES JOHN, Captain
Born June 13, 1916 at Vesta Heights, Penna. Graduated Carl Schurz High School. Enlisted November 9, 1939 at Chanute Field, Illinois. Attended Radio and Mechanics School, Chanute Field before entering pilot training. Eliminated from pilot training in June, 1940. Re-enlisted for navigation training in November, 1940 and graduated with rating of navigator and commission as Second Lieutenant at McChord Field, Washington in June, 1941. Remained in China-Burma-India Theater after Tokyo mission until July, 1942. Subsequently served in North Africa until April, 1945. Relieved from active duty April, 1945. Decorations include Distinguished Flying Cross and Chinese Army, Navy and Air Corps Medal, Class A, 1st Grade.

PARKER, JAMES M., Major

Born February 4, 1920 at Houston, Texas. Attended Lon Morris Junior College and Texas A&M College. Enlisted Houston, Texas on November 21, 1940. Graduated from Advanced Flying School as pilot, July, 1941. After Tokyo Raid, served in North Africa as pilot of light bombardment aircraft. Subsequently served in Europe in Army of Occupation. Separated from service, June 25, 1947. Decorations include Distinguished Flying Cross and Chinese Army, Navy, and Air Corps Medal, Class A, 1st Grade.

POHL, DAVID W., First Lieutenant

Born December 31, 1921 at Boston, Massachusetts. Graduated Wellesley High School in 1939. Entered military service January, 1940 at Boston, Mass. Was youngest of 80 crewmen who took part in Tokyo Raid. Was member of crew interned for thirteen months in Russia. Completed pilot training in August, 1945 and subsequently served with Training Command and Caribbean Defense Command in Panama, Canal Zone. Left service in December, 1947. Received BS degree in Business Administration, Babson Institute, Boston, Mass. Served as marketing analyst specializing in industrial products; Retired 1975. Decorations include Distinguished Flying Cross and the Chinese Army, Navy, and Air Corps Medal, Class A, 1st Grade.

POTTER, HENRY A., Colonel

Born September 22, 1918 at Pierre, South Dakota. Entered military service at Pierre on July 26, 1940. Attended Yankton College, South Dakota and the University of Oregon. Completed navigator training and commissioned second lieutenant in June, 1941. Had Stateside service after Tokyo Raid in Michigan, Colorado, Washington, D.C., Florida, and California. Served overseas in Germany from 1954 to 1958. Holds rating as master navigator. Decorations include Distinguished Flying Cross, Air Medal with 3 Oak Leaf Clusters, Army Commendation Medal, and the Chinese Army, Navy, and Air Corps Medal, Class A, 1st Grade.

POUND, WILLIAM R., Jr., Lieutenant Colonel

Born May 18, 1918 at Milford, Utah. Attended Santa Monica (Calif.) Junior College two years. Entered service May, 1940 at March Field, California. Commissioned and rated as navigator in June, 1941. After Tokyo Raid, flew 50 missions in E.T.O. between September, 1942 and March, 1944. Released from active duty, August, 1948. Died July 13, 1967. Principal decorations include Distinguished Flying Cross, the Air Medal with 7 Oak Leaf Clusters and the Chinese Army, Navy and Air Corps Medal, Class A, 1st Grade.

RADNEY, DOUGLAS V., Major
Born March 17, 1917 at Mineola, Texas. Graduated Mexia High School, Mexia, Texas, 1935. Entered military service, January, 1936. Completed aircraft mechanic's school. After Tokyo Raid, remained in China-Burma-India Theater until September, 1942. Commissioned as an officer in 1945 and subsequently completed pilot training. Served overseas in Alaska as cold weather test pilot and maintenance office. Rater as senior pilot. Retired May 1959. From 1959 to 1970 corporate pilot for Missouri firm. Graduated Rhema Bible Training Center, Broken Arrow, Oklahoma, May 1980; now a minister in Southwest. Decorations include Silver Star with 1 Oak Leaf Cluster, Distinguished Flying Cross, Air Medal with 1 Oak Leaf Cluster, and Chinese Army, Navy, and Air Corps Medal, Class A, 1st Grade.

REDDY, KENNETH E., First Lieutenant
Born June 29, 1920 at Bowie, Texas. Graduated from North Texas State Teachers College with BA degree in 1940. Enlisted as Flying Cadet at Fort Worth, Texas, November 23, 1940. Rated as pilot and commissioned as Second Lieutenant, July 11, 1941. Returned to United States after Tokyo Raid in June, 1942. Was killed in aircraft accident near Little Rock, Arkansas on September 3, 1942. Decorations include Distinguished Flying Cross and Chinese Army, Navy, and Air Corps Medal, Class A, 1st Grade.

SAYLOR, EDWARD JOSEPH, Major
Born March 15, 1920 at Brusett, Montana. Graduated Garfield County High School, Jordon, Montana. Enlisted December 7, 1939 at Fort George Wright, Washington and attended Air Corps Training School, Chanute Field, Illinois. Served throughout World War II in enlisted status both Stateside and overseas until March, 1945. Accepted a commission in October 1947 and served as Aircraft Maintenance Officer at bases in Iowa, Washington, Labrador and England. Accepted regular commission and is still on active duty. Decorations include Distinguished Flying Cross, Air Force Commendation Medal and Chinese Army, Navy and Air Corps Medal, Class A, 1st Grade.

SCOTT, ELDRED V., Lieutenant Colonel
Born September 29, 1907 at Atlanta, Georgia. Completed

three years at Union High School, Phoenix, Arizona. Enlisted in U.S. Army (Infantry) September 9, 1924. Transferred to U.S. Air Corps and graduated from Mechanics School. After Tokyo Raid served in England and France from February, 1944 until February, 1945. Was commissioned as First Lieutenant, April, 1943. Served as maintenance officer in various Stateside assignments and in Korea. Retired September 30, 1959. Employed as Field Operations Analyst by major aircraft company. Died 1978. Decorations include Distinguished Flying Cross and Chinese Army, Navy, and Air Corps Medal, Class A, 1st Grade.

SESSLER, HOWARD ALBERT, Major
Born August 11, 1917 at Boston, Massachusetts. Graduated from Arlington High School, Arlington, Mass. Entered military service December 31, 1940 at Boston, Massachusetts. Graduated from bombardier training and commissioned as Second Lieutenant in August, 1941; completed navigator training, December, 1941. Remained in China-Burma-India Theater after Tokyo Raid until July, 1942. Served in European Theater from September, 1942 until September, 1943 and Mediterranean Theater from September, 1944 until June, 1945. Relieved from active duty November, 1945. Graduated from University of Southern California in 1950 with Bachelor of Engineering (Civil) degree. Now president of heavy construction firm. Decorations include Distinguished Flying Cross, Air Medal with two Silver Oak Leaf Clusters and Chinese Army, Navy, and Air Corps Medal, Class A, 1st Grade.

SIMS, JACK A., Colonel
Born February 23, 1919 at Kalamazoo, Michigan. Graduated from Western Michigan University in 1940 with BA degree; received Master's degree from University of Chicago in 1949 while in service. Entered military service June, 1940 and was rated as pilot and commissioned as Second Lieutenant in July, 1941. After Tokyo Raid, remained in India flying submarine patrol. In August, 1942, was assigned to B-26 unit and served in Africa where he completed 40 combat missions. After WWII served as chief of Contract Frauds Branch, Office of Special Investigations, Air Force Headquarters; Liaison officer, Far East Air Forces (on General MacArthur's staff during Korean conflict); faculty member, Air Command and Staff College, Maxwell Air Force Base (later graduating from Air War College); Chief Officer, Air Force Liaison, House of Representatives; chief, USAF/RAF Exchange Program, Air Attaché, American Embassy, London; Executive Assistant to Deputy Chief of Staff, Programs and Resources, Air Force headquarters. Decorations include Legion of Merit with 1 Oak

432   *Appendices*

Leaf Cluster, Distinguished Flying Cross with 1 Oak Leaf Cluster, Bronze Star, Air Medal with 7 Oak Leaf Clusters, and Chinese Army, Navy, and Air Corps Medal, Class A, 1st Grade.

SMITH, DONALD G., Captain
Born January 15, 1918 at Oldham, South Dakota. Graduated Belle Fourche High School and received BS degree from South Dakota State University June 1940. Commissioned as Second Lieutenant, Infantry. Entered service as Flying Cadet in July, 1940. Completed flying training and rated as pilot in March, 1941. Returned to United States after Tokyo Raid and assigned 432nd Bomb Squadron at Barksdale, Louisiana. Killed in western Europe as result of injuries sustained in airplane crash on November 12, 1942. Decorations include Distinguished Flying Cross and Chinese Army, Navy, and Air Corps Medal, Class A, 1st Grade.

SPATZ, HAROLD A., Sergeant
Born July 14, 1921 at Lebo, Kansas. Graduated Lebo High School, June, 1939 and entered military service November 25, 1939 at Fort Riley, Kansas. Received training as aircraft mechanic at Glendale, California from September, 1940 until March, 1941. Captured by Japanese after Tokyo Raid and executed on October 15, 1942. Decorations include Distinguished Flying Cross, Purple Heart, and Chinese Breast Order of Yung Hui.

STEPHENS, ROBERT J., Flight Officer
Born February 28, 1915 at Hobart, Oklahoma. Graduated from Hobart High School and entered military service as private in November, 1939 at Fort Riley, Kansas. Completed enlisted Bombardier School, June, 1940 and Mechanics School, February, 1941. Remained in China-Burma-India Theater after Tokyo Raid as bombardier until July, 1943. Served in various Stateside assignments for remainder of service. Commissioned as Flight Officer February 11, 1944. Rated as Aircraft Observer. Retired for physical disability on December 1, 1944. Died of natural causes on April 13, 1959. Decorations include Distinguished Flying Cross, Air Medal, Purple Heart, and Chinese Army, Navy and Air Corps Medal, Class A, 1st Grade.

STORK, J. ROYDEN, Captain
Born December 11, 1916 at Frost, Minnesota. Graduated San Diego High School, San Diego, California, 1935. Attended San Diego State College 2½ years. Entered military service November 25, 1940. Graduated from Advanced Flying Training June 1941. Remained in India after Tokyo Raid for 16 months as pilot of B-24.

After return to States, was assigned to Foreign Equipment Evaluation duties and then as pilot ferrying aircraft for Air Transport Command. Released from active duty October 1945. Employed as make-up artist in Hollywood. Decorations include Distinguished Flying Cross, Air Medal, and Chinese Army, Navy, and Air Corps Medal, Class A, 1st Grade.

THATCHER, DAVID J., Staff Sergeant
Born July 31, 1921 at Bridger, Montana. Completed high school and enlisted in military service, December 3, 1940. Completed Airplane and Engine Mechanic Course, Lincoln, Nebraska, December, 1941. After Tokyo Raid, served in England and Africa until January, 1944. Discharged from active duty in July, 1945 after Stateside assignments in California. Decorations include Silver Star, Distinguished Flying Cross, Air Medal with 4 Oak Leaf Clusters, and Chinese Army, Navy, and Air Corps Medal, Class A, 1st Grade.

TRUELOVE, DENVER VERNON, Captain
Born November 10, 1919 at Clermont, Georgia. Completed three years college and entered military service on May 13, 1940 at Atlanta, Georgia. Completed Bombardier and Navigator training in April, 1941. After Tokyo Raid served in North Africa. Killed in action on April 5, 1943 over Italy. Decorations include Distinguished Flying Cross, Air Medal with 3 Oak Leaf Clusters, Purple Heart, and Chinese Army, Navy, and Air Corps Medal, Class A, 1st Grade.

WATSON, HAROLD FRANCIS, Lieutenant Colonel
Born April 3, 1916 at Buffalo, New York. Completed four years of college. Entered military service August 31, 1940. Completed flying training and commissioned as Second Lieutenant in September, 1940. Was severely injured in bail-out and was patient in Walter Reed Hospital, Washington, D.C. until July, 1944. Remained in service after World War II and served at bases in Colorado, Washington, Alabama, Georgia, Louisiana, Oklahoma and California. Served in Japan from May, 1954 until October, 1955. Retired on October 31, 1961. Decorations include Distinguished Flying Cross, Purple Heart, and Chinese Army, Navy, and Air Corps Medal, Class A, 1st Grade.

WHITE, THOMAS ROBERT, Major
Born March 29, 1909 at Haiku, Maui, Hawaii. Graduated from Redlands High School, Redlands, California in 1927. Graduated from California Institute of Technology with BS degree in 1931. Took post graduate work at Harvard University and University of

Southern California. Awarded M.D. degree at Harvard Medical School in 1937. Took postgraduate training at Johns Hopkins and interned in Baltimore and Honolulu. Commissioned as First Lieutenant, Medical Corps, Army Air Corps, June 1941. Entered active duty August 1941. Graduated from School of Aviation Medicine, Randolph Field, Texas, December 1941. Served as flight surgeon and gunner on Tokyo Raid. During WWII served in England, North Africa, Sicily, and Italy. Returned to private practice in California and Hawaii; now retired. Decorations include Silver Star, Distinguished Flying Cross, and Chinese Army, Navy, and Air Corps Medal, Class A, 1st Grade.

WILDER, ROSS R., Colonel

Born January 10, 1917 at Taylor, Texas. Attended University of Texas and Southwestern University. Received Bachelor of Business Administration degree. Entered military service November, 1940 as Flying Cadet. Graduated from flying training and commissioned as second lieutenant May, 1941. Was co-pilot on B-25 that sighted and sank Japanese submarine on December 24, 1941 at mouth of Columbia River. After Tokyo Raid, served as Bombardment Squadron commander in England, North Africa, Italy and Corsica. Returned to United States in May, 1944 and served as base commander at bases in Texas and Oklahoma. Reverted to inactive status in June, 1947. Was Regional Director of General Services Administration. Died June, 1964. Decorations include Distinguished Flying Cross, Air Medal with 9 Oak Leaf Clusters, and Chinese Army, Navy, and Air Corps Medal, Class A, 1st Grade.

WILDNER, CARL RICHARD, Lieutenant Colonel

Born May 18, 1915, Holyoke, Massachusetts. Graduated Amherst (Mass.) High School in June, 1932. received BS degree in Agriculture from Mass. State College in 1938. Commissioned in Cavalry Reserve from ROTC, June, 1937. Entered service as Flying Cadet, June, 1939. Rated as navigator, July 1, 1941. After Tokyo Raid, remained in India until July, 1943. Returned to States and served at various bases as a navigation instructor. In 1946 was assigned to Alaska and subsequently served in Newfoundland and Germany until relief from active duty in November, 1954. Working as a Supply Cataloguer for Marine Corps. Retired from Air Force Reserve August 1962. Decorations include Distinguished Flying Cross with 1 Oak Leaf Cluster, Air Medal, and Chinese Army, Navy, and Air Corps Medal, Class A, 1st Grade.

WILLIAMS, ADAM RAY, Master Sergeant

Born September 27, 1919 at Gastonia, North Carolina.

Completed one year of high school. Entered military service on September 1, 1938 at Charlotte, North Carolina and served with Field Artillery before transfer to Army Air Corps in 1939. Assigned 37th Bomb Squadron at Barksdale Field, Louisiana. After Tokyo Raid, remained in China-Burma-India Theater until June, 1943. Discharged on July 4, 1945. Decorations include Distinguished Flying Cross, Silver Star, Purple Heart, and Chinese Army, Navy, and Air Corps Medal, Class A, 1st Grade.

WILLIAMS, GRIFFITH PAUL, Major
        Born July 10, 1920 at Chicago, Illinois. Completed two years college and enlisted as Flying Cadet in November, 1940 at Hemet, California. Commissioned as Second Lieutenant and rated as pilot in July, 1941. Assigned 89th Reconnaissance Squadron. Remained in China-Burma-India Theater until July, 1942. Later assigned to Twelfth Air Force in North Africa and was shot down in July, 1943. Was a Prisoner of War from July 4, 1943 until April 29, 1945. Retired on January 31, 1952. Decorations include Distinguished Flying Cross, Air Medal with one Oak Leaf Cluster, and Chinese Army, Navy, and Air Corps Medal, Class A, 1st Grade.

YORK, EDWARD J., Colonel
        Born August 16, 1912 at Batavia, New York. Graduated from Batavia High School in 1928 and enlisted in the U.S. Army (Infantry) in July, 1930. Served at several posts, including Chilkoot Barracks, Alaska, before winning an appointment to the United States Military Academy. Commissioned as Second Lieutenant upon graduation and was assigned to pilot training at Randolph and Kelly Fields where he received his wings in August, 1939. Was interned in Russia after Tokyo Raid for thirteen months. Shortly after returning to U.S. in 1943 was reassigned to B-17 unit in Italy. Following World War II, was sent to Warsaw, Poland as Air Attache. Returned to U.S. in 1947 and assigned as Commandant of Air Force Officer Candidate School. Graduated from Air War College and has had service in the Pentagon and in State of Washington. Served as Chief of Staff of USAF Security Service, San Antonio, Texas. Retired 1966. Decorations include the Distinguished Flying Cross, Legion of Merit, and Chinese Army, Navy, and Air Corps Medal, Class A, 1st Grade.

YOUNGBLOOD, LUCIAN NEVELSON, Major
        Born May 26, 1918 at Pampa, Texas. Two years of college. Entered military service on September 10, 1936 at Fort Sam Houston, Texas. Graduated from Advanced Flying School and commissioned Second Lieutenant in July, 1941. Remained in China-Burma-India Theater after Tokyo Raid until May, 1943. Assigned to bases in South

Carolina, New York and Kansas for remainder of World War II. Departed for service in Newfoundland in February, 1946 and returned to States in August, 1948. Killed in aircraft accident in the Serranias Delburro Mountains, Mexico, February 28, 1949. Decorations include Distinguished Flying Cross, Silver Star, Air Medal, and Chinese Army, Navy, and Air Corps Medal, Class A, 1st Grade.

HONORARY TOKYO RAIDERS

Over the years several men have been made honorary members of Doolittle's Tokyo Raiders for their assistance in planning annual reunions, preserving historical records, participating in some aspect of the mission, or providing a complete account of the raid for posterity.

BENTZ, GERALD E.
  Born January 25, 1922 at Wisner, Nebraska. Served in U.S. Navy during World War II in American and European Theaters of Operations. Now Vice President, Public Relations for Mutual of Omaha Insurance Company and United of Omaha. Assists the Raiders annually as reunion coordinator.

GLINES, CARROLL V., Colonel
  Born December 2, 1920 at Baltimore, Maryland. Graduated Glen-Nor High School, Glenolden, PA. Entered Air Force pilot training May 1941; graduated and commissioned January 2, 1942. Served in American, Caribbean, European, and Alaskan theaters. Staff assignments included service with Office of the Secretary of the Air Force and Assistant Secretary of Defense. Final assignment before retirement from service in July 1968 was as Chief, Public Affairs, Alaskan Command. Graduated University of Oklahoma with BBA and MBA degrees in Management and The American University with MA degree in Journalism. Post-service positions have been Associate Editor, *Armed Forces Management* magazine; Editor, *Air Cargo* magazine; and Editor, *Air Line Pilot* magazine. Author of 20 books including *Four Came Home, Doolittle's Tokyo Raiders, The Legendary DC-3*, and *Jimmy Doolittle*. He is the historian for the Raiders.

GRAHAM, CHARLES J., JR.
  Born February 21, 1923 at Venice, California. Graduated Venice High School. Attended Santa Monica College and University of California at Los Angeles 1941–1942. Entered Air Force pilot

training June 1943; graduated and commissioned March 1944. Relieved from active duty as First Lieutenant 1947. Corporate pilot for the Texas Company; joined North American Aviation Company as utility pilot in 1948. Customer Relations Manager and Manager, Special Projects for Rockwell International. Assists Tokyo Raiders during annual reunions.

LEONARD, STEPHEN
Born September 11, 1918 at Kendallville, Indiana. Graduated from Washington and Lee University, Lexington, VA with B.S. in Business Administration 1940. Received Doctor of Jurisprudence degree from Indiana University Law School 1942. Assistant United States Attorney, Associate General Counsel for the National Labor Relations Board and Legislative Assistant for the United States Senate. Private practice includes experience in corporate, criminal, and regulatory law. Assists Tokyo Raiders as legal advisor.

LIU, TUNG-SHENG, Civilian
Born December 3, 1917 at Wei-Tying, Kiangsi, China. Graduated from National Tsing Hua University. China. Served as interpreter and assisted several crews in escaping Japanese troops after bailouts in China. Came to the United States in September, 1946 as student at University of Minnesota. Received Master of Science degree in Aeronautical Engineering in 1947. From 1947 to 1956 worked as instructor and reserch scientist at University of Minnesota. From 1956 was employed as supervisory aeronautical engineer for the Aeronautical Systems Division, Air Force Systems Command, at Wright-Patterson Air Force Base, Ohio. Among many assignments was Air Force Chief Engineer for the C-5A aircraft. Retired from civil service February 1978. Becamse a U.S. citizen in June, 1954.

MILLER, HENRY L., Rear Admiral, United States Navy
Born July 18, 1912 at Fairbanks, Alaska. Graduated from United States Naval Academy June 1934. Prewar service included three years' duty on the battleship *Texas* and the carrier *Saratoga*. After return from duty aboard *Hornet* with Tokyo Raiders, commanded Air Group 23, based on the carrier *Princeton*. Commanded Air Group 6 for remainder of war, based on the *Hancock*. Subsequently served with Office of Naval Research, Atlantic and Pacific Fleets, and Office of Chief of Naval Operations. Graduate of Industrial College of the Armed Forces. Made Honorary Tokyo Raider for his part in training personnel at Eglin Field, Florida and later at a California base before boarding the *Hornet*. Promoted to Rear Admiral July 1959. Decora-

tions include Distinguished Flying Cross with 4 Gold Stars, Air Medal with 5 Gold Stars, Legion of Merit with 3 Gold Stars, and Army Commendation Ribbon. Retired September 1, 1971.

PITTENGER, RICHARD M.
     Born October 12, 1912 at Pittsburgh, PA. Served in U.S. Coast Guard and War Shipping Administration during World War II. Contact with Tokyo Raiders dates from postwar employment as Vice President, Public Relations for Farmers Insurance Group, where Captain Richard E. Miller, bombardier on Crew No. 2, was employed before enlistment. Has assisted Tokyo Raiders during annual reunions. Is chairman and president of Farmers Insurance Group Safety Foundation.

THE MEN . . . 3. Air Force Officers and Enlisted Men
           on *Hornet* But Not on Raid

          Lieut. James P. Bates, Pilot
          Lieut. Samuel M. Belk, Navigator
          Lieut. Warren A. Beth, Pilot
          Lieut. Wiley M. Bondurant, Navigator
          Lieut. Daniel W. Brown, Navigator
          Lieut. Heston C. Daniel, Pilot
          Lieut. Robert M. Hackney, Co-Pilot
          Lieut. Bert H. Hartzell, Navigator
          Lieut. Harvey M. Hinman, Pilot
          Major Harry Johnson, Jr., Liaison Officer
          Lieut. Louis E. Keller, Co-Pilot
          Lieut. Joseph R. Klein, Co-Pilot
          Lieut. Arvid E. Malmstrom, Co-Pilot
          Lieut. James D. Mathews, Navigator
          Lieut. Glen C. Roloson, Co-Pilot
          Lieut. Henry J. Sabotka, Co-Pilot
          Capt. Vernon L. Stinzi, Pilot
          Lieut. Charles H. Sullenger, Navigator

          Cpl. Donald H. Arbogast, Radio Maintenance, Gunner
          Cpl. Louis H. Ahearn, Mechanic
          Sgt. Joseph N. Baldwin, Maintenance
          Sgt. William E. Batchelor, Mechanic
          Sgt. Jess W. Brazell, Mechanic
          S/Sgt. Albert S. Brisco, Mechanic
          Sgt. Lilburn N. Cate, Mechanic
          Sgt. Curtis L. Cloud, Maintenance
          S/Sgt. Mike Coloff, Mechanic
          Sgt. Harry W. Dullinger, Armament, Gunner

Sgt. Lowell J. Fichner, Mechanic
Sgt. Robert L. Habben, Mechanic
Sgt. Gordon B. Hansen, Mechanic
Sgt. Leonard N. Hanten, Maintenance
Sgt. James F. Hattan, Mechanic
Sgt. Thomas W. Hill, Clerk
Cpl. Maurice J. Hilton, Radio Maintenance
T/Sgt. Wendell C. Horne, Bombardier, Aerial Gunner
Cpl. Foster S. Johnson, Radio Maintenance
S/Sgt. Raymond K. Johnson, Mechanic
Cpl. Laurell E. Julius, Mechanic
S/Sgt. Harrison D. Lacquey, Armament
Pfc. Wayne H. Lash, Armament, Gunner
Sgt. Francis M. Lee, Mechanic
T/Sgt. Joseph A. Lopez, Armament, Gunner
T/Sgt. Wilson L. Minich, Mechanic, Gunner
Sgt. James B. Murphy, Mechanic
Sgt. Charles E. Reed, Maintenance
Cpl. Richard L. Schwartz, Mechanic
S/Sgt. Douglas P. Smith, Mechanic
Cpl. Leslie A. Sucker, Armament
S/Sgt. Roy R. Sweigard, Maintenance
Cpl. Charles T. Treadwell, Armament
S/Sgt. Lawrence E. Wikoff, Armament

THE PLANE . . . 4. History of the B-25

The B-25 Mitchell medium bomber, manufactured by the North American Aviation Company, was named after General William "Billy" Mitchell, a staunch advocate of air power who was court-martialed for his strong views. The B-25 was an improvement of an earlier North American design called the NA-40 which had been built in response to a 1938 Army Air Corps request for a twin-engine attack bomber. The NA-40 first flew in 1939 but its top speed of 265 mph and bomb-carrying capability of 1,200 pounds were deemed insufficient. North American engineers then designed the NA-62 which was ordered direct from the drawing board and designated the B-25.

The first B-25 flew on August 19, 1940. Top speed was 322 mph and a bomb load of 2,400 pounds could be carried. However, the first nine B-25's had an inherent directional instability during bombing runs. By a simple wing design change from an unbroken dihedral to a dihedral which gave the wings a drooping effect, the instability problem was solved in all subsequent planes.

The Doolittle Raid was the first combat mission over enemy territory for the B-25, although some of the earliest models had been used for submarine patrol off both American coasts. Mitchells were used extensively in the Southwest Pacific but also served in the Aleutians, China, India and the Mediterranean and Caribbean Theaters.

In March, 1942, the first of 870 B-25's were delivered to Russia under lend-lease. Mitchells were also produced for Great Britain, the Netherlands, China and Brazil. The U.S. Navy also procured 706 B-25's, designated PBJ-1, for use in the Pacific Theater.

As increasing numbers of B-25's came into the Army Air Forces inventory and saw combat service, many modifications were made to increase their firepower and dependability. The Tokyo Raiders made a number of recommendations as the result of their experience and their ideas were incorporated into improving subsequent models. Most notable later development was the installation of a 75mm cannon which appeared on the B-25G and was the largest weapon ever installed in an American bomber.

The B-25J was the last model of the B-25 series and boasted a top speed of 275 mph at a gross weight of 33,500 pounds. Three thousand pounds of bombs could be carried in this model in addition to eight 5-inch high-velocity rockets.

A total of 9,815 Mitchells were delivered to the Army Air Forces. 24 of them were B-25's; 40 were B-25A's; 119 were B-25B's; 1,619 were B-25C's; 2,290 were B-25D's; 405 were B-25G's; 1,000 were B-25H's; and 4,318 were B-25J's.

5. Bibliography

Arnold, Henry H. *Global Mission.* New York: Harper & Brothers, 1949.

Craven, Wesley F., and Cate, James L. (eds.). *The Army Air Forces in World War II.* Vol. I. Chicago: The University of Chicago Press, 1948.

Emmens, Robert G. *Guests of the Kremlin.* New York: The Macmillan Co., 1949.

Glines, Carroll V. *Four Came Home.* New York: Van Nostrand Reinhold Co., 1966.

Glines, Carroll V. *Jimmy Doolittle: Master of the Calculated Risk.* New York: Van Nostrand Reinhold Co., 1980.

Gordon, Gary, *The Rise and Fall of the Japanese Empire.* Derby, Connecticut: Monarch Books, Inc., 1962.

Halsey, William F., and Bryan, J. III. *Admiral Halsey's Story.* New York: McGraw-Hill Book Co., 1947.

Karig, Walter, and Kelley, Welbourn. *Battle Report: Pearl Harbor to Coral Sea.* New York: Rinehart and Co., 1944.

King, Ernest J., and Whitehill, Walter Muir. *Fleet Admiral King: A Naval Record.* New York: W. W. Norton, 1952.

Lawson, Ted W. *Thirty Seconds Over Tokyo,* ed. Robert Considine. New York: Random House, Inc., 1943.

Morison, Samuel Eliot. *The Rising Sun in the Pacific, 1931–April 1942.* Boston, Little, Brown and Co., 1948.

Reynolds, Quentin. *The Amazing Mr. Doolittle.* New York: Appleton-Century-Crofts, Inc., 1953.

Sakai, Saburo, with Caidin, Martin, and Saito, Fred. *Samurai!.* New York: E. P. Dutton & Co., Inc., 1957.

Taylor, Theodore. *The Magnificent Mitscher.* New York: W. W. Norton, 1954.

Toland, John. *But Not In Shame.* New York: Random House, Inc., 1961.

Tuleja, Thaddeus V. *Climax at Midway.* New York: Berkley Books, 1960

Watson, C. Hoyt. *The Amazing Story of Sergeant Jacob DeShazer.* Winona Lake, Indiana: Light and Life Press, 1950.

6. Reunion Sites

Jimmy Doolittle and his surviving Tokyo Raiders have met each year since the end of World War II with the exception of 1946, 1951, and 1966. They have been the guests of grateful citizens who remember the magnificent uplifting effect their mission had on American morale. They remain forever grateful to their hosts in the following cities:

1945 Miami, Florida
1946 No reunion
1947 Miami, Florida
1948 Minneapolis, Minnesota
1949 Galveston, Texas
1950 Palm Springs, California
1951 No reunion
1952 Miami, Florida
1953 San Diego, California
1954 Galveston, Texas
1955 Los Angeles, California
1956 Tampa, Florida
1957 Fort Walton Beach, California
1958 Las Vegas, Nevada
1959 Tucson, Arizona
1960 Colorado Springs, Colorado
1961 Camden, Arkansas
1962 Santa Monica, California
1963 Seattle, Washington
1964 Fort Worth, Texas
1965 Dayton, Ohio
1966 No reunion
1967 Oakland, California
1968 Fort Walton Beach, Florida
1969 Biloxi, Mississippi
1970 Cocoa Beach, Florida
1971 San Antonio, Texas
1972 Los Angeles, California
1973 Houston, Texas
1974 Oakland, California
1975 Coral Gables, Florida
1976 Omaha, Nebraska
1977 Memphis, Tennessee
1978 Rapid City, South Dakota
1979 Charleston, South Carolina
1980 Newport Beach, California
1981 Columbus, Ohio

INDEX

Akers, Frank, Commander, 85
Arndt, R. W., Lt., 112–113, 114
Arnold, Henry H., Gen., 137–138,
   380
   and B-25 maintenance, 64–66
   appoints Doolittle, 22–26
   arrangements with China, 70–73,
      87–88, 89
   early bombing plans, 5–9, 12–13
   permits Doolittle to fly mission,
      53–54
   plans bombing of Japan, 24–31, 37
   reports after raid, 383–384
Asano, Ryozo, **339**

B-25 bomber, **49, 109, 110, 113, 158**
   aboard *Hornet,* 79, 83, 91
   adaptation for mission, 34–41
   history of, 439–440
   Japanese exhibit of, 335–336
   loaded aboard *Hornet,* 69–74
   maintenance problems, 63–66,
      68–69, 83, 91, 100
   model in Air Force Museum, 401
   plans to use, 17–18
   selection of, 25–26
   speculation about after raid, 381,
      392
   take-off, 98, 106–122
B-26 *Marauder,* 23–24
Bain, Edwin V., Sgt., **263,** 264, 270
   biography, 410
Balloon bombs, 395
Barr, George, Capt., **306, 334,**
   364–366
   biography, 373, 410
   capture of, 310–312, 367,
      371–373
   narrative of, 305–312
   torture of, 349

Baumeister, Karl, Capt., 43
Bentz, Gerald E.
   biography, 436
Birch, John M., Rev., 193, 194,
   321–327
   report of, 324–327
Birch, William L., 2d Lt., **237,** 238
   biography, 411
Bissell, Clayton, Col., 88–89,
   260–261, 277, 382–386
Bissell, Wayne Max, 1st Lt., **218,** 221,
   224
   biography, 411
Bither, Waldo J., Major, **241,**
   242–243, 244, 245
   biography, 411
Bitter, Rev. Bruno, 330
Blanton, Thadd Harrison, Lt. Col.,
   241, 245
   biography, 411–412
Boettcher, Robert R., Ens., 103
Bombings *see* Japan, bombing of
Bombsights, 50, **51**
Bourgeois, Robert C., 247, **248,**
   249–251, 256, **257**
   biography, 412
Bower, William M., Col., 47, 52, 166,
   241, 240–241, 242–244, 245,
   401–402
   biography, 412
Bradley, Follet, Gen., 215
Braemer, Fred A., Capt., 54, 122,
   128, 129, 134–135, 323
   biography, 412
Browning, Miles, Capt., 66
Butler, J. C., Ens., 112, 114

Campbell, Clayton J., Lt. Col., 247,
   248, 249, 251, 256–257, **257**
   biography, 412–413